GALLIPOLI

GALLIPOLI

THE NEW ZEALAND STORY

CHRISTOPHER PUGSLEY

Published in New Zealand by Libro International, an imprint of Oratia Media Ltd, 783 West Coast Road, Oratia, Auckland 0604, New Zealand (www.librointernational.com); and in the UK by Frontline Books, an imprint of Pen & Sword Books Ltd, 47 Church Street, Barnsley, S. Yorkshire S70 2AS, UK (www.frontline-books.com)

New Zealand
ISBN 978-1-877514-64-7
Ebook ISBN 978-1-877514-65-4

UK
ISBN 978-1-84832-788-7

First edition published by Hodder and Stoughton 1984
Second edition published by Sceptre Paperback 1990
Third edition published by Reed Publishing (NZ) 1998; reprinted 2003
Fourth edition published by Penguin Group 2008
This edition published 2014

Page design by www.CVdesign.net.nz
Cover design by Susan Pugsley

Cover imagery
Front cover: A picture for the folks at home. *(WW1 Photographic Collection A.A. Perry Negatives, Auckland War Memorial Museum)*
Back cover: Approaching Anzac Cove. *(WF-002662-124, Morison Collection, NAM Waiouru)*
Back flap: Author portrait by Harriet Bright. *(National Portrait Gallery collection)*

Printed in China by Nordica

Contents

LIST OF MAPS

Foreword

Commemorations based on myths or misunderstandings are a disservice to those we honour. With the centenary of the Gallipoli landings fast approaching, the contributions of our historians become particularly vital — and few can match Christopher Pugsley's extraordinary scholarship, informed analysis and passion for his subject.

His *Gallipoli: The New Zealand Story* has become the 'go-to' text on Gallipoli, a reliable and comprehensive account of New Zealand's role in that fateful campaign. He outlines the measures taken before 1914, which were to make New Zealand war ready in a way that it has not been before or since. But this preparation and the training in Egypt could not prepare our soldiers for what they faced when they were accidentally put ashore north of their intended landing on the Gallipoli peninsula. Impossibly steep terrain thwarted the battle plans, they suffered heavy casualties and lost many of their officers in the first few days, and it soon became clear that they were going to be fighting 'with their backs to the sea, clinging to narrow ridges'. Throughout the campaign they faced a determined Ottoman foe. For eight long months, our men attacked and were counterattacked and suffered sniper fire and shrapnel, monotonous and inadequate food and the stresses of life in the trenches. The stench of death from the bodies of mates and foe alike, littering the slopes, was to stay with veterans throughout their lives. The lessons learned at Gallipoli forged them into a tough fighting force and informed the training and command of New Zealand forces on the Western Front.

In the 1984 television documentary *Gallipoli: the New Zealand Story* Lieutenant General Sir Leonard Thornton said that for New Zealanders Gallipoli 'is the most potent place name of the outside world'. That sentiment is an enduring one. Our story is one of New Zealanders going to war with their mates, from small towns like Rawene, Taihape, and Ashburton; we were absorbed into provincial regiments (Auckland, Wellington, Canterbury and Otagos); we linked up with the Australian Imperial Force in Australia; and then finally in Egypt, as others identified us as New Zealanders, Fernleaves, Pig Islanders or men from the Shaky Isles, we did so too. For Māori, this was to be the first campaign that Te Hokowhitu A Tu fought, following a shift in official attitudes towards what role they might take in the conflict.

When Christopher Pugsley first published *Gallipoli* in 1984, there were some 300 veterans still with us. Few other New Zealanders — including their family members — had heard their stories or had any real understanding of what the veterans had been through. New Zealand's starring role in the ill-fated August offensive, the tragedy of Chunuk Bair, and the achievements of Lieutenant Colonel William George Malone were all largely unknowns.

That they are now more widely known is due to ground-breaking work in the 1980s, by the likes of Christopher Pugsley, writers like Maurice Shadbolt, and Jane Tolerton and Nicholas Boyack, who recorded the stories of 84 First World War veterans. The historical work that has followed from this time means we now know so much more.

This new edition is timely. I know from my own experience how historians have made an immeasurable difference to my visits to the rocky slopes of Gallipoli — and as more and more New Zealanders make their pilgrimage to Anzac Cove and the hills beyond it, they will also want to come to grips with what happened there and to read the compelling personal accounts contained in this book. In doing so, they will more fully appreciate the tremendous sacrifices of their forebears and carry on the torch of remembrance to future generations.

Lt Gen The Rt Hon Sir Jerry Mateparae, GNZM, QSO
Governor-General of New Zealand

Men of the Auckland Battalion getting into the boats off the *Lutzow*, 10 a.m., 25 April 1915. *(Album 382, p.6 n1, Auckland War Memorial Museum)*

Foreword to the first edition

For my generation, brought up in constrained reverence of Anzac and of the ANZACs, the insistence of history fell on reluctant ears. We subscribed to the legend of victory in defeat, of a brilliant feat of arms against overwhelming and fanatical enemies. We recognised that the Australians had shared the glory and the sacrifice; but there was little acknowledgement that we were outnumbered ten times over by our British allies, or that the French expeditionary force was larger than our own.

Noble Antipodean sacrifice in a close-run campaign was the version which our betters had adopted and embellished in their desire to make sense of what had happened. We were not to know that a tragedy of errors had been played out on the Gallipoli peninsula, and that others had suffered grievously and fruitlessly, like ourselves.

By the time the chroniclers got to work on the dissection of cause and effect, of mishap and failure, the legend was almost unassailable in the New Zealand consciousness — and so it has remained. This in spite of the fact that over many years the sad evidence has been presented and re-presented that this over-ambitious campaign was at best a 'muddling through' in the classic British pattern, doomed to fail against a courageous Turkish opposition. The only shred of comfort was in the success of the final humiliation of evacuation by stealth.

Yet when all is said, something of lasting significance for us emerged from the Dardanelles debacle. The experience came to be seen as giving tentative expression to a new national consciousness, setting us apart as New Zealanders, not merely British, and more than the affiliates of Australia.

It is this emergence that Christopher Pugsley seeks to capture in his unique approach to Gallipoli. Resisting the temptation to call on his own unparalleled knowledge of the events of the day and the hour throughout those bloody months, he allows the story to be told almost entirely through the spoken and written words of the participants. This gives extraordinary poignancy to the tragedy of knowing that the outcome will be nugatory and that so many of the narrators will survive for only a few days or weeks.

This is not a book about strategy or the tactics of battle, except where explanation is necessary to set the scene. Such analyses can be found elsewhere. Here we have essentially a first-person account, almost always through New Zealand eyes.

Like it or not, these events and the men who suffered them had a seminal effect on the development of our character as a people. It is impossible to view these antecedents without pride and painful sympathy. These men, who endured so much, richly deserve any legend. Of them their sacked British commander-in-chief, General Sir Ian Hamilton, was later to admit rather ruefully, 'I did not know, to tell you the truth, that they were nearly as good as they turned out to be.' On these pages, and between the lines, one can see how good they were.

Lt Gen Sir Leonard Thornton, KCB, CBE

Approaching the beach (Anzac Cove) from the boats that were carrying the Auckland Battalion, 25 April 1915.
(Album 382, p.6 n6, Auckland War Memorial Museum)

Preface to the 2014 edition

It is difficult to believe that it is 33 years since my first visit to Gallipoli in December 1980, and 30 years since the first publication of this book. I have walked Gallipoli many times since in good company, including with family and friends. Like me they all fall under the spell that the peninsula weaves. Each visit the same questions are asked: could the campaign have succeeded and what does it mean today? Sometimes the answers differ. It will always be so, but that too is part of the fascination.

Going to Gallipoli changed my life, but mine has been a voyage of exploration far removed from the daily dangers faced by those who fought in the campaign. This is the first edition that I have edited and changed. The core of the story remains the same, but I have benefited from the scholarship of many other historians and enthusiasts.

I acknowledge the work of John Crawford, Glyn Harper, Sir Peter Jackson, Terry Kinloch, Ian McGibbon, Gavin McLean, Richard Stowers, John Tonkin-Covell, Matthew Wright and others in adding to the New Zealand story, and to many historians overseas including John Moses, Bill Gammage, Peter Stanley, Ashley Ekins, Peter Hart, Jenny Macleod, Peter Chasseaud, Peter Doyle, Robin Prior, Edward J. Erickson, Tolga Ornek and others. On the peninsula I owe a particular debt to my friends Uncle Sabri Yolajan, Kenan Çelik, Serpil and Bill Sellars, T.J. and Bea, Ramazan, and all those who gather at Kenan's call and debate the campaign at the Limon Restaurant in Eceabat.

I am grateful to the following institutions for permission to publish maps, photographs and illustrations: Alexander Turnbull Library, National Library of New Zealand; Archives New Zealand; Auckland War Memorial Museum; Australian War Memorial, Canberra; Hocken Library, Dunedin; National Army Museum, Waiouru; The Press Collection, Fairfax Media; Puke Ariki Museum, New Plymouth; Wairarapa Archive; and Wingnut Film Archive. In particular Clare Olssen and Sebastian Meek have done wonders in accessing the illustrations and in producing the high-resolution images. Thank you to Jordan Black for all of her hard work in producing the high-resolution images and to Charlie Tait for producing the coloured masterpiece from the black and white original.

It is a pleasure working with Peter Dowling and his Libro International team at Oratia Media. Carolyn Lagahetau has been a superb editor and Sam Hill a thorough indexer and proofreader, and Arantxa Zecchini-Dowling and Alessandra Zecchini did the major work of scanning and correcting the original text. I thank Craig Violich of CVdesign for designing the book and my daughter Susan for the cover.

My family have lived with Gallipoli for 35 years and it was a pleasure walking the ground with them in 2010. Deanna has followed the drum as the wife of a soldier for 18 years and continues to do so. This edition is for her with all my love. The mistakes and omissions are my own, but I thank everyone who over the years has shared Gallipoli with me.

Christopher Pugsley
Waikanae Beach, 2014

Author's note

I have many people, far too many to name, to thank for their assistance and kindness during my research and writing of *Gallipoli — The New Zealand Story*. As well as those sources listed in the bibliography, there are the large number of Gallipoli veterans interviewed, not all of whom are mentioned but whose interview tapes and transcripts are now part of the archives of the Queen Elizabeth II New Zealand Army Museum.

My greatest debt is to my family who lived through Gallipoli with me: my parents, and especially my wife, Deanna, who had the burden of typing my draft as well as keeping a family together.

Maurice Shadbolt was the catalyst who made it happen and gave me the confidence to complete the task. Major General R.G. Williams, Chief of General Staff, and Allan Martin, Director-General of Television New Zealand, had the vision to allow me to spend the year working with Television New Zealand.

'Doc' Williams and Sir Leonard Thornton trekked the Peninsula with me and in countless hours of discussion put the story into perspective. Allan Martin, Sir Leonard Thornton, D.O.C. Williams and E.P. Malone read the draft and offered valuable criticism.

Special thanks are due to the Bluestockings — Colleen Hodge, Julienne Stretton, Liz Greenslade and Diane Fowler — for their invaluable contribution to research, and to Mike Wicksteed and John McLeod who tied up many loose ends. All the institutes and libraries listed have my thanks and I am particularly indebted to the staffs of the Queen Elizabeth II New Zealand Army Museum, Base Records Wellington, and the New Zealand Defence libraries in Waiouru, Wellington and Papakura.

Thanks to all those who have shared Gallipoli with me since it was first published in 1984. I am grateful for offered corrections and additions; any omissions remain my own.

I gratefully dedicate this edition to the parents of my wife and I: Olwen and Frank Pugsley, and Joan and Ray Osborne.

Christopher Pugsley

1

THAT AWFUL
DARDANELLES MUDDLE

It was something different, something nobody counted on.
Allen Curnow, 'The Unhistoric Story', *Collected Poems 1933–1973*

It was 4.30 a.m. The tightly packed, darkened boats slowly approached the shore. On the cliffs above, a flare, then a shot. This was followed by a ragged fusillade as the cliff tops above the beach were etched by a line of fire. It was into this fire that the Australians of the 3rd (All Australian) Brigade scrambled through the shallows and onto the beaches of the Dardanelles Peninsula on Sunday 25 April 1915.

The firing echoed across the water towards the ships still steaming up the Turkish coast towards the landing beaches. One of the leading ships was the *Lutzow*, flagship of Major-General Sir Alexander Godley, Commander of the New Zealand Expeditionary Force (NZEF). With him in the convoy were 6324 New Zealanders, who, with the 4th Australian Infantry Brigade, made up the New Zealand and Australian Division. This, with the 1st Australian Division, composed the Australian and New Zealand Army Corps, and a new name was born in the English language: ANZAC.

The *Lutzow*'s deck was crowded with sleeping men. Below in one of the cabins, three young officers, lieutenants Westmacott, Baddeley and Allen, platoon commanders of the 16th Waikato Company, were also sleeping soundly. Spencer Westmacott was the first of the three to wake:

'I had hardly turned over to go to sleep again, when the rumble of guns made me jump out of my bunk and the two others joined me at the porthole. They were the guns at Cape Helles where the 29th Division must by now be going ashore. Day was just breaking. There was a slight mist along the shore. Save for flashes from ships' guns we could see nothing in the half light. It was nice and cool with the promise of a glorious day. It was a little after 4.00 a.m. I said, "We may not rest so comfortably tonight. Let us go to sleep again." and we did very quickly. My words were prophetic. Before another night both my friends were dead …

'We were up and dressed at 7.00 a.m. and went to Holy Communion under Fielden Taylor in the saloon … Breakfast was at 8.00 a.m. We visited our men. They were all happy and well fed. I asked Sergeant Major Hobbs how the sergeants had been fed. He told me they had no complaints. They had not had much cooked food for all the way across, but "plenty of 'am Sir, very good 'am". Those were the last words we had off duty together. We went on the top deck. The ship lay at anchor several miles off shore, which was clear to see, a rugged coastline. There were ships all round us, a magnificent sight, with bright sunlight shining upon a calm blue sea and clear sky. The high cliffs, north of Gaba Tepe, afterwards called Anzac, were straight ahead.

'Yes, and there they were, real shells bursting like puffs of cotton wool against the clear blue sky at the summit of the cliffs. Pictures had always shown a simultaneous flash and smoke. We noted that the flash came first, leaving the smoke afterwards. Interesting. Someone was getting it under those bursts at that very moment. To right and left of us, a mile or so away in each case, our warships lay close in shore pounding away at the enemy's position, and between us and the beach, at the foot of the cliffs, a stream of destroyers, picket boats and lighters crowded with men, plied their way back and forth ceaselessly. As we watched, at about 9.00 a.m. a heavy roll of musketry from a ridge to the left of where the troops were landing grew to a roar and then died away to a few occasional dropping shots. Colonel Chaytor's eye caught mine … His eye lit up and he nodded his head at me, as if to say "Now we shan't be long."

'News from the shore commenced to circulate along the decks. We were told that the leading troops were safely landed; but there had been considerable opposition, which had been overcome with heavy loss to the enemy. Like good soldiers nobody enlarged upon our own. A destroyer came alongside, and from her bridge an unshaven young officer looking very untidy hailed us through a megaphone to say, "Colonel MacLagan has taken three Krupp guns." The news ran like wild fire through the ship and there were cheers from all the decks. Colonel MacLagan commanded the Third Australian Brigade … 'The Colonel and battalion headquarters had gone ashore with the leading troops. Third Auckland under Dawson and Sixth Hauraki under Stuckey went next, with the New Zealand Engineers …

'All fully equipped we now went below to the troop decks and inspected our men who had fallen in and were awaiting us. All ranks were in caps like the British infantry. This applied to the Australians too, being a Corps Order. We had noted with disapproval that when 3rd Auckland went ashore a few men wore hats; but their discipline was slack. Once again we checked over their equipment, satisfying ourselves that each man's water bottle was full. When we had seen the three days' extra rations, the men fastened their haversacks, showed their extra hundred rounds in their breast pockets, and the usual hundred and fifty in their pouches and closed them too …

'We gave the order "Charge magazines". In went ten rounds and the cut offs were closed. I loaded my R.I.C. revolver, and there was a short silence so I said, "We are about to go into action. We are all ready and remember that if anyone is hurt no one is to leave his place to take him to the rear. That applies to me as well as all the rest of you. The stretcher bearers are there to help the wounded. Remember also that I will allow no man to open fire, until we see something to fire at." The leading platoon now began to climb upon deck and the others in turn filed after them …

'On deck we formed up our platoons in close order and waited. I had fifty-six other ranks, the company strength being two hundred and twenty-three. Biscuit tins full of water were placed at intervals on the deck and our orders were to drink all we could of this as our water bottles were not to be used without permission, probably not until night, and the water we drank now would abate our thirst till then. We doubted this … but we did as we were told … Young Cliff Barclay passed me going to his platoon of 2nd Canterbury further along the deck. He said, "We are going ashore in a minute. The lighters are coming alongside." We wished each other good luck.

'It was shortly after 10.00 a.m. Alderman said a few words to the whole company, "We are going ashore now; but I do not think anyone is going to be killed today." At which there were roars of sceptic laughter from his listeners. They were all in such high spirits. It was glorious to lead such men.

'Alderman and some of ours filled the first lighter. My platoon were in the second and two platoons of the Canterbury Regiment, whose colonel Macbean Stewart and his battalion headquarters also came and took their places forward. Critchley-Salmonson, their Adjutant and I sat near them on the port side, our legs hanging over the water. Jack Anderson of divisional H.Q., who was being left on board … waved to me and I waved back. We were quiet enough. There was no talking at this stage. A destroyer was to take us in. The tow rope tightened. We were under way.'[1]

The events of this day would see the name ANZAC pass into legend. As the New Zealanders sat packed in the lighters and barges approaching the Gallipoli coast, few thought back to those heady days of August 1914 when the war had begun. New Zealand had entered the war 'ignorant of its causes and innocent of its meaning'.[2]

War on New Zealand soil existed only in the memories of the oldest of our inhabitants. Our experience of war was shaped by the Boer War. To New Zealanders, flocking to enlist in 1914, those memories were of cheering crowds waving the men off as they sailed to South Africa and the excitement, songs and patriotic speeches on their return to a hero's welcome. Few had been killed.[*]

War was something remote, fought far away from these shores, always in the Empire's cause. New Zealand had never been threatened nor had experienced war's presence. 'The public would sing men off and cheer them home with no understanding of what they had been through.' The First World War was never of New Zealand's making; the causes of the conflict were not entirely clear but that did not matter. Britain had declared war on our behalf, and that was enough.

Of the young men clamouring to join up, few consciously enlisted for King and Country. Patriotism was a comfortable cloak worn unthinkingly, an accepted tenet of New Zealand faith. Men joined for more immediate and personal reasons. Now there was the chance to go away and see the world, to escape this isolated spot on the globe

---

[*] New Zealand's casualties in South Africa were: 70 killed in action, 25 accidentally killed, 133 died of disease, and 166 were wounded. Some 6500 New Zealanders served in South Africa from 1899 to 1902.

and do something. Indeed, we did not even consciously go to war as New Zealanders. Nothing in our experience had forced us to consider our relationship to the land in which we lived.

This war was to change that; but when 8574 men sailed from these shores in October 1914, they sailed not as New Zealanders but rather as a number of highly competitive provincial teams: Otago, Canterbury, Wellington and Auckland. Jealous of their reputations, more conscious of their differences than of any national identity, they were sailing overseas to play a series of games whose results, in their minds, were preordained. The British Empire would win. The only real concern was that the New Zealand Expeditionary Force would not arrive in time for the competition.

The destination? No one was sure. The most likely rumours were England, then France. It could be India and garrison duty or the Cape again, against the Boers. It did not matter, they were off — off to find adventure and the rest of the world. Turkey's entry into the war found them in Egypt for training with the Australian Imperial Force (AIF). It was Egypt and the contact with Australians as well as with British and Indian troops that forced New Zealanders to look at their identity for the first time. As always it was the Australians who made the biggest impact. The term 'Australasian' suggests two similar peoples with a joint heritage. Egypt was to accentuate the differences. The Australians were more numerous, more confident, more aggressive and far more prepared to believe in and try to live up to the myth of the 'wild colonial'. The New Zealanders were more reticent, less confident, and more prepared to accept standards of dress and discipline rather than oppose them simply because they had been imposed by English officers.

The fleshpots of Cairo were a strong attraction to fit young men, both New

New Zealanders on board *Itonus* watching the bombardment ashore, 25 April 1915. *(Bollinger Collection, NAM Waiouru)*

Zealanders and Australians, bored with training and frustrated at missing out on fighting in France. Everyone went to see the sights, and many indulged. C.E.W. Bean, the Australian historian, wrote in his diary: 'There were rowdy British Territorials and rowdy drunken New Zealanders, but my own observation was that the Australians were easily the most noticeable and the most frequent offenders were Australians. I think we have to admit that our force contains more bad hats than the others; and I also think that the average Australian is certainly a harder liver.'[3]

By contrast, Bean saw the New Zealander as colourless, without the 'extraordinarily good points' that in Bean's eyes atoned for the Australian's visible vices. Both looked askance at the character and deeds of the other; one New Zealander writing home expressed a view common in the letters and diaries of New Zealanders of the period: 'For taking the Australian, and more especially the town bred man, is a skiting bumptious fool who thinks nobody knows anything but himself. If we meet or see them in a restaurant or anywhere in town there is generally a row of some kind.'[4]

Each blamed the other for outbreaks of bad behaviour. Some Australians noted that New Zealanders were 'soft on the blacks'. They were far too inclined to treat them as they would a Maori without recognising that New Zealanders were demeaning themselves as white men by not recognising that the 'gyppo' was a lesser being on the human scale.[5] ANZAC did not, as the term suggests, indicate a close and indistinguishable union of the two forces. Rather, it emphasised the uniqueness of each of the nationalities, Australian and New Zealand, working together, but highly individual and increasingly proud to be so. Within the New Zealand Expeditionary Force the provincial rivalries still existed.

Hard training for war on the desert sands still allowed plenty of time for rugby. In the afternoons, the battalion rugby team's time was sacrosanct. Its members were excused fatigues and drills. Regimental and provincial pride demanded success in the inter-regimental rugby competition. But a national identity was growing. New Zealand was becoming important for itself. When they sailed from Wellington, many saw it as a chance to be 'home' for Christmas. Home was Britain, but Egypt changed that: the reality became the towns and farms they had left behind. Home was Ashburton, Ohakune, and a hundred other New Zealand towns and settlements. They travelled across the seas only to find that what they wanted most was back in New Zealand. 'It seems great to be such a long way from home but we are all New Zealanders and now that we are away from our own country we all stick together like glue.'[6]

Indeed it was as New Zealanders that other nationalities identified us, not as 'Otago' or the 'Canterbury boys' but as 'Fernleaves'* or 'New Zealanders', and it made sense to do so ourselves. Much of the credit for forging this national identity is due to Major-General Sir Alexander Godley, Commander of the New Zealand Expeditionary Force. Of Anglo-Irish stock, Godley was a professional soldier without

---

* 'Fernleaf' and 'Fernleaves' was the slang term for New Zealanders. 'Kiwi' was not used. According to Brophy and Partridge in *The Long Trail*, 'Kiwi' meant a ground-duty air force man. A 'Kiwi King' was any officer fussy about spit and polish, derived from the brand of *Kiwi* shoe polish.

means in an age when means and breeding were expected of the officer class. He had to achieve in order to survive in his profession.

No other British officer wanted the position of Commander New Zealand Military Forces when it was offered by the New Zealand government in 1910. New Zealand was isolated and the money was seen as not good enough for a first-class man. Godley accepted it on the grounds of 'Imperial Service', but he was not in a position to refuse. He needed employment and like many others southbound before him, Godley journeyed to the Antipodes to make a name for himself. He succeeded.

By 1914 he had forged a national army of citizens in arms and he took it to war. In Egypt he drove his mixed division of New Zealanders and Australians hard. He demanded levels of training far higher and more ambitious than his Australian counterpart, Bridges, expected of his Australian Division. Godley's message was 'Drive, Drive, Drive' and never a word of praise. He would not tolerate the indiscipline that racked the Australian Force on its first contact with the drinking holes and brothels of Cairo. From the outset Godley cracked down on any signs of ill-discipline, and the worst offenders were shipped back to New Zealand. His New Zealanders would conform. They would salute officers, maintain dress standards and had to prove by their performance in training that they 'were almost as good as British regulars', the highest accolade that Godley and the Imperial officers attached to the New Zealand Expeditionary Force could bestow.

Praise and a true understanding of the men he commanded were foreign to Godley. A tall, austere figure, he lacked the awkward geniality of Sir William Birdwood, the Commander of the ANZAC Corps. The New Zealanders were conscious of being driven hard and they resented Godley for it. Apocryphal tales spread among the troops emphasising Godley's harshness, and equally how this influence was reinforced by his wife!* Yet love him or not, he was imparting a standard of training and discipline that became the hallmark of the New Zealand Expeditionary Force during its existence. His administration was of an equally high standard. Nothing escaped his attention. Wet canteens were established to keep the men out of the stews of Cairo and his policy for the prevention of venereal disease was particularly enlightened. Over the objections of his subordinate commanders, who believed abstinence was the only 'manly' way to avoid this self-inflicted disease, Godley had treatment centres established in every New Zealand unit where men could obtain prophylactic ointments and seek remedial assistance after a 'doggy time' in Cairo.

In April the ANZAC Corps sailed to Mudros Harbour on the Greek island of Lemnos as part of the Mediterranean Expeditionary Force commanded by Sir Ian Hamilton. This hotchpotch force of French, British, Indian and ANZAC troops was

---

* Lady Godley accompanied her husband to Egypt, as did the wives of the other Imperial Officers serving with the New Zealand Forces. She established convalescent homes in Egypt for sick and wounded New Zealanders and was mentioned in despatches for her services. Her letters show a keen concern, but it was hidden under an efficient manner. 'I have very hard work competing with these untidy and independent New Zealanders and Matron and I are perfect dragons ... but we still have to do most of it ourselves.'

to be committed to an 'adventure unprecedented in modern war', an opposed landing on the Turkish mainland to seize the Gallipoli Peninsula and open the straits of the Dardanelles to the battleships of the Royal Navy.[7] The British Regular 29th Division would land in the south at Helles and advance up the Peninsula. The French would land at Kum Kale on the Asiatic shore as a feint, while the ANZACs would land further up the Peninsula, advance across it, and cut the Turkish communications that ran from north to south. It was an ambitious project. In hindsight, it seems obvious that Sir Ian Hamilton saw this as another colonial war. The Turks were just another hill tribe to be overawed with the guns of the Royal Navy. A show of force by the Empire on land, and any Turkish opposition would be swept aside. The difficulty would be in getting ashore.

New Zealand's contribution was 6324 men. One infantry brigade was part of Godley's NZ & A Division. Theirs was to be a modest role in the plan for the landings on 25 April 1915. Bridges' stronger Australian Division would land first at 4.30 a.m., before the dawn. His 3rd (All Australian) Brigade would seize a bridgehead. They would be followed by the two remaining Australian brigades, who would expand and consolidate the ground won. Only then would Godley's smaller division of two brigades land. It would remain in reserve, behind the Australians. Godley expected hard fighting for his New Zealanders but not on 25 April. 'We shall have plenty to do, after they have gained a footing, in either attacking the enemy in position further up the Peninsula, or pursuing him if he retires.'[8]

It should have been Australia's day. They landed before dawn but instead of doing so on the beaches near the open expanse of the Maidos Plain that crossed the Peninsula from west to east, the Navy blundered and set them down two kilometres north. Instead of a low coastal ridge and an open plain, the Australians faced a lunatic landscape of clay slopes and ravines, all cloaked in an impenetrable prickly scrub. They landed around a headland on the northern point of an unnamed beach some 600 metres long and a cricket pitch wide. This part of the coast was all but deserted as the Turkish command considered this the least likely area for a landing.

It was a mistake on the Navy's part: the importance of which is still being argued. Even though the isolated pockets of Turks guarding the coast were soon driven inland, from the beginning the fight was as much with the landscape as it was with the Turk. It was this landscape that broke and scattered the Australian battalions as they waded ashore, across the narrow beach, and started up the heights above them. This was not immediately apparent. By 9.00 a.m., some 12,000 Australians were ashore and, although disorganised with large gaps in the line, they were advancing inland.

It was then that Godley's New Zealanders landed. The New Zealanders of the *Lutzow* were first ashore, Westmacott among them. His company commander had not been speaking in jest when he had said, 'I do not think anyone is going to be killed today.'[9] Everything so far seemed to justify Hamilton's belief in the poor fighting qualities of the Turk. The Australians could be seen swarming over the hills and both Birdwood and Godley appeared confident that New Zealand would have little to do that day.

The high promise of the morning was not fulfilled. A yet unknown Turkish divisional commander, Mustafa Kemal, had heard of the ANZAC landing. Recognising the threat, he committed his leading regiment to a counter-attack about the time the Auckland Battalion was lining up in four ranks on the beach. As they stood gaping at the sights and breaking ranks to pick up shrapnel balls for souvenirs, Kemal's battalions were advancing on the Australian line. Though heavily outnumbered, the Turks knew the ground and were in organised units. The Australians, by contrast, were widely separated in small groups, often out of touch with the men on their flanks. From 10.00 a.m. the Australian advance was held, and the Turkish counter-attacks threatened to break the overstretched Australian line.

The major threat developed on the coastal ridge around the heights of a hill known as 'Little' or 'Baby' 700, because of its height in feet above sea level. Here the battle was at its most bitter. In turn, Australian then Turk held and lost the hill. It was in defence of this hill that the Auckland and Canterbury battalions were committed into action. The New Zealand Infantry Brigade headquarters had not yet arrived off the beach; the New Zealand brigade commander was sick with the measles. Indeed, everything indicated how little Godley's staff had expected action that day. The New Zealanders from the *Lutzow* would claw their way inland, becoming as disorganised in the tangle of ridges as the Australians before them. It would be Westmacott's platoon and men of Alderman's 16th Waikato Company who would first face Turkish fire on the slopes of Baby 700. From the outset they would be on the defensive, never attacking, merely trying to hold the line and fill the gaps where Australians before them had been killed and wounded.

Overshadowed by the large numbers of Australians ashore, the New Zealanders would demonstrate a thinking tenacity that would become a characteristic unmatched by any nationality, other than perhaps the Turk. Three thousand one hundred New Zealanders would cross the beaches that ANZAC day[*], but few, apart from some 1500 from the *Lutzow*, would see action other than to cringe from the burst of artillery shrapnel overhead. By day's end the New Zealanders would lose Baby 700. It would never be recovered; most of the New Zealand dead would remain unburied and unrecorded behind the Turkish lines. The day would claim some 600 New Zealanders as casualties — more killed and wounded than in the three years of the Boer War. Yet, for Westmacott and others, the deeds they performed on the slopes of Baby 700 that day would go largely unrecorded and unappreciated. As the New Zealanders themselves saw it, it was the Australian achievement that deserved the praise. 'No orders, no proper military "team work", no instructions, just absolute heroism.'[10]

It was a view held by the watchers afloat. On one of the battleships, Ashmead Bartlett, the official correspondent, drafted his despatches on the exploits of that day. He too wrote of it as Australia's day and in his initial draft he made no mention

---

[*]   5100 would land by 1 May 1915. Some 1000 returned to Egypt with ships carrying wounded. These were drivers, batmen, groomsmen of the Army Service Corps who were originally to land once all the fighting echelon was ashore — they would trickle back to Gallipoli during the month of May.

of 'New Zealand' or 'New Zealanders'. By chance, a naval staff officer noticed the omission as he censored the despatch. A friend of Godley's, he inserted the words 'New Zealand' and 'New Zealanders' wherever he thought appropriate. These despatches would trumpet the deeds of the ANZAC Corps around the world. It is by such actions that legends are born.

It was grim reality in that first week as both Australians and New Zealanders fought dourly to hang onto the gains of the first day. With their backs to the sea, they clung to two narrow ridges of land that linked inland as the two arms of a triangle, with the third arm being the sea coast and the beach, but the apex of the triangle, Baby 700, the height, was now held by the Turks. It was an impossible situation. The ANZACs were holding on by their fingernails. A Turkish advance at any point meant disaster. Two hundred metres on the left flank at Russell's Top or 30 metres in the centre at Quinn's would mean the destruction of the ANZAC Corps.

Anzac, as this foothold on Turkish soil became known, was in a state of siege. Few sieges have involved so many men for such a small piece of ground. The Turks fought to drive the ANZACs into

Life in the trenches. *(025A, ALO 645, Stereo Glass Plate, Wingnut Archive)*

the sea, the ANZACs fought to secure their foothold by seizing the apex, Baby 700. Only when these heights were seized could the ANZACs move from the defensive to the offensive. Within the besieged lines, the Australians and New Zealanders each fought true to type. 'The jealousy that existed between New Zealand and Australia in Cairo vanished in one blow on the first day at Anzac.'[11] The Australian was there to kill Turks, not to dig holes! Unmatched in the attack, apathetic and reluctant in defence, no one but he could have won a footing at Anzac, but the Australian temperament made him unsuited to the monotony of holding on.

The New Zealander had no opportunities to attack. From the start he was used to plug the line, to hang onto the gains of the first day, and from the outset the New Zealander demonstrated an appreciation that the shovel and pick were as important as the rifle and bayonet. The cost was high. The Canterburys lost their Commanding Officer, Lieutenant Colonel D. MacBean Stewart, on that first day. All the officers and sergeants of the 16th Waikatos, including Alderman, Baddeley, Allen and Westmacott, were killed or wounded. But as they fell, so others took their place. Dawson of the Aucklanders held Quinn's Post that first difficult night. Wallingford, an expert with rifle and machine gun, was everywhere the line was threatened. Fielden Taylor, the padre, earned the devotion of all New Zealanders.

One of the commanding officers, Lieutenant Colonel W.G. Malone, confirmed a reputation that had grown around him during the hard days of training in Egypt. He had the drive, determination and sense of organisation to excel in the defence. Under him, the left flank of Walker's Ridge and Russell's Top was secured during the savage, senseless fighting of the first week. It would never again be seriously threatened by the Turk. He would perform the same service in early June at the critical centre of the ANZAC line. In turn, his Wellington battalion would garrison Courtney's and Quinn's posts. Under his leadership and practical commonsense, stinking pits held by frightened men dominated by superior Turkish fire and bombing would be transformed into impregnable positions. Malone established standards of organisation of defences, covered shelters, sanitation and hygiene that became models for the other battalions at Anzac to aspire to. Malone earned a reputation as landlord of Quinn's Post, and Quinn's became known as Wellington Battalion property, and other battalions as they served their time in the line at Quinn's had to leave it as they found it.

Gallipoli was a soldier's war. Both the Australian and the New Zealander would show their amateur status at Gallipoli but they quickly became expert. Though they were individually brave, and possessed an initiative and a degree of skill of improvisation unknown to the British soldier, these individual attributes could only partially compensate for their inexperienced commanders. Large-scale operations required careful coordination, reconnaissance and planning. This was invariably lacking in the first months at Gallipoli. Such poor planning caused the failure of Godley's first divisional attack on 2 May 1915. This over-ambitious effort doubled his New Zealand losses after a week ashore to 1200. Many of the mistakes would be repeated. It became clear that Godley's undoubted ability as a trainer was not matched by an understanding of the capabilities of his men in combat, their strengths and their weaknesses.

The rugged nature of Gallipoli terrain imposed limitations on a commander at every level. It demanded that commanders be well forward to recognise crises as they arose and be able to quickly communicate any orders necessary to meet the situation. Godley never met this challenge. To Godley a battalion was a battalion, be it 900 strong men fresh from training in Egypt and anxious to see active service, or 400 scarecrows, worn and gaunt after three months' service on the Peninsula, with dysentery endemic among the ranks and most of the officers and NCOs (non-commisioned officers) gone. His faith in his New Zealanders' ability was constant, they were good for 'irregulars', but this was a faith born out of detachment. As the campaign progressed, his New Zealanders increasingly felt they counted for nothing in his eyes and hated Godley because of it.

The failure of the 2 May attacks satisfied Hamilton that Anzac held little prospect for a successful breakout. It was a view shared by the Australians and New Zealanders in the trenches: 'It's a … failure but we can't chuck it.' So the Australian and New Zealand Corps was to hold its perimeter while Hamilton attacked with his Regular 29th Division in the south at Helles. The two strongest brigades, the New Zealand Infantry Brigade and the 2nd Australian Brigade, were shipped south as reserves for this attack. At Helles the New Zealanders found that amateurism and poor planning was not an ANZAC preserve.

The cricket-strip-wide beach at Anzac Cove was the centre of life within the perimeter. It was here that stores and water were drawn, reinforcements came ashore and wounded were evacuated. Men going to the cove would have a wash, take the chance to search for lice (note the man on the right), have a yarn or look up friends in cushy jobs on the beach. *(NAM Waiouru)*

On the third day of the Helles battle, the New Zealand Infantry Brigade, some 2600 strong, attacked the Turkish line alone. They advanced over open farmland from 1000 metres behind their own front line. Opposing them were at least twice their number of Turkish infantry, dug in and expecting an attack. Four New Zealand battalions of infantry advanced against nine battalions of Turks, with no clear orders or objectives. Turkish artillery and machine-gun fire cut them down before the British front trenches were reached. The attack was repeated later in the day and the 2nd Australian Brigade suffered the same fate. Two senseless and avoidable Balaclavas, but without anyone reaching the Turkish front line. Most never saw a Turk. Casualties were heavy, some 900 were killed and wounded among the New Zealanders alone.

In three weeks the New Zealanders at Gallipoli had suffered as many battle casualties as there had been Pakeha casualties in the Land Wars and casualties in the Boer War. The Infantry Brigade was now less than half-strength, the critical losses being among the officers and non-commissioned officers. The Auckland and Otago battalions had been shot to pieces. Morale plummeted. Praise was heaped on the New Zealand and 2nd Australian brigades for their heroism, and the term 'White Gurkha' was used as an accolade. Yet this 'puff' did little for New Zealand's spirits and no one

Members of the New Zealand Divisional Signals with Corporal Cyril Bassett, the New Zealand Gallipoli VC, second from right. 'All my mates ever got were wooden crosses.' *(Robert William Robinson Collection – PA1-o-438, Alexander Turnbull Library)*

in authority outside the brigade appeared to recognise that the attack had been a shambles and that 'blame should be attached to some quarter'.[12]

After two defeats the New Zealand Infantry Brigade was not a happy organisation. The brigade commander was a sick man, increasingly at odds with his commanding officers, and the feeling grew among some of the officers that New Zealanders 'have nothing to learn from the imported (Imperial) men. They are not practical men.'[13]

The remnants, now made up with reinforcements, returned to Anzac in mid-May. They met up with the New Zealand Mounted Rifles, who had come as dismounted infantry to hold the Anzac perimeter. Now, for the first time, Godley had both his New Zealand brigades under his command on operations. Life had assumed the monotony of trench warfare. From May until August they would hold their share of the line at Anzac.

It had become an Antipodean colony, reminiscent of the gold-rush camps of the Coromandel or the South Island. Life at Anzac reduced existence to the basics: lice, flies, dysentery, no sleep and little water. Gallipoli was a struggle to survive. Each man's world was his area of the trench, two to three metres deep, and perhaps the same in length, with a niche in the trench wall covered by a blanket where he rested by day and tried to sleep. His belongings were a greatcoat, webbing, rifle and bayonet. His dress was a singlet and shorts. Dirty, unkempt, bearded, he bathed in the sea whenever his duties took him to Anzac Cove, risking death from Turkish shrapnel to do so. His food was beef and biscuits, the first salty, the last rock-hard. Bacon fat and rotten cheese and jam that ran like thin watery juice completed his fare. A lack of fresh vegetables, no exercise, the dirt and the monotony of the diet saw him waste away. His water allowance was a half-gallon a day.

New Zealanders marvelled that the greatest Empire on earth waged war in this fashion. Food, though monotonous, was plentiful, but everything else was lacking, from ammunition for the artillery and grenades for the infantry, to iron and timber for the trenches. They became masters of improvisation. Jam tin bombs matched the abundant Turkish supply of hand grenades. Periscopes and periscope rifles were made with glass cut from ships' mirrors and scavenged box wood. Barges would disappear overnight and become support and framing for trench and dugout. Stealing became an art form, but only from officers and other battalions, never from your mates.

The infantry and the mounteds proved equally adept at sniping and patrolling. They treated the rugged foothills of the coastal ranges as they would the scree slopes of their runs in the Canterbury foothills. Death from the sniper's bullet or from shrapnel bursting overhead was always present. Its presence was everywhere. You could not sink a post without striking a body. Bodies littered No Man's Land, were built into the trench wall, or were tidied into tiny cemeteries behind each post. The stench of the dead in the hot sun became as familiar as the flies and the lice, a smell so distinctive that it remained with veterans for the rest of their lives.

In the end the ANZAC persevered, living for a letter from home, waiting for each sunset to relieve him of the heat, the flies and Turkish artillery. There was little faith and less hope. He lived for his mates and for home. He distrusted his commanders. The Empire ceased to be sufficient excuse for no medical supplies, no canteen stores, no attempt to arrange fresh rations and, worst of all, no mail. The New Zealanders turned in on themselves, scorning the Tommies and those British officers whose only answer to another failure was a patronising arrogance and the loudly expressed belief that it would have worked with a 'few regulars'. Little hint of this reached New Zealand. 'The world outside has great confidence in their men but I often wonder if they realise or try to realise what a hell the firing line is and know that every man desires and cannot help desiring immediate peace.'[14]

By August, few of the New Zealand main body remained. Those who were left were worn men, but the majority of the force were newly arrived reinforcements. The promise of breaking out inspired sick men to hang on so that they might be with their mates for this last throw. And all knew that one last throw was about as much as they had left. Half in hope, half in fear, nagged by a growing belief that this time, on percentages, it was their turn, the New Zealanders prepared for the breakout battles of August 1915. Helles had failed and now Hamilton turned to Anzac in order to achieve the goals set on that first day, all those months before.

August was New Zealand's battle; for 36 hours the New Zealand Infantry Brigade held Chunuk Bair, the vital heights on the ranges above the coast. For 36 hours there was the faintest prospect of success, the possibility of an advance to the Narrows. Perhaps the fate of Turkey and its participation in the war, and if conclusions are drawn from this the history of the world in the twentieth century, rested unknowingly on the shoulders of those worn men belonging to the smallest nation taking part in the campaign.

It was not without cost. The New Zealand Mounteds, in a brilliant but now forgotten prelude, opened the way. The New Zealand Infantry, racked by internal dissent among its commanders, dithered and delayed. Opportunities were lost. The situation has similarities with a future campaign and another New Zealand brigade at Maleme in Crete, 25 years later. Finally, Malone's Wellingtons seized the heights of Chunuk Bair on 8 August 1915, and if New Zealand has a day, and a dawn service, it should be in memory of this largely forgotten hour when New Zealanders first saw the Narrows from the hill.

But having won it and held it against Turkish counter-attacks, it would be a New Zealand-born brigadier general who would play the major role in its loss and it would be Godley who would equally fail to grasp this, his moment of greatness. By 10 August it would be finished. The British battalions who relieved the exhausted New Zealanders would be thrown off the heights by Mustafa Kemal. Under Wallingford, the New Zealand survivors with their machine guns would stabilise the line and hold onto a spur below the crest. It would not be enough, and the fate of the campaign would be sealed. The animosity and infighting within the New Zealand Infantry Brigade took its toll. It ensured that New Zealanders would never receive full recognition for their achievements in the August battle. Vindictiveness within the brigade would see the now dead Malone of the Wellingtons blamed for losing Chunuk Bair. Hamilton would accept this, and his despatches published in 1916, while praising Malone's bravery, also made it equally clear where the fatal error lay. Malone had failed to dig in on the 'true-crest', and as this was left in Turkish hands, failure was inevitable, regardless of the bravery of Malone and his men.

This story has passed into legend and has become a myth of Gallipoli, subscribed to both by C.E.W. Bean and John North in their major works on the campaign. Failure and the suspicion of blame broke the surviving New Zealanders' spirits. They saw the dead blamed and the mediocre and incompetent praised. One New Zealander, Cyril Bassett, was awarded a justly earned V.C., the first awarded to a New Zealander in this war. Seven were awarded to the Australian Division for the battle at Lone Pine. Today, Lone Pine has a familiar ring in both Australia and New Zealand. Chunuk Bair was all but forgotten, until revived by Maurice Shadbolt's play *Once On Chunuk Bair*. But after August men spoke of the V.C.s that should have been awarded. 'Richard Warden, the great scout of the Auckland Battalion, killed on Chunuk Bair — the unknown soldier who was the heart and soul of the Wellington forward trench on Chunuk; Major Wallingford M.C., the hero of Anzac, and Fielden Taylor, the chaplain.'[15]

So many deeds, so few survivors and a belief held by both Godley and Brigadier General Russell, Commander of the Mounteds, that officers, regardless of their bravery, had been merely doing their jobs and therefore did not merit the V.C. All this led to an imbalance and the suggestion that the Australians have more to remember, the New Zealanders more to forget.

Finally, with disease and sickness rife, the New Zealanders were relieved in September and shipped to Lemnos to rest and re-establish the New Zealand brigades.

Nine hundred men sailed away, out of the thousands of New Zealanders who had fought on the Peninsula. They would return, still at half their original strength, now largely made up of reinforcements and convalescents. The siege would continue, but now it would be a different campaign. The extra acres won in the August offensive allowed a greater degree of freedom. Administration had improved, though the daily round of sentry, supports and fatigues would continue to be a soldier's lot. Other than the landscape, nothing was the same. What Gallipoli had been was the tale told by the silent mummified corpses forward of The Nek and on the slopes of Chunuk Bair. Already, to the new arrivals, the Gallipoli story had passed into legend.

In December 1915, the long anti-climax ended. Anzac was evacuated. It was a brilliantly conceived and executed operation. The irony is that if only the care and forethought that marked the end had been evident at its beginnings, in April and early May, how different it might have been.

Now the ANZACs were a veteran and professional team. The backbone of experience was provided by the few survivors still serving from those who had landed before August. Russell of the Mounted Rifles commanded NZ & A Division, and Godley the ANZAC Corps. Back in Egypt, the New Zealand Division was formed. Russell would command it throughout the remainder of the war. He would build on the reputation won at Gallipoli and would refuse a corps command in France to stay with his New Zealanders. Godley, as Corps Commander, would remain Commander of the New Zealand Expeditionary Force. His administration of this force would establish a policy that is largely followed still in the relationship between New Zealand forces serving overseas with larger allied forces. This particular skill of Godley's lay beyond the perception of the New Zealander in the trenches. As Corps Commander he was now, for them, thankfully all too remote. The good he had done was forgotten, except by the government and perhaps the public at home. In the eyes of the men who had served him at Gallipoli, Godley had failed their trust.

Gallipoli was initially a bitter memory. 'We will not be terribly proud of our Gallipoli "Bar". Ours is not to reason why, but just to do and die; but who has blundered?'[16] However, though the taste of defeat must have been gall to men who believed they had achieved everything asked of them, and yet saw others lose what they had won, Gallipoli was a major step in our recognition of ourselves as New Zealanders. It is a process that continues today. No one point can be labelled as the time we stood up uniquely as ourselves.

O.E. Burton wrote: 'Somewhere between the bloody ridge of Chunuk Bair in August 1915 and the black swamp in front of Passchendaele in October 1917, New Zealand quite definitely found individuality and nationality.'[17]

Identity and a growing consciousness of individuality were forced on us from the time the main body of the New Zealand Expeditionary Force arrived in Egypt. Even if we did not, others labelled us 'New Zealanders'. Finally, Gallipoli confirmed a difference in approach, and showed that although we had much in common with our nearest neighbours, the Australians, and with the men from the British Isles, their ways were not always our way.

As the largest single body ever to sail from these shores, the first of the New Zealand Expeditionary Force found 'that the great distance from their own country created an atmosphere of loneliness. This loneliness was emphasised by the fact that the New Zealanders rarely received the same recognition in the press, and many of their gallant deeds went unrecorded or were attributed to their greater neighbours. But they had a silent pride that put these things into proper perspective.'[18] 'Silent' is the word invariably used of New Zealanders — in France the New Zealand Division was called 'The Silent Division'. Not for them the singing to and from the trenches. In appearance and speech they displayed 'a peculiar inhibition, a seeking as it were, to avoid all distinction'.[19] In battle, this reticence matched with a practical professionalism set them apart.

A consciousness of loneliness and isolation had seen young New Zealanders willingly join the colours to see the world. Now the distance from New Zealand strengthened the bond with the raw new land they had left. 'Home' ceased to be a dream of England. It became the remembered reality of small town and country New Zealand. The hills of Gallipoli conjured up the images of home: the hills above Paekakariki, or the scree slopes of inland Canterbury. Men would gaze out to sea as the sun set over the hazy outline of Imbros and think of home 'and for a moment we were back in Ashburton again'. The regional battalions reinforced this homesickness — each district served together, Auckland, Canterbury, Wellington, and Otago, and common thoughts, often not expressed, were sensed. Even today, outside perhaps of Auckland, New Zealand has still 'a village pattern of relationship'.[20] This was true in the trenches of Gallipoli and grew until it encompassed the entire Expeditionary Force.

Comradeship or 'mateship' was the direct result of this relationship. 'If I let my mates down how could I go back and face the people at home?' There was no escape from who you were. Everyone knew you or could quickly establish a link through some mutual acquaintance. This became the key to both our identity and our growing reputation in battle. This was the sense of responsibility that forced the Aucklanders forward to certain destruction on the morning of 7 August 1915. This commitment to each other led to 36 hours of clinging onto the slopes of Chunuk Bair when commonsense should have indicated that they were beaten men. These men with 'their flat laconic idiom' found a confidence 'born in war', nurtured in war. It would make them one of the most formidable divisions in France and its characteristics would be seen again in the Second World War, almost 20 years later. 'They were mature men, these New Zealanders — quiet and shrewd and sceptical. They had none of the tired patience of the Englishmen, nor that automatic discipline that never questions orders to see if they make sense. Moving in a body, detached from their homeland, they remained quiet and aloof and self-contained. They had a confidence in themselves such as New Zealanders rarely have, knowing themselves as good as the best in the world could bring against them.'[21]

This discovery of identify and nationality was not immediately shared with New Zealanders at home. Our sense of nationality would percolate through from the experience of New Zealanders at war, but what they saw in 1914–18, and then in

1939–45, would not be widely recognised until the last quarter of the twentieth century. New Zealand itself would largely remain locked into a dream of a world before 1914. The confidence and vitality 'born in war' would be consumed in the fires of Gallipoli and then of France and Flanders. All that energy and promise was dissipated in the frustration and agony of years of battle.

Today, it is fashionable to decry as myth the idea of a 'lost generation of 1914'. Statistically, survivors were plentiful; men of Gallipoli fought, came home to a hero's welcome, and took their place back in society. According to records, 8556 New Zealanders fought at Gallipoli; 7473 were casualties — 2515 killed in action, 206 killed by accidents and disease, 4752 wounded. The figure indicating the wounded is deceptive; many of the 8556 were wounded more than once and this is included in the total. Even so, casualties as a percentage of New Zealanders involved were very high. Yet they do not take into account the enormous wastage from disease, the dysentery and enteric fever that were permanently crippling more men than shell and

The first New Zealand wounded arrive in Wellington on the SS *Willochra*, 15 July 1915.

bullet. Hardly a man of those who landed before August 1915 served on the Peninsula without being evacuated through wounds or sickness. At the evacuation in December 1915, there were perhaps five or ten originals from the landing in each company of some 223, and most were returned convalescents.

For the majority of those who sailed from New Zealand in 1914, Gallipoli was their only war. By January 1916, before the casualties began flowing from France, 3111 New Zealanders had returned to New Zealand unfit for further overseas service, and there were 4857 sick or wounded in hospitals throughout the Mediterranean and England. Gallipoli had exacted a heavy toll. France and Flanders, the Sinai and Palestine would further erode those who had seen Gallipoli service. But even by January 1916 they were figures of legend.

> *There are plenty of slouch hatted soldiers in town,*
> *Doughty and debonair, stalwart and brown;*
> *Some are from Weymouth or Salisbury Plain;*
> *Others have 'pushed' in the Western campaign;*
> *Call them 'Overseas soldiers' or 'down under' men,*
> *Declare that each one is as daring as ten;*
> *Call them 'Cornstalks' or 'Fernleaves' — all out for a fight —*
>
> *But don't call them ANZACs, for that isn't right.*
>
> *The ANZACs — their ranks are but scanty all told —*
> *Have a separate record illumined in gold.*
> *Their blood on Gallipoli's ridges they poured,*
> *Their souls with the scars of that struggle are scored;*
> *Not many are left, and not many are sound,*
> *And thousands lie buried in Turkish ground,*
> *These are the ANZACs; the others may claim*
> *Their zeal and their spirit, but never their name.*[22]

Those who still served were absorbed in the struggle for survival on the Western Front; Gallipoli was the past and unspoken. It was the same for the many who returned to New Zealand in 1915 and 1916. It was a hero's welcome and they found that their loved ones cheered them home without any real understanding of what they had been through. Nor could they tell them — it was an age when gentlemen did not tell women of lice, flies and dysentery, and of men dying in agony untended.

In New Zealand there was a reluctance to know. If you tried, it became too difficult. Where did you start? And so war's truths would continue to remain remote; 'no alien bayonets would glitter on these shores'. The New Zealand press would extol suffering in the old, old way. Noble deeds by brave sons dying for King and Empire. The war had brought prosperity to New Zealand, and pride and guilt made the New Zealand public want to believe that this carnage had a purpose. Grief and questioning remained a private act. The returned veterans found themselves strangers in the land they loved and one which they perhaps appreciated far more than those who had stayed behind. The sick and wounded were institutionalised under government care, and paraded each 'Landing Day' in their blue uniforms, while the pace of New Zealand life passed them by.

It was the same with those discharged as unfit for further active service. New Zealand has never lived comfortably with its history and never with its heroes, and this was certainly true of the Gallipoli heroes. They were far from heroic, suffering from the aftereffects of wounds and sickness. Employers appreciated that 'they had done their bit' but they were looking for fit men. So they fitted in as best as they could, grew embittered at the lack of work and lack of recognition, and locked away Gallipoli and the sense of identity they had found there in their hearts. They had seen the Narrows — but it was a feeling of unity or kinship that they never passed on. Theirs was a generation blighted by war. So many dead, and the rest exhausted by the toil of a war, they allowed Massey's generation to continue to run New Zealand.

They failed to give a lead. New Zealand continued to be a country searching for the world of 1914 and the security of Empire, and not accepting everything had changed. The 1920s and 1930s were years of struggle, years of unfulfilled promise. 'The Great War — the first Great War — cut deep into a generation of men and tired out those who survived. In the bad years there was a wide gulf between the ignorance of our youth, and the old men who had run the country for so long. The old men were tired old men and played for safety. The young men wanted action and belief, and found neither. Between the two generations there grew up a genuine hatred, rare and peculiar to those times.'[23]

It is more than that. Three generations are involved and the one that is missing is the generation that fought the 1914–18 war. They stood aside, in the years of depression, the bad years, and let the generation before them continue to rule with the same vision. They were lumped in with the 'old men', and in a sense they were old.

War had tested them and pushed them to the limit and they were not prepared to go that far again. It was the men of their generation still untested and keen for the struggle who would lead New Zealand, men such as Savage, Nash and Fraser, who had opposed the war in 1914–18.

The world and New Zealand had changed, and there was no going back. Never again would we commit ourselves so innocently and unthinkingly. In 1939–45 New Zealanders once more glimpsed 'the Narrows', found anew that sense of identify 'born in war', nurtured in war. It would be on the foundation built by our reputation from 1914–18. Consciously or not, Gallipoli and its costs left its mark on New Zealanders.

But New Zealand's story of Gallipoli faded into legend. A *Popular History* was published in 1919, but no official New Zealand history was ever produced. We left our story to be told by C.E.W. Bean, in his epic two-volume work *The Story of ANZAC*, and while it is a study of depth and objectivity, the New Zealander plays an anonymous and at times misleading role. We became submerged into an Anzac epic, where the deeds and even the name were synonymous with Australia. That is why today 'The Landing' and 'Lone Pine' and 'The Nek' have a familiar ring but the 'Daisy Patch, 'Chunuk Bair' and 'Hill 60' are unknown.

There was little examination of the importance of Gallipoli to New Zealand: one novel, a play, a handful of personal recollections. There was no encouragement to remember. Horace Moore-Jones, whose watercolours of the Gallipoli landscape were a common sight as prints in the 1920s and 1930s, offered his works to the New Zealand government in 1917 after displaying them throughout New Zealand to packed galleries. Our government declined and they were bought by Australia.

Our country found it easier to live with monuments in stone in every settlement and town. Whatever the public saw in Anzac Day, the ANZACs themselves saw in the day a touchstone for those feelings of confidence, comradeship and identity that they had experienced as 'New Zealanders' at Gallipoli, in France and in the Sinai. It overlaid the struggle and the sacrifice and became a memory to treasure. Perhaps one day the country would feel it too.

> *Men of our islands and our blood returning*
> *Broken or whole, can still be reticent;*
> *They do not wear that face we are discerning*
>
> *As in a mirror momentarily lent,*
>
> *A glitter that might be pride, an ashy glow*
> *That could be pity, if the shapes would show.*[24]

This then is their story, told as much as possible in their words and with their photos. Both diaries and cameras were forbidden on the Peninsula, but this was the New Zealanders' first big trip overseas, and everyone wanted to keep a record. 'Cameras were forbidden, but one has to take a risk. I still have the number "A" Kodak and if it could speak, it would tell of the days it was buried, carried in ammunition boxes, in the open shirt, stuffed in the lining of a greatcoat, it also suffered from heat and wet and shortage of films. Many of the films stuck together and were useless, and after a lapse of 9 months, developed; some prints to be stolen by a Gippo Chemist. However, I present to you what remains and hope you will understand the circumstances of their origin.'[25]

This is the soldiers' story. It is incomplete because much of it has died with them. It is subjective because it is their words and their photos. Personalities stand out; in some cases this is due to the evidence that survives, while equally important stories have been lost.

Every man who served on Gallipoli endured, and established a reputation and a sense of identity that is important to us today. Through it we can establish who we are. This, then, is the tale that diaries, letters and the oldest of old men once told. This is Gallipoli's and New Zealand's story.

2

THE LOUD BEATING
OF THE DRUM

And I was a fool leaving
Good land to moulder,
Leaving the fences sagging
And the old man older
To follow my wild thoughts
Away over the hill,
Where there is only the world
And the world's ill, …[1]

"War is declared Jack!" "What war?" I said. "Civil war in Ireland?" For the papers had been full of Home Rule and Irish unrest for weeks back, and as it was two weeks since we had seen a paper and the newest we ever got were two days old when they reached us, there was time for quite a lot to take place in the world, without our knowledge or comment. "German," said Mcintosh briefly. "Fool's war — madness, I call it. Picking a quarrel with all the world at once. Fools!" He gave a final grunt of farewell and jogged heavily away.'[2]

The immediate prospect of war burst in to New Zealand's public consciousness in the last days of July 1914. This immediacy evoked scenes of widespread public enthusiasm. Everywhere there appeared a national confidence in New Zealand's preparedness for war and willingness to fight. These scenes have never been repeated on the same scale since. New Zealand's international history in the twentieth century is very much the story of a nation at war, but never again would we embrace the prospect of war as cheerfully and innocently as did those boisterous and patriotic crowds in 1914.

'I was chopping bush on the Motu River, about 48 miles out of Gisborne. Had a contract for clearing 170 acres. I only had one mate with me, Reg McRae, and we had been out there some 12–13 weeks. I had a dream one night. that England had declared war on Germany and that I would be wounded and my mate Reg would be killed. I

Train stop at Taihape in 1914. *(F.G. Radcliffe, G7059-1/2, Alexander Turnbull Library)*

Service to king, empire and country was a tenet of New Zealand society. Christchurch Boer War veterans receive their medals from the Duke of York, later King George V, in a parade at Hagley Park, 1901. *(F67958-1/2, Alexander Turnbull Library)*

told Reg about my dream the next day ... I said we were at war with Germany.

'"No such luck," said Reg. Just a bit after midday, the boss came down, he had the paper. Reg said, "By Jove, Charlie, your dream came true."

'The boss said: "It's not true yet, but the whole of Europe's at war. The Duke and Duchess of Austria have been killed, and they're blaming the joker that done it on to Serbia, and they have declared war on Serbia. Russia declared war on Austria, Germany has declared war on Russia, and France and England are in a treaty with Russia and it looks as if they are both coming in at any time."

'The boss then asked: "What are you going to do?"

'"Well, I'm going to the war," said Reg.

'So I says, "Hold on, you can't go to the war. We've got a contract here to do and there's a lot to do in it yet!"

'So the boss says to us, "If England goes to war and if you want to go, I'll cancel the contract and pay you day wages and take it off your bill at the store."'[3]

Service to King, Empire and country was a tenet of New Zealand society. It was a virtue extolled in most outward expressions of New Zealand society, the press, architecture, dress and in the schools. Young boys trained as school cadets from the age of eight years and remained involved in some form of military activity until the age of 25 years. The basic school text, the *New Zealand School Journal*, contained as its principal theme stories of patriotism and tales of the heroes of the British Empire. School children were encouraged to use these Imperial figures as models for their own lives. To be a New Zealander in 1914 was to be taught that 'The Empire itself looks to you to be ready in time of need, to think, to labour and to bear hardships on its behalf.'[4]

This outward display was imperial in theme but had national undertones. Anthony Trollope perceived this in 1873: 'New Zealand considers herself to be the cream of the British Empire ... The New Zealander among John Bulls is the most John Bullish. He admits the supremacy of England to every place in the world, only he is more English than any Englishman at home.'[5]

Its effect is imprinted in the diaries and memories of the period. Ewen Pilling, a student at Otago University, mirrored the thoughts of many of his countrymen as he wrestled with the implications of war.

'Can any one of us be persuaded into the belief that his duty lies in safety here at home, while the other fellow goes out to endure all manner of hardship, to be wounded, yea to die for his country? Has the call come to me? ... I believe that the Empire to which I belong stands on God's side in the cause of righteousness and Justice in this world, and that his servants must array themselves against the power and evil influences and ambitions of a nation like Germany. I believe God calls me in this way.'[6]

Dan Curham, then an office worker in Wanganui, recalled that, 'It was a mixture of patriotism and adventure. I was always interested in battles, deeds that won the Empire. There was not the doubt and questioning that we have now. We were more simple-minded I think. We used to look at the map and see all the red areas. We were "wisely ruled" and "loyal to the Crown".'[7]

Most took patriotism for granted. It was a comfortable cloak that they had worn unthinkingly since childhood. War in New Zealand was something in the distant past. Our only experience in foreign wars had been the Boer War of 1899–1902. In New Zealand's eyes it had been a glorious adventure, short, sharp and victorious, with New Zealanders playing a highly public if minor role. Ten contingents of mounted rifles had been sent to South Africa to serve with Imperial Forces, a total strength of 6500, with 8000 horses.

Each contingent had served in South Africa for 12 months. Towns 'had cheered them at their departure' with parades and speeches, and 'the loyal shouts of the inhabitants greeted the soldiery' on their return. The New Zealand Mounted Rifles built up an enviable reputation as scouts and horsemen well suited to the irregular guerrilla war waged by the Boer on the veldt. They were lauded as natural soldiers. It was a reputation that the New Zealand public was more than willing to believe.[*]

'The average young New Zealander … especially the young New Zealander who lives in the country, is half a soldier before he is enrolled. He is physically strong, intellectually keen, anxious to be led though being what he is, he will not brook being driven a single inch. Quick to learn his drill, easily adapting to the conditions of life in camp since camping usually is his pastime and very loyal to his leaders when those leaders know their job.'[8]

War was seen as an international tour involving countries of the world in a series of matches with preordained results. The Empire would win. New Zealand's only concern about involvement was a fear that our boys would not get there in time to play the series. If Germany was going to fight the British Empire then Germany must be in the wrong. New Zealanders had unquestioning faith in the righteousness and might of the Empire.

'When New Zealanders went to war, they were ignorant of its causes and innocent of its meaning. No alternative was suggested by the politicians or the press, or the parsons.'[9]

War in the service of the Empire was a noble cause, a crusade, and anyone who gave his life in such a war should be seen as a martyr. This was the message of the press and pulpit, but it was not patriotism alone that stirred young men to go to war. In 1914 they flocked to the drill halls and clamoured to join up for other reasons too. While some New Zealanders, such as Ewen Pilling, could accept the war as a crusade, such fervent belief was exceptional. For most young men in 1914 war was adventure, escape, a chance to see the world. 'No one ever thought of not coming back.'[10]

On the East Coast the boss of Charlie Clark and Reg McRae had come back with the news that England was at war. So they took him up on his offer and went

---

[*] This was built largely on the performance of the first contingents; later contingents suffered in the quality of the recruit, who was committed immediately to anti-guerrilla operations with little training and no administrative support; pay, welfare, mail and hospital care were lacking. This led to 'strikes', which threatened New Zealand's reputation.

To avoid this, the 8th, 9th and 10th Contingents were to serve as a New Zealand Brigade under a New Zealand Commander, Colonel. R.H. Davies, with proper administrative support. The end of the war in 1902 prevented this.

Corporal Charlie Clark (left) and his mate in the 17th Ruahine Company. *(Clark Family)*

Dan Curham. 'It was a mixture of patriotism and adventure.' *(Curham Family)*

The 'Rawene Boys' enlist for war. 'No one ever thought of not coming back.' *(Harris Collection, Auckland War Memorial Museum)*

The Boer War: a glorious adventure with each man a hero. This image shows the reality of a guerilla war on the Veldt where farms were burned and stock was slaughtered to force the Boer Commandos to surrender. *(W.F. Raynes Collection, 81923-1/2 Alexander Turnbull Library)*

'We thought of ourselves as natural soldiers.' Private Kivell (second from left in the rear rank) and his tent mates at annual camp. *(NAM, Waiouru)*

into town. 'I went into Gisborne and all the bushmen from the district were in and there were bushmen out on the town and I was one of them and I liked a spot too. So we had a few drinks and we all marched over and put our names down to go into the War.'[11]

For most New Zealanders it was their one chance to get away and do something different. It was a mood that gripped young men's hearts country wide.

'I was working on the Wairua Falls power line and I rode to Whangarei the following day and enlisted. Riding home … I met Friedrich Petersen, who had in his younger days been a member of the German Army. I told him I had enlisted and he said, "I fink the Ghermans vill vin," but I was not unduly concerned because I wanted to see something of the world and joining the Army seemed to me a chance of doing so on the cheap.'[12]

Henry Lewis, then an apprentice motor mechanic in Wellington, remembered: 'I had been living with a stepmother and she didn't suit me so good so I thought that it would be an opportunity to make a break — I'll go to war. We were very loyal in those days to the British Empire … I wouldn't say that had a great deal to do with it, but it was just to go with the boys and be with them.'[13]

Cecil Malthus, 12th Nelson Company: '… we certainly doubted whether we should be in time to see any fighting.' *(Malthus Family)*

George Skerret worked on the wharfs at Bluff. 'There was a parade called for the Territorials and I volunteered. I don't know why, I think it was because I wanted to be with my mates. King and Empire was the last thing on my mind. Not everyone was keen to join but many changed their minds when they saw that everyone was going.'[14]

'When I joined up most of the volunteers in our regiment had been members of a rowing club I was in and the football team I used to play with. I know the Wanganui Rowing Club almost shut down because most of its members went into camp for active service.'[15]

University classes emptied, representative games were cancelled, sports fixtures were abandoned. To be left behind was unthinkable. If your mate was going, then somehow you had to get away too. Each regiment was responsible for recruiting its quota for the Expeditionary Force, and had strict instructions to eject anyone under the age of 20 years.

But as the Territorial training age started at 18 years, there were many under-age applicants. Good men known to be under age were accepted. 'I was 19 and in the Territorial Force. A few friends of mine and I took our training seriously and we were in the local infantry battalion. When I went to enlist, the recruiting warrant officer told me I was too young, so he put me in the medical corps.'[16]

Regimental staff were prepared to close an eye to under-age enlistments and many youthful applicants of Otago Medical School ended up in the field ambulances of the Expeditionary Force. Similar situations were faced by the military in each district. 'Polly' Parrant of Petone was a Territorial in the Mounted Rifles: 'I had not attended parades and should have been prosecuted. I met Hastings, my captain in the Territorial Force, on the day after war was declared. He said, "I don't think we will get to war but I want volunteers." Initially he did not want to take me because I had not attended training but after a talk he agreed. He said he thought we would be an army of occupation or something like that, and we wouldn't see any active service. I didn't go to work the next day and when I told my mother she said, "You're crazy! People will not take a boy like you." But I was one of the first into camp at Awapuni.'[17]

Indeed, the mothers were less enthusiastic. 'I was working on a farm in Central Otago when the papers brought news of the War. I joined because it was the proper thing to do. I was under-age, 19, but I put my age up as no one checked. My mother quizzed me on this but she let me go, after talking with my uncles, as they said I would get away anyway. I joined the 10th Otago Company, the local Territorial regiment, with its headquarters in Oamaru.'[18]

Inland from Otorohanga, at the head of the Waipa River, a young farmer was preparing to go into a territorial camp to study and then sit for his promotion examinations. He was an infantry second lieutenant in the 16th Waikato Regiment of Infantry. Part-time soldiering was his only relaxation from breaking in the rugged acres of bush on the slopes of the Rangitoto Range. He had come north, as had many

'To be left behind was unthinkable. If your mate was going, then somehow you had to get away too!' Volunteers for the Main Body NZEF march through Christchurch, August 1914. *(The Press, G11949-1/1, Alexander Turnbull Library)*

others from the South Island, lured by the prospect of land at a shilling an acre in the King Country. Spencer Westmacott had toiled on Rangitoto since 1910, and now he was conscious of the prospect of war, a prospect he had dreamed of since he was a boy, but at 28 years old, it seemed it would always be a dream unfulfilled.

'I lay long enough reading *From Midshipman to Field Marshal* to be reminded for the unnumbered time that the romantic days were past when men went to war; but if I could not enjoy that experience myself I could recapture some of the excitement by reading about it — and with that thought I soon put out the candle and went to sleep.

'Up betimes, I milked the cow, had breakfast, tidied up, saddled my horse and changed out of my dungarees into blue undress uniform, which I thought to carry better that way than rolled up in a swag; I strapped the latter onto my pommel, and mounting my horse I drove the cow before me and rode slowly down the creek. Did anyone ever go to war driving a cow before him? I could not allow imagination to play on that subject, and felt self-conscious and ridiculous as I handed the quiet animal into Mrs

Herbert Spencer Westmacott, a dream fulfilled. *(Westmacott Family)*

Morton's keeping. She, good soul, only admired the uniform and saw no absurdity in it and so I rode on down the Waipa Valley alone.'[19]

It was 2 August 1914. Spencer Westmacott would be wounded and disabled at Gallipoli. He would not return to his farm at Rangitoto until 1926, and then he would find his hard-won slopes had reverted to secondary growth.

On 4 August 1914, England's ultimatum to Germany led to spontaneous demonstrations throughout the country. In all the main centres people flocked to the paper offices and waited for news. Similar scenes were witnessed in Dunedin, Christchurch, Wellington and Auckland. Flags were flown, patriotic songs were sung, and 'at intervals rousing cheers were given for Territorials in uniform who happened to pass along the street'.

Already preparations for war were well under way. On that day the Governor, Lord Liverpool, had issued a proclamation mobilising the New Zealand Garrison Artillery to man the guns protecting the ports.

On the same day the New Zealand government cabled to the British government asking permission to call for volunteers.[20] A reply was received on 6 August accepting the generous offer and indicating that 'One Mounted Rifles Brigade, one Field Artillery Brigade and one Infantry Brigade, with supply columns in proportion, would be a suitable composition.'[21]

On 5 August at 3.00 p.m. in Wellington, Lord Liverpool, with Prime Minister William Massey and the Leader of the Opposition, Sir Joseph Ward, present, read out a message from the King and New Zealand's reply that she was 'prepared to make any sacrifice. The noise of applause and cheering was cut short when the Governor read: "War has broken out with Germany.[22] Crowds took to the streets. New Zealand was joyously at war.

'Next day it was quite clear we were at war. We discussed every aspect as we smoked our pipes in the spells between periods. Enquiries as to when and where we could offer our services resulted in our being told there were as yet no instructions and no form of application. We were most of us, in my class, young enough to be eager to go. But I was surprised to find there were some who were not, especially Hawkins, who was most dubious. He was a married man with a young family, he said. He did not know if he would have to go.' Hawkins was not alone in his doubts. 'It staggered me later to find officers in my billet, much my senior, especially two mounted rifle men, who had no intention of going.'

Nor was this reluctance confined to any particular rank. Westmacott speaks of three young town kids in the Territorials coming into the drill shed and asking one of the sergeant majors of the permanent staff: "'We don't have to go if we don't want to, do we Sergeant-Major?"... He said, "Hullo, what's this? White spots on the liver eh? No ye don't have to go if ye don't want to."

'On the other hand there was Captain Bluck that I had known on the strike. In the passage I heard him holding a long distance conversation over the telephone with his wife. He had said he would be going and after a pause with a note of surprise in his voice, he asked "You are not crying are you?" I fled. Bluck was a dairy farmer with a young family.[23] Bluck would sail with the Auckland Mounted Rifles. He would be one of the first officers of that regiment killed at Gallipoli.

New Zealand was well prepared for war in August 1914. The country's keenness to fight was matched by a military organisation that had developed rapidly since the passing of the 1909 Defence Act. This Act had established a system of compulsory military training.

The organisation had been outlined by Field Marshal Lord Kitchener on a visit to New Zealand in 1910. All New Zealanders from the ages of 14 to 30 years were liable for part-time military training. Boys from 14 to 18 years served in the senior cadets, and young men from 18 to 25 years served as territorial soldiers with the regionally affiliated regiments and battalions — hence the name 'Territorial'.

Service in the reserve was a requirement from the age of 25 to 30, but legislation allowed for this service to be extended up to the age of 55 years in the case of a national emergency. The same legislation allowed the Territorial Force to be mobilised by proclamation for service in New Zealand, and Section 26(1) of the 1909 Defence Act made provision for members of the Territorial Force to volunteer for special service outside New Zealand.[24]

The New Zealand government asked for an Imperial Officer to introduce this system of compulsory military training. The British government was keen to oblige,

3.00 p.m., 5 August 1914. Governor-General Lord Liverpool with Prime Minister Sir William Massey and Sir Joseph Ward, leader of the opposition. 'War has broken out with Germany.' New Zealand was joyously at war. *(NZ Herald)*

Field Marshal Lord Kitchener of Khartoum reviewing school cadets at Christchurch with Sir Joseph Ward in top hat. He visited New Zealand in 1910 and inspected the New Zealand Militia. His recommendations established the Territorial Force Scheme. *(NZ Herald, Auckland War Memorial Museum)*

Major General Sir Alexander Godley. 'It was a long way to go and I could not help feeling that one might in the Antipodes be out of sight and out of mind.' *(Wilson and Horton Collection)*

but it was not an attractive appointment. The New Zealand Defence Forces, particularly under 'King' Dick Seddon, had always been a political football, and the Colonial Office was well aware of the unhappy reports of previous British officers appointed to oversee our forces.

There were fears that the system of compulsory military training would suffer the same fate, that the New Zealand Prime Minister, Sir Joseph Ward, 'will still be influenced by political pressure and will keep the real power in his own hands — with disastrous results to military efficiency.'[25]

The British government offered Colonel Alexander Godley. Godley was of Anglo-Irish stock and a nephew of John Robert Godley of Canterbury fame. He came from a military family of good connections but little money. On his father's death, the young Godley was brought up dependent on the favour of his more wealthy relatives. He was sponsored through Sandhurst and as a subaltern joined the Dublin Fusiliers. He had no prospects outside the army, and he had to survive in a period when British Army officers needed a private income.

In 1910 Godley was not really in a position to refuse the New Zealand offer as others had. He sought advice; many said not to go, but Sir John French, Sir Ian Hamilton and Henry Rawlinson, while agreeing that it was a gamble, advised him to take it: 'The offer was, of course, a most tempting one; but it was a long way to go and I could not help have a feeling that one might in the Antipodes be out of sight and out of mind; more especially as I had been given to understand that I had a very good chance of being given a command of a regular brigade.'[26]

It was a doubt felt by many southbound travellers before him, but Godley agreed and was accepted by the New Zealand government. It was a good decision. The problems that had plagued previous New Zealand commanders largely escaped Godley. This was a tribute to the commander's skill in persuading both the public and politicians of the needs of the military. It is his great achievement that by 1914 New Zealand could boast of 'a real national army'.[27]

It was an impressive force for an isolated country of one million people. The New Zealand Army was planned as a field army of two infantry divisions, each of 12,000 men, as well as four mounted rifle brigades, each of 1500 men. There were coastal defence forces to watch the coastline and garrison artillery to man the guns in the forts that protected the main New Zealand ports.

By 1915 it was planned that this force would reach its ceiling of 30,000 men, and in the longer term Godley anticipated that, with reserves, the New Zealand Forces could draw upon 89,000 partially trained men. Godley proved equally adept as an organiser, administrator and trainer of men.

The country was divided into four Military Districts: Otago, Canterbury, Wellington and Auckland. Each provided one quarter of the Territorial Force. Each Military District was subdivided into areas, and local units were raised and recruited from each area. For example, in the Canterbury District there were four battalions of infantry, organised into an infantry brigade, and three regiments of mounted rifles organised into a mounted rifle brigade, as well as artillery, engineers, ambulance and supply units.

The 'Territorial' was a citizen in arms. Under the Defence Act he was required to carry out annually 31 drill parades of one and a half hours, 12 half-day parades, and seven full days of training in camp as well as completing 'the prescribed course of musketry'. Failure to attend resulted in the likelihood of prosecution and the risk of a fine or imprisonment.

Godley had brought a number of Imperial officers and non-commissioned officers to help him administer and train the territorials. He established the New Zealand Staff Corps (NZSC) for career officers and the New Zealand Permanent Staff (NZPS) for career warrant and non-commissioned officers. Cadets were sent for officer training to the newly founded Royal Military College of Australia at Duntroon, where ten places were allowed each year for New Zealanders. These measures allowed Godley

New Zealand's reputation for military prowess was built on the quality of our mounted infantry. The Canterbury Mounted Rifles Regiment marches past in an inspection at Sockburn Camp, August 1914.

(1914 Glass Plate Slide Collection, The Press newspaper – Fairfax Media)

to provide a nucleus of permanent, trained officers and non-commissioned officers for each district and for each battalion and regiment. From the beginning Godley kept in close touch with his colleagues in Britain and deliberately laid the foundations for an expeditionary force 'which this country will clamour to send at once if war broke out.'[28]

In 1912 Godley wrote to the New Zealand Minister of Defence, Sir James Allen and said, 'Of the large Continental powers there remains Germany who is our probable opponent in the next great war. In such a war the New Zealand overseas Expeditionary Force might be employed as follows:

a) For an attack on German overseas territory.
b) As first reinforcements to the British Expeditionary Force.
c) For operations in Egypt.'[29]

Samoa and German New Guinea were identified as likely German overseas territory to be seized by New Zealand, 'as a subsidiary operation' by a small force. But the Expeditionary Force proper could be better employed in Egypt: 'In the event of Turkey, instigated by Germany, advancing against Egypt from the East.' If not Egypt, there was Europe: 'Despite the distance from Europe, it would seem best that the Dominion troops should be given the opportunity of fighting with the British Expeditionary Force in the main theatre of operations … It is therefore suggested that as soon as it is considered safe to sail, it should proceed to Egypt, and be sent from there to the front with Imperial troops.'[30]

This was accepted. In 1912 Godley visited Sydney and met with the Australian Minister for Defence. A scheme was devised whereby a combined expeditionary force would be committed if either country were threatened. This force would be a division of 18,000 men, two thirds provided by Australia and one third by New Zealand.[*]

This provided the basis of the New Zealand offer to any future expeditionary force that was made in April 1913, when Sir James Allen, New Zealand Minister of Defence, visited London and, with Colonel Robin, New Zealand's representative on the Imperial General Staff, met with the Army Council. It was agreed that New Zealand's share in such an expeditionary force would be a headquarters, one brigade of infantry, one brigade of mounted rifles, a field battery of artillery totalling six guns, and associated engineer, medical and service units. This amounted to one quarter of the existing New Zealand Territorial Force.

Godley and his staff planned that this force would be drawn from the existing provincial regiments. Each existing regiment would mobilise one quarter of its strength, either a rifle company or a mounted rifles squadron, and this would enable

---

[*] In *The Story of ANZAC*, Vol. 1, p.28, C.E.W. Bean describes these negotiations but says that by the outbreak of war New Zealand's arrangements had not been effectively organised. This is incorrect. The speed of mobilisation and the efficient administration of the Advance Party and Main Body in August 1914 shows that these aspects had been well anticipated and planned for by Godley and his staff. It was certainly far ahead of Australian planning.

The New Zealanders were recruited as provincial battalions and regiments and were a source of provincial pride. James Allen, Minister of Defence, addressed the Canterbury Mounted Rifles Regiment of the NZEF at Sockburn Camp, August 1914. *(1914 Glass Plate Slide Collection, The Press newspaper – Fairfax Media)*

New Zealand to provide a constant supply of trained reinforcements to keep her contribution up to strength. Godley's training ensured that this force would be ready as soon as it was called for. In 1912, camps were held by battalions and regiments in the provincial areas. In 1913 units were concentrated into brigades for annual camp, and in 1914 divisional levels camps were held. These were some of the largest manoeuvres undertaken in New Zealand until the divisional camps of the 1950s. Godley was highly innovative; aeroplane reconnaissance featured in his exercises of 1913, and his formation of a Post and Telegraph Corps and Railway Battalion was unique among the Dominions of the British Empire.

This pace of military development is unparalleled in New Zealand's peace-time history and Godley himself wrote: 'For 1913, I was determined to hold brigade camps in spite of a good deal of opposition from my staff, who insisted, with some reason, that we were trying to fly before we could walk, and that it was a far too ambitious project. However I was firmly of the opinion, and always have been, that important as preliminary training and grounding may be, it is still more important to let people see the higher organisations and the higher training up to which they have to work. In this particular instance I felt pretty sure that there was no time to be lost in establishing the higher formations before we should be called upon to furnish an expeditionary force.'[31]

Godley kept in close touch with the feeling in Whitehall. In 1913 he returned to England, where he discussed the likely employment of a New Zealand expeditionary force with Douglas Haig and Sir Henry Wilson. Before his return to New Zealand, elements of the mounted rifles had experienced a rapid, if unofficial, mobilisation. This was in the wharf strikes of December 1913. Prime Minister Massey, doubting the ability of the police to handle the situation, ordered Godley's deputy, Colonel Heard, to call out the troops. Heard refused and Massey started enrolling 2000 special constables from the country districts.

Despite Colonel Heard's formal refusal, Massey's 'Specials' were largely Territorial Force. In both islands, throughout the country districts, local Territorial commanders contacted their men and gave instructions. They rode in as 'Massey's Cossacks'. They were quartered in military barracks, armed with long batons, organised on military lines into squadrons and troops, and maintained military discipline. It was in every sense a military operation.

In Wellington, Colonel Andrew H. Russell was Chief of Staff of the Wellington 'Specials'. A sheep farmer from Hawke's Bay, he had come in with fellow landowners and their drovers, farmhands and stockmen. In every case his squadrons were commanded by Territorial officers. From the Wellington 'Specials' alone, two of the squadron commanders and eight of the troop leaders would sail away to war with the Expeditionary Force or with the early reinforcements. Five of the ten would die at Gallipoli.[32]

It was the same in every New Zealand port. Godley both supported his deputy's actions and applauded the initiative shown by his Territorials: 'At Wellington the Mounted Rifles, camouflaged in this way, had made short work of the strikers. Mounted, and armed with stock whips, they rode through the town, and not only effectively dispersed riotous gatherings but pursued the rioters into the houses, and then dealt with them in such a manner that they had little stomach for a continuance of law-breaking.'[33] It was said, and the country districts were more than ready to believe, that 'the country had come to town to save the Country'. At the end of the strike Massey would award medals to his Specials. Few foretold that it was to be a dress rehearsal for war and that in eight months Russell would once again bring his Mounteds to town to fight for New Zealand.

Godley had the men, the organisation and the training. He also convinced the government to purchase the necessary military equipment. Artillery batteries were equipped with the most modern of British field pieces, the 18-pounder field gun. Two batteries, one in Palmerston North and one in Dunedin, were equipped with modern 4.5-inch howitzers. They would initially be the only such guns at Gallipoli and were invaluable in the hilly country. D Battery of Wellington was to be equipped with mountain guns but the four guns delivered in 1914 were found to be obsolescent and they were returned to Britain. It appears that they were then sold to Turkey and it is possible that they were next experienced by New Zealanders on the ridges above Anzac Cove.*

---

* Four Vickers 2.95-inch mountain guns were to be replaced by a new 2.75 inch Breech Loading Mountain Gun. (*AJHR*, H19, 1913, p.24.) C.E.W. Bean in *The Story of Anzac* (Vol. II, p.65), says that they were bought by Turkey from the New Zealand government. They may have been the guns intended for New Zealand, but Turkey purchased them directly from Britain.

It was the same with small arms and machine guns. Two machine guns were issued to each regiment of mounted rifles and each infantry battalion on the same scale as laid down for each British regular battalion. Each of the infantry soldiers was equipped with a .303 inch Magazine Lee Enfield (MLE) (Long) Mark I, which had been standard issue during the Boer War. These rifles were purchased in large quantities second-hand from the Canadian government and the Enfield factory in Britain, at considerable savings in cost. The most modern pattern rifle in service was the MLE (Short) Mark III. Sufficient of these had been imported to equip the artillery, engineers and mounted rifles. In all aspects, from webbing to weapons, New Zealand had bought sufficient stocks to equip her expeditionary force. Much of the material, such as clothing, boots and small arms ammunition, was manufactured in New Zealand.

We have never been better prepared for war at any stage in our history, although the *Encyclopaedia of New Zealand* takes a more dismal view: 'There were only a few modern guns for them, many old-fashioned rifles, and little else.'[34] The *Encyclopaedia* speaks of 'miraculous improvisation'. This was not the case; New Zealand had for the three previous years been involved in a period of sustained military growth without precedent in our history. Since 1909, defence expenditure had quadrupled and the effective strength of our forces had grown from 14,249 volunteers to 25,905 territorials. The scheme was not yet completely effective and would not be for another two years, but the planning had been done and New Zealand's likely war roles anticipated.

In May 1914, at the divisional annual camps, General Sir Ian Hamilton, Inspector General of Overseas Forces, reviewed the Territorial Force throughout New Zealand. He toured both islands and inspected 18,807 territorials and 17,868 cadets — a total of 36,675 men, or 70 percent of the Defence Forces. After a series of practical field exercises, Hamilton concluded that 'the military machine in New Zealand had been subjected to a severer trial than that of any portion of the Empire' ever inspected by him.[35] His conclusions were: 'It is well equipped; well armed; the human material is second to none in the world; and it suffers as a fighting machine only from want of field work and want of an ingrained habit of discipline.'[36] The first he concluded could never be made good unless the force went to war or was mobilised for a period of time. Egypt would provide New Zealanders with their fill of the second, as they would prove in the hard desperate days at Gallipoli.

Such expansion had not been without protest. Why was it that of all the forces of the Empire, only Australia and New Zealand had compulsory military training? There was growing opposition, particularly in Christchurch and in the mining centres of the West Coast and the Coromandel. This was based on the 'somewhat improbable alliance between middle-class liberalism and militant labour'.[37] In the year ending 30 April 1914 there were 3181 prosecutions against territorials for obstructing or absenting themselves from parades and 2779 were convicted. Among senior cadets there were 1601 prosecutions and 1367 convictions. Though these were but a small percentage compared to the number attending parades, there was evidence of a growing public concern about why we needed such strong defence forces.

Ashburton boys seeing the sights of Christchurch after enlisting for war service. 'Well, I am passed fit to go and fight for my country.' *(NAM Waiouru)*

Godley had no doubts; unquestionably our forces were being prepared to assist in a Continental war against Germany, but that was not something that he could tell the public. It was left to General Sir Ian Hamilton to provide an answer in an Auckland speech during his inspection of tour. He foretold the growing threat of 'Asiatic barbarism',[38*] and in a curiously muted reaction by the New Zealand press, this appeared to be accepted as being as good a reason as any. Such matters soon became academic. War justified the government's efforts, and the anti-militarist, anti-compulsory training movement was submerged under the wave of patriotic feeling. It would not resurface until the conscription issue of 1916. Now Godley's preparations were put to the test. Already on 30 July, his staff had despatched confidential preliminary notices to each of New Zealand's four military districts, giving warning to defence staff of all necessary mobilisation instructions in the event of war.

The plan was for each of the four military districts to provide sufficient volunteers on a quota system from each battalion and regiment to make up both an infantry battalion and a mounted rifles regiment. For example, in the Canterbury Military District, the Canterbury Infantry Battalion, 1000 strong, was made up of companies of men, each 250 strong, from each of the Territorial Battalions. Each company took its identification from the Territorial Battalion from which it was drawn. The four companies were: 2nd South Canterbury drawn from Ashburton to the Waitaki River, 1st Canterbury drawn from Christchurch and its suburbs, 12th Nelson drawn from Nelson Province, and the 13th North Canterbury and Westland drawn from North Canterbury, Marlborough and the West Coast.

There were four regiments of mounted rifles, one from each district. Auckland, Canterbury and Wellington formed part of the Mounted Rifles Brigade while the Otago Mounted Rifles was a separate independent regiment. Each regiment numbered 608 men and was made up of three squadrons of 169 men commanded by a major. Each squadron numbered four troops, equivalent to an infantry platoon, commanded by a subaltern (a lieutenant or second lieutenant). And, as with the infantry battalions, each squadron was drawn from one of the Territorial Mounted Rifles Regiments in the district.

---

* 'It would be madness for us to allow any Asiatic movement to attack us in detail, to watch White Australia overthrown and to wait until the flood of Asiatic barbarism reached our own shores.'

The Wellington Mounted Rifles Regiment of the Expeditionary Force was drawn from the three Territorial Regiments within the Wellington District, the 2nd Wellington West Coast Squadron drawn from Wanganui and Taranaki, inland to Ohakune, the 6th Manawatu Squadron and the 9th Wellington East Coast drawn from Wairarapa and Hawke's Bay.

Each of these Territorial regiments and battalions was responsible for the 'selection, enrolment, medical examination and attestation of all volunteers'. This was carried out locally at the regimental headquarters. Godley hoped each unit would make up its numbers from 'serving Territorials within the unit' or by special enlistment of men with previous military experience living in its own geographical area. Volunteers had to agree to serve for the duration of the war 'and for such further period of service as is necessary to bring the Expeditionary Force back to New Zealand to be disbanded'. Only those aged 20–34 were to be included, and it was the responsibility of each regiment to check. Preference was given to single men, and everyone had to pass a medical examination before attestation.

To join the Mounted Rifles one had to come equipped. Volunteers were expected to bring their own saddlery and horse. Saddles were to be 'of a large strong type and must be in thoroughly good order in

Lieutenant Colonel Charles 'German Joe' Mackesy, 11th North Auckland Mounted Rifles. The abbreviated title for the regiment was NAMR, which was said to stand for 'Nearly all Mackesy's Relations'. *(C22394, Alexander Turnbull Library)*

every way'. The saddlery, if up to standard, would be bought by the government and the amount credited to the owner. Volunteers also had to bring a suitable horse which, if passed by a veterinary officer or regimental board, would be paid for at its market value. 'Such value should not exceed £20. Horses for Mounted Rifles must be from four to seven years of age, practically sound, from 14.2 to 15.2 hands in height, but animals under 14.3 hands will only be accepted if otherwise specially suitable. No greys, duns, or light chestnuts will be taken. Geldings are preferable to mares!'[39] Once enlisted, volunteers would be sent forward in drafts to concentration centres in each district: Alexandra Park or 'Potters Paddock' in the Auckland District; Awapuni Racecourse, Palmerston North, in the Wellington District; Addington Park, Christchurch, in the Canterbury District, and Tahuna Park, Dunedin in the Otago District.

The medical examination was the major hurdle to overcome. This was to be conducted by an officer of the New Zealand Army Medical Corps. In the smaller centres this was not always possible and the local G.P. was enlisted to carry it out. In larger towns, teams of doctors examined the large numbers of applicants. As the *War Diary* stated, no one was to be accepted whose height was under 5'4" or whose weight exceeded 12 stone,[40] except in special cases, which were never specified. Fred Rogers, a wagoner at New River Flat in Southland, was over 6′ in height and over 12 stone in weight. 'As this was over the limit they put me down as 11 stone 13lb. One chap under 5′4″ was from the rowing club and the local boys used to take him down to the club rooms at night and stretch him to meet the requirements.'[41] History does not record if the efforts were successful.

In Gisborne, Charlie Clark and his bushmen mates had trooped over to go to war, but were told that they would have to wait as application forms and details for enlisting volunteers had not yet arrived. 'So we stopped in Gisborne until we found out what we were going to do. We wasn't stopping there for nothing remember. So we went over to them and demanded a hearing … So they said well come over that afternoon and they put us all under the doctor. I went over there and there was seven bushmen ahead of me before I went in … and those bushmen were put aside for heart trouble with strained heart. And the other fellas said, "Oh well you won't get through." But those doctors told me there was nothing that they could find wrong with me, only a couple of bad teeth. One of the doctors said, "That stops him." "No," the other doctor said, "we can have that looked after on board the boat."'[42]

In 1914 medical rejections were averaging 25 percent of all applications, but as with any representative team there were pressures, particularly on the local doctors, to put men through and ignore minor disabilities. This became such a problem that re-examinations were held in camps and unfit men were returned home. Roderick McCandlish, a farm boy from Whangaehu, wrote to his mother on 14 August 1914 from Awapuni Camp: 'I suppose you are wondering what has become of me. Well I am passed fit to go out and fight for my country. I can tell you I got the shock of my life when Willie got passed out and they picked about half a dozen holes in him. He was knocked up over it and a fellow must feel pretty rotten, getting sent back after saying goodbye to everyone.'[43]

The *Southland Daily Times* reported on 13 August 1914: 'There was a goodly number of men rejected by the medical examiners and many of the rejects displayed keen disappointment and were obviously much annoyed. In some instances the men so treated loudly clamoured for the application of another test.'[44] The more practical of those rejected were not so loud. They swallowed their disappointment and journeyed from town to town until they found a practitioner who would pass them. Dentists did a prosperous trade, as 'bad teeth could put you out'. Advertisements appeared offering quick and cheap extractions.

By the time the Main Body enrolment for the Expeditionary Force was complete, the medical system was working smoothly, even if sometimes in the wrong order: 'I duly received my notice to appear again at the Drill Hall for medical examination. On reporting I was told to "stand over there" and strip, which I duly did. A medical officer then measured my height, weight and chest measurements and handed me over to someone else who put me through an eyesight test, using coloured pieces of wool for the purpose. My eyesight evidently being all right I was handed over to a third man who told me to "sit down on that chair" and cross my legs. This was to test me out in some way for all he did was to tap my knee with his hand and then transfer me over to the fourth man. This one tested my hearing and then handed me over to the fifth man who grabbed hold of the scrotum sack and told me to cough. After duly coughing to the best of my ability he examined my teeth … and then handed me over to Number six who made me hop round the room first on one leg and then the other, after which I was allowed to don my clothes again and go home.'[45]

Godley chose his commanding officers and key headquarters staff. He selected Colonel Andrew Russell for command of the Mounted Rifles Brigade. Russell was New Zealand born and a sheep farmer from Hawke's Bay. Educated at Harrow and Sandhurst, he had graduated into the British Army, and spent five years with his regiment in India before joining his father in Hawke's Bay in 1892. In 1914 Russell was commanding the Wellington Mounted Rifles Brigade of the Territorial Force and he had impressed both Godley and Hamilton with his handling of the brigade during annual camp manoeuvres, as well as his handling of the Wellington 'Specials' during the 1913 Wharf Strike.

Arthur Bauchop was the only other serious contender for the command of the Mounted Rifles. A sawmiller from Port Chalmers, he had served in South Africa with the 4th Contingent of New Zealand Rough Riders. By the end of the war Bauchop had risen to the rank of major, been awarded the CMG and was highly regarded as a commander of mounted troops in action. On his return to New Zealand he accepted a permanent appointment as Lieutenant Colonel in the New Zealand Militia. In 1914 he was commanding the Otago Military District. Godley believed that despite Bauchop's reputation as a commander on active service, his administrative skills and ability to handle a brigade did not match Russell's. This feeling may have been strengthened by Bauchop's removal from the British Staff College at Camberley in 1912 because of poor marks. 'Bauchop was not very happy at not having been given the command of the Mounted Rifles Brigade, but I have had it out with him, and said distinctly that I do not think his qualifications were so good as Russell's and he now quite understands the position.'[46]

Bauchop was appointed Commanding Officer of the Otago Mounted Rifles, which was the independent mounted rifles regiment in the Expeditionary Force. John Findlay, a farmer from South Canterbury who had seen service in South Africa, was brought back from the reserve to command the Canterbury Mounted Rifles. William Meldrum, a lawyer farmer from Hunterville and Commanding Officer of the 6th Manawatu Mounted Rifles, was given command of the Wellington Mounted Rifles. Charles Mackesy, from North Auckland, was appointed to command the Auckland Mounted Rifles. A noted horseman, he was Commanding Officer of the 11th North Auckland Mounted Rifles. 'German Joe', as he was known, was a German Lutheran who had settled in New Zealand from the United States. On mobilisation he rode down to Auckland like a patriarch of old, bringing his sons and male relations with him. Not for nothing was the 11th North Auckland Squadron or NAMR, of the Auckland Mounted Rifles, known by the nickname 'Nearly all Mackesy's relations'.

Godley's selection of commanders for his Mounted Rifles was a comparatively easy task. New Zealand was noted for its mounted men. This is where our reputation was made in the Boer War and it was this arm that had most impressed Hamilton during the inspection. Command of the Infantry Brigade presented a more difficult problem. Godley did not believe any of his serving Territorial officers had sufficient experience. He selected a regular officer, Frances Earl Johnston, a New Zealander who had joined the British Army and was serving with his regiment in India. In 1914 he took leave from his regiment and as a major returned to New Zealand. In July 1914 he was appointed Temporary Lieutenant Colonel in the New Zealand Forces and posted as Commander, Wellington Military District. He was at once involved in supervising the district annual camps and in checking preparations for mobilisation. Johnston must have impressed Godley, for on the outbreak of war he was appointed Commander of the New Zealand Infantry Brigade of the Expeditionary Force, with the rank of colonel. It was a rapid promotion; Johnston was then aged 42. The only other possible contender for this command was Colonel Edward Walter Clervaux Chaytor, a New Zealander and member of the New Zealand Staff Corps. Chaytor was staff-trained; Godley valued his staff ability and retained him on the headquarters of the Expeditionary Force as Assistant Adjutant-General.

The four infantry commanding officers were of varied backgrounds. The Otago Infantry Battalion was commanded by Major Thomas William McDonald, aged 45, an officer of the New Zealand Staff Corps. Two existing territorial commanding officers from Otago, John McClymont, Lieutenant Colonel Commanding 14th South Otago Regiment, and John Moir, Lieutenant Colonel Commanding 10th North Otago Regiment, were superseded. However, Godley appealed to both officers to serve as company commanders.

15th North Auckland Company of the Auckland Infantry Battalion on parade in camp at Epsom Park racecourse. Sergeant Joe Gasparich is the first left in the front rank. *(Alan Lawson Collection – PA1-o-1312, Alexander Turnbull Library)*

McClymont received the following telegram. Similar telegrams were sent to officers throughout the country:

> *Trust you will command company Expeditionary Force furnished from your*
> *Regiment with rank of major. The company represents on active service the*
> *regiment which you have so successfully commanded and trained in peace*
> *and it is imperative that the best officers should go with these big companies.*
> *In other parts of the Dominion many officers temporarily reverting to*
> *lower rank to have chance of going on active service. Wire reply Glenavon*
> *Auckland and meet me Dunedin on arrival First express Thursday.*
>
> *General Godley* [47]

In the climate of the time it was a hard request to refuse. The other battalion commanders of the Infantry Brigade were Douglas McBean Stewart, an accountant, aged 37, Commanding Officer of the 1st Canterbury Regiment in the Territorial Force, who led the Canterbury Infantry Battalion; William George Malone, a lawyer farmer, aged 56, Commanding Officer of the 11th Regiment (Taranaki Rifles), who took over the Wellington Infantry Battalion; and Arthur Plugge, headmaster of Dilworth School, aged 36, who commanded the Auckland Infantry Battalion.

The speed of mobilisation was impressive. On 7 August the New Zealand government received a cable from Britain: 'If your Ministers desire and feel themselves able to seize German wireless at Samoa we should feel this was a great and urgent imperial service.'[48] The New Zealand government agreed and Godley was ordered to mobilise a force. This contingency had been planned for. It had been anticipated by Godley in 1912 — 'I had received a private letter from Henry Wilson, the previous year, in which he stated that in the event of a war with Germany this would probably be the first step New Zealand would be asked to undertake.'[49] It was Friday night, a Territorial parade night, when the instructions went out, and by Tuesday 11 August Godley could report that the force of 1413 all ranks was on parade on the Wellington wharfs, fully armed, equipped and ready to embark. They were all Territorial volunteers from Auckland and Wellington. It would be a further three days before transport and escorts were ready. On 29 August 1914 the Samoan Expeditionary Force landed at Apia in German Samoa, one of the first German territories to fall in the First World War.

Mobilisation of the Main Body of the Expeditionary Force was equally swift. Embarkation date was planned for 28 August 1914 and in the camps men were being assembled and kitted out. Delays in providing sufficient Royal Navy escorts held up the force, first until 18 September, then until 25 September. Around the country, from every town, drafts of volunteers were railed to the concentration camps: '12th August 1914. Entrained at Carterton after a "send off" in Victoria Hall and monster procession led by the Band to the Railway Station.'[50] For everyone it was adventure, receptions, parades, tearful farewells, being feted at every stop along the way, and then the first letter home:

Addington 18 Aug. 1914

Dear Mother,

Have just time to scribble a line before lights out. Arrived here at 7 o'clock and were some time getting our gear. Had a lovely time coming over. Good weather. Snow on the Otira. Please post me my nugget outfit and a spare tin or two of nugget. There was some in the bottom of my tin box. Also post my heavy striped shirt and that pink singlet.

Have to go and make my bed now. Will try and write again Thursday. Best of love to you and Nora

Ned.

Please excuse my sending wire collect. Could not get change and had to get a boy to take wire as we are not allowed out. [51]

If you were serving in the Territorial Force you came into camp fully kitted out.

Urgent
NOTICE TO MOBILISE

To Pvt P. M. Thompson
   NZ Drug Co.
   Burnside.

You are hereby called up for Active Service. You are to proceed to the Garrison Hall, Dunedin on Thursday 13 August 1914 at 9.00 a.m. You will bring with you the following articles to the place of assembly:

To be Worn: Complete service uniform, Service Boots, accoutrements, arms, water bottle filled with cold tea or water; strong pocket knife; about two yards of strong cord; haversack containing sufficient cooked rations for the day; Overcoat folded — worn if wet.

As Baggage. Rolled in waterproof sheet in as small a space as possible — one double or two single blankets, dubbing for boots, empty pillowslip, change of underclothing and a shirt; pair socks, towel and soap, brush and comb, shaving material; few needles, pins and strong thread, fork and spoon and plate; pannekin distinctly labelled with name, company, regiment.

R. N. Fraser Capt & Adjt
4th (Otago) Regiment [52]

Godley had hoped for the Main Body to be all Territorials. It could not be. The strength of the Territorial Force in 1914 was 25,685. Some 10,000 of these were under enlistment age, and of those remaining 1400 had already sailed to Samoa. Medical rejections further reduced the numbers. But the main reason was the organisation of the military districts. Wellington, one of the major centres, was excluded from providing infantry because it had made the major contribution to the Samoan Force. The other major centres, Christchurch, Dunedin and Auckland, were asked to contribute on the same basis as the more rural areas. Dunedin, Christchurch, Wellington and Auckland had the eligible manpower but their quota was based solely on the number of major units of the Territorial Force that were recruited in their area. So Auckland provided a rifle company and a mounted rifles squadron and its share of divisional troops in the same numbers as Taranaki, Nelson and North Otago.

Auckland had little difficulty in reaching its manpower targets. Indeed, it could have filled its quota many times over had the positions been available. It was the same in Dunedin, Christchurch and Wellington, but in the smaller centres, while most filled their quotas, it meant recruiting every available Territorial who wanted to go, turning a blind eye to those who were under age, and accepting good men who were not in the Territorials but who had previous military experience. The Auckland, Canterbury and Wellington Military Districts quickly met their manpower contributions to the force. Otago, particularly outside Dunedin, had difficulties. Eventually, men of the Wellington district who could not get into the Wellington Infantry Battalion were shipped south to make up the numbers in the Otago Infantry Battalion.

New Zealand in 1914 had a larger urban than rural population,[*] but the quota method ensured that the Main Body of the Expeditionary Force would have a strong rural flavour. They were largely men off the land, or men from small town New Zealand closely associated with the farming industry. Later reinforcements would be largely from the main urban centres, but the character and reputation of the force would be established by the 'country' minority.

Each battalion and regiment drew most of its companies from the rural areas. Urban companies could be counted on one hand. There were the 3rd Aucklands, the 1st Canterburys and the 4th Otagos, and the men of the artillery batteries. District recruiting had reinforced the 'village pattern of relationship'. Each district drew its character from the land and the industries associated with the land, and each section of 12 men, each platoon of 50, each company of 250, reflected the aspirations and associations of its area. There were miners, sawmillers and railway men from Westport; wharfies, fishermen and farm labourers from the Bluff; and shepherds, carters and farm labourers from Ashburton. This strong local identity typified each group. They were 'the boys' from Greymouth, Waihi, Taihape, Milton and every other town. That was how they joined and went to war. It would be the home town first, the regiment second, and for the moment no one saw themselves as New Zealanders. That was an issue they had not yet had to face.

The Mounteds were almost all from the land. In the Canterbury Mounted Rifles, for example, 24 of the officers listed their occupations as farmers, 6 were accountants

---

[*] The 1914 *New Zealand Official Year Book* estimated a population of 496,799 in the counties compared with 505,598 living in boroughs.

and in banking, 11 were lawyers, 2 were regular soldiers, and there was a warehouse manager, a land agent and a merchant. Among the men, 60 percent were from farming occupations, 6 percent clerical and 4 percent professional, while the remaining 30 percent were unidentified labourers, transport workers and tradesmen mostly from the smaller centres of inland Canterbury.[53] But the Mounteds too reflected the areas from which they were drawn — from the patrician pastoralism of the Canterbury Plains to the smaller dairy farms of the Waikato and North Auckland. Each regiment had its own identity, and as with the regiments the squadrons would be equally distinctive. Enlisted in the 6th Manawatu Squadron of the Wellington Mounted Rifles, Rod McCandlish wrote: 'One thing I notice is that there are very few working men going out to fight. The greater part of the chaps here have been to College and every other one comes from the Wanganui School. The young High Commissioner's son,* a very decent chap, he and I chum up a good bit, he asked me to come in his section. That means working and living with him through the war but I am in with some other very decent fellows so I did not accept although it would make things pretty right when I arrive in London.'[54]

There was the same flavour to the 9th Wellington East Coast Squadron, with the farmers and their drovers and farmhands from Hawke's Bay and Wairarapa. They would find much in common with the Canterbury Mounted Rifles. The 2nd Wellington West Coast Squadron was different again; they were farmers, bushmen and sawmillers from inland Wanganui, Raetihi and Ohakune. All the other trades of small town New Zealand were represented, even a biograph operator from Stratford. Godley's Main Body was 74 percent New Zealand born, professed to be 86 percent Protestant, 94 percent single, 63 percent under 25 years of age, and 82 percent with previous military training (see Appendix III).

In August and early September men in the camps were kitted out and started the routine of training, drill, route marches and musketry. There was little indiscipline as each man was afraid that one wrong step would make him miss the trip. Each commanding officer was determined that his unit would be the example to the rest of the force. Colonel Malone of the Wellingtons wrote: 'August 20th–23rd Completing equipment and organisation of the regiment. Training same. Men improving as the O [Officer] C [Commanding] Brigade says astoundingly. They are of all classes. Sons of wealthy run holders, farmers, school masters, scholars, M.A.s, B.A.s, musicians, tradesmen, mechanics, lawyers and all sorts. They will make good soldiers and the Regiment, I trust, will lead the other Regiments in the Brigade. I will do my best to make it.'[55]**

---

* Clutha McKenzie. Sir Thomas McKenzie was the New Zealand High Commissioner in London.

** Malone's Wellington Battalion wore their brimmed felt hats with four distinctive dents, later known as the 'Lemon Squeezer'. Malone instituted this headdress in his Territorial Battalion, the 11th Taranaki Rifles, and on his appointment to command the Wellington Battalion of the NZEF, made this the headdress in the battalion. In 1916 it was adopted by the New Zealand Division. It is still worn in the New Zealand Army on ceremonial occasions.

Pride and anguish: the Canterbury Contingent are farewelled from Lyttelton. *(1914 Glass Plate Slide Collection, The Press newspaper – Fairfax Media)*

Eight thousand adventurers. 'We were off to see the world.' *(1914 Glass Plate Slide Collection, The Press newspaper – Fairfax Media)*

There was an unreal quality about those balmy days of August 1914. Despite the news from overseas, it was hard to believe the country was at war. 'For most of them these were lazy holidays after the hard life of the bush and the sheepruns. The army was generous in its supply of food, and much good butter, jam, meat and bread, which would have been luxuries indeed in the months to come, went to waste in Awapuni incinerators. And day after day came cars from towns and farms and stations within two hundred miles, bringing tuck-box after tuck-box containing the choicest products of the home larders …

' … Usually, during the day, in independent troops of thirty or forty men, they wandered about the district, among the pleasant suburban homes of Palmerston, along shady country roads or up into the hills. They walked or cantered for an hour or so, and then, selecting a likely-looking homestead, they would unsaddle and unbridle their mounts and leave them to graze the succulent grass at the sides of the road, or roll if they wished, while a man was put at both ends of that stretch of road to prevent their straying. Then the others would lie in the shade or sun themselves on the bank opposite the homestead, sleeping, smoking, reading or playing cards. Scarcely ever did the oracle fail to work. The door of the house would open and a fair maid appear anon, a mother and a sister. The first would come tripping down the path to the soldiers and inquire:

'"Mother says would you like some tea?"

'"Well," they would reply, "it wouldn't be a bad idea, would it? But, I say, wouldn't it be a lot of trouble?"

"Oh, not at all."

'And she would skip away back to the house, to the innards of which, mother and sister, regarding the preamble as a mere formality, had disappeared to get things under way. A brief interval was followed by the appearance of large trays of cups, the whole of the household crockery from the drawing-room, breakfast-room and kitchen, with scones and cakes, and all the luxuries of the storeroom, and, perhaps, apples from the barn. The good family, as is only in keeping with proper hospitality, would join in the feast; …'[56]

The Canterbury Mounted Rifles embarking at Lyttelton. *(1914 Glass Plate Slide Collection, The Press newspaper – Fairfax Media)*

The presence of 3818 horses gave a distinctive tang to shipboard life. *(1914 Glass Plate Slide Collection, The Press newspaper – Fairfax Media)*

On 23 September the transports were ready to sail from Auckland, Wellington, Lyttelton and Port Chalmers with the troops from each of the provinces. On the 24th the Auckland transports *Waimana* and *Star of India* put to sea with the Auckland contingent. Escorted by the HMS *Philomel* they were to rendezvous with the rest of the convoy off the North Cape. On 24 September there was a farewell parade in Newtown Park for the Wellington soldiers. Malone was typically critical: 'Too much speechifying and praying. Before show over rain fell.'[57] They then marched back through the crowded streets and embarked upon the four transports: *Maunganui*, *Orari*, *Arawa* and *Limerick*. That evening the Port Chalmers and Lyttelton transports, *Ruapehu*, *Hawke's Bay*, *Athenic* and *Tahiti*, arrived in Wellington Harbour, and all transports except Godley's flagship, *Maunganui*, put out into stream, ready to sail on Friday, 25 September. However it was postponed and the Auckland ships recalled. Massey and his government were not prepared for the Expeditionary Force to sail without sufficient naval escorts to meet the threat posed by the German Pacific Squadron.* The

---

* 'The New Zealanders absolutely decline to despatch their expeditionary force — all in transports and
  ready to sail tomorrow or next day — unless we can provide them with a sufficiently powerful escort ... The
  Admiralty think there is no real risk, but I am inclined to agree with the New Zealanders, and as there are
  no available ships at hand ... we have been obliged to tell them to wait for what may be as long as another six
  weeks.' p.235, H.H. Asquith, *Letters to Venetia Stanley* (Oxford University Press, 1982)

frustrations grew; the war would be over before New Zealanders got there!

The mounteds were camped at Trentham, the artillery in the Hutt and the infantry on board ship. Training was carried out in the hills around Wellington and rifle practice conducted at Trentham. The delays had seen the force grow. Now, instead of an artillery battery as originally planned, a Field Artillery Brigade of three batteries of 18-pounders would sail with a Brigade Ammunition Column, and a Howitzer Battery of four 4.5-inch howitzers would follow six weeks later with the Second Reinforcements.

Already reinforcements were marching into camp, and in Britain a British Section of the New Zealand Expeditionary Force had been recruited and trained. To those enlisting for war in England there were no doubts about identity. Charles Saunders was Superintendent Engineer of the Twickenham and Teddington Electric Light Company Power Station: 'Being a New Zealander I would like to go to the War, as such, so I rang up the High Commissioner Office and learned that probably a contingent of New Zealanders would be formed.'[58] Saunders turned

'A Mother's Farewell'. *(PH2003 1, WW1 Photographic Collection, Auckland War Memorial Museum)*

down a commission with the Royal Engineers 'to join as a private with the New Zealanders', and the numbers of the British section grew to some 200 men.

'We were very conspicuous with our slouch hats in the streets and little boys used to gape at us a lot. We had "New Zealand" in white on a crimson ribbon on both arms just below the shoulders and one little paper boy looked hard at it and slowly and laboriously spelt it out, looked into my face, then said to his mate "New Zealand and Gor Blimey' e's white!"'[59]

In New Zealand, the delays were giving some men time to think again about the prospects of adventure. For many, it had not met their expectations. All it had been was training and drill. "Form Fours", "Right Turn", etc. How sick we get of it.'[60] In October the escorts arrived, and the men embarked. George Bollinger of the Wellington Infantry Battalion wrote in his diary: 'Wednesday 14 October 1914. In Port, Wellington City: General leave was granted from 8.00 a.m. to 2.00 p.m. Wharves make a very busy scene owing to horses being shipped. British and Japanese cruisers in Port. Roll call at 2.30 p.m. This parade was one to be remembered; majority of men were drunk and disorderly, and several were missing. The wharves were crowded with thousands of sad faces.

'At 4.00 p.m. the whole of the Transport Ships — eight in number — swung out into the stream. How hard it is to realise that we are at last about to leave the shores of "God's Own Country".'[61]

3

A RAGTIME ARMY

Egypt, land of sun and sunset
Where our footsteps pause a while;
While the dirty unkempt Arabs
Barter fruit with native guile,
Half the world we've crossed to reach you,
Hearts were light and hopes were high.
But we're only 'Standing by'.
Soldiers' song, Egypt 1914[1]

At 6.00 a.m. on the morning of 16 October 1914, all Wellington was awake, and the wharfs and the streets along the bays were lined with people, for the Main Body of the Expeditionary Force was sailing. Since the 14th the ships had anchored in the stream where they had been joined by the Auckland transports. Now led by the menacing grey of HMS *Minotaur* and the black-hulled Japanese cruiser *Ibuki*, the fleet, to the rumble of anchors and belching clouds of steam, started to move. 'In single line ahead, the fourteen great grey ships, their smoke trailing away over the port quarter before a fresh wind, passed down the wild rocky gap of the entrance. The grey seas rolled in a long swell, grey, flying clouds hid the eastern mountain tops. The passengers of an in-bound steamer had hurried on deck, clad lightly against the chill wind, and sent a faint cheer to each passing ship.'[2]

The farewells and tears of the crowds ashore and the cheers of the garrison artillery skylined above the forts at the harbour entrance were whipped away by the wind. To the men crowding the rails, hanging on to the winches and in the lifeboats, peering into the wind and madly waving, there was an overwhelming sense of relief. At last they were off! No more fears that the next inspection and the next roll call would have them relegated to the reserves. They were sailing to war. They had no idea what this meant, but that did not matter. It would most probably be over by the time they arrived — all the papers spoke of Allied victories — but if it was not, then the Dominion boys would teach the Germans a thing or two.

Godley, his staff and commanders understood the destination to be England for training, and then service in France. That was also the best bet among the men. French speakers such as Second Lieutenant C.M. Cazalet, the Interpreter attached to Godley's Divisional Headquarters, would have their time fully committed giving French language lessons in the days to come. Others were not so sure, or did not care — to be going was enough. During the weeks of training, Godley's Imperial staff and the ex-British Regulars had been quick to point out how much they had to learn before it could be conceivable that they could serve alongside British Regular soldiers. So it could be India, replacing British Regulars as garrison troops? The Cape where the Boers had once again broken out in rebellion? Egypt as garrison?

For many this would be their last sight of New Zealand, but few thought of the possibility of not returning. War was a quest, an adventure. The first days were rough and the rolling grey seas and the westerly swell laid most of the Expeditionary Force low. Those that could staggered on and tended the horses, who gave a distinctive flavour and tang to each of the ten transports. Seasickness cancelled the first parades and Sunday's church service. 'We awoke to find we had run into heavy weather. Men all got on deck and the place was soon covered with huddled heaps of men, undoubtedly all thinking of home. I could not refrain from a sick smile as a trooper with a sad and white face strolled down the deck playing "Home Sweet Home" on a concertina.'[3]

Seventeen men had grown tired of waiting and had deserted in Wellington and there must have been some on board who secretly wished they had joined them, especially when the novelty of sailing gave way to the monotony of shipboard routine.

'Reveille 6.00 a.m. Physical Training for men from 6.30 to 7.00 and for officers from 7.00 to 7.30, Breakfast 8.00, Parades 9.00 to 12, being an hour's squad drill, an hour's rifle exercise, a half hour lecture and a half hour semaphore signalling practice. Dinner in two sittings, 12 until 2, parades from 2 until 5 and this repeated the morning's programme. 7.30–8.15 Potential NCO training, 8.30–9.15 NCO instructional classes and 8.00–9.00 every evening a lecture for all officers.'[4] This was on HMNZT No 10. *Arawa* carrying the Wellington Regiment. Malone, their commanding officer, drove his officers to make every minute count. No slackness would be brooked for a moment, and as the days at sea progressed all his subordinates experienced his wrath until they met his standards.

'My officers are not seeing with me too readily. They each want their own way and some of them have a supercilious air when I am telling them what I want and mean to have done.'[5]

Not all the ships had a commanding officer with the force of Malone aboard, and keeping the men busy and gainfully employed on those overcrowded troopships was to tax the most ingenious of minds in the long weeks to come before the voyage ended. The Expeditionary Force numbered 8574 men and 3818 horses; Godley's headquarters corresponded to that of a division: 'For example, there is an officer of the Military Secretary's Department to look after all records of officers, promotions, appointments, Gazettes etc; an A.A.G. to keep track of all personnel and to keep all records as regards discipline etc., etc., an A.Q.M.G. to keep an eye for the New Zealand Government on all the business part of the show, especially the Finance for which he has a small Pay staff; an Assistant Director of Ordnance, and a Base Depot organisation commanded by Shawe, late Rifle Brigade, who will I am sure, manage it well. I hope that these officers will prevent all the confusion and trouble that was given by the contingents during the South African War.'[6]

In the force, Godley commanded an infantry brigade of four battalions; a mounted rifles brigade of three mounted rifles regiments, plus an independent mounted rifles regiment as part of divisional troops; a brigade of field artillery of three batteries each of four 18-pounder field guns; an artillery brigade ammunition column; a signals company; a company of the divisional train or supply company, and two field ambulances. The immediate reserves, or First Reinforcements, as they were called, were also carried. They consisted of 738 men. Also sailing with the convoy were ten veterinary officers, and ten chaplains (one for each transport), an x-ray specialist, an extra medical officer for Godley's headquarters, seven members of the Imperial Reserve, one member of the Russian Army, five officers rejoining their regiments in Britain and cadets going to Sandhurst, a canteen supervisor as well as the families of the Imperial officers and staff serving in New Zealand who were travelling back with their husbands to Britain — or so they believed.[7]

The ten transports were jammed with men, horses and equipment plus ten million rounds of rifle and machine-gun ammunition for the force and 6000 rounds of artillery ammunition. In these conditions the officers of most of the units found the organisation of realistic training too difficult.

'After all, there was a limit to the brass work to be polished, the decks to be scrubbed, the boat drills to be gone through, the musketry courses that were possible in such limited space, the military knowledge that could be imparted by means of lectures, the odd jobs that could be found for orderlies, and yet there seemed no limit to the number of men. So for the greater part of the time the majority lay around in the sun smoking and playing cards, yarning and sleeping but coming to life in a rush when the bugle called all and sundry to "Come to the Cookhouse Door."'[8]

One thing broke the monotony and that was food. From living like kings in New Zealand on the best that the country could provide, shipboard fare was all too different. 'God bless those cooks and their proverbial stews and tough roast beef' was the cry.[9] The diet was: Breakfast — porridge, coffee, bread and butter. Dinner — tough roast beef and potatoes or 'bog oranges', beans and cold tea or a mug of soup. Tea — bread, butter, jam and cheese. Tea was remembered by all as the worst meal. It was the subject of much wry humour in the ship's newspapers that flourished.

'Orderly Officer: "Any complaints men?"

Private: "Yessir, taste this, Sir."

Officer: "H'm, rather thin and greasy, otherwise not bad soup!"

Private: "Yessir, that is what we thought, but the Cook says it's tea."'[10]

Food could also provide a flashpoint among the bored and discontented troops.

'After one meal of barrelled beef which was not edible on account of its saltiness and toughness, potatoes, mostly bad, bread that was sour and doughy, and water, very warm and sickly to the taste — taking all things into consideration the men considered they had a grievance and all hands lined up and called for the officers to come out and give them a hearing which after some delay they did, and they told the men to go away and the matter would be seen into but the men stood fast as complaints about food were set aside before and nothing had been done. Our spokesmen said that our stew was not fit for dogs and its appearance on our tables was far too frequent, and the dinner today was not eatable, and it must be remedied for the men would not stand for such treatment.[11]

In another incident on the *Athenic*, poor food and a hot, crowded mess deck tried the patience of the men too far: 'So it happened that when the orderly officer appeared that day with the traditional "Any Complaints?" he was greeted with an almost unanimous roar of anger, and the next moment was hit fair in the face with an old hunk of cheese. I regret to say it was thrown from our table.'[12]

The ship's canteens were another source of discontent. The canteens had been under private contract in Wellington but after continued complaints of overcharging, the government stepped in and took over the management before the convoy sailed.

'When the government took them over we did expect we would get looked after, but beyond bringing the price of the 3d softdrink down to 6d they did nothing. Except for soda water our canteen was emptied out after the first week, and only a few shillings worth of stuff was sent aboard at the port of calls.' Despite orders prohibiting dealings with the crew, 'the crew used to sell us our own or somebody else's food done up fit to eat. The Butcher sold iced lemon water and made not less than 10/- per night. The Bakers made a pile with little rock cakes and buns at 1d each.'[13]

As a private only received 1/- a day, finances, even on board ship, could become a problem.

'Having just had afternoon tea this may sound like leisure and good living. It consists of a cake of which I dare not give a name, cut into pieces about two inches square in most cases it is difficult to tell whether it is cake or pudding, and a mug of tea, the latter is generally considered passable. This we buy from the cooks who reap the profit and are paid for their troubles handsomely as the prices are, tea, two pence a mug and the cake a penny a piece so it generally costs us four pence for our afternoon luxury and when tea time comes we buy a tin of fish for six pence. The day cost us ten pence leaving us a profit of two pence for our daily labours which is generally spent in tobacco and matches when the two pences amount to a 1/-. So you see that if we only draw a shilling a day we cannot save enough to buy a sheep station and pay a deposit.'[14]

The frustrations and restrictions of military routine and the additional impositions of shipboard life stripped away much of the glamour of sailing across the wide seas to find the rest of the world. All ranks had to come to terms with the complete lack of privacy, no matter what a soldier was doing. The tier upon tier of bunks in the closely packed holds of the crowded ship meant you could never be alone. A soldier had to learn tolerance or he would go mad.

'From this time for one, two, three even four years, a man could not eat by himself or sleep by himself. If he looked at his sweetheart's photograph there was probably an audience, more or less appreciative; if he opened a parcel there was his own section at least to assist him, if he was cheerful his exuberance might be infectious or it might provoke the wrath of someone who was indulging in a fit of melancholy; if he was miserable he was regarded as a bringer of gloom, a wet blanket; if his mate was offensively drunk he could not do more than edge a few inches away from the odorous reality of the exhilarated one, and sometimes hardest of all, he could not die by himself.'[15]

Men learned to live with each other and the bond of 'mateship', forged first in the camps, the troopships and under training in Egypt and then endured in the stresses of combat at Gallipoli, proved to be the foundation stone of New Zealand's fighting reputation. A 'good mate' was everything, and it was on the troopship they found that you could escape unpleasantness by having a yarn to your mates. It was here that the value of the home town men you joined with came through: 'Talked Ashburton in groups of twos and threes. A good few Ashburtonites were discussed and old jokes raked up, and ... for a while we were not aboard ship in the Red Sea but in Ashburton.'[16]

It was on board ship that a now shaven and uniformed Charlie Clark met up with Reg McRae, also clean-shaven, and they stood looking at each other, each not recognising the reasonably spruce, beardless man opposite, until realisation dawned and the two bushmen were reunited.

The voyage also allowed medical authorities to give all necessary inoculations and dentists to catch up on those needing dental work. The soldiers viewed this in the same manner as they would the first day of combat. 'Today everyone's nerves have been reached with the rumours of a dental parade ... and, also inoculation for fever. It

'Sailing off to see the World': the New Zealand transports in the Indian Ocean. Photograph taken from the *Limerick*. *(WF-002662-6, Morison Collection, NAM Waiouru)*

is very funny to see one fellow go to another fellow and open his mouth wide and say, "Do you think he will pull those out?" and when his fears are satisfied … by a man who knows no more about it than himself, he will continue, "Does this inoculation hurt?" It did. Both Dentist and Doctor have been busy all day, some chaps having as many as eleven teeth out, and in spite of my having six out some months ago I had to get as many more out today and a nice condition some of us are in now for eating tough beef … not painless, this time, but gouge them out like a navvy in a shingle pit. Tonight some of us are going round with our faces, and others with their arms in a sling or handkerchief tied round to let people see that it is sore and avoid bumping it.'[17]

On 25 October, after the first series of inoculations, Lance Corporal Jack Gilchrist of the Otago Battalion died on the *Ruapehu*. It was later diagnosed as ptomaine poisoning, but the initial rumour throughout the force was that inoculations did it. This would have immediate repercussions. His burial at sea stayed in the minds of the men and brought home to many for the first time the purpose of the voyage.

'Calmest day we have yet experienced. Burial at 4.00 p.m. Both lines of transports and escorts heave to together and engines ceased. *Ruapehu* was in centre. We stood to attention for fifteen minutes … Circumstances and stillness made the affair horrible.'[18]

Godley and his commanders were now to face the problem of men refusing inoculations. 'Inoculation is not compulsory and the Authorities forgot to make it a condition of enrolment — some 20 privates of the Ruahine Company are objecting to being inoculated, also Sergeant Majors Dallinger and Foster. I had the two latter up before Colonel Johnston (OC Troopship). I had the men up and did my best to get them to agree.'[19]

It was caused by the wording of the Attestation Form. It had asked, 'Are you willing to be vaccinated or re-vaccinated?' and all had to agree before signing on. However, the voyage had given time for the 'barrack room lawyers', particularly with the rumours of why Gilchrist had died, to convince many of the men to balk at 'inoculations' which, they insisted, had not been a condition of enrolment. Many would finally consent but 35 men would still refuse and were returned to New Zealand from Egypt. It showed the temper of the force. The material was first class and most had experienced some form of military training, but they still saw themselves as citizens in arms, truculent and prepared to go to the letter of the law if they had a mind to. It was an object lesson to Godley: 'It is of course, very difficult to control many of these men who have never been accustomed to discipline or ever had to do anything except exactly what they please.'[20]

Major Hart wrote in his diary of the soldier's life on board ship: 'They have their drill and physical training to perform, are vaccinated where necessary, inoculated for typhoid, and when they recover from that the Doctors inspect them, then they go before the Dentist and all unsound teeth are pulled or stopped, the CO inspects their feet, then he holds a kit inspection, next the Doctor lectures them on a multiple of subjects and sins.

'Their beer is stopped, cigarette smoking is prohibited, they have to leave 3/5's of their pay in New Zealand, and every time after leaving a port many of them are brought before the CO for "overstaying their leave" or similar crimes, and packdrill is inflicted or further pay stopped. It is surely an interesting life and quite puts in the shade the experiences we read of "the poor married man".

'I forgot to say that if he takes his trousers off or any other belongings, they are usually stolen, and he has to repeat the procedure before he can show himself out.'[21]

The accepted code was, 'If someone pinches your belongings you do the same.' All the regimental staff were concerned with was that each man came on parade fully equipped. Hats were always going missing and the hatless were driven to borrowing from someone who was not going on parade because of sickness and fatigue.

'My turn came again to appear on parade without my hat. I made up my mind I would continue to come on parade hatless and take the consequences rather than get a hat in the recommended way. However, after parade one of my mates, Jack Bree, said he thought he could fit me out with one. Below his bunk mattress, flattened out ,were no less than six hats. He excused such hoarding by declaring, that "the way things were shaping he had better get in a good supply."'[22]

'It is common to see a fellow come up on deck to sleep and have no bedding whatever — and in about five minutes he may be curled up in a complete outfit and walk off with it. Consequently, some other person has to perform the same sleight of hand — and so the entertainment is kept up.'[23]

Food was a favoured target, either from the canteen or the officers' mess. 'Several bags of biscuits were stolen through a port hole in the rear of the canteen, so a few doctored bags were placed purposely very handy with the result that several of the boys were very ill for a few hours — biscuits may now be left near the port hole till they rot, no one would risk them.'[24]

Hobart was the first port of call, 'no leave', but a route march was held 'that rapidly generated into a triumphal procession. The whole population of the town was in the streets thronging around the marching men, walking beside them, breaking into the ranks, pressing on everyone Tasmanian apples, bunches of roses, cigarettes, parcels of cake, handshakes, kisses. It was a most marvellous burst of spontaneous welcome.'[25]

Here they linked up with the troopships carrying the Tasmanian troops of the Australian Force. Inevitably, there were comparisons made and from general to private a critical eye was cast at Australian soldiers. Godley wrote to Allen: 'I am told that the Tasmanian ships that left yesterday … had a great many absentees, and that a considerable number of men had to be put forcibly on board at the last minute … Their behaviour was so bad that they were forced to send them out into Norfolk Bay, to wait for us till tomorrow morning, as today was a half holiday and a Show going on and they did not dare leave them in the town.'[26]

This reflected the soldiers' view, and displayed evidence of a growing national pride. 'It seems great to be such a long way from home but we are all New Zealanders and now that we are away from our own country we all stick together like glue … I can tell you that this is the life and getting along at home is only existing. I am sure I don't know if I'll ever settle down to work again. We do not work and are fed and trained up to think that we are just it and fear nothing or nobody and the Tasmanians say they have to admit that we are a better and smarter looking lot of troops than their own.'[27]

As in Wellington, the welcome ashore and the attractions of Hobart led to a list of absentees, seven men from the Auckland Battalion off the *Waimana* and four of the Canterbury Battalion. Men missing ship and desertions would be a feature of every port of call. The Aucklanders from Hobart would rejoin but the Canterburys remained absent and were classed as deserters. 'The men have been that humbugged since joining the force that there is a good deal of discontent.'[28]

The next port was Albany in Western Australia. Here the New Zealand convoy met with the 26 ships of the Australian Expeditionary Force. There was no leave in Albany, although the troops were taken for a route march through the town. This was too much for some — after all, they had joined to see the world. It was the first test of many for the young officers of the Expeditionary Force and they grew in experience.

'On more than one occasion, notably at Albany when the men were very discontented at not being allowed ashore and there was the makings of a riot, by having the piano out on deck among them and getting some choruses going round the instrument, an unreasonable temper died away in song.'[29]

One soldier would desert at Albany, but the convoy of 43 ships and escorts soon set sail. Destination, it was rumoured, the Cape of Good Hope. 'I wonder if such a sight as this has ever been witnessed before — thirty-eight ocean liners and five battleships.'[30]

Days were swelteringly hot and after the first day out the convoy steamed north and the information passed that Colombo was the next port of call.

Nine days out of Albany, at 6.30 a.m. on 9 November, Private Falconer of the Wellington Regiment, and the acting wireless operator of the *Arawa*, picked up an S.O.S. call from Cocos Island, some 50 miles away.

'HMAS *Sydney* immediately moved off at full speed westward and there was terrible excitement on board.

'At 11.00 a.m. we received word that the *Sydney* was in action with the *Emden* at Cocos Island. The *Ibuki* and *Melbourne* steamed off with battle flags flying. Half an hour later a message was received that the *Emden* was done for and had beached to save her crew — It has been an exciting day and we can see big demonstrations in Sydney tonight.'[31]

Everyone was conscious of the damage that could have been caused had the *Emden* met with the convoy. 'It was amusing to see the Australian transports last night. Hitherto they have been a blaze of light. Last night hardly a light showed anywhere.'[32]

Now, until Colombo, only Crossing the Line would break the monotony of the heat during the day and the tropical rains at night which prevented the soldiers sleeping on the decks. 'Today I am going on ships guard. The guard mounted at 8.00 a.m. and will change at 8.00 a.m. tomorrow. In such a heat, sentry-go is no joke. Already several men have been overcome by the heat, and have been found sleeping at their posts.'[33]

Colombo was a welcome sight. 'Beautiful place — Got ashore in afternoon for two hours. Perkins, Rawnsley, Kirk and self got rickshaws and went round the town to Hotel. Had two iced beers, lovely after weak tea. Rickshaw 1/- an hour. Coolies salute "Dust your boots, Sir", and all the rest of it — Ceylon natives in shops awful frauds and rooked soldiers frightfully. If you beat them down and walked out of shop they chased you and let you buy practically at your own price.'[34]

As in Hobart, large numbers of men were late returning from leave and two men deserted. C.E.W. Bean, the Australian official correspondent, noted in his diary: 'Several local people spoke rather feelingly about the behaviour of New Zealanders in town last night and we certainly saw numbers of them laid out in all directions on the landing stage. They have only dry canteens and they are liable to break out at every port they come to … '[35]

The Australians also felt the New Zealanders were soft on the natives. 'The New Zealand men are not used to dealing with "real niggers" and place same on level with Maoris.'[36]

Godley was unhappy with the incidents in Colombo, particularly as they were now with the Australians. He blamed his officers. 'They, with plenty of noticeable exceptions, are a weak point … instead of looking after their men, went off on their own account and left the men to their own devices. Fortunately, thanks to the good behaviour and good sense of the latter no harm was done …'[37]

He gripped up his commanders and retribution was meted out: 'The orderly room where offenders are tried was very busy this morning. There being 85 men up for not coming back to the ship in time … they (had) done the town in great style and hired natives to bring them off in the small hours. In consequence (they) are now doing 14 days in the stokehold. All further leave is stopped till we get to our destination and they all know that disobeying orders is not worth the candle.'[38]

Aden was the next port reached and no leave was granted. On leaving Aden, Godley found out the convoy's destination from Major General William Throsby Bridges, the Commander of the Australian Force: 'Unforeseen circumstances decided Force train in Egypt and go front from there. Australians and New Zealand to form Corps under General Birdwood.'[39]

It rankled with Godley that he received the news second-hand. It was expected that the men would not know from one day to the next what was happening but the Commander of the New Zealand Expeditionary Force should at least be told: 'It is very humiliating to get such news at second-hand, and through the Australians, and I cannot imagine why our High Commissioner did not cable to me, if the Australian High Commissioner could cable to Bridges.'[40]

And so after six weeks the long and arduous voyage was approaching an end. As one censored letter home put it: 'Early in the morning … we steamed into … It was here that we were informed of our disembarkation at … The chaps took it very well although most of us were somewhat disappointed at not being home for Christmas. After being for six weeks on the ship we were glad to get off no matter where.'[41]

At 6.00 a.m. on 3 December 1914 the convoy berthed off Alexandria. Godley issued a Special Order to his troops: 'Owing to unforeseen circumstances it has been decided that the New Zealand Expeditionary Force shall do its training in Egypt before proceeding to the front instead of in England, as had been originally intended.

'This is a most fortunate change of plans for us as it means we shall escape the inclement English winter and have long days and the best of weather in which to train.'

He forwarded this view to Allen: 'then to get to the front, we shall I hope, only have the short voyage to Marseilles and in the meantime our troops may have the practical reality of a brush with the Turks or Bedouins.'[42]

Generally the Commander of the New Zealand Expeditionary Force was happy with arrangements: 'I imagine that we shall be made up to a division in some way, and that then the Australian Division and ourselves will form a corps under General Birdwood. I know him well, and like him, and shall be glad to be under him, and he is, I believe, a very good man in the field. He was Military Secretary to Lord Kitchener when the latter was Commander-in-Chief in South Africa, and has lately been secretary to the Army Department in India.'[43] Birdwood would command the Australian and New Zealand Army Corps — ANZAC.*

The New Zealanders were to encamp in the desert at Zeitoun on the outskirts of the modern European suburb of Heliopolis, about six miles from Cairo. The Australian Force under Bridges were encamped near the pyramids, some 15 miles [24 kilometres] from the New Zealanders. 'Entrained at 11.30 for Cairo. The journey took 4½ hours and on both sides of the railway the whole way the land is (under) close cultivation.

'Large canals and water races irrigate the land thoroughly and it is like a huge Chinaman's garden, growing vegetable maize, barley and lucerne etc. There are no fences, labour is apparently plentiful. Men, women and children work in the fields. Their implements are the same as those used in the days of Moses. Immediately one gets out of reach of the irrigation supply the country becomes a desert.'[44]

Zeitoun fell into this category: 'Great Scott! What a place! Foreign service is liable to land men anywhere. We certainly did expect to find some grass, but not so this time — simply sand, sand, sand, everywhere. We are camped on the Sahara Desert.'[45]

This patch of desert, laid out in streets for a yet undeveloped suburb, was soon transformed into a city of tents. Commanding officers busied themselves with questions of rubbish disposal, incinerators, water supply and sanitation, and the layout of the tent lines.

'Few will forget the pitching of the camp under supervision of the Commanding Officer, assisted by the Adjutant, Sergeant-Majors, and the Sergeant Bugler. Tent occupants paraded in front of their tents. Two men got inside and held the pole, four men held guy ropes and others stood by with mallets ... Bugle sounded, men seized guy ropes ... and ... lifted the pole, moving it according to instructions from an NCO. For a half an hour it was bedlam, all in authority seemed to be competing as to who could shout the loudest. Everybody was in a sweat, especially men inside tents, but they could not come out until the Commanding Officer ... checked the whole camp.'[46]

Then it was straight into training. The horses had not yet recovered sufficiently from the sea voyage to be ridden, but the men started immediately on drill, route matching and musketry. Godley wanted his New Zealanders ready for active service

---

* ANZAC came into being when the clerks on Birdwood's Headquarters had a rubber stamp made 'ANZAC' for registering correspondence. This was credited to Sgt K.M. Little, a New Zealander serving on Birdwood's headquarters. After being in common use among the clerks for some time, Maj. C.M. Wagstaff proposed ANZAC as the telegraphic codeword for the Corps. The initials gradually spread into common use. See Bean, *The Story of ANZAC* (Vol. I pp.124–25), also K.M. Little, Papers.

by February. 'We drilled all day on the desert and found it terribly tiring work. Our Colonel told us we would be in action within a month, but what a game of bluff soldiering is; anything to make the men work well.'[47]

There was tremendous rivalry between each of the provincial units. Each commanding officer was determined that his would be the best. Each had his own method and the personalities in the New Zealand camp started to stand out. One of these was Colonel Malone of the Wellington Battalion. An Englishman, he had settled in Taranaki with the Armed Constabulary in the 1880s, and had seen service in the Parihaka incident. A lawyer farmer, he was a perfectionist in everything he did. As a territorial soldier commanding the Taranaki Rifles, Malone had studied the theory of war, and was now determined to excel with his battalion in the practice. A strong-willed man, he would not budge if he thought he was right. This did not always make for easy relationships and in Egypt his men 'cursed him for a martinet who kept them toiling like the coolies of the land.'[48]

'We start Battalion training today. The Brigadier [F.E. Johnston] is in a hurry to rush us along at schemes and the top of the work. I am determined to begin at the bottom. He has been used to troops who, before they go to their Regiments after enlisting have six solid months' recruit training. A very different thing to ours, where the men have only been four months together and two of those at sea on a Transport with no room to work. We went away to our training area, and after two hours marching in different formations, I put the men onto "Musketry" under section commanders, as change and rest. Just then our Corps Commander General Birdwood came up with

It was straight into training. The Wellington Battalion on the range. *(WF-002662-53, Morison Collection, NAM Waiouru)*

General Godley and our Brigadier. General Birdwood … quite agreed with our work and specially approved the hour's musketry … General Godley … also approved … They left after a bit.'

Colonel Johnston (the Infantry Brigade Commander) returned and wanted to know why Malone had carried out squad drill despite his instructions. 'He was somewhat put out. I stood to my guns and told him that the parade was mine, that I was responsible for the efficiency of my battalion, that I knew better than he did what weak places there were, and that I was actually putting in more work, by two hours a day, than any other battalion in his Brigade, and that if I gave him six hours of work, according to his programme, I could do what I liked in the other two hours.'[49]

After an argument, Johnston reluctantly agreed. Johnston and his staff and the fellow commanding officers always found Malone a difficult man to deal with, but could not question the high standards that he achieved with his battalion. This friction created an undercurrent of ill-feeling that would have repercussions on Gallipoli. In the infantry brigade, Johnston, the Brigade Commander, Major Temperley, his Brigade Major and Captain A.B. Morton of the NZ Staff Corps were highly thought of.

Of the battalion commanders, Lieutenant Colonel Stewart of the Canterbury Battalion was another Malone, 'rigidly orthodox and very strict, looking to find fault'. The Otagos' original commanding officer had gone sick and been replaced by Lieutenant Colonel A. Moore of the Royal Dublin Fusiliers, previously the battalion adjutant. He, at 35, was the youngest of the commanding officers. His promotion found satisfaction with the men: 'We can at least be expected to be treated as men now, and not as children as heretofore.'[50]

Lieutenant Colonel W.G. Malone. 'Telling them what I want and mean to have done.' *(WF-002662-23, Morison Collection, NAM Waiouru)*

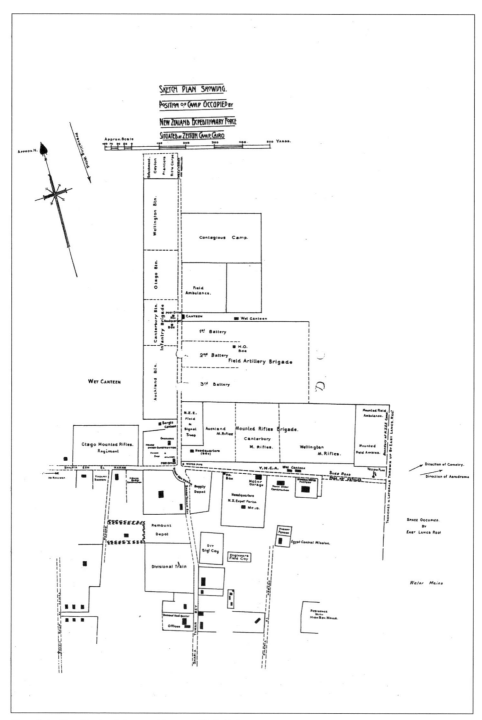

Plan of the New Zealand Camp at Zeitoun. *(Archives New Zealand)*

The Auckland Battalion was the least happy. Arthur Plugge, the commanding officer, was regarded by all as 'amiable but weak'. Discontent existed because he favoured the company drawn from his Territorial Regiment, the 3rd Auckland Regiment. Westmacott, a platoon commander in the 16th Waikato Company, recorded his views: 'The whole thing savoured of intrigue to convenience 3rd Auckland; but that would not have been so, had the impression not been created by certain people in 3rd Auckland, notably the Colonel and Dawson [Company Commander of the 3rd Auckland Company]. One was made to feel that the latter had the Colonel under his thumb in some way and that the rest of us would fare badly.'[51]

Egypt moulded the partly trained raw New Zealanders from 'citizens in arms' into soldiers. 'Today has been our worst so far and I daresay we will get harder … We are realising every day that we have a frightful lot to learn.'[52]

Godley and his staff officers were always present, checking progress. As the men slogged across the desert sand they would see the tall aloof figure on horseback watching impassively. 'Sometimes Lady Godley, accompanied by a maid, both on beautiful horses, would ride along with him.'[53] To his men Godley remained an enigma. Unsmiling, with never a word of praise, his figure became the focus of all the grumbles and discontent. This over-flowed and Lady Godley became, in the men's eyes, 'the eminence grise' behind the constant demands of training. Legends were born from it; on one field day as the men passed under Godley's eye, with Lady Godley in the background, Westmacott overheard one of the characters in the front rank of the platoon remark: '"Oh! How nice! Make them run again, Alec!" … mimicking a female voice which was lost in a gust of laughter … By the time the joke had reached the end of the column no doubt it was stated as a fact.'[54]

'We drilled all day on the desert and found it terribly tiring work.' The Wellington Battalion in full marching order. *(WF-2662-85, Morison Collection, NAM Waiouru)*

It was something that the men were prepared to believe and it became history in the minds of most Main Body veterans, and an event to which many were prepared to stand witness for the rest of their lives.

As a sop to training, the men had Cairo.

'P.M. Perkins, Hamilton and self visited Cairo. Trams run every 20 minutes from Heliopolis. Splendid trams — half as long again as New Zealand ones … Terminus lands right in Cairo … Had feed at London Cafe. Splendid Orchestra. Beer iced and flavoured most temptingly. Fifteen piastres a jug and half which poured out about two long beers each. Eggs and bacon 5 piastre … Next visited Shepheards, famous Hotel … packed with officers and tourists! Did not see a great deal of Cairo but, from observations, most forcibly convinced it is an awfully immoral place.'[55]

It was the temptations of the flesh that Godley feared as the biggest problem facing his raw New Zealanders. Even before landing he had warned them against the delights of Egypt. He was determined that the outbreaks of ill discipline on the voyage out would not be repeated in Egypt:

SPECIAL GENERAL ORDER
Headquarters, New Zealand Expeditionary Force,
H.M.N.Z. Transport No. 3,

30th November, 1914, at Suez.

Special General Order by MAJOR-GENERAL SIR A.J. GODLEY,
K.C.M.G., C.B., Commanding New Zealand Expeditionary Force.

IMMEDIATE steps are to be taken to advise all ranks as to their conduct while in Egypt, particularly as to their conduct towards natives. The natives in Egypt have nothing in common with the Maoris. They belong to races lower in the human scale, and cannot be treated in the same manner. The slightest familiarity with them will breed contempt which is certain to have the most far-reaching and harmful consequences. Every member of the Force in Egypt is charged with the enormous responsibility of maintaining the prestige of the British race.

All ranks should avoid conversation with the natives except on matters of business. They are to be treated with ordinary courtesy, and their point of view being so different from that of Europeans or Maoris, it must be remembered that men must exercise the greatest care in checking themselves or their comrades from becoming too free in their manner. All ranks are asked to co-operate in preventing a repetition of the regrettable incidents noted in Colombo, of men mixing with the natives, imitating their manner of speech, and indulging in badinage in conversation, which acts only tend to lower the prestige and good name of the Force.

In connection with the foregoing, the extreme danger of having any intercourse with native women is to be brought to the notice of the men. Syphilis in a most virulent form is rampant in Cairo, and men having connection with prostitutes are running the gravest possible risks. Forms of venereal disease are far more severe in Oriental countries than in New Zealand or England, and such diseases are certainly far more common.

The native drinks are generally the vilest concoctions possible; are most potent, an almost certain cause of illness, and cannot be taken with impunity.

Officers Commanding Units are to explain the contents of this memorandum to all ranks in addition to merely reading it to the men. The efficiency and good name of the Force as a British Force being, as it is, so dependent on the conduct of all ranks, too much trouble cannot be taken in educating every one in their duties and responsibilities in the novel surroundings in which they shortly will be placed. Egypt being held as it is by force of arms, the self-respect of every individual man of the Force is a factor which cannot be overestimated.

E.W.C. CHAYTOR, Colonel,
Assistant Adjutant-General[56]

SPECIAL GENERAL ORDER.

Headquarters, New Zealand Expeditionary Force, H.M.N.Z Transport No. 3, 30th November, 1914, at Suez.

Special General Order by MAJOR-GENERAL SIR A. J. GODLEY, K.C.M.G., C.B., Commanding New Zealand Expeditionary Force.

IMMEDIATE steps are to be taken to advise all ranks as to their conduct while in Egypt, particularly as to their conduct towards natives. The natives in Egypt have nothing in common with the Maoris. They belong to races lower in the human scale, and cannot be treated in the same manner. The slightest familiarity with them will breed contempt which is certain to have the most far-reaching and harmful consequences. Every member of the Force in Egypt is charged with the enormous responsibility of maintaining the prestige of the British race.

All ranks should avoid conversation with the natives except on matters of business. They are to be treated with ordinary courtesy, and their point of view being so different from that of Europeans or Maoris, it must be remembered that men must exercise the greatest care in checking themselves or their comrades from becoming too free in their manner.

All ranks are asked to co-operate in preventing a repetition of the regrettable incidents noted in Colombo, of men mixing with the natives, imitating their manner of speech, and indulging in badinage in conversation, which acts only tend to lower the prestige and good name of the Force.

In connection with the foregoing the extreme danger of having any intercourse with native women is to be brought to the notice of the men. Syphilis in a most virulent form is rampant in Cairo, and men having connection with prostitutes are running the gravest possible risks. Forms of venereal disease are far more severe in Oriental countries than in New Zealand or England, and such diseases are certainly far more common.

The native drinks are generally the vilest concoctions possible ; are most potent, an almost certain cause of illness, and cannot be taken with impunity.

Officers Commanding Units are to explain the contents of this memorandum to all ranks in addition to merely reading it to the men. The efficiency and good name of the Force as a British Force being, as it is, so dependent on the conduct of all ranks, too much trouble cannot be taken in educating *every* one in their duties and responsibilities in the novel surroundings in which they shortly will be placed. Egypt being held as it is by force of arms, the self-respect of every individual man of the Force is a factor which cannot be overestimated.

E. W. C. CHAYTOR, Colonel,
Assistant Adjutant-General

Christmas in Egypt, 1914. 'Most of us were somewhat disappointed at not being home.' Corporal Henry Dixon on the right, with some of the 'Knuts' ('hard cases') of the Army Service Corps in the mess hall at Zeitoun.

(W.W. Martin Collection – PA1-o-308, Alexander Turnbull Library)

Godley did not confine his efforts to words alone. He wrote to Allen: 'Really the only trouble I foresee is venereal, I am afraid we are almost bound to lose about ten percent of the men through it. The women here are all full of it, and there is a great deal of syphilis and gonorrhea ... I am also arranging privately, without putting anything on paper, for the Medical Officers of each battalion to have a supply of ointment and syringes for injection, and letting the men know that on return from their jaunts they can get the use of these from orderlies on duty; this may save a good many ...'[57]

This was an enlightened policy for the day and one that was never made public to the people of New Zealand. Godley feared that it would be seen as condoning the men's indulgence, so it remained 'a purely private arrangement'. It met strong opposition from some of his own subordinate commanders, including Malone.

'Then, to my horror, the G[eneral] O[fficer] C[ommanding] (ours) has approved certain measures for preventing certain consequences of vice, so as to enable them to indulge in vice with no fear of disease. At present we appeal to the man's better nature and to his morality, at the same time letting him know the awful punishment of certain vice in this country. To do what is proposed to be done is to destroy all moral restraint and lead to worse things.'[58]

But as Godley rightly foresaw, admonition was not enough. Already Cairo was 'a perfect pandemonium ... Australians and some New Zealanders frightfully drunk and singing uproariously in cafes.'[59] Soon each battalion line had its treatment tent operating 24 hours a day, where men could pick up prophylactic ointments on their way into town and be 'syringed' on their return, no questions asked.

In Cairo, the Wazzir was the brothel quarter. 'When the Colonial Troops arrived ... a man's lust could be gratified at the cost of a very few piastres and houses of ill repute were as numerous as the churches in Christchurch.'[60] Even if you did not indulge it was one of the sights that you had to see. 'The houses ... are from four to five stories in height and on one evening I counted as many as eighty dear little things leaning over their balconies or out of their windows with little or no clothing on, beckoning by word and gesture to the soldiers passing underneath to enter and taste the grapes inside.'[61]

The city catered for every taste; a drunken soldier could stagger to the Wazzir or, if he preferred, 'There are many dancing salons … They open about 11.00 p.m. a fine big hall, bar in one corner, orchestra in another, and chairs and tables all round with a free space for dancers in the middle. There are pretty French girls … by the score. Most charmingly dressed, they come up and chat, the waiter ever on the alert bowls up and you have to shout. All drinks … cost 1/- each, so you can imagine how costly it is to get drunk. If you wish to dance she will dance with you, and if you wish anything else — tres bien.'[62]

The Australians and New Zealanders, fit and with money in their pockets, enjoyed all the temptations that Cairo had to offer. Those inflicted with venereal disease were treated as criminals.*

A large venereal disease hospital was established near the Australian lines and run by the Australians for both Australians and New Zealanders. It was surrounded by barbed wire and guards to prevent men breaking out.

Men unfortunate enough to be so caught earned the sobriquet 'barbed wire' soldiers, 'and it was rumoured that there were sufficient officers and men to form a whole battalion from colonel down — not omitting the padre.'[63] Indeed it was a padre, an Australian Salvation Army chaplain, who earned the affection and admiration of the force by leading an assault on the compound to break in and tear down the barbed wire that was so objectionable to the men.

'A ragtime Army standing by.' Trooper John Black and his mates of the Wellington Mounted Rifles, taken at Zeitoun Camp before Gallipoli. From left to right, rear to front: Tom McCullough, Charlie Nicholl, D. McCullough, John Black, Nugent Cuff, Jerry Black, Leslie Watson, Jack Graham and Eric Watson. *(John Black)*

> In camps with barbed wire guarding
> Things of disease and shame
> Were the loving boys we had given
> To die for an Empire's name.[64]

Godley was determined that his New Zealanders would conform and, by hard work, reach a standard 'almost as good as a regular'. This meant a full day's training, including drill and inspections. There were time limits on leave; all men had to be back in camp by 10.30 p.m. Such measures encouraged men to stay in camp. Wet canteens were set up in the battalion lines where good beer could be bought by the bucket at 1d a pint. It cut down the trips into town as 'a poker school could have a happy evening in their own tent'.[65]

---

* By 10 April, 445 New Zealanders were hospitalised for VD, an average of 100 a month. 206 of these would be sent to hospitals on Malta on the SS *Atalantia* on 26 March 1915 to relieve the pressure on hospitals in Egypt.

Discipline was strict, courts martial common, and on 21 December the *Athenic* sailed for New Zealand carrying 58 members of the force: 9 invalids, 4 others with syphilis, 38 who had refused inoculations and 10 incorrigibles for misconduct. A further five venereal cases were sent back to New Zealand on the *Orari* the following week. Godley's message was clear: if you did not meet the standards, you were sent home. It was a very public disgrace. Names were published in Routine Orders, men were paraded in front of their units, and as each man had joined with his mates, lived and trained in sections and platoons made up from men of his district, everyone knew. Such measures succeeded and Godley could report: 'both the Johnstons say it has had an excellent effect on the discipline of their brigades.'[66*]

Not that New Zealanders were saints. Like their sons in Egypt in 1940, they broke camp, got drunk, were robbed by the Egyptians and robbed them in their turn. Such incidents increased as the novelty of Egypt wore off. But Godley's efforts and his imposition of discipline made his New Zealanders look almost saintly by contrast to the Australians. 'There was a time about Christmas when the sights in the streets of Cairo were anything but pleasant for an Australian who had any regard to the good name of Australia,' wrote C.E.W. Bean. 'There was a great deal of drunkenness and I could not help noticing that what people in Cairo said was true — the Australians were responsible for most of it.'[67] This apparent breakdown of discipline in the Australian Force prompted a letter from Birdwood, Commander of the Australian and New Zealand Army Corps, to Major General W.T. Bridges, the Commander of the 1st Australian Division. It was privately circulated by Bridges among his subordinate commanders.

It called on Bridges to bring his Australians back into line: 'But there is no possibility whatever of our doing ourselves full justice unless we are every one of us physically fit, and this no man can possibly be if he allows his body to become sodden with drink or rotten from women, and unless he is doing his best to keep himself efficient he is swindling the Government which has sent him to represent it and fight for it.'[68]

At the same time Godley could report, with evident satisfaction: 'Sir John Maxwell [Commander in Chief in Egypt] stopped all leave for 36 hours last week and had a round up of all absentees in Cairo, with the result that one man of ours was apprehended and over two hundred Australians, and General Bridges told me yesterday that he still had 61 unaccounted for.'[69]

Even though Australians and New Zealanders were both part of this new Australian and New Zealand Army Corps, and even though the initials ANZAC would soon echo the deeds of both countries, their relationship in Egypt was distinctly brittle. Competitiveness was natural; both Godley and Bridges wanted their men to be seen

---

* Lt Col. G.N. Johnston, commanding the NZ Artillery Brigade, and Col. F.E. Johnston, commanding the NZ Infantry Brigade. Brigadier General Russell, Commander of the NZ Mounted Rifles Brigade, had a generally older and more mature stamp of men and from the start maintained a firm grip on the discipline of his brigade.

Curio stalls grew as fast as the camp. The ANZACs had money and the Egyptians were keen to see it spent. *(WF-002662-24, Morison Collection, NAM Waiouru)*

as the best. But it was more than this; a growing national pride, a touch of envy on the New Zealanders' part at the size of the Australian Force, and critical comments from both sides made for uncomfortable partners. Australians viewed us as 'pale imitations' of themselves. We, in turn, at every rank were equally censorious: Malone was deeply prejudiced against Australians and conscious of it. During the voyage to Egypt he wrote: 'The Australians were alight again last night. They seem a slack lot. Perhaps it is my prejudice against Australians. I have it, I know, but cannot say why. I must be juster and only judge on first hand evidence. Yet there is evidence of slackness on their part and a comparison unfavourable to them can be made every day.'[70]

Australian doings in Egypt spread this view among New Zealand officers — Colvin Algie, a captain in the Auckland Battalion, wrote in his diary: 'It was rather spoilt by the behaviour of some Australians who came in and got a bit drunk. These gentry, as in South Africa, have earned none too good a name and are disliked by most of the business people. I cannot help making comparisons, although they are odious, but our boys are doing remarkably well here and are quite a credit to everyone they belong to.'[71]

This attitude is echoed in the diaries and letters of New Zealand soldiers: 'The Australian, and more especially the town bred man, is a skiting bumptious fool, who thinks nobody knows anything but himself.'[72]

Among the New Zealanders there was a growing sense of identity, a national pride emerging. 'The papers and the French and English people here are making the

Australians sore over the fuss they are making of us fellows. For instance, in the route march through Cairo the Australians were there. The papers gave a full account of it and said all sorts of nice things about us but did not mention the Cornstalks at all. They have written several letters to the papers complaining about being overlooked and drawing attention to the fact that Australia is eight times as large as New Zealand … I dropped in to a theatre on Sunday night and one of the main items was a song … about the soldiers from New Zealand … we nearly brought the house down. I suppose the Australians there said, "Those damned Pig Islanders have scored again!"'[73]

Such rivalry, combined with plenty of drink, led to incidents: 'If we meet or see them in a restaurant or anywhere in town there is generally a row of some kind.'[74] There was much that the two forces had in common. They both tended to scorn the Tommy private and the Gyppo, and many Australians and New Zealanders served in each other's forces. Regiments who trained alongside each other found much to admire. Russell's Mounteds formed close ties with the Australian Light Horse, even if they held different views of the infantry.

But for all that, Godley's New Zealanders were too small in number to form a separate New Zealand Division and so a close association with the Australians was inevitable. It was agreed that Godley would command a division made up of the New Zealand Infantry Brigade, the New Zealand Mounted Rifles Brigade and the New Zealand Artillery Brigade. To this was added the 1st Australian Light Horse Brigade under Colonel Harry Chauvel, and the 4th Australian Infantry Brigade under Colonel John Monash, which had not yet arrived in Egypt. Godley wrote to Allen: 'It is of course a very abnormal division. Personally I am very glad to have the mounted troops, and if we only had a little more artillery I should be perfectly satisfied with it in all respects, but we shall be woefully short of artillery.'[75]

Godley formed Engineer and Army Service Corps companies from his reinforcements from New Zealand and also the New Zealand contingent from London when they arrived in December. However, his force would continue to rely on his sole artillery brigade, unlike a normal divisional organisation that had a brigade of artillery for each brigade of infantry or mounted rifles. The name, too, became a compromise. 'We have hitherto called it the New Zealand Division, but now that we have got two Australian Brigades in it … they naturally feel that they should be represented by name also, so I think the best way out … will be to call it the New Zealand and Australian Division, New Zealand coming first, as it is the nucleus on which the Division has been built, and as all the staff is New Zealand …'[76]

It was letters in the mail that joined Godley and his men like an umbilical cord to the land they had left. 'First New Zealand mail arrived today and great were the rejoicings in camp.'[77] Home suddenly became very important as the men began to appreciate more and more what they had sailed away from. 'We got a pile of papers by the mail and I have to thank someone for a *Press*. It looks quite homely to see *Herald*s, *Chronicle*s, *Auckland*s and *Canterbury Times* kicking around the tent, we took and pasted some pictures up whare fashion. All the officers that come down the line come in and have a look at our Maori belles, bush pictures and New Zealand pictures in general.'[78]

Some were sent home. This is a parade of Wellington Battalion men who refused to be inoculated, before being sent back to New Zealand, December 1914. *(WF-002662-25, Morison Collection, NAM Waiouru)*

Other soldiers went to town. Two New Zealand soldiers buying corncobs from a street vendor. *(W.W. Martin Collection*
– PA1-o-309, Alexander Turnbull Library)

Post Office, Zeitoun Camp with New Zealand Signal Company motorbike parked out front. 'The first New Zealand mail arrived today and great were the rejoicings in camp.' *(WF-002662-25, Morison Collection, NAM Waiouru)*

'It's not a patch on the stuff we get back home.' Major Bobby Young and Lieutenant Leonard Jardine of the 9th Hawke's Bay Company enjoying a beer. *(WF-002662-59, Morison Collection, NAM Waiouru)*

Letters home were full of life in Egypt and life in camp: 'We draw 28 bob once a fortnight, for a few days after pay day we live pretty high. The boys buy buns, cakes and all sorts of luxuries to make a good feed with our rations and a good many of them don't show up at meals at all but patronise the native tucker shops … but towards pay day the tables are full, the boys all stay home at night and talk finance and argue the point in general. The troop I am in comes from all up the Main Trunk line, I am about the only lowlander in it. There are some great arguments about dogs, horses, bushwhacking, fencing etc. One can hardly realise that we are so far away from home.'[79]

The biggest thing that had happened to New Zealand was the sailing of the Expeditionary Force and everything about the 'boys' in Egypt was news. Despite censorship, every rumour, every hint of scandal, both real and imagined, reached home and generally received publicity. 'There has been a big scandal over our stores I am sorry to say. All the gift stuff we were supposed to have given to us free has disappeared and in some cases has been sold to us through our canteens.'[80]

Some saw the sights. A farrier corporal and a trooper of the New Zealand Mounteds visit the pyramids. Note the horseshoe above the corporal's stripes; both men have their spurs pinned to their epaulettes. *(WW Martin Collection – PA1-o-308, Alexander Turnbull Library)*

Boastful letters home about doings in Cairo had a way of rebounding on the sender. 'From what we see in the New Zealand papers that have reached here they are printing some awful rot about the country and our doings here. And one chap in our Squadron who has been writing to the papers got such a twist the other day that he has not turned up in the Mess Room for several days. If I were guilty of writing such slobbery stuff, drunk or sober, I would never show my face among the troops again. What gets over me is how anybody with ordinary common sense would publish some of the tales we see in the papers.'[81]

Such publicity also perplexed Godley. Bad press over compulsory military training had jaundiced his view of the New Zealand media, and all too quickly he discovered the uniqueness of his position as Commander of the New Zealand Expeditionary Force. Any other British major general could get on and train his men, knowing that dealings with government and media were the concern of his superiors. Not Godley, however. As well as being answerable to Birdwood, his Corps Commander, for the training of his men, he was also answerable to the New Zealand government for the conduct of the force. Every week the mail brought a time bomb that had been sizzling en route for the five or six weeks that the mail took to arrive. James Allen, Minister of Defence, was a master of detail, and a power in Massey's cabinet. The deeds and

New Zealand Artillery trumpeters practicing at Zeitoun. *(WF-002082-67, Captain W. Deans Album, CMR, NAM)*

achievements of our men overseas were politically important to a government holding precarious tenure in office. Allen wanted all the answers from his Force Commander, and Godley's cry of exasperation at his predicament still echoes from the pages: 'And really, if you come to think of it, when one considers all the big things that might have gone wrong, those you write about are very insignificant and of very small moment. After all, even if there is a certain amount of drinking and venereal, even if a man does get stabbed; even if some few gift stores are lost, even if men have to be sent back for misconduct, if grumbles are published, these are very small things, when you think that you have a force of eleven thousand well trained men of splendid physique, nearly all fit, beautifully mounted, thoroughly well equipped, and ready, and only too willing to go and fight for the Empire … Many really big and important things might have gone wrong, but none of them have.'[82]

Called to account on one hand, Godley found on the other that he could not go direct to his government for additional men and material. Any such request had to go through the Secretary of State for War, Lord Kitchener. It was an unenviable position; Allen would rap Godley over the knuckles if he asked directly in his letters for another brigade of infantry or a battery of howitzers: 'As regards the communication with the War Office for alterations in establishment beyond what we had agreed to … communications should come direct from the War Office to us in New Zealand.'[83] Godley must have fumed in private, but, always the diplomat, he would apologise by return mail: 'I quite understand the difficulties which you mention of dealing with more people than one, and that one should be the War Office, but, on the other hand, it is very exasperating here to have to sit and wait patiently for things to go, as they do now, through, first, our Army Corps Commander, second, the Commander of the Forces in Egypt, third, the War Office, and also probably the High Commissioner, before they reach you, and of course one naturally thinks that it could be much quicker settled if it could be done direct.'[84]

It is to Godley's credit that he maintained a good relationship with Allen and developed it so that by the end of the war he was dealing direct on many matters. His tact allowed the New Zealand Expeditionary Force to evolve into a small national army within the framework of the larger British Forces in which it served. It laid the groundwork for Freyberg's charter of the 1939–45 war.

This was in the future, but while in Egypt, Godley's abilities as a trainer of men and administrator soundly established for all the high standards of the New Zealand Force. It was the foundation of our reputation in this war, but it would never be appreciated by the troops. Godley never courted popularity; he had not the awkward geniality and the gift of self-publicity of Birdwood. He remained apart from his men, seeking satisfaction in their achievements, never their praise, demanding higher and higher standards, but never offering a word of encouragement.

'About 11.00 p.m. the General and staff arrived and inspected the bivouac … All hands were of course sound asleep. Then he inspected the sentry groups. He suddenly thought he would like to see an alarm and how quickly the men could get into the posts. He ordered the alarm signal and two shots to be fired. The men turned out in record time and without a word and in 5½ minutes were lining the brow of the hill where the camp was. Then he set them to work to dig trenches and dig themselves in at that hour. He left before the job was finished … This is one thing the men love him for.'[85]

4

RUMOURS OF THE DARDANELLES

When Asquith asked whether the Australians and New Zealanders 'were good enough' for an important operation of war, Kitchener replied that 'they were quite good enough if a cruise on the Sea of Marmara was all that was contemplated'.
Martin Gilbert, *Winston S. Churchill 1914–1916*

Egypt was rapidly losing its charms. All the action was in France and 'Bill Massey's Tourists' were stuck among the desert sands; letters home were now full of complaints. 'Life here is becoming as monotonous as a permanent job … We are all sick of this show and want to be doing something somewhere.'[1] On 25 January there was the promise of action against the Turks, who were reported advancing on the Suez Canal. Word came through in the evening for the New Zealand Infantry Brigade to mobilise by train to the canal.

'The men were delighted at moving off and seemed to talk all last night. When the news came that the infantry brigade was to go the bands began playing and everybody was singing patriotic songs. The last detachment left about 2.00 p.m. and as each half battalion passed along the lines and down to the station the mounted men and artillery cheered them to the echo.'[2]

The New Zealand Brigade deployed along the canal: the Wellington and Otago battalions, commanded by Colonel Malone at Kubri, five kilometres from Suez, and Brigade Headquarters under Colonel F.E. Johnston with the Auckland and Canterbury battalions at Ismaila. Positions were reconnoitred and trenches dug. Men waited and watched. 'Ships large and small passing through all day. Some were crowded with passengers who cheered again and again as they passed … They threw dozens of tins of cigarettes and tobacco and stuff and our fellows swam out in the canal to pick them up …'[3]

It was at Serapeum on 2 February 1915 that the 12th Nelson Company of the Canterburys had the first major action of New Zealanders in the war. Turkish soldiers attempted a crossing of the canal in aluminium pontoon boats. Heavy rifle fire from Major Brereton's Nelson Company sank most of the boats and caused many casualties. This day also saw the first New Zealand casualties: 'We had … one man wounded, Bill Ham, of 10 Platoon, but the poor chap died the next day. He was shot in the neck and the spine was broken …' Sergeant Williams of 9 Platoon was also wounded by Turkish shrapnel: 'Billy Williams had all the Cockney's gift for profanity, and on this occasion he excelled himself.'[4]

That night, the Turks probed with fire all along the New Zealand line at Kubri, where the Wellingtons were manning the trenches. All was blackness and a sandstorm was raging. 'At 12.10 p.m. we were awakened by the sound of rifle fire, and immediately we took our place in the trenches. We had quite made up our minds that a ribbon would be the outcome of this lot …'[5] There was to be no ribbon, for no Turkish attack materialised. After this, life on the canal settled into a monotony of sentry duty, trench fatigues, digging and wiring.

'The men are not taking this war against the Turks very seriously, and they always refer to the raiders at night as "a harmless lot of orange sellers" and when the guns of the warships boom they remark, "Another orange seller came up to the canal on the wrong date."'[6]

Now instead of action it was mail from home that was more important. On 9 February Bollinger wrote: 'Today reports, "Not a Turk within 20 miles of the Canal". We are taking things easy and wondering what will be our next move if Turks do not return. Continuation of training will go very hard after this. I feel sure we will go to Europe.'[7]

On the banks of the Suez Canal. 'Ships passing through all day … They threw dozens of tins of cigarettes and tobacco and stuff and our fellows swam out into the canal to pick them up.' *(WF-002662-83, Morison Collection, NAM Waiouru)*

At the end of February the New Zealand Brigade returned to Cairo. 'On the journey to Cairo we met the remainder of the N.Z. and A Division who have been out bivouacking. We reached our old camp at 4.00 p.m. and soon had tents pitched. Wild, though may they not be wild, rumours are afloat to the effect that we will not be here more than a week, and that our destination is somewhere in the direction of the Dardanelles.'[8]

That same week, an Australian infantry brigade marched out of camp and entrained for Alexandria, to sail to an unknown destination. This was the 3rd Australian Infantry Brigade under Colonel Sinclair MacLagan. They would find themselves on board ship in Mudros Harbour on the Greek island of Lemnos, 100 kilometres from the Gallipoli Peninsula. On the island water was scarce; there was no accommodation or wharfs sufficient to land the brigade, so they remained on board ship. They had no orders and the puzzled Australians received no inkling why they were there, only that it had some connection with the Royal Navy's bombardment of the Dardanelles Forts.

For the next month the Dardanelles were to remain no more than a source of rumour to the New Zealanders. As Bollinger feared, it was more training. 'I think it can be safely said that the work of the month has been both difficult and trying. Divisional training is no joke … the Division moved off in three columns to attack a position far across the burning desert … we were put on a forced march for two solid hours in the heat and glare of the sun. March discipline was strictly enforced and every man from the OC down was disallowed the privilege of drinking water. About three miles had been coveted when the first man dropped and from then on men were simply dropping right and left.'[9]

The men cursed and grumbled. Hope would lift on every rumour of going. They sweated on, little realising that the Division was having its final polish. Captain A.B. Morton NZSC, Staff Captain on the New Zealand Infantry Brigade headquarters, wrote: 'I watched the Brigade march into camp one day last week after a hard day in the desert and it was a fine sight. The men looked a picture of health and readiness for action. They were wearing the coolest kit they could find — "shorts" and a singlet or shirt, hat, puttees and boots … in addition each man had his rifle, bayonet and web equipment … The men have learned the rules of the game and are ready to play it as it should be played.'[10]

But the men had little confidence in ever leaving Egypt. 'A fortnight has elapsed since I wrote … nothing worth recording has happened … We have had several disappointments … such as packing up, striking camp, and going out as if we were going to entrain for a shift, but every time it has been simply for practice or a review and we return to camp at nightfall grumbling or growling in hearty fashion … I don't think we will ever get to the Front.'[11]

'Our fellows have been issued with a thin drill uniform this week which looks as if we were to be in a warm climate. The warships are making progress at the Dardanelles and according to today's paper there is a French force now en route to that place so perhaps we shall be on the move soon.'[12]

'The people in New Zealand must be quite tired of getting letters telling them how we are off to the Front "next week". I wonder if they are as tired of it as we are? Of course we know that it cannot be helped, as everything lately has depended on the bombardment of the Dardanelles.'[13]

Reinforcements drawn from each region for each battalion were sent from New Zealand every two months. The First Reinforcements had sailed with the Main Body and by the time Godley's men left Egypt, they had received the Second and Third reinforcements, each nearly 2000 strong. Also to join were New Zealanders of the British Section recruited in England, and a Maori contingent, 500 strong. The British Section arrived first, on Christmas Eve. Two hundred and forty strong, it was a varied mix of professional men — engineers, Rhodes Scholars, opera singers, actors, farmers — who had been holidaying in Britain. Many were over age; one would meet his two sons in Egypt; another, Horace Moore-Jones, was 47 years old. An artist, Moore-Jones had studied painting at The Slade and been working for *Pearson's Magazine* as an illustrator. Like many with him, he had shaved and dyed a greying moustache and hair, adjusted his age and enlisted. 'Aunty' Moore-Jones would never find military life easy. Yet his watercolour landscapes of Gallipoli Peninsula and his paintings of 'Simpson and his Donkey' would be part of the moulding of the ANZAC legend.

They received a mixed reception: 'The New Zealand lot from London came in this morning and the Colonel called for three cheers for 'em and they walked over his garden and then he gave them bloody hell.'[14]

Many were not happy to be in Egypt and resented being split between the Engineers and the Service Corps for they had trained as infantry. One of these was

The principal players in the New Zealand Anzac story: The GOC (Major-General Sir Alexander Godley) with the staff of the NZ & A Division and his brigade and battalion commanders before the Gallipoli campaign.
(34259, Alexander Turnbull Library)

Charles Saunders, who had given up a commission to join as a New Zealander. 'We British Section men were very disgusted when sent to Egypt, as we had reckoned on going to France and so getting at the Germans … Abbey and I used often to discuss the possibility of getting to Alexandria and so to Marseilles and on to the front with a French Regiment.'[15]

It was the opposite with the Maori Contingent. They were pleased to get to Egypt, as initially a Maori contingent had not been acceptable because of 'the known unwillingness of the Imperial Government to use native troops in wars between Europeans.'[16] The service of Indian troops in Egypt and in France changed that, but the Maori Contingent found that they were regarded as suitable for garrison duty only. They arrived in Egypt at the end of March with the Third Reinforcements and impressed Godley and Birdwood with their dress and bearing.

However, not all were as complimentary. Malone wrote: 'Mostly big hulking gone-in-the-knees walking men. I think the War Lords don't quite know what to do with them. They look soft, and, I fancy, were not killed with work on the transports.'[17]

Despite pleas to be allowed to remain and fight with the rest of the New Zealand Force, the Maoris were ordered to Malta as garrison. They sailed with some 206 other New Zealanders, all venereal cases, who were shipped to Malta as the hospitals in Egypt were being emptied in planning for projected operations. Major Herbert Hart, Malone's Second-in-Command, commented: 'The Maoris have been giving displays, hakas etc. to Generals and other big guns ever since their arrival. Today one exhibition was witnessed by Sir Henry McMahon, High Commissioner, Generals Maxwell, Birdwood, Godley and all the chief people of Cairo — and myself.

'On Monday the Maoris go to Malta; for more haka displays presumably.'[18]

Unknown to the soldiers, the ANZAC Corps had been earmarked since February for operations in the Dardanelles.

'In order to assist the Navy a force is being concentrated on Lemnos Island to give co-operation and to occupy any captured forts. At present 2000 Marines in the Island, to be followed about 13 March by 8000 more.'

'You should warn a force of approximately 30,000 of Australians and New Zealand Contingent under Birdwood to prepare for this service.'[19]

It was planned as a navy show and was the brainchild of the First Sea Lord of the Admiralty, Winston Churchill. The stalemate of the Western Front and Russian cries for assistance against Turkish attack in the Caucasus had given Churchill the chance to convince an apathetic British cabinet of the potential gains to be won in the Mediterranean. The old pre-'Dreadnought' class battleships of the British Navy would, with French ships of the same class, batter the Turkish forts guarding the Dardanelles Straits, steam through into the Sea of Marmara, arrive off the Turkish capital of Constantinople and awe the Turkish government into submission.

Brilliantly conceived, but yet to be equally executed, it held great prospects for knocking Turkey out of the war, bringing relief to Russia, and bringing in the Balkan States on the Allied side. It was agreed to. Hopes of success were high. In February, the Navy bombarded the outer forts. Little real damage was caused, but news of the

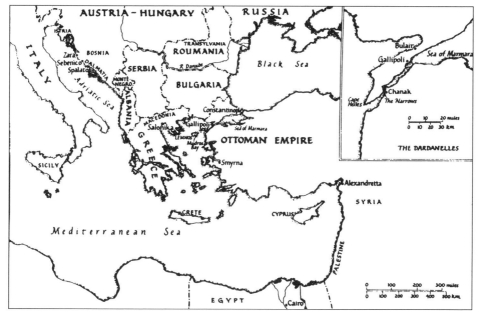

The Eastern Mediterranean, 1915. *(From H.H. Asquith letters to Venetia Stanley)*

attack 'created a vast international sensation. The Bulgarians hastily broke off their flirtation with the Central Powers; the Greeks offered three divisions for an attack on the Gallipoli Peninsula; the Russians, anxious not to be out of the dismemberment of the Ottoman Empire, spoke of attacking Constantinople from the east and bringing up an army corps for the purpose; the Italians made distinctly friendly noises. In Constantinople itself there was almost a panic.'[20]

By the end of February the outer defences had been successfully bombarded. Small parties of Royal Marines from the warships had landed against little opposition and put large numbers of guns in the forts out of action. The high cost of the landings on these same beaches two months later would show how well the Turks had absorbed these lessons.

It was now felt necessary to commit soldiers 'to help the Navy to reap the fruits of success.'[21] Sir Ian Hamilton, no stranger to the Australian and New Zealand Forces, was made commander of a Mediterranean Expeditionary Force.* This force would number some 70,000 men. It included a French Division of mainly colonial troops; the 29th Division, under Major-General A.G. Hunter-Weston, the only British Regular Division not yet committed to France; the Royal Naval Division, another brainchild of Churchill's, commanded by Major-General Paris and made up of two brigades of seamen, stokers, etc. for whom no sea jobs were available; and one brigade of Royal Marines. This Naval

---

* Asquith, the British Prime Minister, described Hamilton as 'a sanguine enthusiastic person, with a good deal of superficial charm ... and much experience of warfare ... but there is too much feather in his brain.' Despite this, it was at Asquith's insistence that Hamilton commanded the Mediterranean Expeditionary Force.[22]

Division was equipped with a hotchpotch of rifles and artillery, anything left over after the needs of the Western Front had been met. As a result, their weapons were few and of doubtful quality. The force was joined by the ANZAC Corps commanded by Birdwood. By now the ANZACs were considered by all, including their own commanders, as magnificent material, but as yet untried and untested — amateurs. When Asquith, the British Prime Minister, asked whether the Australians and New Zealanders 'were good enough for an important operation of war, Kitchener replied that "they were quite good enough if a cruise on the Sea of Marmara was all that was contemplated."'[23]

The events of 18 March 1915 made it a far more serious business than a cruise. On this day warships of the French and Royal navies tried to force the Narrows and subdue the inner forts lining both sides of the Straits. They failed, at a cost of three battleships sunk and three badly damaged. Though the losses were quickly made good, the Navy had lost heart. It was now a combined operation of war in which Hamilton's army was to play the major role. 'The Army's part will not be a case of landing parties for the destruction of the forts, but rather a case of a deliberate and progressive military operation carried out in force in order to make good a passage for the Navy.'[24]

Hamilton returned to Egypt to organise his forces and prepare for the first large amphibious operation against a defended shore in over a century. It was a tremendously difficult undertaking. There was no guide to assist him in his planning. Ominously, the previous amphibious operation, against Walcheren Island in 1809, had been a disaster. Ever optimistic, Hamilton pushed on with a small staff against every conceivable obstacle: no information, troops and equipment scattered throughout the Mediterranean, objections from Birdwood and all the divisional commanders, who saw little prospect of success.

The difficulty as Hamilton saw it was getting his troops ashore. Little consideration was given to the fighting qualities of the Turkish soldier. The Turks' poor performance at the Suez Canal and the initial ease of the marine landings during the bombardment of the forts convinced Hamilton that once his army was ashore, any Turkish opposition would be brushed aside with the assistance of the Navy's guns. It would be planned, in many respects, as one of the last of Britain's colonial wars with the gunboats off-shore and the Empire's troops landing to subdue the hill tribesmen. The preparations were conducted in a blaze of publicity, and all Europe awaited the outcome.

Cairo was abuzz with the Dardanelles. On 29 March, Sir Ian Hamilton inspected the Australians and New Zealanders. '20,000 troops on parade … and we had the biggest dusting since reaching Egypt … dust in our ears, eyes, mouth and every-where …'[25] Anything could be endured, for the word was the Dardanelles! Charles Saunders, now reconciled to being an engineer, wrote: 'Abbey and I congratulated ourselves that we had not been rash and deserted as we had thought of doing. We knew we were in for something big by reason of having such a distinguished General as Sir Ian Hamilton in charge, as he was probably the third man of the Army and would only be spared from France for something big.'[26]

Godley wrote of Hamilton to Allen: 'He is very glad that he is to have us under command. I am sure that he really is, and we are glad to be with him.'[27]

Godley's NZ & A Division would take only part of his New Zealand force; this would be the Infantry Brigade, the Artillery Brigade, engineers, and services. Together with the 4th Australian Brigade it would be a weak division of only two brigades instead of the normal three, and, like the Royal Naval Division, it was 'woefully short of artillery'. Godley and his staff held little hope of Russell's Mounted Rifles Brigade rejoining them: 'I do not think that when we go the mounted troops will come for some time; we must get through the Dardanelles first, which will be a purely infantry and artillery job — exactly the opposite to South Africa, and Mounted Troops are at a discount. The only chance will be if, after getting through the Dardanelles, we get onto the plains of Hungary.'[28]

The Wazzir, the aftermath of Good Friday.
(G. Creamer Collection)

Some 1600 New Zealanders from the Infantry Reinforcements would remain in Egypt, as well as Russell's Brigade and Bauchop's regiment of Otago Mounted Rifles. The total number of New Zealanders who would sail for the Dardanelles was 6324. This included 522 reinforcements who were to act as 'hold' parties to unload stores and remain on board ship until called for. There was fierce competition among the reinforcements who were being left in Egypt to find a place among the men going to the Dardanelles. One of these was Ewen Pilling, a Third Reinforcement. In Egypt he rejoined the Otago Battalion and found it full of 'old friends, and found many with whom I had swotted, debated, played cricket, and football, and skylarked in the old school and university. It is good to be with them … On Friday rumour had it that the Main Body was very soon to leave for the Front. The thought of again losing my friends and being left behind was too much. Orders that embarkation rolls were to be made up came out on Saturday. I bustled round and after losing a great deal of sweat, found a platoon with two holes in it. Adamson and I offered ourselves and the name of "University" worked the miracle. We were told it would cost us our stripes. "Ha Ha! What matter that? We will go as lance-privates if you like!" Now we are in the Main Body.'[29]

They were days of packing, sorting kit, sharpening bayonets, but the men would have one last fling. On Good Friday, 2 April, New Zealanders, Australians and Tommies ran riot in the brothel area. 'They started at 5.30 p.m. by removing furniture from these buildings and burning it in the middle of the street. The "Redcaps" arrived and matters started to get worse. The Redcaps were the object for a lot of missiles and they fired into the crowd, wounding five soldiers. The riot grew and the Redcaps had to retreat. We heard the shots fired and rushed around to see the Redcaps galloping away with death written on their faces. Now the soldiers had things their own way. Two thousand soldiers must have gathered in the street. The rioting party paid attention to about 200 yds of building. They smashed every window and door in the street and removed all furniture and had a tremendous fire in the street. The fire engine arrived but as soon as a hose was unreeled, it was cut to pieces. At last a hose was connected and the natives on board turned it on the crowd. This was the "Last Straw". The natives' heads stopped batons and bottles. The hose was taken from and turned on them, and they only retreated, when their engine was pushed on the fire.

'Still the battle raged, pianos, chests of drawers, chairs, bed stead, etc came out wholesale from windows storeys high. To make matters worse the troops had raided all shops in ground floor and obtained as much liquor as they could drink. At 7.00 p.m. a company of infantry arrived. They loaded, fixed bayonets, and marched down the street amid hooting. They were subject to a lot of missiles and some of their rifles were thrown on the fire. They finally had to unfix bayonets. Suddenly flame burst out from a four storey building. The Redcaps dare not come back. Cavalry now began to arrive. Plenty of tact was used; the row quietened down. A second fire engine arrived under cavalry escort and fire was put under. We left at 8.00 p.m. but there were still thousands in the street. On arrival at Camp we heard all leave was stopped from 12 o'clock on Sunday, and we were leaving on Wednesday.'[30]

How it started no one could tell, although there were plenty of stories. The Australians blamed the New Zealanders, who in turn blamed the Australians. Four were wounded —three Australians and one New Zealander, so, based on the respective size of the forces, 'honours' were equally shared.

There were many eyewitness reports, but all who had been there claimed to have been spectators. It was always someone else having all the action! It did not end there. On the Sunday the troops were confined to camp. When the projector in the camp cinema broke down and the proprietor refused to refund their money, they burnt it down; 'an ice cream shop also received some attention and had to close in a hurry.'[31] It was an eruption of pent-up frustration and tension by trained, bored and anxious troops who felt that even now there might be yet another delay.

But it was true! They were off. There was time for letters home.

Zeitoun Camp

April 8th 1915

My Dearest little lass,
Just for what is in all probability my last letter to you from our camp at Zeitoun. I am going to dash on hurriedly and trust to the sporting spirit of our pal the Censor ... Oh! At last it has come and I trust and pray it will not find us wanting. In the mess room where I am writing some of the boys are having a 'last night's' entertainment. Frank Blanford (the well known New Zealand entertainer) is at the piano and Harvey Baxter is giving us a treat with his violin. Just now they have been playing 'Because' and how it makes me think ... All the little evenings in the front room return with a vividness that is real, and we spend tonight together in New Zealand again ...'[32]

Sailing for the Dardanelles. 'How the world goes round and we with it.' HMS *Queen Elizabeth*, with warships and transports in the distance. *(G00224-2, Auckland War Memorial Museum)*

'Mudros Harbour, a big landlocked sheet of deep water, about as big as Wellington Harbour'. In the foreground, the Wellingtons rest before re-embarking. *(WF-002363-5-1978-1949-5, W.A. Hampton Collection, NAM Waiouru)*

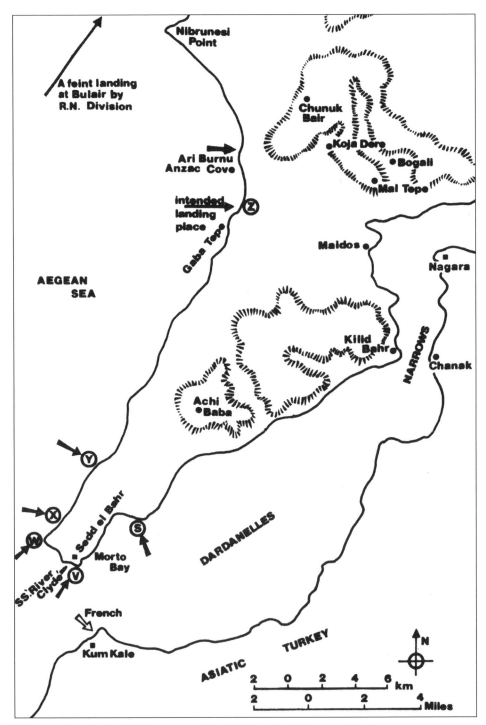

The approach to Gallipoli.

'Sunday 10th April. Reveille … We moved off quickly and quietly … After a tiresome journey we reached Alexandria at 10.00 a.m. and embarked right away. We are on a miserable tub called the "Achaia". She is a German prize boat. At 5.00 p.m. we moved into the stream all extremely happy to see, we hope, the last of a "Niggers Paradise" … Farewell Egypt.'[33]

Godley's division was to sail on 13 ships, mostly captured or interned German passenger ships and transports: *Achaia*, *Itonus*, *Katuna*, *Lutzow*, *Goslar*, *Annaberg*, *Haider Pasha*, *Seeangbee*, *Australind*, *Ascot*, *Seeangchun*, *Californian* and *Surada*. Alexandria was crowded with transports, and ships left independently for the rendezvous at Mudros Harbour on the island of Lemnos.

'Our course is about due North and there is no doubt that the Dardanelles is our destination. Few of us, in fact none of us, ever thought we should get our baptism of fire on Turkish soil. How the world goes round and we with it.'[34]

The *Lutzow*, carrying Godley and his headquarters with the Auckland and half the Canterbury battalions, arrived at Mudros on Thursday 15 April. The NZ & A Division was complete by 20 April when the *Goslar* arrived, carrying the Infantry Brigade headquarters and the engineers. Mudros made an immediate impact. 'Most glorious harbour, great sight, about 100 transports and dozens of battleships and cruisers. Aeroplanes, submarines, and torpedo boats galore. Also submarine nets right across the harbour. Finest harbour yet seen. Evidently gigantic preparations have been made for terrific assault on Turkey. Excitement extreme.'[35]

Commanding officers got the first indication of the task ahead. Malone wrote: 'The harbour was full of shipping of every nation as the French, British and ANZAC troops assembled. There was talk that the Peninsula was strongly defended "and that we shall get a warm reception". Apparently they cannot force the Dardanelles without a land force to demolish or complete the demolition of the Turkish Forts, and that will be our job after we have driven back the Turkish Army. The job is going to be a big one. There will be difficulty about water There is none on Lemnos (for an Army) and we will have to depend on ships for all our water and supplies.'[36]

Spencer Westmacott was with his platoon on the *Lutzow*. 'Inside the boom all shipping was safe, lying at anchor. We had never seen such an Armada before. The green island looked a paradise after the sands of Egypt, though the hills were treeless. As usual I was allotted a boat. These were very good and made of some kind of three ply. Instead of men hauling them out of the water, they were hoisted and lowered by steam. We commenced at once to practise landing operations. These consisted of parading the companies of infantry in full kit and going ashore in turn, packed in the boats as close as the men could sit, their rifles between their knees. We would land, extend along the shore, advance to the nearest hill top and take up a fire position, and when satisfied everyone was ready to fight, pile arms and allow the men to roll in the long cool grass which grew up to ankle height. In this way we would spend two or three pleasant hours, until our turn came to re-embark and go back into the crowded ships.

'During these times on the island, the men, so long as they did not stay beyond the call of a whistle, could amuse themselves as they pleased. Most were content to laze in that mild atmosphere. Lemnos was one of the isles of Greece "where burning Sappho loved and sang". What a privilege to have a breathing space before battle in such classical surroundings! It seemed only right it should end in battle. It only needed a poet to sing of our emotions in after years. We had our poet in Rupert Brooke; but alas, though we did not know it then, his voice was stilled forever there. He died of blood poisoning and was buried on April 23rd by some of his brother officers, one of whom was named Freyberg.

'Towards the end we had a number of errands to run, including a visit to Sir Ian Hamilton's Headquarters ship, where everything looked clean and comfortable with plenty of space, as became the surroundings of a C in C. I was not invited below, and having delivered the bag with despatches, paced the deck whilst awaiting return documents.

'Meanwhile our boat fell away from the gangway, clinging to a line, with a number of others, which rose and fell six feet or so at a time, all bumping into each other and trying to fend off the ship's side. Most, like my own, were manned with soldiers, who were willing and did their best. A naval boat came alongside in quite different style and a fine looking seaman with two red stripes on his arm mounted the ladder. Whilst waiting he looked over the side during an extra wind squall at the mass of confusion below. "This is awful Sir," said he to me. "I been fifteen years in the Royal Navy and never saw anything like this before. No good can come of it." It sounded as if he

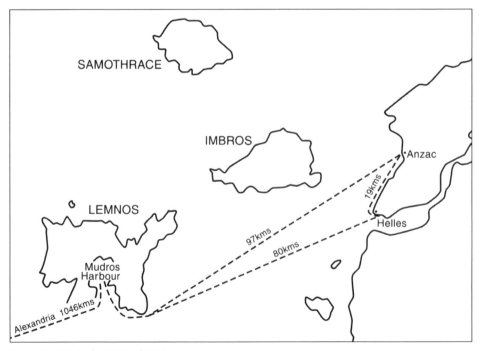

Sir Ian Hamilton's plan, 25 April 1915.

forecasted disaster and I told him we were only soldiers unused to handling boats. He would find we would be all right ashore …

'On the Sunday we practised landing as usual, and the Reverend Fielden Taylor, chaplain of the Canterburys in our ship, took advantage of the occasion to hold an open air service. It was a fine day and he went off with the first tow early and standing on a grassy mound said a prayer and gave a short address. The men having piled arms lay on the grass around him, listening attentively — it was entirely voluntary — and they came and went — he certainly had a quiet magnetism and held his congregation; but it was more than that. Everyone there knew in a vague sort of way that many of us would presently die, and whilst no one seemed unduly depressed at the prospect, we were in solemn mood and ready to pay heed to the preacher's words which were something like this: "As you have lived, so you will die, and it does not very much matter" uttered in quiet conversational tones which we all found strangely satisfying, even comforting. Perhaps they are one and the same. As each tow of boats came ashore, newcomers approached and sat down, whilst the first to arrive were recalled for the return to the ships. He was there when I arrived, and continuing in the afternoon when I left. I believe with prayer and exhortation he went on all day. A Sermon on the Mount it seemed. Comparing notes after, I do not believe any of us forgot it …'[37]

Final conferences were held between the Navy and commanders and staff. Disquieting aspects about some of the administrative planning emerged.* Godley wrote to his wife: 'I have written to General Birdwood to say I am not satisfied about the hospital arrangements. All our wounded and sick, however slight, are to go all the way to Alexandria and I want them to establish a stationary hospital here at Lemnos.'[38]

It was the same with the navy and sorting out the detail of the landing. The number and size of ships looked impressive, particularly HMS *Queen Elizabeth* with her 15-inch guns, but the Navy Staff's approach to the planning of the operation appeared somewhat casual. Braithwaite, the GSO1 of the NZ & A Division, noted in his diary: 'There seems to be slight divergence of opinion between the Army and Navy on some points viz. intercommunication and covering fire — the Army naturally wants everything cut and dried, the Navy appears averse to this.'[40]

There were few beaches suitable for landings on the Peninsula and reconnaissance had shown that the Turkish Army had made good use of the five weeks since 18 March. Hamilton's plan aimed to confuse the Turkish defender as to the beaches that would receive the main weight of the Allied assault. To do this, landings were widely dispersed on almost every suitable beach on the Peninsula. The main effort would be in the south at Helles. Here on V, W, X, S and Y Beaches, the cream of Hamilton's force,

---

* Planning was confined to Hamilton's Operations Staff, and Birdwood's staff, who had carried out a great deal of anticipatory planning, were excluded. Relationships were particularly strained between Birdwood and Hamilton's Chief of Staff, Maj. Gen. W.P. Braithwaite. Birdwood was particularly critical of Hamilton's failure to use his administrative staffs: 'The Adjutants-General, the Director of Medical Services and the Quarter Master General probably knew less about the destination and purposes of the expedition than anyone in Egypt, and no attempt was made to enlighten them.'[39]

Hunter-Weston's 29th Regular Division, would land. The 29th would advance north up the Peninsula, seizing what were believed to be the vital heights of Achi Baba.

This landing would be at dawn and heralded by the supporting fire of the warships of the Allied navies. In keeping with Homeric tradition the plan included a converted collier, *River Clyde*, being used as a modern wooden horse. She would ground herself below the Fort of Sedd El Bahr at V Beach and let down soldiers from ramps and doors cut into her sides.

Opposite them, on the Asiatic shore, the French would land at Kum Kale suppressing any guns that might interfere with the British landings. This was a feint and it was anticipated that the French would then withdraw and reinforce the British.

The Anzac landing site, Z Beach, was along the coast near a headland called Gaba Tepe, some 20 km north of Helles. Gaba Tepe was a low promontory covering a wide cultivated plain running between the rugged Sari Bair Range to the north and equally difficult country of the Kilid Bahr Plateau to the South. This plain offered a perfect route from west to east across the Peninsula. The ANZAC Corps would land at Z Beach north of the wire entanglements and machine guns protecting Gaba Tepe. Its soldiers would seize the high ground of the Sari Bair Range and Gaba Tepe and then advance across the Peninsula. At the same time, well to the north and opposite Bulair, a further feint attack would be carried out by the transports of the Royal Naval Division, supported by warships bombarding the Bulair lines.

Surprise was the essence of the Anzac landing. A Covering Force of brigade size would land before dawn and seize a beachhead. The task went to the 3rd Australian Infantry Brigade under Colonel Sinclair MacLagan. It was just reward for their wait at Lemnos since early March. The 1st Australian Division under General Bridges would land and expand the perimeter won by the Covering Force. Finally, the NZ & A Division would land ready to continue operations across the Peninsula to cut the Gallipoli-Maidos, Boghali-Kojadere roads. Mai Tepe, a low conical hill overlooking the roads, was named as the Anzac objective. 'The seizure of this position will threaten to cut the line of retreat of the enemy's forces on Kilid Bahr Plateau and will prevent reinforcement of plateau during attack of 29th Division … Its capture is of vital importance, and should have far reaching results.'[41]

Hamilton's staff estimated the enemy's strength on the Peninsula to be about 34,000 men in four divisions. Locations were believed to be one division at Bulair, one or more in the centre from the Anafarta villages to Kilid Bahr, and one in the south between Achi Baba and Cape Helles. It was an accurate estimate.

Marshal Liman von Sanders, a German officer attached to the Turkish forces, had been given command of operations on the Peninsula. His plan of defence was a string of outposts along the coast to impede the invader and warn of his presence. Behind this he concentrated his six divisions in three main areas: two were concentrated at Bulair, and two on the Asiatic shore below Kum Kale, as he considered those the areas of greatest risk. Cape Helles to Suvla Bay was guarded by the 9th Division. In the Anzac area there was one battalion guarding the coastline, the 2/3 Battalion of the 27th Regiment. Two companies were around Gaba Tepe, and two companies covered the coast from Gaba Tepe along the coastal foothills to the valley of the Aghyl Dere. The remaining two battalions of the 27th Regiment were placed in reserve above Maidos.

It was the same at Helles, with a thin screen of companies from the 26th Regiment along the coast, with part of a battalion in reserve at Krithia. The third regiment of the 9th Division was held as divisional reserve on the Kilid Bahr Plateau. Von Sanders' last division, the 19th, was held in reserve between Koja Dere and Boghali. This was commanded by a Colonel Mustafa Kemal.

Hamilton's plan exploited the beaches least expected by the Turk. However, the nearness of Turkish reinforcements would demand that the troops, once landed, must rapidly advance and seize their objectives before the defenders could react. Details of the operation filtered out to the soldiers. Birdwood appeared less confident than Hamilton about the ease of the operation. In his message to his troops he impressed the likely difficulties upon them. It was practical man-to-man language and made a deep impression. Letters and diaries recorded it word for word:

> *Officers and Men,*
>
> *In conjunction with the Navy, we are about to undertake one of the most difficult tasks any soldier can be called on to perform, and a problem which has puzzled many soldiers for years past. That we will succeed I have no doubt, simply because I know your full determination to do so. Lord Kitchener has told us that he lays special stress on the role the Army has to play in this particular operation, the success of which will be a very severe blow to the enemy — indeed, as severe as any she could receive in France. It will go down in history to the glory of the soldiers of Australia and New Zealand. Before we start, there are one or two points which I must impress on all, and I most earnestly beg every single man to listen attentively and take these to heart.*
>
> *We are going to have a real hard and rough time of it until, at all events, we have turned the enemy out of our first objective. Hard rough times none of us mind, but to get through them successfully we must always keep before us the following facts. Every possible endeavour will be made to bring up transport as often as possible; but the country whither we are bound is very difficult, and we may not be able to get our wagons anywhere neat us for days, so men must not think their wants have been neglected if they do not get all they want. On landing it will be necessary for every individual to carry with him all his requirements in food and clothing for three days, as we may not see our transport till then. Remember then that it is essential for everyone to take the very greatest care not only of his food, but of his ammunition, the replenishment of which will be very difficult. Men are liable to throw away their food the first day out and to finish their water bottles as soon as they start marching. If you do this now, we can hardly hope for success, as unfed men cannot fight and you must make an effort to try and*

refrain from starting on your water bottles until quite late in the day. Once you begin drinking you cannot stop and a water bottle is very soon emptied. Also as regards ammunition — you must not waste it by firing away indiscriminately at no target. The time will come when we shall find the enemy in well entrenched positions from which we shall have to turn them out, when all out ammunition will be required; and remember:

Concealment whenever possible,
Covering fire always,
Control of fire and control of your men,
Communications never to be neglected.

W.R. Birdwood [42]

There were many who were pessimistic about the undertaking. 'Moore the Munster Fusilier commanding 1st Otago was one of these officers … He tried to maintain his usual light facetiousness; but we decided after that he was not feeling cheerful. He had been in Buller's Army in Natal, knew what stiff fighting was, and whilst making light of it outwardly, was worried at the magnitude of the task before us.

'All communication with the shore having now ceased, we got our detailed orders, and studied them with the aid of the maps. It seemed rather a dispersion of force. We were to land at widely different points, but the Australian and New Zealand Army Corps had one objective, and Brigadier General MacLagan's third Australian brigade were to land first at daybreak and push forward to a defined line to cover the landing of the rest of us. It was impressed on us that on our part of the field, the main feature was a commanding hill numbered on the map 971, the Turkish name being Chunuk Bair*

If we got astray in the advance, we could not go wrong if we located it and made for it. To capture it would be the first objective of the corps after making good our landing. The New Zealand Infantry Brigade — ourselves — were to land after the Australians, go into reserve, and advance through the Australians the following day. We were disappointed not to lead. But one has to do what one is told.

'That afternoon we communicated the gist of our orders to our men, who of course were very interested and if there were any faint hearts they were not noticeable. We had parades in full marching order to see everyone was in possession of all that was ordered, and had it on his person. As none of them had any other possessions in the ship this left the hold empty of everything but surplus tins of meat, of which they had been issued more than usual rations. On deck we were cramped for space, that allotted me being an alleyway between the deck houses and the bulwark not six feet wide, and with swollen packs there was only just enough space to pass along the tanks. The men

---

* Chunuk Bair or 'Hill of War'. Throughout the campaign soldiers mistook Chunuk Bair for 971 or Koja Chemen Tepe. They assumed they were one and the same, as Chunuk Bair could be seen as the highest hill on the skyline from the ANZAC perimeter, while 971 was masked from view. See chapter 5 for a detailed description of the ground.

were in great spirits, their humour only just repressed by order. I was inspecting identity discs when a voice at the far flank of the platoon shouted stentoriously, "Gangway for a naval officer!" A shrinking little Greek fireman in peaked cap and greasy flannel passed along our ranks.'[43]

Each man was heavily laden. On the *Itonus*, Lieutenant Colonel Malone had meticulously noted in his diary:

'The men are going to carry a big load, 200 rounds of ammunition each, weight 12 pounds [5.4 kilos]. In all they will carry close to 75 pounds [34 kilos] … Each man is carrying extra to the regulations — an oilsheet, some firewood, an extra iron ration, and an extra half day's food, 50 rounds of SA ammunition, one pound of raisins.'[44]

Iron rations consisted of a tin of bully beef per day, hard biscuits, and a tin containing tea, sugar and some beef cubes. In addition the men were savouring the first issue of free cigarettes. 'These were "Major Drapkins" and were regarded as the best of all issues to be received on the Peninsula.'[45] The quality of free cigarettes, like the high hopes of the men, was not to be maintained. 'Of later issues … "Rough Riders" and "Carrolls" and "Silk Cut" were surplus stock manufactured for the South African War — and they tasted like it.'[46] But now all was bustle and excitement. 'Three months of very hard training over the hot sands of Egypt, with gritty food and hosts of flies, followed by cramped conditions in the *Lutzow*, made the rank and file, who were in perfect physical condition, yearn for the adventures they had been promised. And now here we were, about to be released.'[47]

On the 23rd rough weather and rain led to a postponement of 24 hours. The landings would now take place on Sunday 25 April 1915. Godley was writing every day to his wife: 'It all looks very promising … and if we are only successful here, I can't believe that the war can go on much longer … I have been sorting my kit and leaving my suitcase and big tin despatch box to go round, I hope, through the Dardanelles, and be available for use in Constantinople …'[48] On the 24th he wrote: 'Yes I do hope that I shall come back to you in the train for the third time.'[49]

At 2.00 p.m. that day the fleet left the harbour watched by Captain A.B. Morton, Staff Captain on the NZ Infantry Brigade Headquarters. 'The huge battleship *Queen Elizabeth* led the way and in her wake followed battleships, cruisers, torpedo boats and destroyers in a long line. It was a wonderful sight, all these huge grey ships steaming silently and almost without a ripple … as they swung around and passed through the "gap" in the barrier at the entrance to the harbour. We have seen many interesting and historical sights since we left New Zealand, but no sight could approach the significance and tremendous import of this magnificent fleet starting afresh to the conquest of the Dardanelles. We felt as we watched it with fascinated interest, that this indeed was the first line of a new page in the history of the Empire.'[50]

5

THE GREATEST DAY
IN OUR LIVES

This I have no doubt will be the greatest day in our lives.[1]

The SS *Lutzow* was the first ship of the 13-ship convoy to arrive carrying the New Zealand and Australian Division. At 8.00 a.m. on 25 April 1915 it was some four kilometres off the landing beaches. Its passengers were 1725 New Zealanders, consisting of Godley's Divisional Headquarters, the Auckland Battalion under Lieutenant Colonel A. Plugge, and half of the Canterbury Battalion under Lieutenant Colonel D. MacBean Stewart, plus signallers, field engineers and artillery. Most of the soldiers had slept on the decks and were woken in the early dawn about 4.30 a.m. to the sound of gunfire. Private E.J. Baigent of the Canterbury Battalion remembered: 'Dawn was breathlessly awaited. Everybody was on deck. The hilarious spirit of yesterday was missing in the cold half-light of dawn. My thoughts kept constantly changing, first to those at home, and then trying to picture the position a few hours hence. The guns broke the silence first at Cape Helles and also relieved the tension.'[2]

As it grew light the soldiers crowding the decks could see that they were part of a huge flotilla slowly steaming north up the coast, past warships bombarding Cape Helles where the British 29th Division was to land. The troops mustered to the boat decks as the company sergeant majors and platoon sergeants started their final checks on webbing, rifles, ammunition and equipment.

Cheers and comments and snatches of information were shouted from neighbouring ships — 'No news in particular but blowing the bastards to hell' — as the *Lutzow* was directed into her anchorage and slowed to a stop. 'The sea was like glass and the weather perfect — surely a good omen.'[3] So it seemed, for all the news that could be gained was promising. Godley caught the mood as he quickly penned a last few lines to Allen, the Minister of Defence: 'Sunday 25, 9.00 a.m. We are just going in to disembark. Everything has gone extraordinarily well. The sea is as calm as a duck pond, and MacLagan with his covering brigade is well ashore, and has thoroughly established himself.'[4]

Everything apparently was going according to plan, except that the landing beach was some two kilometres north of that intended. Instead of landing on the long expanse of beach below the low foothills just north of Gaba Tepe as planned, the Navy had set the Australians ashore on the northern tip of a narrow unnamed cove. This narrow bay, today enshrined in legend as Anzac Cove, became the centre of all activity from then on. It is a sandy beach enclosed by two headlands, some 600 metres long, with a strip of sand 20 metres deep, and is overshadowed by the steep slopes climbing to a flat plateau and the spurs of the Sari Bair Range. The hinterland is considerably more rugged than the open plain beyond the intended landing beaches above Gaba Tepe.

'Bloody rough country for infantry,'[5] summed up a New Zealand private. General Birdwood, after an earlier reconnaissance, stated: 'The country there is so difficult and broken that it is impossible to attempt a landing there while it is dark.'[6] It was a view also held by the Turks. But land they did, and though alerted, the thin screen of Turkish Infantry on the coast, some 200 men of the 2nd Battalion of the 27th Regiment, were rapidly driven back by 'the impetuous Australians.'[7]

On the *Lutzow* that morning, Godley had every confidence that Bridges' Australian Division had the situation well in hand. Already the last of the Australian brigades were landing. Soon it would be time for his New Zealand Infantry to land, followed later in the day by Monash's 4th Australian Brigade.

Godley shared Hamilton's assessment of the dubious fighting quality of the Turk, and probably thought that the disembarkation of his division would be an administrative problem only. He certainly did not expect his brigades to be committed to operations that day; action was for the future. His confidence can be seen in his arrangements for the landing. Colonel F.E. Johnston, his New Zealand Brigade Commander, had fallen sick on 23 April. Johnston had 'not been feeling well for the last days, and Dr Murray who saw him — he would not allow he needed a doctor before — says he has gastro-influenza.'[8]

Godley was informed on 24 April: 'I think under the circumstances, that I shall probably ask General Birdwood to let his Chief General Staff Officer, Brigadier General Walker, take command of the brigade temporarily ... But I will not make up my mind till I have consulted General Birdwood, which I shall have the opportunity of doing tomorrow [25 April], as I am to go on board the *Queen*, where he is with Admiral Thursby, to get orders as to the action of my Division, as soon as most of it has disembarked.'[9] The *Goslar*, a notoriously slow ship that carried his New Zealand Infantry Brigade headquarters, was one of the last ships in the convoy. It is inconceivable that a commander with the slightest expectation of his soldiers being committed into action would have allowed them to disembark without a commander and without a headquarters. When Westmacott's company commander, Major W.W. Alderman, a seconded officer from the AIF, told his 16th Waikato Company, 'We are going ashore now: but I do not think anyone is going to be killed today,'[10] he was echoing the feelings of Godley and his staff.

After all, very little went according to plan. The high hopes of the morning were not fulfilled. The Navy's blunder in landing MacLagan's Covering Force on the wrong beach would be a fatal blow to the hopes of success. Hamilton and Birdwood's planning relied on surprise; on the Australians landing, forging inland and establishing themselves before the Turkish defenders could react.

The original landing site, Z Beach, though close to Gaba Tepe, had been chosen because it was away from the wire and defences on the promontory. It offered some 1300 metres of open beach on which to land. It was as lightly defended as Anzac Cove, and offered a relatively rapid route across low foothills and then up the ridge lines to the Covering Force objectives.

None of these advantages existed in Anzac Cove. The Australians' battle that morning was to be with the landscape, and it defeated them. Though they pressed inland in small groups, the lunatic tangle of gullies and ravines over which they had to cross-grain threw Bridges' plans and organisation into chaos. This confusion would allow a much smaller Turkish force the time and opportunity to threaten the landing with disaster.

It is important to understand the landscape on which the troops landed, as it was to shape the New Zealand and Australian experience at Gallipoli. The heights up which the Australians scrambled that morning were those of the Sari Bair Range, a thorny, scrub-covered line of dissected gravel and clay ridges running southwest from the narrow valley containing the two villages of Anafarta.

In the north-east are its highest features: Koja Chemen Tepe, or 971, Hill Q and Chunuk Bair. Of these, Chunuk Bair, always confused by the soldiers with 971, gives

Everyone was on deck. 'No news in particular but blowing the bastards to hell.' HMS *Triumph* and HMS *Majestic* bombarding Turkish positions at Gaba Tepe, south of the ANZAC Corps landing. *(E.B. Paterson Collection – PAColl-0914-1, Alexander Turnbull Library)*

the best view to the south-west down the rolling ridge towards Gaba Tepe. From it can be seen the open cultivated Maidos Plain that cuts across the Peninsula and meets the Dardanelles Straits at the small harbour of Kilia Liman, the proposed route of Birdwood's Corps to the Narrows. Beyond it again is the black bulk of the Kilid Bahr Plateau and, on the rare exceptionally clear day, the long low ridge of Achi Baba can be seen far to the south.

From Chunuk Bair run three spurs that, as they move inland from the coast, were named on the landing day First, Second and Third ridges. Third Ridge runs south from Chunuk Bair and was the objective for the Covering Force. MacLagan's 3rd Australian Brigade were to seize and hold this ridge from Chunuk Bair in the north to where the ridge petered out among the olive trees and wheat fields of the Maidos Plain. It was an ambitious length of ground for the 4000 men of the brigade to hold, but it overlooked both the north-south road in the valley and the Koja Dere village, and the Maidos Plain. It offered good fields of fire over relatively open country. It was on this ridge that the remaining Australian brigades would reinforce MacLagan's force. Behind them the NZ & A Division would then land in reserve, await orders, and prepare to advance. Continuing along south-west of Chunuk Bair parallel to the coast are two smaller crests. These became known as Battleship Hill, or Big 700, and Baby 700. Both gave good observation over approaches to Chunuk Bair from the south, but it is Baby 700 that dominates the First and Second ridges.

The First Ridge runs south-west from Baby 700 across a narrow saddle, later to

The scene on the beach (later known as Anzac Cove) as the New Zealanders arrived. Soldiers move up the slope up from the headland at Ari Burnu onto Plugge's Plateau, on the route taken by New Zealanders to reach the front line. *(Judge Gresson Collection – PAColl-3604, Alexander Turnbull Library)*

become infamous as The Nek, onto a narrow plateau, which is Russell's Top. On the seaward side of Russell's Top are steep gravel cliffs, falling to the beaches some 500 feet [152.4 metres] below. Two spurs run from Russell's Top to the beaches. The northern spur, Walker's Ridge, is deeply eroded. It allows access in single file up narrow goat tracks onto Russell's Top. It is a tough, heart-stopping climb, even without rifle and pack. The southern spur, the Sphinx, presents a sheer, apparently unscaleable face to those on the beach below.

Russell's Top ends abruptly in a narrow, eroded razor-backed ridge of gravel and sand, which falls steeply away on both sides. This impassable obstacle, the Razor Edge, links Russell's Top with Plugge's (Pluggy's) Plateau, the arms of which are MacLagan's Spur to the south, ending at Hell Spit, and Queensland Point to the north, known to the Turks as Ari Burnu. MacLagan's Spur and Queensland Point enclose Anzac Cove.

On the inland slopes of the First Ridge the ground falls steeply into a dog-leg valley. This tortuous valley climbs gradually towards the junction of First and Second ridges with Baby 700. The steep sides of the valley are dissected by side gullies and watercourses which, though dry in April, turn into gushing torrents in the winter months. The stretch from the dog-leg to the sea earned notoriety as Shrapnel Valley. The upper arm, which can be seen from Baby 700, became Monash Gully. Together they separate First and Second ridges.

Second Ridge continues from Baby 700 and runs as a narrow spur. It falls steeply into Monash Gully to the west, but more gradually into Mule and Legge Valley to the east.

The small indentations on the ridge where dried watercourses fall sharply into Monash Gully were to become pockets of cover where men could seek shelter from the shrapnel and sniper fire. They have passed into ANZAC legend as Quinn's, Courtney's and Steele's posts. Further along, the ridge opens into a broad plateau known as 400 Plateau, where on 25 April a lone pine stood etched sharply against the blue of the sky. Further south again are a series of finger spurs that run towards Gaba Tepe until they merge into the low-rolling mounds inland from the proposed Z Beach. These merge into the small headland of Gaba Tepe, a hill just high enough to mask the Maidos Plain from watchers at sea.

Though disorganised by this unanticipated rough terrain the Australians drove inland and scattered the Turkish defenders. By nine o'clock they had occupied Second Ridge and small parties had advanced to Third Ridge. 'Who can stop us? Not the bloody Turks.'[11] Colonel MacLagan was disconcerted by the disorganisation of his battalions. He appreciated that he lacked the strength to hold Third Ridge and ordered his men to dig in and consolidate on Second Ridge until the remainder of the division was ashore. The principal threat came from Lieutenant Colonel Şefik's 27 Regiment, who arrived from Maidos and pushed back the outposts on Third Ridge opposite 400 Plateau (or Lone Pine) and it was this that prompted Colonel MacLagan to direct the 2nd Australian Brigade, the next brigade ashore, to reinforce his covering force in the south and not move towards Chunuk Bair as originally planned.

This change of plan meant that the northern flank leading to the heights of Chunuk

Bair was starved of reinforcements. MacLagan recognised the key to successfully holding Second Ridge was Baby 700. If the Turks held Baby 700, they could fire from it along Second Ridge as far as the 400 Plateau. They could also observe along Monash Gully. MacLagan was racing against time. Already he could see Turkish reinforcements moving north to the high ground. To consolidate his position he now pushed every man available towards Baby 700. As the New Zealanders landed, the hill was held by three groups. On the inland slope Major Kindon of 1st Australian Battalion held a line facing Battleship Hill, his men a mix from every unit of the Australian Brigade. On the seaward slopes another party was digging in at The Nek. This was under Captain Lalor, grandson of Peter Lalor — the man who had led the only armed insurrection in Australian history, that of the Eureka Stockade on the Victoria goldfields. A platoon from Lalor's party, commanded by Lieutenant Margetts, had been ordered forward of The Nek to hold the crest and seaward slopes of Baby 700.

It would be here among the low thorny scrub that covered the slopes of Baby 700 that New Zealanders would first fight the Turks on Gallipoli. They would be only a very small part of the total force ashore. Some 1500 New Zealanders of the 3100 to land that day would be ashore by midday. It was these men, the New Zealanders from the *Lutzow*, who would stake New Zealand's claim to Anazc Day. They would fight and die on the slopes of Baby 700 and in the serrated gullies of Second Ridge.

The struggle of the day for the New Zealanders was in four acts, though none of the participants could have recognised the intervals between. In speaking of 'acts' we are using a historian's licence to record and relate the many separate and desperate struggles involving New Zealanders that day.

The first and the most critical act, involving most of the first New Zealanders ashore, was the battle for the inland slopes of Baby 700 as they fought to hold the thinning Australian line. This involved the Waikatos, Haurakis and the South Canterburys, though individuals from all companies ashore fought with these groups.

Over the ridge, the second act was played out simultaneously with the first. It was the struggle for the seaward slopes of Baby 700 around the narrow saddle — The Nek. It was to involve the *Lutzow* men from mid-afternoon onwards through the night of the 25–26th. The third act narrates the frustrations of the remaining New Zealanders as they landed piecemeal into the confusion of Anzac in the late afternoon and evening.

The final act was the battle for the yet unnamed Quinn's Post and Second Ridge. Here, men of the Auckland Battalion, inextricably mixed with Australians, would fight into the night, clinging by their fingernails to the slopes nearest Baby 700 after the Turks had forced them back. Here, Major Dawson, commanding the 3rd Auckland Company, first held that vital, seemingly untenable niche that later became famous as Quinn's Post. It is a story that has remained largely unrecorded; much now will never be known in its full and tragic detail. It is a soldier's tale, and many New Zealanders would die that day on ground that would not be walked on again by New Zealanders and Australians until 1919.

C.E.W. Bean was one of those who were to arrive in 1919. There he found the pitiful remnants of the first day's struggle, on the inland slopes of Baby 700. 'One of the two who lay farthest appeared to be a New Zealander, for the cover of a New Zealand entrenching tool lay beside the little patch of torn clothes and human remains. Part of the Narrows was clearly visible from his summit.'[12]

Godley's headquarters was the first ashore of the NZ & A Division. Lieutenant Colonel P.C. Fenwick, ADMS (Assistant Director of Medical Services), was with this party: 'We were all ready to land but were kept waiting and waiting until about 9.00 a.m. Some barges were moored alongside and a string of boats outside of these on the starboard side. Hughes came along and told the staff to get into the boats. Colonels Braithwaite, Chaytor and Manders, Major Hughes, Captain Beck and I got into the first boat. We were frightfully hampered by our kit — overcoat, revolver, glasses, map case, haversack, three days rations, firewood, Red Cross satchel, water bottle — like elephants. It was a certainty that we would drown if we got sunk.

'After waiting, a steam picket boat came along in charge of a very fat rosy midshipman. He took our string of boats in tow and we were off. Our boat grounded about 50 feet from the shore and we all hopped out. Of course I fell into a hole up to my neck. I could hardly struggle ashore and when I did the first thing I saw was Beck sitting on a stone, roaring with laughter at us. Billy Beck* was the first New Zealander of Godley's force (there were New Zealanders serving in the Australian Division) to get onto Gallipoli.'[13]

Godley remained on board the *Lutzow* and Colonel Chaytor, the Assistant Adjutant General, assumed command of his headquarters and linked up with Bridges' headquarters to establish the situation. It was now 10.30 a.m. and inland the Australians were meeting increasing opposition. The Australian brigades were established in a line along Second Ridge with isolated groups further forward, but units were intermingled and gaps were evident along the line. From 10 o'clock onwards on both flanks the forward Australian line were being halted or driven back by increasing numbers of Turkish soldiers. For as the first tow of nine barges left the *Lutzow*, the Turkish divisional commander of the 19th Division, Mustafa Kemal, was committing the first of his regiments in counter-attacks against the Australian line. Kemal recognised the threat presented by an Allied Force seizing the high ground of the Sari Bair Range.

'It was at 0630 hours that from a report which arrived … it was learnt that a force of enemy had climbed the heights of Ari Burnu and that I was required to send a battalion against them … My firm opinion was, just as I previously judged, that an enemy attempt to land in strength in the neighbourhood of Gaba Tepe was now taking place. Therefore I appreciated that it was impossible to carry out my task with a battalion, but that as I had reckoned before, my whole division would be required to deal with the enemy.'[14]

His 57th Regiment had been warned out for an exercise that morning. Kemal at once placed himself at its head and made towards the sound of the guns, ordering

---

*   It seems mildly ironic that in this first major operation, the first New Zealander to land was the Ordnance Staff Officer of the Division.

the rest of his division to follow as soon as possible. From an observation point at Scrubby Knoll on Third Ridge, Kemal observed Australians advancing north up the ridge towards Chunuk Bair. 'It was about 1000 hours when the 57th Regiment began its attack.'[15]

The combination of Sefik's 27th Regiment attack earlier that morning, and now Kemal's attack down the line of the ridge, meant that although outnumbered, the Turkish had greater strength at the point of attack and so the lead battalion of the 57th Regiment drove back the forward Australian parties on Battleship Hill, and a critical battle now developed for the crest of Baby 700. It was the Turkish soldiers of the 57th Regiment who would fight the New Zealanders that day and they were to suffer casualties as savage as those of the New Zealanders, who were now wading ashore on the crowded beaches of Anzac Cove. By the day's end not only the fighting qualities of Australians had grown in the New Zealanders' estimation; the Turks, from the outset, were to prove a tenacious and formidable enemy.

This, then, was the situation Colonel Chaytor had to deal with. MacLagan in his turn was becoming increasingly concerned about the situation on his left flank around Baby 700, while continuing to face a threat on his right where the battalions of the 27th Regiment were counter-attacking. He was rapidly running out of men and he pleaded with Bridges for reinforcements.

Bridges had none to send. He conveyed the situation to Birdwood who, with his headquarters, was on the battleship HMS *Queen*. By now, Godley had joined him. Godley here told Birdwood of Johnston's illness and his need for a commander for his New Zealand Infantry Brigade.

At Godley's request, Birdwood agreed to the transfer of Brigadier General Harold 'Hooky' Walker, the Chief of Staff ANZAC Corps, to command the New Zealand Infantry. It was here, in Birdwood's company, that Godley learnt the news of the deteriorating position on the left flank. One can imagine the private chagrin of this reserved, proud and ambitious man. The soldiers he had raised, trained and drilled in formation manoeuvres in Egypt, his New Zealanders, were now to fight their first battle under Australian command. In this, their first major action, Godley would be a bystander. It must have been a bitter pill. He made no mention of not commanding 'his New Zealanders' this day, anywhere — to Allen, to his wife, or in his memoirs. Rather, he wrote: 'Only a comparatively small part of my division had yet landed. I therefore established myself at Bridges' headquarters in order to keep in close touch, to utilise my units as they landed to best advantage, and to secure the ground which his men had gained.'[16] It is the impression of a man firmly in command.

Ashore, the first task for Chaytor and the staff of the New Zealand and Australian Division was to form an 'ad hoc' brigade headquarters to support Brigadier General Walker. Captain R.E. Coningham, Royal Engineers, Indian Army, a staff officer of Godley's division, acted as Brigade Major; and Captain Wallingford, NZSC, the machine gun officer of the Auckland Battalion, became the Brigade staff. Jesse Wallingford was to earn a Military Cross for his efforts during his first days at Anzac. To all he became the man who sensed when and where the situation was becoming

Mustafa Kemal. It comes to few men the opportunity to play such a decisive role in a campaign. *(Moorehead, Gallipoli)*

critical. Instinctively he would be there, rallying the wavering, or using his beloved Maxim guns to best effect. He featured in all the major crises of the campaign. This was to be the first. 'He … was the strongest, most capable, coolest officer on Walker's Ridge for at least the first three weeks.'[17]

'At first no definite orders or instructions could be obtained but at 10.30 a.m. General Walker met the General Staff who gave us verbal instructions to the effect that one brigade (the New Zealand Infantry Brigade) would extend left of 3rd Brigade Australian and one brigade (4th Australian Brigade) would be held in reserve.'[18]

Westmacott was with Critchley-Salmonson, the Adjutant of the Canterburys, in a barge approaching the shore. Though Lieutenant Colonel Plugge and Dawson's 3rd Auckland Company were first to land, Westmacott's 15th Platoon and Alderman's Waikatos were the first New Zealanders to see action that day. The first act, the battle of the inland slopes of Baby 700, is largely Westmacott's story: 'Never while I live, shall I forget the grandeur of the scene. In front was the coast, rugged and steep; but with easy country to the right front and beyond Achi Baba with huge 15-inch shells bursting on it, from HMS *Queen Elizabeth*.

The fire was deliberate. Minutes would pass between each shot which seemed to scrape up the mountain side, bursting on top like a volcano throwing tons of earth high into the air. It was a cheering sight to us; but terrifying to the enemy. To our right, close in shore, stood a balloon ship with an observation balloon glistening high in the sun. Right and left, broadside onto the shore were the battleships steaming slowly and firing at the Turkish positions in crashing salvoes which went booming and echoing among the hills. About halfway to shore we passed, on the left, HMS *Queen* with General Birdwood on the bridge … Cotton wool puffs over the ridges ahead showed where the Australians were holding the ground won and being shelled.

'A lighter was towed past us filled with wounded lying quietly for the most part, one or two here and there sitting up, or propped on an elbow to look at us. I think they made us feel rather envious. They had been under fire. We had not. We felt they were one up on us. They were soon behind us and we were looking forward.

'Our men sat smoking for the most part, their rifles between their knees. They were crowded as close as they could sit and quite imperturbable, gazing towards the shore. Colonel Stewart sat near me on the small deck near the bows. Similarly placed astern, Regimental Sergeant Major Mooney and Hobbs, the latter puffing away at his pipe, sat amongst a group of sergeants. I thought what fine soldiers they looked, and then

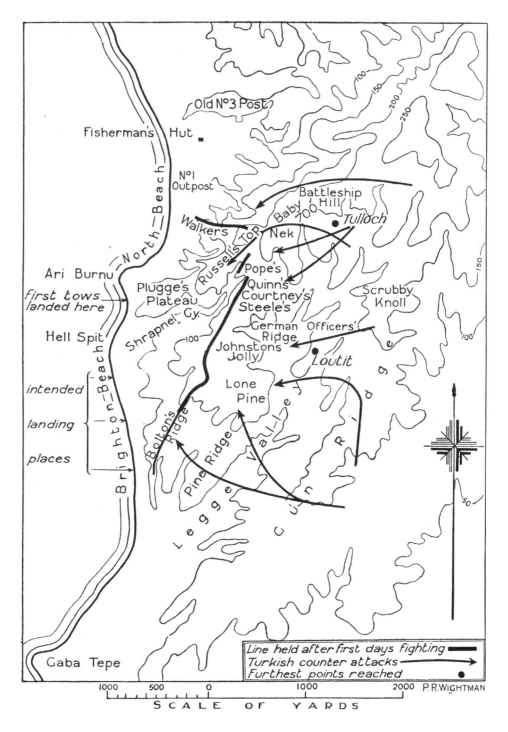

Anzac Day, 25 April 1915. *(P.R. Wightman, Lucas, The Empire at War)*

Major T.H. Dawson, Auckland Battalion, on the *Lutzow*, has a celebratory cigar as he waits to disembark on 25 April 1915. *(Album 382, p.3 n6, Auckland War Memorial Museum)*

of their wives and families, Mooncy with his baby daughter, Hobbs fifty-six years old with five children, and not a grey hair in his head, a veteran of South Africa in the Scots Guards. I do not suppose when he came to New Zealand he ever expected to see fighting again. He looked placid enough as he approached his last battle.

'With the tow rope tightening and sagging we continued towards the shore. At bow and stern was a naval rating standing erect, and for some reason each was supposed to be disguised as a colonial soldier, this simply seemed to mean he was more untidy than usual and wore an Australian slouch hat, obtained where I know not. These were there to keep the towed lighters running straight. We approached the shore and the beach became visible. Lines of wounded lay in the sand. Officers and men were moving about. A party of Australians were building a jetty by throwing stones into the water. A man stark naked was bathing in the sea. A stream of wounded was straggling down from the hills. Parties of men were at work making tracks up the cliffs. From the ridges beyond came the sound of fighting. The beach seemed sheltered and very quiet.

'Our destroyer ran close up and turned to the right running parallel with the shore. Our sailors cast us all loose, and we drifted on, closing in on the beach under our own way. The leading lighter approached the jetty of stones aforementioned and the men prepared to go ashore when ordered. A handsome staff officer, with fair hair and moustache, clad in light breeches and puttees, a helmet on his head, no jacket and his sleeves rolled up to the elbow, came down to the edge of the water and shouted "Come out of the boats, the New Zealanders". We continued sitting and gazed at him while he grew red in the face. We considered that he should call for the officer in charge of us and say, "Get your men out of the boats". Instead, after repeating himself, he got sarcastic and shouted, "Are the New Zealanders afraid of wetting their feet?" At that I saw Salmonson raise himself with his hands and we both jumped into the sea together, going into the water right up to our waists at once. The men poured over the side after us en masse, without a word from us, those further astern going right in up to their necks. Their readiness to follow us unbidden seemed magnetic. At this moment a Turkish shell burst overhead.

'We waded ashore, shook ourselves, and met Captain Thoms of the N.Z. Staff Corps, who directed us to the left. The water squelching out of our boots and clothes as we walked, we straggled along to the forming up point in a small gully, picking out way past the wounded on the ground. A certain amount of confusion was apparent. There were packs, rifles and other articles of equipment all over the beach and at one point a number of packs had been built up to form a barricade, rather an ineffective one I fear. Our

A destroyer towing the first New Zealanders from the SS *Lutzow* towards the shore, about 10.00 a.m., 25 April 1915. *(Album 382 p.7 n3, Auckland War Memorial Museum)*

men still carried miscellaneous things besides their rifles, the machine guns four, and the tins of water from the ship. Rounding a spit of land from the slope of the hill, on the way to the gully where we were to form up, we came under rifle fire; but it was not serious for I saw no one hit though I stood there till all my men had passed.'[19]

The scene on the beach as the New Zealanders landed is well captured by a photo taken from Plugge's Plateau looking along the beach. The dark mass of the Auckland Battalion can be seen forming up on the centre of the beach as others of the battalion wade ashore or clamber down the improvised piers. As the companies formed up by platoons in four ranks, personal impressions included the shell fire as Signaller Fred Senn recalled: 'Stray bullets were zipping all around, but our real welcome was a field gun shell which screeched from the right just over our heads and burst at the water's edge not more than fifty yards along the beach. There were no casualties from this one, but it made us realise that we were now in amongst things and that there would be many others to come.'[20]

But the overwhelming impression as the New Zealanders waited for the second tows to land was the achievement of the Australians earlier that morning. Sergeant Richard Ward, who was Westmacott's platoon sergeant, afterwards wrote: 'As we approached the "landing" … the Turks, who had got the range absolutely correct, poured in shrapnel very hard, and several of our men who were tightly packed on our lighter were hit. Our lighter could not get right on the beach, so we had to jump into the water, and waist deep we had to wade to the shore … All along the beach were dead and dying Australians (3rd Brigade) who had landed at dawn with splendid courage and drove the Turks back over the ridge of hills.'[21]

Every letter, every diary, records the praise and admiration for the Australian effort: 'No orders, no proper military "team work", no instructions. Just absolute heroism.'[22]

It was an impression that would grow as the days passed. It would end the antagonism between Australians and New Zealanders that had been present in Egypt. Rivalry would always exist but now it would be mellowed by a mutual admiration.

Plugge formed his battalion in four ranks in close column of platoons and they moved north along the beach. First came 3rd Auckland Company, then 6th Hauraki Company, 15th North Auckland Company and 16th Waikato Company. Evidence of the hard fight following the first landing became more apparent, for it was here in the shadow of the Sphinx that the 12th Australian Battalion had come under effective rifle and machine-gun fire as it had landed earlier that morning. 'Rifles, packs, overcoats, bodies, equipment and letters scattered open in great quantities gave the impression of an army that had been thrown ashore shipwrecked.'[23]

The Auckland Battalion in column of four files straggled across the broken ground below the Sphinx. In the waist-high thorny scrub, it was difficult to maintain the files and formation was soon lost. Westmacott, in the rear company, the 16th Waikatos, had barely passed Ari Burnu when the head of the battalion came to a halt at the foot of Walker's Ridge, where it packed itself into a confused and untidy scrum as the leading company, the 3rd Auckland Company, sent forward its scouts to search for a route up the steep and narrow slopes. 'As I waited there Colonel Braithwaite came up to me and, pointing at the company in the lead as he did so, said, "Is that your number one company?" and I replied, "That is the third Auckland company sir."

'After which he asked in his usual tone of irascible irritation, "Is it Dawson's company?" "Yes Sir," said I. "Then it is your number one company," he said emphatically as if I were a damn fool. I held my tongue, though I was irritated as it had always been impressed upon us that we were to adhere to territorial designations, and reflected I would have been slanged in any case, whatever I called it. He went forward hurriedly and left me. 'Colonel Braithwaite bustled up to Colonel Plugge and said loudly, "Reinforce the First Australians on the left. Reinforce the First Australians on the left." Then Plugge turned towards me and said, "Yes that's it, Westmacott, reinforce the First Australians on the left."'[24]

Westmacott now led the long Auckland file: 'It was the first and only order I heard my colonel give that day, and it was not his fault either. The regiment was very confused and bunched, owing to Dawson's company having run into an unclimbable cliff and being turned about towards the rest of us. No parade ground formation seemed possible here, and Braithwaite's close presence with his excitability made me eager to move away from him. I called to my platoon to follow as they were and led the way up, by what seemed the shortest route along the hill side. At a later day I would have been more deliberate in my movements; but I had been ordered to take the lead and did not wish to show any sign of hesitancy when going under fire for the first time. I came quickly to where a party of Australian engineers were making a zigzag track to the top, and almost immediately cut off an angle of it by making a run up. I was followed by some of my more active men and from where I was above them helped others by taking their rifles by the muzzle and pulling them up till six men were with me, when I saw it was too steep for most of them and told the others to follow the track already well defined and half formed.

'The men at work were steadily improving this thoroughfare to the top, picks were breaking down the hard clay and shovels were sending it flying. Our men were pressing up, crowding the workers; but it was the only way and we had to get on. Also, wounded Australians were coming down here and there. We had not the heart to stop them; but they delayed us a little. This perhaps had an advantage as some of the men were getting a bit blown. Alderman joined me at one of these checks, quite out of breath and relieved to pause a moment. Someone tried to pass a box of Australian ammunition forward past us, it did not fit our long rifles, and Alderman said, "Don't worry about that, lad, until we can get forward." I said, "But I think we ought to pass it on, Sir. The Australians must have their ammunition." I had more wind than most after climbing Rangitoto for over four years, and the box went on from hand to hand ahead of us.

'Only about a minute's spell was indulged in here, until our men began to bunch up behind us, and our next move upward carried us to the hill top, where we found the track entered a Turkish trench which followed the contour of the cliff from which it stood back three or four feet and was fairly straight for the most part. It gave a good field of fire out to sea; but obviously any troops who succeeded in reaching the beach were almost immediately in dead ground, unless the defenders climbed out to hang over the cliff edge. This perhaps accounted for our initial success and progress on reaching the shore. It was a little puzzling as we had expected from our orders to find ourselves on fairly flat ground at the beach level. It was only afterwards that we learned the landing had been made in the dark at the wrong place. No General would have dared to launch troops at those cliffs.'[25]

They climbed the steep spur above the wireless station at the north of Anzac Cove onto the plateau that was later to bear Plugge's name. The intention was that Plugge's battalion would move along this plateau onto Russell's Top and then on to Baby 700. It was Brigadier General H.B. Walker, the new commander, who had ordered Braithwaite to redirect the Auckland Battalion over Plugge's Plateau. He decided the steep knife-edged Walker's Ridge was far too narrow and the long climb in single file would result in the battalion being committed in a piecemeal and disorganised fashion. So it was, that, for the remainder of the day, New Zealand troops would be initially directed along the beach to the left until met by a staff officer from Walker's Brigade Headquarters. They would then be turned about and move inland over the spur above the beach leading up over Plugge's Plateau.

Indeed, the very disorganisation that Walker had feared had begun. Apart from receiving the order to move over the plateau above the wireless station, only some of the officers may have had the slightest idea what they were to do or where they were. Not only were they north of the intended landing but the maps issued to the officers 'proved to be useless both in themselves and in the light of the events. I imagine they had been filled in by someone sitting on the deck of a ship off the Peninsula and concerning himself only with the main approximate contours. They hardly gave a hint of the great complexity of tangled ravines of Anzac.'[26] For the men trudging back humping their packs and cursing quietly as the additional ammunition boxes were passed forward, it was a case of following on. If the line stopped or was broken, inevitably they were separated and mixed with other platoons. Retracing their steps, the Auckland Battalion met the two companies of the Canterbury Battalion moving towards the left as directed: 'There was great confusion, as the men of the various companies had not only become mixed with one another, but in some cases had attached themselves to the Auckland and various Australian battalions; while Aucklanders and Australians were picked up by the officers commanding the various Canterbury parties.'[27]

Many men had no idea where they fought or whom they fought alongside on that chaotic day. Lieutenant Colvin Algie was one: 'Landed with 15 men (Hauraki) about an hour after the rest of the company. Couldn't find Haurakis when I got ashore so attached myself to 3rd Coy (Auckland).'[28]

'"Keep going Westmacott," were Alderman's last words to me so I now went like smoke along the trench which bore to our left, which, I gathered, from what had been said on the forming up point, was the direction in which we would find the First Australians, from whom I could expect to get a clear idea of what was required of us. However, soon, several of my men behind called to me, "Mr Westmacott a message." I stopped and word came, "Halt and let the rear close up," and I waited whilst my men crowded up, there was only room for single file, the trench being about three foot wide. Everyone was hot and red faced with the pace at which we had climbed and come on. They wiped their foreheads and smiled when I caught their eyes. Another message arrived, repeated from man to man, with care, as they had been taught, "All packs off." We complied. I told everyone to put his pack in rear of the trench. I placed mine under a bush, specially noting its position behind an angle, and never saw it again. Whilst doing this a company of Australians in single file who had reached the top, just here, by another track, passed over our heads straight towards the firing line, which was across a wide valley on the inland side of the hill top where we were. We exchanged greetings with them till the word came for us to advance again, and I now came on several dead Turks, both on top and in the trench. We had to walk on the latter. In that hot sun their presence was just noticeable though they had only died soon after dawn; but not yet unpleasantly so.

'Now I came to the end of the trench and my first problem. It opened down a hillside. To the left was a steep and scrubby slope with no track. To move along it would be slow progress. To the right there was a track, obviously the enemy's entry to the trench, which went on down an open razor back and was under fire for some

Unloading a mule from the *Lutzow*, 25 April 1915. *(PAColl-0130-1-1, Alexander Turnbull Library)*

New Zealanders coming ashore at Anzac Cove, 25 April 1915. *(Thomas Jackson Grant Estate Collection – PAColl-0130, Alexander Turnbull Library)*

distance. If we took the left hand hillside it was so steep we would be climbing along it slowly under fire all the way. The bullets were smacking on the bare clay of the razor back almost at my feet as I paused there. Each course before me seemed unpleasant; but I could not remain under cover of the trench and continue the work I was there to do. I took the quick decision to go down the hill and up the bottom of the valley to the left, as affording the best cover to our men. Waiting till they had closed up I called to them to follow and led the way down.'[29]

Westmacott found himself staring down a steep thorn-covered cliff, which fell away to both sides from a narrow eroded razor edge of clay and gravel that linked Plugge's Plateau to Russell's Top. It was the same sight that had greeted the Australians earlier that morning. Some of them had tried to scrabble across the barely passable razor edge ridge, but the majority had followed the cliff face down to the right where it fell into Shrapnel Valley. Westmacott saw that the left gully led back towards the ground below the Sphinx over which the battalion had moved that morning, and with shrapnel bursting overhead and spent bullets smacking into the gravel face below him, he also moved right, down a zig-zag path into Shrapnel Valley. 'It was a time to double. I saw no use in waiting to see them out of the trench or any kind of heroics, and no one lost any time about following just as fast as I went. On our right we passed a Turkish tent covered with branches of scrub. The Australians had been before us and I did not stay to examine it. We never paused until we reached the valley bottom where I thought we were in dead ground again, and halted whilst the men came down. The ground was damp; but there was no stream. On the reverse slope of the opposite ridge where the track we had followed went upwards, an Australian was standing, with rifle and bayonet. In answer to my enquiry he pointed to a spade stuck in the ground beside him, and told me he had been posted there to prevent anyone touching it in case it was a booby trap. "Beware mines," said he knowingly. The company were clustering behind me and I called for Number 15 platoon men to join me, which those present did …

'Here John Hill of the Second South Canterbury came down to me. He said his platoon was with us in the rear, having somehow lost touch with their battalion and followed us forward. He was a little troubled as to his position and asked the question, "If an officer loses his own CO he joins himself onto the nearest senior officer does he not?" knowing the answer to be yes; but seeking moral support, for I found he had three platoons with him under subaltern officers, Cliff Barclay being one, and no senior. On my reassuring him, he asked, "Who is your senior officer?" I told him, "Major Alderman" … He reported to him. They came on with us.'[30]

As they came down the zig-zag path they found themselves in a narrow scrub-covered valley surrounded by steep cliffs and narrow re-entrants — it was the top of Shrapnel Valley. The New Zealanders turned left up the valley and, following the parties of Australian ammunition carriers, moved in single file inland in search of the Australian left flank. Private H.S. Sing wrote home of the move: 'We had to go tight into the middle of it and jingo didn't we catch it. The Australians had driven the enemy back over onto the Second Ridge by the time we got there but still we were getting picked off by snipers who were still hiding in the scrub.'[31]

Behind Westmacott's platoon, Walker's worst fears had been realised. Turkish shrapnel fire was now peppering the slopes of Plugge's Plateau, the slow file of New Zealanders had little idea where they were, and the line was being broken by Australians carrying ammunition forward and wounded straggling back. 'The rough ground, the thick growth of stunted ilex, the enemy fire, were all disorganising the line. The natural impetuosity of some, the physical strength of others, carried them on ahead. From this time the battalion as such ceased to exist.'[32]

The rear companies of the Auckland Battalion stopped and sheltered in the trenches on Plugge's Plateau, for Shrapnel and Monash gullies were still congested with the leading companies. Turkish shrapnel started to take a heavy toll. Private Steele of the 15th North Auckland Company remembered: 'The machine-gun section (of which I was then part) was ordered 500 yards [457 metres] to the left and to go up at once to the aid of the Australians. Off came our packs and, each carrying his portion of the machine-gun and its equipment, we started up the hill. The engineers had cut a path up the face … Shrapnel screamed over our heads and we would seek cover lying close to the ground. Lt Bob Frater gave the order for us to advance and collect, as we got the chance, over the ridge in the next gully. We were under a perfect hail of shrapnel and bullets … I would jump up, run about 10 yards and then dive under a bush or behind a small ridge. In a few seconds off I'd go again, watching where the shrapnel was bursting for the shells would generally fall 50 yards from the one before.'[33] Steele was later wounded in the leg on Plugge's Plateau.

Rather than quickly reinforcing the left flank, 'the earliest of the NZ reinforcements were disorganised by the turning of the Turkish fire up Plugge's, and all of them, attempting to follow their instructions, became split up in the tangle of Rest Gully and Monash Valley.'[34] For MacLagan, commander of the Covering Force, it was a frustrating period. He was increasingly concerned about the deteriorating situation in the left flank. From his vantage point on the eastern slopes of Monash Gully he could see the effects of the Turkish fire upon Plugge's Plateau and the movement of the New Zealanders back down into the tangle of Shrapnel Valley and Monash Gully. He sent the message back that all reinforcements should move from the beach up Shrapnel Valley and not over Plugge's, but though New Zealand signallers had laid line to Walker's headquarters and though the New Zealand Brigade was under Australian command, no record exists of Walker being told of the effects of this fire; and for the rest of the day New Zealand reinforcements continued to move in over Plugge's.

As Westmacott reached the bend in Monash Gully he sent out a patrol up its eastern slope to establish the position of the left flank. 'They saw men waving to them from the top to go on up the gully. The figures on the hillside were those of MacLagan and his staff. The New Zealanders turned and filed up to the head of Monash Gully and so to the lower slopes of Baby 700 just beyond The Nek.'[35]

'"Now then," said I to the nearest, "I want four men to go up onto the ridge, find out who is up there and report back to me. Who is going?" Jack Peterson of Te Kuiti, now a lance corporal, Dick Sircomb of Otorohanga, Arthur and Ned Cowdray, all sprang forward. "No! I will not let both Cowdrays go together. Come along another man!" I spoke quickly and with emphasis and another man, Mackinnon, immediately took Arthur Cowdray's place. From then on the latter remained close to me, covering my back wherever I moved. Gillanders was another man who offered for this; but he also, being now a corporal in charge of a section, I kept back. Off went the patrol, opened out in scout formation and disappeared onto the top. We waited, watching the short knee-high scrub with which the hill tops were covered, until Dick Sircomb reported back, "The First Australians are on the ridge between two and three hundred yards along, Sir." "Right," said I, "come along," and led the way up to him.

'The men came straggling up in what might be called file, but was really stringing along as the slope was steep and bare, though not very high, being near the head of the gully. Once on the crest, a few yards along the track which was well defined, I noted to the left a shallow depression which grew gradually to a gully towards the cliff and the sea. This in itself was like a wide trench. I ordered the men to file along it, take three paces' extension and lie down on the gently sloping bank in the enemy's direction so that they could use their rifles, if need be. When they had numbered off and lain down I found I had 28 men. I divided them into two sections under Corporal Grant on the right and Gillanders on the left. The Australian seven prolonged the line to our left and when I strolled along to them found they had conformed to our formation. I said they would act under me and asked if they understood things. They smiled and looked willing and a likely looking man of the natural leader type answered that they were glad to act with us. I did not see the man I had noticed before, with the South African medal ribbons, at this stage and fancied he had fallen out.

'It was quiet here, the depression about eight foot deep at the bottom, the sides gently sloping to the ridge in front and behind, and the artillery fire was going over us. I strolled along to about the centre of my line and said, "If you take my advice you'll have something to eat because you don't know when you'll be able to have another meal." Several men asked, "May we have a drink of water, Sir?" to which I replied, "No water may be touched till evening and then not without permission. It may have to last three days," and suiting the action to the word commenced to eat a biscuit. The men laying their rifles beside them did the same. Looking back I saw some of the company had taken the wrong spur to out right and were halfway to the top; but were already turning back. I could see two officers who I supposed to be Peake and Allen directing them.

'Baddeley now came up the track, followed by his men. He had a pipe in his mouth though not a great smoker … He formed his men up exactly as I had done in one long line close to and covering mine and they commenced opening their haversacks and bringing out their biscuits. Baddeley and I smiled at each other, and spoke a few words — our last on earth together — and as we went on eating biscuits I noted his platoon was about the same strength as mine.

'Alderman now arrived very much blown, I told him the situation as I knew it, which was not much and that I was giving my men a spell for some food. We all three had a small council of war. He pointed out that the rest of the company, having gone astray as we could see, would be some time coming up to us, and decided that

I was to go and reinforce the First Australians at once with my platoon. Baddeley was to follow with his and come into line when there was room. He himself would wait until the rest of the company came up before supporting us. As I left he said, "Wait a minute. Which way are you going?" and I gave the only possible reply I thought, "Straight along the ridge, Sir."

'It was but a few paces to my post in front of the centre of my platoon whence I ordered the men to put away their food. There was a pause whilst they did up their haversacks once more, and fastened their belts.

'The hill top was covered with scrub knee-high. The track which we had followed all the way up ran diagonally away from us slightly towards our left front. The gully on our right was steep; but not unscalable as we found to our cost later on. The ridges beyond, which were held by the enemy, ran parallel with us and up towards a high hill which was on our right front, overlooking our line of advance. On the left of our ridge the country fell away precipitously down to the sea; but we could not see this as our direction was carrying us each minute further away from it leaving more space on our left flank into which, without loss

Private Arthur Cowdray, 16th Waikato Company. 'He gave a surprised stare, then quietly laid his head on his rifle on the ground in front of him and was dead.' *(NZ Herald)*

of time, Baddeley advanced his number sixteen platoon. Swish! Swish! Swish! We strode on through the scrub, each man gazing forward as he walked. One stumbled and gave a laugh as he regained his place. "It was a dead Turk," said he, and so it was, and there were more of them, quite a number lying at intervals and right across the track where the First Australians had got them when we heard the heavy firing in the morning. The bullets were cracking round us now. We were getting it on the right; but there was nothing to indicate its direction. We could see no live enemy …

'Steadily we moved on. Suddenly, from in front appeared an Australian officer running like a deer. "Hullo. There you are … For God's sake push on!" he shouted as he came. I signalled my men to "Halt — Lie down," and the officer also stopped, panting. I sat down and he did too. It seemed no place to stand about. He sat there, beating the ground with his hand, his breath coming in great gasps. When he recovered a bit I said, "Now, what's the matter?"

"For God's sake push on," he replied. "They are getting Hell in front, and I am going back for reinforcements." This between gasps.

"All right," said I, "I am going to reinforce in a minute. Those are my orders; but I want to know what to expect. Tell me all about it. What do you mean by 'getting Hell'?"

"Well, they've formed a firing line in front —"

Roy Lambert, 3rd Auckland Infantry. Killed in action, 25 April 1915 *(NZ Herald)*

"'Who have?'

"'The First Australians and they're getting Hell.'

"'That's what I want to know, that the First Australians are there all right. What do you mean by Hell? Are the Turks attacking with the bayonet or what?'

"'No! No! They are losing a lot of men. They have formed a firing line on the other side of the hill and are holding on; but they need reinforcements badly and I'm going to get some.'

"'Very well,' said I, 'That's all right. We shall reinforce at once. Now as you go on down this track about a hundred yards you will find my Company Commander in a dip on your right. He is an Australian officer. Tell him what you have just told me and give him the message from me, that I am pushing straight on.' I heard afterwards that this message was never delivered.

'The officer jumped up and ran on. I rose and waved my men to advance again ... The bullets were passing all round us, making a crack as loud as a rifle, and seemed very close to the ears. I marvelled we were not all hit, and thought, "If I can come through this, I will survive anything."

'I judged it time to pause and get our bearings, so I raised my arm in the signal to halt and take cover again, which the line did, as one man.

'I lay down in the scrub ... I was able, by cautiously raising my head, to see how we lay. We were approaching a gully, our line being almost parallel to it. It was the head of the steep gully on out right which as it shallowed towards the top curved to our left towards a ridge or neck of land which connected our hill top with a higher feature overlooking us beyond. The track which at first we had been following up, and then on the hill top had crossed, curved away from us and went on over the neck apparently following the top of the cliffs along the coast which I could see from where I was. Though shallow to our left front, the slope was steeper in front. It was no use staying where we were, for we had little field of fire, though that we were under heavy enough fire ourselves, even if the crack of bullets did not convince us, was evident by the dead and wounded Australians who lay in the scrub everywhere around us. It was easy to find our way now by these bodies on the ground.

A little further forward then, must we go, to be properly effective, so I rose crouching and signalling my platoon up, crept the last few yards which brought me to the edge of the gully ... We reached the edge of the gully; but the situation was extremely puzzling to me, for as yet I had found no officer in charge. Where were they all? Failing anyone to tell me anything I stood up to try and locate the enemy. I got up quickly and at once the fire was tremendous. I suppose each man fired so suddenly at sight of me without taking careful aim that all went by me … A quick glance found was enough to tell me no more than I knew before, but I had obviously been seen by the Australians in front for a voice there called impatiently to me, "Don't stop up there. The firing line's down here …"

'I decided there must be an officer there, and the firing line being on the forward slope, must be in a trench. I decided to go on and signalled the men with an under-arm wave to follow, and looking to right and left long enough to see them arising to obey my order led the way down the slope. The fire was very heavy, terrific it seemed to me. I doubled less than twenty yards jumping over dead men, and tripping over a bush, fell forward into what had been the firing line of the First Australian infantry. From the time we moved for this last rush we were met by such a hail of bullets I expected each moment to be our last.

'A.C. Cowdray who had covered my back steadily up till now, fell beside me behind the bush and having seen me fall asked, "Are you hit, Sir?" and I answered,

Second Lieutenant H.S. Baddeley, 16th Waikato. Killed in action, 25th April 1915. *(NZ Herald)*

"No thanks, Cowdray. Keep your head down," for the bullets were grazing the scrub a few inches above and cutting the twigs off the bush in front of us. "This," it ran through my mind, "is just like old Edwards told me about at Rangiriri." Poor old First Australians! Their firing line had almost ceased to exist. Who had called out to me when we were on the ridge I shall never know. There was no trench. Lying on the forward slope without protective cover, every man there had been killed or wounded. They had fought on there, unsupported, rather than retire, and I saw at once that the same fate awaited me and the few of my men who had got so far forward … Nothing remained but to stay where we were and hope that something would happen to ease the pressure upon us.'[36]

Westmacott and his men could see higher features beyond, Battleship Hill and the crests of Chunuk Bair, but they had no time to look at the ground ahead. The platoon sergeant, Sergeant Ward, wrote: 'With our commander Mr Westmacott leading we approached the firing line of the Australians (who had been waiting for us as reinforcements) under a perfect hail of bullets and shrapnel. I somehow got into the centre of some Australians and lay down as close to the ground as possible as the bullets were flying thick about two feet above our heads. Mr Westmacott lay down about ten yards in front of me and Corporal Grant, the only man of out platoon, near me. I had not been there more than five minutes when an Australian next to me got his rifle up to fire and just as he pulled the trigger, a piece of shell struck him on the head and split his head from top to chin. He was killed instantly. I felt very sick then, this being the first man killed near me.'[37]

By now it was approaching 2.00 p.m. Major F.J. Kindon, the Second in Command of the 1st Australian Battalion, had held his thinning line of men from every Australian battalion against increased Turkish opposition. 'When the New Zealanders arrived, Kindon seemed to have only four or five effective men left with him. The others who could be seen were dead or wounded. Not another man was visible on either flank. To the left was the summit of Baby 700. It seemed a long endless slope, always gradually rising with little tracks running through it.'[38]

'So we lay amongst the dead and wounded Australians. One lying just in front of me made me feel ashamed that I was sheltering behind a wounded man, and that I must move away; but taking him by the foot I found he was already stiffening and must have been dead some hours. These men had most of them gone down in the fusillade we had heard from the ship about nine in the morning. A warm sun had been shining on them ever since, and the wounded were calling for "Water!" and "Stretcher bearers!" A man to my left rear called, "Where's our bloody artillery?" Strange the moral effect of the guns! But "Water!" was the worst cry. Otherwise all lay quiet. Behind us on the hill we had first ascended from the beach, was an Indian mountain battery. They would fire steadily for a few minutes and then seem to be silenced by the weight of Turkish gun fire, whose shells seemed to be bursting right on top of them. We thought that was the end of them; but presently they would start firing again. They were only small guns; but their presence was most encouraging, and they remained in action on and off all the time. Apart from ship's guns, these were the only artillery support we had.'[39]

Westmacott and Baddeley's platoons were on the inland slopes of Baby 700 facing Battleship Hill. It appears that the rest of Alderman's company took up a position on the crest of the hill behind them. The Waikato line helped cover a gap that existed between Kindon's line and a party from Kindon's 1st Australian Battalion under a Captain Jacobs, who were on the lower slopes of Mortar Ridge to Kindon's right rear. Every advantage was with the Turks. Men lying in the scrub were often firing at ranges of 10–20 metres because of the high scrub. To the right flank they could see men moving along the ridge to the high ground and brought rifle fire to bear but as officers and NCOs had to rise, kneel or stand to give directions and orders, too often they fell victim to Turkish snipers. 'From then on Gallipoli — the battlefield — was only seen from the prone position' and 'even small rises looked like hills'.[40]

The situation was becoming more and more precarious, even with the arrival of the New Zealanders. Turkish snipers were infiltrating behind the line of Westmacott's right and were sniping from the rear. On the crest the Australian line had been forced back and the Anzac line on Baby 700 had both flanks in the air.

'From the front, from the right, and now from the right rear the rifle fire was coming. The last got several of us, though we did not know it at the time, for a sniper lay there just on the edge of the plateau and picked us off as we showed up, one by one. I think he had crawled up out of the gully after our right flank had passed, I learned this afterwards. Cowdray was the first to get hit. He was talking to me one moment, the next his blood was pouring down his face from his forehead. He gave a surprised stare, then quietly laid his head on his rifle on the ground in front of him and was dead.

I felt his death dreadfully … I could not help talking to his body as if he still were alive, calling him "poor little boy" and telling him "never mind" …

'Soldiers now appeared about six hundred yards off moving inland from the sea coast. My obedient men had lain until now under all this fire without firing a shot. Some to my left rear saw these men first and called to me "There they are, Sir! There they are! May we open fire?" I called back, "No don't fire. They may be our own men," as they were undistinguishable at that range from ours who, if they were there, were moving in the right direction to soon take the pressure off us, and I wished they were. I believe them now to have been a flanking party of a larger force of Turks advancing to the hill in front of us, following the top of the cliffs and turned inland by a curve in the coast line. I got my glasses out and whilst focusing on them they disappeared behind the hill.

'Raised on my elbows I continued to examine the landscape in front through the binoculars, when I received a blow on my right arm close to the shoulder which turned me right over. I was now on my back and my arm completely useless. Reaching down I found something that seemed cold, fat and heavy at my left side on the ground. It was my own right hand. I was lying on my smashed right arm, though how I got there I know not. I looked at my wrist watch. The time was ten minutes past two. I reached for my pipe, but could not get hold of it, as it was in the right side pocket of my jacket. Turning cautiously over on my face again, my arm fell into position. I gave some groans, and was very ashamed of them. They were concern for myself. The arm was not painful but numb, I got relief by rolling on my left side, taking hold of it and pulling it tight.

'Suddenly, perhaps a hundred yards away to our left front, a line of Turks appeared. They were only a section of about eight; but there were others behind, a small party leading would be the point of an advance guard, moving in quick time and absolute silence as trained soldiers should, well extended and searching the scrub as they came on, their rifles at the ready. They were well equipped and uniformed, wearing the Enver helmet. Like all the Turks we had seen they were of good physique, sturdy peasants, drilled fighting men. They were following the track.

'I shouted, "Fix bayonets — Rapid fire." My good Sergeant Ward lying behind us, called, "Now then! Don't forget. Firing with the bayonet on, put the sights up a hundred and fifty!" Our fire ripped along the ridge and the whole of that leading section went down in the scrub; but more were to follow. I reached for my revolver, knowing I must use my left hand, with which I had schooled myself to shoot accurately; but instinctively trying to rise on my right and getting no action, went face downward in the dust and got my mouth full of dirt …

'Our men were fine shots and now, at last, they were getting their own back. The fire from the ridge behind and to the left was so steady and rapid that the Turks went down like nine pins — as they came in front of the ridge. One moment they were moving towards us, and the next collapsing into the scrub, perhaps crumpling is the better word. The foremost ones got no nearer than sixty yards from us. They at no stage tried to rush; but moved steadily on. No doubt many unwounded took cover in the scrub, as we had done, and hoped for better times; but as the advance came to a standstill these began to get up in ones and twos and run back to the ridge. The broad flat packs on their backs made a good mark. Not a man got more than a few yards before he pitched forward on his face. Not one reached the ridge. For a few wild moments I wanted my men to continue firing until there was no sign of life in our enemy who lay visible; but was soon ashamed I should feel like that. I am always sorry for wounded and prisoners, but I was not then.

'The blue sky looked clear above me as I turned over and looked up at it. It was not long afterwards that I learned we had met the head of the Turkish counter-attack and beaten them back. But it was only a check.'[41]

The line facing the Turkish advance from Battleship Hill had thinned to breaking point and, with Turks pressing in on both flanks, gave ground. Sergeant Ward remembered: 'Our major [Alderman], who was also very badly wounded and away to our right, gave the order to retire because our men were falling all around us and the reinforcements [6th Hauraki Company] had not caught up to us to help. The men began to retire in splendid order and were a sight to watch and to think one had such splendid men to lead.'[42]

By this time, Westmacott's platoon had been reduced to a handful of men. Ward half carried, half dragged his wounded platoon commander back over the crest past the second line held by the South Canterburys and the Haurakis under Captain Sinel. Private Sing, was also forward with the Waikatos reinforcing Kindon's line, said:

'I stayed there for some time then we had to retire because the odds were too heavy. We retired slowly at first then they gave it to us hot. We had to shift. They started to chase us. We had to run. I can tell you I don't think I ran so fast in all my life.'[43]

Baddeley and the majority of his platoon were never seen again, but the remaining Waikatos and Australians, alternately moving and firing, retired over the crest on to the second line, where they formed a mixed group of Waikatos, Haurakis and South Canterburys supported by three Maxim guns of the Auckland Battalion which had positioned themselves behind the firing line at The Nek.

On the seaward slopes of Baby 700 forward of The Nek, another equally intense battle had raged all morning and into the afternoon. Lalor, the original commander of this position, had been killed. Turks were moving along the tops of the cliff-faced spurs between Battleship Hill and Baby 700. Australian reinforcements, totalling some four mixed companies, had already been swallowed up in the battle for this position: 'All that the men and even the officers knew was that the great effort of the expedition had been launched and that it was their duty to see that it did not fail. That attack had manifestly not gone as was intended. The high hopes of the morning advance had long faded. They were up against the fire of some Turkish Force. A comparatively scattered fire at first, but now incessant and always growing. Each man could only keep touch with one or two others on either side of him in the scrub, and, as one after another was hit, the line was thinned to breaking point. But they knew that all the other parts of the line must be depending on them to hold the flank. If the line gave, it meant failure. With an unknown and increasing force ahead of them — with the long hours passing, and the enemy showing no signs of exhaustion — yet the determination of each individual man and officer still held them to that hill.'[44]

In the afternoon individual New Zealanders separated from their units, and searching for them, had moved forward over Russell's Top and joined with the Australians on this flank. They fought on without officers or recognised leaders, keeping in touch with their immediate neighbours in the scrub, moving forward or falling back as the Turkish pressure grew or eased. A Lieutenant L.J. Morshead, later famous in the Second World War as the Commander 9th Australian Division and defender of Tobruk, had brought his platoon forward. He was one of the few surviving officers on this flank. By now the line had been drawn back on The Nek and Malone's Gully for the fifth time and 'it was difficult to prevent the exhausted nerve-racked men from retiring too far.'[45]

It was about 3.00 p.m. that a party of New Zealand infantry 'came up the steep gutter of Malone's Gully from the sea. For some reason they had not been turned back by Walker's headquarters below the Sphinx, and had continued north along the beach, then up the very steep gully which ends at The Nek. It appears that they were the remaining platoons of Major D. Grant's South Canterbury Company. Separated in the melee of Aucklanders and Canterburys below Plugge's, this group of at least two platoons, most probably under Lieutenants R.A.R. Lawry and O.H. Mead, had been directed to the left around the base of Walker's Ridge. Despite Turkish snipers active on the seaward spurs of Baby 700, they climbed that backbreaking 500 feet [152.4 metres] and linked up with the Australians holding the head of Malone's Gully and The Nek.

It is not known who was in command of this group but an Australian survivor of the battle on this flank, then Lance Corporal H.V Howe, wrote of how the New Zealand officer decided to attack a Turkish trench dominating the northern exit from the gully onto the seaward slopes.[*] It had been attacked before but Turkish machine guns on the crest of the hill could fire straight along the line of the trench, causing heavy casualties and forcing the attackers to withdraw each time back into Malone's Gully.

The New Zealander was told that 'the trench was enfiladed and could not be held when taken; and that an advance would be useless.'[46] However, if the position on Baby 700 was to be stabilised it could only be done by holding the crest. The officer ordered his men to attack the trench. 'When for the third time the trench was rushed, the Turks did not defend it, but ran back.'[47] As the assaulting New Zealanders jumped into the trench the Turkish machine-gun swept it, killing the officer leading the charge and killing and wounding most of those with him. Only those attackers who were sheltering in the communication trenches leading over the spur from Baby 700 escaped this enfilade fire. They were under heavy rifle fire from Battleship Hill. Lying there waiting for the fire to lift, the New Zealanders could see Turks advancing over

---

[*] It is likely that the officer was Major David Grant, O.C. of the South Canterbury Company. Lt Col. Fenwick found his body in Malone's Gully during the Armistice on 24 May. See chapter 8.

the slopes of Battleship Hill and it was obvious that a major attack was in progress. Again this was by the battalions of the 57th Regiment of Kemal's 19th Division. The New Zealand survivors were in danger of being cut off, and they scrambled back towards The Nek.

By late afternoon, the Anzac lines on both the inland and seaward slopes were being pushed back. The fight now pivoted on the Auckland Maxim guns positioned at The Nek and scattered parties of Australians and New Zealanders along the edge of Second Ridge. The guns had been positioned soon after the Waikatos had moved up Monash Gully.

'Here we found the Australians were being driven back from the top [of Baby 700] for the third time … and were retiring down the spur towards us. We found we could not do any good by advancing so Lieutenant Frater retired the guns, three of which had now turned up with their teams … He lined the three guns across a narrow part of ridge about 75 yards in width … with the lowest point of the saddle between [Russell's Top] and [Baby 700] some fifty yards ahead of us and distant from the skyline [of Baby 700] by 350 yards. We had no time to erect proper cover for the guns, but just trusted to the natural cover afforded by the bushes which are far from bullet proof.'[48]

Forward of the guns the last of the Auckland Infantry, mixed with elements of the 2nd South Canterburys, moved forward. 'Your son [Roy Lambert] arrived with his lot and laid down alongside me for a second or two to recover his breath … I directed him to the saddle ahead to which place the main body of Auckland infantry and Australians had, by this time, retired, after another abortive attempt at carrying the hill. The trouble with taking Turkish trenches … was not their infantry but their shrapnel … The small force ahead of us was mustered together by Captain Sinel (6th Haurakis) and an Australian Major. There could not have been more than 50 all told, and they made a last stand here, supported by our three guns. Your son was killed … During the Armistice a month later, the men who fought in this and died in this action were buried. Your son's body was found 50 yds ahead of three piles of C[olonial] A[mmunition] C[ompany] ammunition, all that remained to mark the place we fought on, as the scrub had long been shot away.'[49]

It was a soldier's battle. The ground made it difficult for commanders to control their men. It was impossible to see anything ahead without standing, and to stand was to fall victim to Turkish sniper or shrapnel fire. All the New Zealand commanders forward on Baby 700 that day were killed or wounded. The Waikatos had every one of their officers and sergeants killed or wounded, except for Ward, Westmacott's platoon sergeant.

For the commanding officers, Stewart and Plugge, it was frustrating. They had no idea where their companies were and they could not communicate with them. Signallers had laid line from Division to Brigade Headquarters but communications forward were by runner or semaphore flags. It was by flag that Brigadier General Walker on Ari Burnu kept in touch with his units on the high ground. Fred Senn was one of his signallers: 'General Walker with rolled up sleeves and in shorts, and armed only with a swagger cane, binoculars and a map case, followed by Coningham and Wallingford similarly attired but also carrying revolvers, compasses and a signal pad, decided to leave the "point" and proceed up the spur towards the Plateau. Dick Morgan and I were told to go off with them to handle the communications … We were in touch with Russell's Top all the time and sent and received messages … Morgan and I were now learning a bit about war and decided there would not be much future in standing up wagging a morse flag, so we looked for and mostly found partial cover. In one of these spots, a dry watercourse with a clay bank as a perfect back-drop, I was wagging the flag with only my head over the top when a burst of machine-gun fire plugged into the bank a few inches from my head. From then on flag and head were not both visible together.'[50]

No information came back, or when it did it was hours old. In the late afternoon, Lieutenant Colonel Stewart of the Canterburys moved forward to contact his men. He met with Walker on Plugge's and gathered every available man, Australians and New Zealanders, stragglers, including some of his own battalion. They moved up Walker's Ridge and advanced towards The Nek. As he moved forward the Turks counter-attacked.

'Stewart evidently saw the line of Morshead's men near Malone's Gully, for Morshead received from him three messages at short intervals. The first was an order to retire upon the Canterbury line; the next — "Stay where you are, we will come up to you." In the interval between the last two the shrapnel fire upon The Nek had been tremendously heavy. A few minutes later Stewart was killed.'[51]

It was now after 4.00 p.m. On the beach the Otago Battalion was landing. Inland the first two acts were almost over. The line, a mixture of Waikatos, Haurakis and South Canterburys, with remnants of the Australian units, were under increasingly heavy shrapnel and rifle fire. They clung to the lower slopes of Baby 700. If these lines were to hold, guns and fresh troops were needed. For the present none were available. Bridges' last reserve, two companies of the Australian 2nd Battalion commanded by Colonel Braund, had been committed after Stewart up Walker's Ridge. They reached the junction of Walker's Ridge and Russell's Top at about 4.00 p.m. and formed a line at the top of the spur. They stayed there lying in the scrub, sniped at from Baby 700 and shelled from batteries on Chunuk Bair.

Of the New Zealand Brigade ashore, Plugge's last companies had moved forward to Baby 700. In the Canterbury Battalion, the South Canterburys were fully committed. The 1st Canterbury Company had sent two of its platoons forward to reinforce Baby 700. Its remaining two platoons were quickly dissolved into parties carrying ammunition forward to the Australian line on Second Ridge, as well as reinforcing Walker's Ridge against a threat from the north along the coastal foothills. Corporal R.J. Petre wrote: 'We landed about eleven. Had to wade ashore. Hit on foot with spent bullet at 2.30. Shrapnel terrible. The Colonel was killed today. With Capt Salmonson and twenty — to hold left flank. Got there alright. Reinforced at 6 by 12th and 13th. Had sentry group all night. Very cold until someone found some Australian greatcoats.'[52] A cryptic diary entry of a boy who was to die at Quinn's Post on 4 June.

Twenty men, Australians and New Zealanders, under an English officer, Captain Critchley-Salmonson, Adjutant to the Canterburys, climbed Walker's Ridge, and from halfway up its slopes fired at Turks infiltrating south along the low foothills bordering the sweep of Ocean Beach. Looking north they could see the beached rowboats from the *Galeka* with their cargo of dead Australians, killed by Turkish fire that morning opposite Fisherman's Hut. This small party alone held this position on the far left of the Anzac Line.

A line, under Captain Jacobs of Kindon's 1st Australian Battalion, had formed a position on Mortar Ridge to close the gap between Baby 700 and Second Ridge. As they lay there on the spur of Mortar Ridge, to their left they could see 'the whole summit and flank of Baby 700 and the Australian line upon it.'[53] In front and to their right they could see Turkish soldiers advancing in open formation from the Third Ridge against the Australian line in the areas later known as German Officer's Trench, Johnston's Jolly and the Lone Pine Plateau.

It was this threat that drew New Zealanders piecemeal into the defence of Second Ridge. The intensity of the Turkish counter-attack against Second Ridge resulted in small parties of New Zealanders from the 3rd Auckland Company and 15th North Auckland Company responding to cries of 'reinforcements' and supporting the hard-pressed Australians all along the eastern rim. Like the Australian line before it, the New Zealand line on Baby 700 was starved for support. 'Joined Leer's line. There they stayed, fighting desperately. One New Zealander whose left hand had been shot off, lay propping his rifle on the ground against his elbow and firing. Presently he was shot through the head.'[54]

These dour battles continued all along the forward slopes of Second Ridge. The gap between the thinning line on Baby 700 and the line above Monash Gully was widening. Lieutenant Cowey commanded the mix of Australians and New Zealanders that clung to the spur of Mortar Ridge. By late afternoon Turks were moving to their

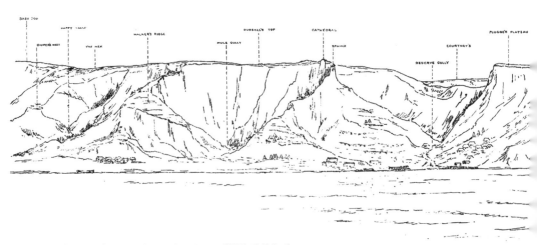

Panorama of ANZAC from 1 Mile NE of Ari Burnu. *(RC04218, Australian War Memorial)*

left and right. Baddeley's and Westmacott's platoons further up the slopes of Baby 700 had been wiped out. For Cowey's party, ammunition was giving out. On the slope of Monash Gully, reinforcements lining the edge of the escarpment fired into the backs of his men, not realising that ANZAC troops were still forward. Cries to stop firing were seen as a Turkish ruse: 'It was difficult to hold the men there. Finally the Turkish fire became so accurate that anyone who tried to cross the forty yards in front of the Bloody Angle was instantly shot.'[55]

It was about 4.30 p.m. when the line finally broke. Suddenly the forward remnants of the Australians and New Zealanders came running back: 'Get to buggery,' they said. 'The Turks are coming on — thousands of them.' Back they came, dragging their wounded with them. Small groups collected in pockets of dead ground where men could escape from the shrapnel fire overhead and rifle fire from Baby 700. The ANZACs lined the eastern edge of Bloody Angle and the future Quinn's Post, and fell back on the guns at The Nek.

The slopes of Baby 700 were empty. The last act was beginning.

All that day, commanders and men could not understand why the men of the *Lutzow* were not quickly joined by the rest of the brigade. In his diary, Lieutenant Colonel Braithwaite speaks of 'the complete hiatus in disembarkation' between 12.30 and about 4.30 p.m.[56] C.E.W. Bean states: 'The transports of the New Zealand infantry were due to arrive at midday, but were not brought to their anchorage until late in the afternoon.'[57]

Yet the same concern about delay is not evident in the diaries and memoirs of those New Zealanders waiting to land. As far as they were concerned everything was going according to plan. Despite Bean's statement, they were off the beaches soon after the *Lutzow* had finished sending her troops ashore. The next ship to land her troops

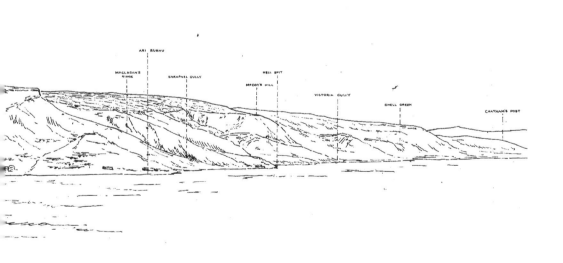

was 'the old cargo tramp called the *Annaberg*. Private Thompson of the 4th Otago Company wrote:

'12 Noon. For the last two hours we have been in sight of Gallipoli. The warships are violently bombarding the Turkish positions. We are quite near our anchorage now, but will not attempt a landing until reinforcements are called for.'[58]

Lieutenant Colonel Moore's Otago Battalion started to land at 2.00 p.m. and were finally ashore soon after 4.00 p.m. But they were not alone at the anchorage. Major Herbert Hart, second in command of the Wellington Regiment, had two companies of this battalion aboard the *Achaia*, which was off the landing at 1.00 p.m.

'The battle was in full swing, the warships were firing continuously, their shells throwing up huge clouds of dust upon bursting ashore. Torpedo boat destroyers were rushing about everywhere taking troops ashore, first from one transport then from another. We could see the men landing and then pushing away to the right, some to the left, others climbing the spurs and rushing forward over the ridges.'[59]

Even that most particular and critical of soldiers, Lieutenant Colonel Malone, on the *Itonus*, which had been delayed in leaving Lemnos, makes no mention of delays in landing: 'At 4.30 p.m. my first troops went ashore. Taken off by HMS *Bulldog*, torpedo boat, I sent two companies of the Canterbury Battalion and half the Taranaki Company, the latter in the main barge we had towed. I went with this consignment.'[60]

Godley's division was arriving as planned. There was no apparent effort to speed up the landing of the troops offshore. Communication with Birdwood's headquarters was by 'the Naval wireless station, which was in not very efficient contact with Army Corps HQ on HMS *Queen*'.[61] Birdwood was not aware of the full seriousness of the situation until he and Godley landed at 3.00 p.m. Godley stayed ashore, and as the Otagos were now arriving, nothing more could be done. While it must have appeared inexplicable to those on shore that the rest of the New Zealanders had not arrived, this merely characterised the difficulty of communications that was to plague the campaign. Only when they landed did they find that all was not going to plan: 'The staff were delighted to see us, and several of them shook hands warmly and said, "We are very glad to see you, Brereton." This was so unusual that it was almost sufficient to cause, in the language of the Army Act, "alarm and despondency in His Majesty's forces", and we realised at once that the situation must indeed be grave.'[62]

Major Brereton of the 12th Nelson Company landed with Malone from the *Itonus* in the late afternoon. The Otagos were ashore and only the remaining companies of Malone's Wellingtons had yet to land. The Otagos were despatched to reinforce the Australians on the left flank. Then they too were directed to return and dig in on Plugge's Plateau. The Turkish counter-attack which was to drive the New Zealanders off the slopes of Baby 700 was pushing against the Anzac line all along the front. It was essential that Plugge's Plateau be held. It was the final possible bastion before Anzac Cove. Private Thompson of the Otagos wrote: 'We effected a landing at Gaba Tepe exactly at 5.00 p.m. and disembarked without a single casualty. We were under fire the whole time, and immediately on landing we were rushed to the left of the position held by the Australians. A little later, however, we were brought back and sent up a big hill to dig in, but we had no sooner got there than the Turks commenced sending shrapnel over. We got it hot and strong and suffered a few casualties, but we had to dig for our lives. That was our baptism.'[63]

Few Otagos saw a Turk, and those they saw were dead. But Turkish observers on Baby 700 could see all movement across Russell's Top and Plugge's Plateau, and in the last of the daylight they used their artillery to great effect. Walker's headquarters had moved to Plugge's as Fred Senn recalled: 'It was about 5.00 p.m. when we reached the plateau and things were pretty hot on top. The Turks were counter-attacking and endeavouring to get shell and machine-gun fire over the top onto the beach. The shells were clearing the Plateau by as little as 4 feet. At this time General Walker, Coningham and Wallingford were watching the position from about five yards from the beach edge of the Plateau, and Morgan and I were ordered to take cover behind the edge. We did not need to be told twice. The Otago Infantry were now ashore, and had just reached the Plateau and were starting to make their way across … One of the low shells passed so close to General Walker's solar plexus that it knocked him flat on his back. We thought he was dead, but when we picked him up, he gasped, "all right". He was only winded, and was still groggy when he noticed that some of the Otagos, suffering heavy casualties and halfway across the plateau were faltering … and

New Zealand soldiers are among those assembled on the beach, 26 April 1915. Note signaller with semaphore flag signalling. The wireless mast on the right is for shore to ship communications. *(WF13022, Malone Family)*

were turning around looking for cover. Calling out "Come on Coningham, they're turning back," he dashed across the plateau with Coningham in tow, waving his cane and shouting, "Come on boys, here's the front line over here." The Otago boys turned round to a man and followed him to the rim overlooking the valley. Here they had a pretty bad time digging in, with many casualties, but were consolidated by dark.'[64]

That massive firepower that was 'blowing the Turks to buggery' had little effect on the soldiers' battle inland. Lack of communications and the low trajectory of the naval guns meant that the only targets engaged had to be on the forward slopes well clear of our own infantry. The only artillery ashore was an Indian Mountain Battery on Plugge's and one lone Australian 18-pounder that was landed after dark. The headquarters of the New Zealand and Australian Divisional Artillery had landed at 10.30 a.m. that morning. The staff looked for gun positions on those inhospitable slopes, but later Bridges directed that no artillery was to land and some sent ashore by barge was returned to the transports. The feeling may have been that one could not risk losing the guns. Offshore, 'the artillery men on their transports were consumed with impatience'.

Darkness was approaching. Inland on the lower slopes of Baby 700 at the junction of the First and Second ridges, the final act of the day had to be played. In a frayed semicircle around the base of the hill, small tired groups of Australians and New Zealanders lay in hastily scratched holes or any likely fold in the ground, peering out into the dusk. The war was fought at a distance of a few metres, bullets cracking overhead, flashes in the gloom, then movement in front, mere paces away, as parties of Turks from Kemal's battalions filtered down the slopes of Baby 700 and from across the gullies onto the Second Ridge.

Just below Baby 700 was a slight shoulder of land, behind which was a narrow dried water bed falling into Monash Gully. Into it retired the men who had held and fought on the crest that long afternoon. Private Frank McKenzie of the Auckland Battalion wrote: 'All the officers in our part had been laid out and there was no one to command. Someone bolted and yelled "retire". We obeyed and ran. As the line got up, there was a hail of bullets. The Australians fell in dozens. In my cramped position my leg had gone completely to sleep and I made a bound and fell over like a turkey with its head off. However, the leap had taken me over the crest into comparative safety. About 15 yards from the crest we dug in like mad with out little entrenching tools — coffin trenches they called them, but they are 6' x 2' x 1. The Turks did not follow up immediately and this saved us — Dawson took charge from now on and held on like a hero.'[65]

Dawson's band held that tiny ledge of sheltered ground that would pass into legend as Quinn's Post. His band was a mix of every company of the New Zealand battalions ashore as well as Australians. They grew to some 100–150 men as the night advanced and stragglers made their way back or reinforcements came up. Throughout the night they held the post, digging in some 10 metres back from the crest, conscious of Turkish movement just over the crest 10–20 metres away.

'The Turks did not know how few we were and they would not come over the crest onto our bayonets. We were better shots and they couldn't show above the crest, so you see we had them … From now till daylight we alternately strengthened our trenches and kept off their attacks which came every quarter of an hour at some point. We went on to our old trench and brought in our wounded, including Richardson, but he died; captured a few Turks who got cut off in their sorties, but owing to treachery, when one held up his hands while his mate shot the Australian who went to bring him in, they shot most of them (the Turks) on sight.'[66]

While Dawson and his band hung on to Quinn's, a similar struggle was taking place at The Nek, by the Auckland guns. It was a mixed group commanded by a machine-gun sergeant of the Aucklanders, Sergeant McLean. Second Lieutenant Frater had been wounded, and refusing help, staggered back to the beach to die. McLean's group were joined by the last stragglers clinging to Baby 700. 'All emptied their magazines into the oncoming Turks and bolted. This party was probably the last of the ANZAC forces to cross The Nek alive during the campaign. Still in full flight and moving fast they fell into the rifle pits around the machine guns. An Auckland machine-gun sergeant was in command. There was room for all in the rifle pits, each of which was about two feet deep. They seemed a home from home after the open ground further forward. The position was open to attack only across The Nek or by troops climbing to the top from Monash Valley, the slope from Malone's Gully was unscaleable. Through the position a clearly defined track ran to the rear. The machine gunners had arrived by this track and knew that it led back to the cliff above the beach and to Divisional H.Q. The gunners had 16 belts of ammunition and most of the men still had almost full pouches — having replenished them continuously during the day from the dead and wounded.'[67]

It was a powerful position they held. They were aware of heavy firing from the left rear and knew this came from their own men, Braund's battalion holding the junction of Walker's Ridge and Russell's Top. There was also a party of New Zealanders dug in some 70–80 metres behind them, probably remnants of Lieutenant Colonel Stewart's party. Conscious of this support, they were determined to hang on with no 'nicking off.'

'Shortly before sunset a strong force of Turks attempted to cross The Nek, moving carelessly, bunching together. There was great excitement among the machine guns. Men whispered to each other, "Let the bastards come." The sergeant ordered everyone to hold fire until the machine guns opened, which they did when the leading Turks were less than 20 yards distant. The attack stopped dead, the relatively few unwounded enemy escaping by jumping into the valleys on either side.'[68]

Night came. There was a nearly full moon, at times partly obscured by cloud, but the men watching and waiting in the pits could see forward about 30 metres. At this distance a man's head and shoulders could be distinguished above the scrub covering the saddle. Twice again that night the Turks attacked. Parties made their way into Monash Gully and up the slopes of the ridge to outflank the trenches holding the bottleneck. The attacks were beaten off. Sergeant McLean was wounded and went back seeking ammunition and reinforcements. He left the post in the command of a corporal of the Canterburys and Corporal H.V. Howe, the only N.C.O.s remaining. A soldier sent back to see New Zealanders in the rear came back with the news. 'Hey Corp, the mob behind us have cleared out.'

Some time later the Turks moved a strong party along Monash Valley and attacked the post from right and rear. They had been heard and the men were ready and waiting. Invisible in the pits, men kept silent, opening fire only when it was impossible to miss. 'The Turks fired a few rounds — mostly at each other and the attack faded.'[69]

The party, which included a dozen badly wounded men, was conscious of being both heavily outnumbered and outflanked: 'We could hear the Turks talking excitedly and advancing down the ridge. We took the machine guns and ammunition and some wounded men and carried all back. Oh! What a task, for we were nearly collapsing.'[70] They pulled back down the track, leaving three badly wounded men who refused to be moved, and retired to a position above the Sphinx. 'An officer appeared from the rear and we determined to hold on. We cleared the scrub immediately in front and fired the only available machine gun. Throughout the wet night we held on until ordered back to our lines about three o'clock.'[71]

As night fell, Bridges made every effort to plug the hole left by the loss of Baby 700. Fortunately the Turks were not aware of the gap between Braund's party on Walker's Ridge and Dawson's at Quinn's. However, small parties of Turks infiltrated onto Russell's Top and sniped into the backs of those defending Second Ridge. Kemal's attacking battalions, particularly his 57th Regiment, had 50 percent casualties, and were badly disorganised. Disaster loomed for the ANZACs, but night brought relief. Turkish artillery ceased and Monash's 4th Australian Brigade was arriving on the beaches.

Monash's leading battalion under Lieutenant Colonel Harold Pope was sent forward with the Taranaki Company under Major J.W. Brunt to secure the head of Monash Gully. Pope's men and the Taranakis were separated in the dark, but by morning Pope had secured a low spur jutting out from The Nek, which became Pope's Hill, and a mixture of Australians and Taranakis found themselves a niche alongside Dawson's party on Second Ridge, later called Courtney's Post. Fire echoed throughout the night as Australian fired at New Zealander, Turk at Turk in the confusion. Brereton's company was sent along the beach to reinforce Braund on Walker's Ridge. Cecil Malthus led with the scouts: 'Unfortunately the two companies [12th and 13th] who were supposed to follow failed to keep connection with us and remained bogged down on the beach for the night, while the half dozen of us toiled on up the slope and spent the next 24 hours with a mixed lot of Australians. By the time we reached the top of the ridge on the left flank [Walker's Ridge] not only had we lost our mates and ourselves, but we had perforce thrown away our carefully packed valises, which we never saw again. We could get no information from the scattered parties whom we passed. A state of muddle and utter exhaustion existed everywhere and the defence [it was already defence and not attack] was terribly weak. Finally we were seized upon by a harassed Australian Lieutenant who begged us to strengthen his handful at the top of the hill. And so, expecting our companies to arrive and reinforce the position we stayed there and dug in. The whole night was spent improving our trench, while a cold misty rain reduced us to cowering misery.'[72]

After the heat and lack of water of the day, that cold night remained in men's memories, and although Kemal pushed his regiments forward throughout the night, ANZACs and Turks had fought each other to exhaustion. Frayed, and full of gaps, the ANZAC lines on First and Second ridges still held. Baby 700 was lost, and the trenches at The Nek abandoned, but Braund, with Australians and Canterburys, held Walker's Ridge. Scattered parties were on Russell's Top. Pope's Australians held Pope's and Dawson held Quinn's. The rest of Second Ridge was defended by the Australians intermingled with New Zealanders. All was confusion but men hung on and dug in.

By nightfall Birdwood had some 16,000 men ashore, including 3100 New Zealanders. Against them were some 12,000 Turks, all of Kemal's 19th Division and the 27th Regiment, which had been guarding the coast. For most of the day, the ANZACs had greatly outnumbered the Turkish defenders. Both regiments, the 57th Regiment and 27th Regiment, which had carried the brunt of the fighting during the day, together numbered not more than 4000 men. They had 2000 casualties, but they pinned the Australians and New Zealanders into the two ridges above the beach, and by nightfall Turkish reinforcements almost matched the ANZACs in strength.

It had been the ground that had swung the balance in favour of the Turks. They were able to attack in strength at opposite ends to a widely stretched half circle that was the ANZAC front line on First and Second ridges. This prevented Birdwood's Corps utilising its superior strength — the ANZACs could not be strong everywhere, and on both flanks of the line the Turks had massed more men and threatened to break the ANZAC perimeter.

Holding Baby 700 would have secured the ANZAC lodgement on the Peninsula, but Bridges and Godley faced night knowing it to have been lost. The beach was confusion itself: 'I climbed ashore over some barges and found myself in the semi-darkness amidst a scene of indescribable confusion. The beach was piled with ammunition and stores, hastily dumped from lighters, among which lay the dead and wounded, and men so absolutely exhausted that they had fallen asleep in spite of the deafening noise of battle. In fact it was impossible to distinguish between the living and the dead in the darkness. Through the gloom I saw the ghost-like silhouettes of groups of men wandering around in a continuous stream apparently going to or returning from, the firing line. On the hills above there raged an unceasing struggle lit up by the bursting shells and the night air was humming with bullets like the droning of countless bees on a hot summer's day.'[73]

Above the beach, cut into the crest of the plateau, Bridges and his staff assessed the situation. Godley was with them, but all the units of the NZ & A Division ashore were under General Bridges' command. Bridges was conscious that his brigadiers had serious doubts about their troops' ability to hold the line without reinforcements. All the troops in the firing line were exhausted, and large numbers of wounded were making their way back to the beach. Ominously they were being accompanied by an increasing flow of unwounded men; men who were often so tired that regardless of the firing and the bustle around them, they slumped on the beach and fell asleep.

In this situation both Godley and Bridges believed that a major Turkish counter-attack in the morning would cause disaster.

Godley later wrote to his wife: 'We have had a devil of a time, and on Sunday night it was touch and go whether we could stand it for the next day. It was the shrapnel that played the mischief and it was almost too much for untrained (or rather irregular) troops to do … Bridges and I had to tell Birdwood it was touch and go, and he decided that we must let Sir Ian know and we sent him a message by Admiral Thursby. He replied that there was no question of doing anything except sticking it out and the Admiral said that in any case it would be impossible to re-embark us.'[74]

None of Bridges' brigade commanders realised that evacuation was planned. When Walker, commanding the New Zealanders, was told, the anger of his reply to Bridges was insubordinate. As for the men, they were too tired to contemplate being beaten. 'They had thought, and a good many of them said, they would get a spell and many of them wandered down to the beach from the trenches to get it, but fortunately the majority hung on.'[75]

Birdwood's objectives at Anzac that day were far too ambitious. Success demanded that everything go in MacLagan's favour, including a sluggish reaction from the Turkish defenders. This was too much to hope for. Then the Australian prospects were dashed when the Navy failed to put them ashore on the planned beaches. From these, the low foothills and good going up the spurs of the Third Ridge would have at least offered a chance, but the rough terrain at Anzac Cove destroyed it.

It is an indication of the magnificence of the Australian effort that they almost succeeded despite the ground, and only the presence of two skilled commanders, first in Sefik Bey of the 27th Regiment and then Mustafa Kemal who finally swung the balance against success.

At Anzac the Navy failed. This was never admitted. In hindsight the ANZAC commanders saw the mistake as a blessing in disguise after the slaughter on V Beach at Helles. But the two landings were different: V Beach and Helles was in broad daylight on a narrow bay with wire covered by rifle fire at each end. On the other hand, Z Beach north of Gaba Tepe had the space to disembark the troops rapidly and was sited clear of the Gaba Tepe defences. The errors in landing were never made an issue of by the Army. The Navy for its part blamed a non-existent current and the midshipmen in charge of the pinnaces. The truth is closer to what Braithwaite recognised in the conferences before the landing: 'The Army naturally wants everything cut and dried, the Navy appears averse to this.'[76] Prior briefings of the pinnace commanders may have played a part but the mistake was primarily due to the Navy being in the wrong place: 'When daylight came,' Captain R.N. Bax of the *Prince of Wales*, which landed part of MacLagan's Covering Force, wrote in his private log, 'we found we had anchored one mile too far to the north.'[77]

Hamilton's plan had succeeded inasmuch as he had his army ashore. In the south at Helles casualties had been heavy, but many of these were due to the inflexibility of Major-General A.G. Hunter-Weston, Commander of the 29th Division. The feint by the Royal Naval Division opposite Bulair had convinced Liman von Sanders that here was the major threat and he kept two divisions on hand to meet it. As part of this diversion a young Lieutenant Commander, Bernard Freyberg of the Hood Battalion of the Royal Naval Division, swam ashore on the night of 25 April and lit flares on the beach to simulate the bivouac fires of disembarked troops.

'After an hour and a quarter hard swimming in bitterly cold water I reached the shore and lighted my first flare and again took to the water and swam towards the east, and landed about 300 yards away, where I lighted my second flare and hid among some bushes to await developments. Nothing happened.'[78] Freyberg would receive a D.S.O. for this exploit. Contrary to popular legend, Freyberg did not serve with the New Zealanders until the Second World War.

Both at ANZAC and Helles there were prospects of success and the attackers greatly out-numbered the initial defenders. However, in both areas Hamilton had not allowed for the Turks' tenacity. Grimly determined to defend their soil, they capitalised on the Navy's errors at ANZAC. At Helles, Hunter-Weston and his subordinates showed no initiative. They got ashore but allowed a much smaller Turkish force to bottle them up. Had the roles been reversed, the Australians would have given Hamilton his objectives of Krithia and Achi Baba by nightfall on the first day. As it was, the failure at ANZAC confirmed the secret impressions of Hamilton, Birdwood and Godley. The Australians and New Zealanders were still 'irregulars' and had been overmatched. In Hamilton's eyes it was now up to his regulars. He wrote to Birdwood: 'Hunter-Weston, despite his heavy losses, will be advancing tomorrow which should divert pressure from you. Make a personal appeal to your men and Godley's to make a supreme effort to hold their ground.

'P.S. You have got through the difficult business, now you only have to dig, dig, dig until you are safe.'[79]

The wrong beach and Turkish tenacity upset all the administrative arrangements. The medical plan was based on a rapid and considerable advance inland and assumed that the wounded would be kept on shore, the most serious cases being evacuated to the Gascon, the sole hospital ship allotted to Birdwood's ANZAC Corps. Field ambulances and the stationary hospitals would be quickly established ashore to receive casualties. Transports had been earmarked for the lightly wounded, but the rough weather and delays at Mudros had prevented these being stocked with supplies and medical staff.

Godley's fears about the hospital arrangements were horribly realised: Lieutenant Colonel P.C. Fenwick was Deputy Assistant Director of Medical Services (DADMS) of Godley's division; he and his superior, Colonel N. Manders, the Assistant Director of Medical Services (ADMS) had landed with divisional headquarters:

'Several dead men were lying on the beach … I moved to the south end to the Clearing Station established by Col. Howse, VC, ADMS 1st Aust. Div. There were numbers of wounded lying here close to the cliff waiting to be sent off to the ships. Every minute the number increased and, as in addition fresh troops came ashore with mules and ammunition, the chaos became appalling. I started to help receive the wounded and got the stretchers stacked close against the cliff. Violent bursts of shrapnel swept over us, and many wounded were hit a second time. Col. Howse was packing boats and lighters with these poor chaps as fast as possible, but the beach kept filling again with appalling quickness. At one time over 400 were lying on the stones waiting to be moved. I dressed as many as I could but it was a dreadful time. The shrapnel never ceased. Later I went some few hundred yards north and opened a Dressing Station with Capt. Craig (Auckland Infantry Battalion). We stopped as many wounded as we could and so lessened the congestion at Col. Howse's station. This state of things lasted all day. It seemed impossible for men to live under the hail of bullets. Capt. Craig dressed over 100 cases under fire. One of his assistants had his finger shot off while helping him. Men were hit constantly in our station and their pluck and devotion in continuing their work under these galling conditions is hopelessly above praise. After dark I got the Naval Transport Officer to give me some boats, and when Craig and I had filled these, a steam pinnace took them off to the ships. At midnight I got four big horse boats, which held twelve stretchers on the bottom and I packed in less severe cases along the sides, sitting, kneeling, lying — anyhow, about 120 all told. I got these four off at last at 1.30, and lay down in the rain at the side of the hill. I certainly was very astonished that I was alive. A more hellish Sunday one could not conceive. Col. Howse told me that he estimated he had evacuated 1500 wounded, to which must be added 120 I got away from my station after midnight, and all I got away in boats during the afternoon.'[80]

By midday, the Australian Casualty Clearing Station had been swamped by the steady stream of wounded moving down the gullies from the firing line. In accordance with instructions, no evacuation of wounded had started until the fighting men were ashore, but by 2.00 p.m. the congestion was so great that barges returning to the ships for further loads of troops took stretchers and walking wounded out to the designated hospital ship and transports for lightly wounded. These were soon crammed with men.

'Steady streams of reinforcements were still arriving in boats and barges of every size and description, but those pushing off again were equally loaded with wounded. Even the most badly injured had to be tipped into the boats without their stretchers which were indispensable ashore and anyhow would have taken the room of six men apiece in the crowded boats. Rows of other wounded were lined along the beach, dumped on a blanket or just on the bare earth or shingle. Those who could move were for the most part cheerfully giving way to more desperate cases, but inevitably there were some who rushed out into the shallows and insisted on clambering aboard the overcrowded boats. They were accepted with contemptuous pity.'[81]

All the arrangements had broken down. There was no time for documentation of wounded; it was a hurried check to see that the field dressing was secure, morphine tablet under the tongue if necessary, and onto the barges. Since many of the transport ships lacked medical personnel and stores, any stretchers sent remained on the ships. So did the medical NCOs sent out with the barges to get them back — they were grabbed by ships and kept to look after the wounded. To get a wounded man from the firing line to the beach was equally difficult. Westmacott was one of the fortunate: 'By this time I could not walk more than a few yards at a time and only very slowly, with assistance, getting up, getting down and staggering along. We now found ourselves over the edge of the steep slope into the gully. Someone said, "It's no good. We'll have to get a stretcher." So they put me down on the ground, where I lay very content with my eyes closed; but feeling the thirst …

'Ward went off and presently returned with a sergeant of the Australian Medical Corps. He cut off the sleeve of my jacket and shirt and bandaged the arm. The bullet had entered the back of it just below the shoulder, shattering the bone and tearing a great hole out in front. The limb dangled. It was still a relief to pull it tight which I did, sitting up, and I felt it was so numb I could have had it off then and there. The sergeant broke some twigs off a bush close by and tied them round the wound, like a splint. For the first time it began to hurt a little as he tied it; but he said it would help me if I could stand it and it was by no means unbearable.

'I asked for some rum to help my thirst, which was, I felt, unquenchable. He had none; But gave me his water bottle full of brandy which bucked me considerably. I now asked him to look at my body wounds which I thought were serious; but they proved not as bad as I thought. Two small shell wounds were nothing; but the bullet wound which knocked me over the second time was a narrow escape, striking near the spine, it had slid, round the left ribs coming out with a large exit on my left side; but doing no permanent damage though I bear a couple of good scars to this day. I now felt much more chirpy thanks, doubtless, to the brandy. They took my jacket off and after emptying the pockets threw it away. I asked them to keep the buttons for me; but they said we could get plenty more. I would have liked them as souvenirs.

'They said it was hard to carry a stretcher down the slope, could I walk to the gully bottom? I said I would try. The sergeant took off one of my puttees, tied it round my neck and slung my arm in it. They stood me up. To the bottom of the gully was about fifty feet I should think, and almost precipitous. I could find foothold like a goat at that time, so used was I to steep country and I reached the bottom in about two spurts, my escort being harder put to it to keep their feet than I was. Collapsing on the soft sand, I lay there on my back whilst the sergeant went for a stretcher. Presently a wounded Hauraki man appeared and sat on the bank beside me. The lower part of his face and jaw were shattered. His eyes looked out of a bloody bandage tied all round his head. Of course he could not speak. Presently, drawing his bayonet, he motioned me to watch, while he wrote with the point in the sand of the bank, "Lieut Morpeth wounded half an hour ago." I felt very pleased, for up to that time I thought I was the only officer of our regiment hit, and felt rather a fool in consequence. The sergeant returned with the stretcher. I had a last drink of brandy and when I returned his water bottle he said, "Do you know Sir that you have drunk all my brandy?" I did feel ashamed of this. Two men lifted me on the stretcher. I was carried up the winding pathway and I do not remember much about it except that we were very slow and sniped at.

'It was dusk as we reached the top of the hill and the landing place was below us. Just over the crest was a small dressing station where they examined my wounds. I asked for brandy and got it. They sent me down the path. I lost my cap here, which

I valued and had clung to all the way. Down the slope, which was crowded with little parties of troops, men were still cutting tracks whilst others were making little shelters to sleep in. Others again were boiling water in their mess tins, heedless of the turmoil and the smoke from countless little fires ascending in thin wisps into the still air. Seawards lay the ships, black hulks upon the still water, while boats of all kinds swirled in with troops who were still disembarking, all along the shore, and picking their way among the wounded, who still lay in rows upon the sand. Overhead still burst the shells, whilst ever and anon came the roll of rifle fire from the hills inland.

'On reaching the beach a surgeon came to my stretcher and asked me about myself. I told him how the sergeant had tied my arm up with twigs, in case it needed further attention. On looking at it the surgeon said, "It is a rough job; but quite a good one. He stopped the bleeding." He examined my other wounds quickly and told me I ought to be all right until under cover when I could be properly attended to. "I tell you what I will do," he went on, "I'll put you on a lighter straight away." There was one lying close to us, on the beach, being filled, at the moment, with wounded. I was hoisted in, two blankets placed over me and what with the day's excitements not forgetting the brandy, was soon fast asleep.

'Some time later I awoke. Darkness was complete by now; but I could see boats on the water and the forms of people moving about on the beach, a light here and there where a surgeon attended his work, and the spark of little fires on the hillside, whilst now and again a shell would burst and illuminate its immediate surroundings in a momentary red glow. Everything was quiet and businesslike. The lighter was towed onto the shore, her nose resting on the sandy beach. A seaman of the Royal Navy was sitting in the bow close to me, and another dimly visible at the stern. The intervening space was crowded with wounded on stretchers and there was an undercurrent of grumbling which I realised from the occasional remarks of one or two lying close to me, though the quiet patience of the men, many of whom

Wounded on the beach at Anzac Cove awaiting evacuation; 'a more hellish Sunday one could not conceive.' *(PS1659-1, Australian War Memorial)*

were suffering, and none crying out. They bore their wounds in silence. Our seaman at the bow was sitting there smoking philosophically, and discussing everyday affairs with one in a lighter lying close to us. I soon got sick of this so I said, "What are we waiting for? Why don't we push off to a hospital ship?"

'Our seaman replied in tones of weariness, "Well Sir, we can't, you see. Both hospital ships have gone to Alexandria. They were full at midday."

'"But," said I, "It will take four or five days to get there and back."

'"Yes Sir," said the seaman. "That is just what it will do," in a tone apparently quite pleased at my mental grasp of the situation.

'"But," said I, "You can't stay here all night." Everyone was listening in the boat now, so I was determined to have local public opinion on my side. "There are wounded men in the boat, and it is going to do them no good lying in the cold like this."

'"Yairs," said a wounded Australian, lifting his voice, "and I'm shot through the bloody belly. It is no good to me stopping out here all night, either."

'"There you are," I continued my oration once more, "Listen to that man. He's shot through the stomach. Just you get us taken on board the first ship you come to whether it is a hospital ship or not. At least we'll be under cover."

'"Well Sir," answered the seaman, "We can't get a tow out."

'"Nonsense!" said I. "Call out to the nearest destroyer or picket boat. Say you are full of wounded and there is an officer here who wants you to be towed out to the nearest ship."

'This was done. Our seaman only needed someone to speak with the voice of authority and after an interval we were made fast to a picket boat and under way. The first ship we came to would not have us, had no doctor on board, they said, and we were towed slowly on, feeling very forlorn, wandering round like a lost dog in the night; but we had more luck at the next ship. We went slowly past the anchor cable and stopped. "Who are you?" they hailed us.

'"Wounded men from the shore. There is no hospital ship. Can you take them aboard? Who are you?" The young naval man in charge of our towing craft spoke for us.

'"*City of Benares* with First Australian Field Ambulance, waiting to land," was the reply.

'"Wait a minute till we see the captain." The interval did not seem long as we drifted on the still dark water, before we were hailed again by the same cheery voice. "All right. Send 'em up."

'It took some time to bring us alongside the ladder. Then it was decided to hoist us up one at a time, and nets and men were sent down, stepping onto the lighter close to me. I said, "Hoist up that chap with the wound in the stomach." But a man leant over me with a lantern and said, "No! We'll hoist up this Briton with the smashed shoulder first." So my stretcher was placed upon a net, and presently I hung between sea and sky, till being lowered on the deck. I was lifted and carried along and finally placed on a table just inside the door of the mess deck of His Majesty's Transport *City of Benares* and my wounded companions of the lighter, to the number of about seventy, were carried in after me, and placed upon the other tables.

'A pleasant faced medical officer visited me. We all received beef tea. I asked if my batman "Fish" whose name was written down, could be signalled for from the *Lutzow* to come over with my kit, and was soon fast asleep.

'So ended the most glorious day of my life.'[82]*

For the wounded on their way to Alexandria, the agony was only just beginning.

Although the *Lutzow* was designated as a hospital ship for 200 seriously, and 1000 slightly, wounded, there were only two medical men aboard: Major A.R. Young, a veterinary surgeon, and a medical orderly, Private O.E. Burton. Together they would deal with a constant stream of wounded, until, with over 300 serious cases on board, they would be reinforced by three doctors, a naval surgeon, and two NZMC officers. By that stage the wounded on board the *Lutzow* had been for 77 hours in the care of the vet and his lone assistant. Finally, with the two NZMC officers and a lone orderly, and still carrying 160 horses, the *Lutzow* sailed for Alexandria at 5.00 p.m. on 27 April 1915. Ormond Burton wrote: 'The voyage was a most dreadful one. The holds were crammed with stretchers. Any able to walk were crowded into cabins or indeed any available space. The doctors improvised an operating theatre where they were able to do the most urgent things and at least get wounds cleanly dressed. They were all I think the equivalent of junior house surgeons who in the ordinary way would never have been allowed to operate except under very close supervision. On the *Lutzow* they tackled the most desperately serious things.

'On the first night I had a hold full of seriously wounded men to myself. Several of them were dying, some with head wounds especially very horribly and painfully. So much needed to be done and so little could be done — fix a bandage here, ease a man over on the hard stretcher, perhaps get him back on it from the deck, a drink, a word here and there, an opiate to some poor chap that he might die more easily. Most of the wounded were very patient and pathetically grateful for the small things possible. Some died in the night.

'In the morning I was given a deck cabin and told to do what I could for all those who were able to come to me. For the next two days while we crossed the Mediterranean the line of men shuffling up never ceased. At least I was able to keep wounds fairly clean and in some cases to make things more comfortable. I hope I did not do very much damage but consultation with the doctors was almost impossible as they were at the point of exhaustion. I suppose the fact that we were at least trying to do something kept up the courage of many. For three full days I do not think I had more than two or three hours' sleep. It was a marvellous relief to get our patients ashore at Alexandria and to know that they were going direct to properly equipped hospitals.'[83]

Private Tony Fagan, of the Auckland Battalion, was evacuated to the *Seeangbee*. 'We arrived at this Japanese boat, the *Seeangbee* and my stretcher was lifted up by the ship's winch and I was lowered through the forward hatch which had no cover over it, onto the deck below which had been a Mess Room. There were two doctors for, I

---

* Spencer Westmacott would lose his arm but recover to serve on Major General Sir Andrew Russell's staff in France.

was told, 600 wounded men on that boat, two doctors, no nurses, no medical orderlies and there we lay. I wasn't even touched all the way to Alexandria. I don't know how long it was, it may have been four nights, it may have been five, one didn't know. I could hear the watch above me, in the crow's nest, singing out in Japanese. I suppose the equivalent to "All's well" every hour. I lay there without any attention at all with all these bandages around me and it began to be a bit nasty by the time we arrived in Alexandria. Alongside me there was a poor Aussie boy who had been shot in the head and had bandages all around his head and blood that trickled down and he was more or less delirious and every now and again he would stumble to his feet and wave a trenching tool handle and shout out, "Kill the bastards!" and then he would fall over and I was very frightened he would fall on me but he didn't and eventually in what I took to be a sane moment, he said to me in a hoarse voice, "Have you got a pencil cobber?" I didn't have a pencil, I couldn't have got one anyhow but somebody gave him a pencil assuming I suppose that he might want to write goodbye to somebody but all the poor fellow wanted it for was to lever the bandages up from his head because they had become too tight and his face was smeared with mucus and stuff, it was horrible really.'[84]

The shiploads of wounded swamped the hospital facilities in Egypt. It was the first indication of the extent of the casualties. Accurate New Zealand losses of the first day are not known. 'I am afraid it will be impossible to send accurate casualty lists for some

New Zealand wounded from the Dardanelles. *(WF-002083-51 –p4a, Charters Album, NAM)*

time, as platoons, companies and battalions were so hopelessly mixed up, not only amongst themselves but also with the Australians, that it is impossible to tell whether many of the men missing are really killed or not, some keep dribbling in, even now.'[85]

It would be three days before battalions could give an estimate of casualties to the Infantry Brigade headquarters. The *War Diary* has a cryptic entry: 'considerable difficulty in getting casualty states'. By the morning of the 29th, New Zealand casualties had been reported as 517 officers and men, not including 'missing'. A fortnight later a meeting was called at Brigade to sort out casualties as there were still 200 men not accounted for, over and above those reported. It was impossible: 'The battle has been continuous since we landed … This is certainly a far bigger job than anyone thought it was going to be.'[86] Men were too busy holding the ANZAC perimeter to worry about who had died the day before — mates were joining them every day.

However, it is likely that New Zealand casualties on 25 April were between 600 and 700, primarily off the *Lutzow*. The official estimates compiled after the war listed New Zealand casualties from 25–30 April 1915 as approximately 372 dead and 703 wounded and missing, a total of 1075, the majority from the first day.

The Auckland Battalion had the most serious losses. Sixteen of its 28 officers were killed or wounded. In the 16th Waikatos Sergeant Ward was the sole surviving senior N.C.O.; all the officers were casualties. On the 26th he was directed by Colonel Plugge 'to get together all the 16th [Waikato] men I could find and let [Plugge] know how many had survived. I was awfully busy and still very tired but found only 34 men of our 226 in the company.'[87] Thirty more struggled in the next day. Finally, 64 survivors were assembled. Losses were 122 killed and wounded, and 37 missing. None of the missing was ever accounted for. The 6th Haurakis had suffered almost as heavily.*

With so many officers and senior NCOs wounded, the reported fate of casualties depended on what the survivors remembered of that confusing day. For example Private Arthur Cowdray, who had been killed at Westmacott's side, was seen to have fallen but was reported wounded along with his brother Ned. This report was sent back from Egypt to New Zealand on 16 May 1915. Only months later, when a search of hospitals in Egypt, Malta, Gibraltar and England failed to find Private Cowdray, would he be posted on 20 July 1915 as 'Wounded and Missing'. Finally in January 1916, with Gallipoli evacuated, he would be posted 'Now Reported Believed Dead 25 April 1915'.

This was not an isolated case. Baddeley, Westmacott's fellow platoon commander, Couston, Dove, Dawson, Frank, Furze, Laurence, Manning, Meekan and Rutland were some of those of the Auckland Battalion, first posted as wounded, then wounded and missing, and finally 'believed dead'. It happened in every battalion. Men lying in the scrub would see a mate fall wounded, and then laboriously crawl back towards the beach. Later when the line had been driven back, they would report him wounded, little realising that he still lay unseen in the scrub on the slopes of Baby 700.

He would remain there, to be bayoneted when the Turks reoccupied the hill. This

---

* O.E. Burton in *The Auckland Battalion* lists the battalion casualties as 78 KIA and 220 WIA, a total of 298.

Beach Cemetery at Anzac. In use from the first day, the cemetery was below Hell Spit and could be seen from the Turkish positions at Gaba Tepe to the south, so all burials were conducted by night. *(NAM Waiouru)*

was common practice on both sides in those first bitter days. Only one New Zealander was taken prisoner on 25 April 1915. This was Private T.H. Burgess of the Auckland Battalion, who died in captivity from his wounds on 25 September 1915.[*]

Most of the New Zealanders killed at Gallipoli have no known graves. Like those that fell on the first day they remained forward of the ANZAC front line. It would be 1919 before New Zealanders would again walk on the slopes of Baby 700. Then, as today, one could ponder on the bones lying scattered among the thorn.

Newspapers in New Zealand broke the news of the Dardanelles landings on 29 April.

FIGHT AT DARDANELLES

It is officially announced that allied troops have been landed on both the Asiatic and European sides of the Dardanelles. The troops landed on the Gallipoli Peninsula have been engaged in hard fighting but are thoroughly making good their footing with the help of the fleet. [88]

---

[*] '12/705 Pte T.H. Burgess. Died Tash Kushla Hospital 25 Sept. 1915. Pte W.J. Surgenor, captured 8 August 1915, saw Burgess before he died. 'He lay there for three days. Every Turk who walked past him clubbed or bayoneted him. Then some stretcher bearers picked him up and he was taken to a camp.'[89]

Gallipoli casualties on the crowded deck of a hospital ship , which also swamped hospital facilities in Egypt. Warehouses and skating rinks were used as hospital wards. *(P02194.001, Australian War Memorial)*

On 30 April, 'the King congratulates splendid conduct and bravery displayed by New Zealand troops'. On 3 May the first reports of casualties appeared. These reported two officers wounded, and in addition private cables notified relatives of a further five wounded.

The first official lists were published on 4–5 May. They reported eight officers killed in action, two officers dead from wounds, 19 officers and 107 men wounded. These were made up from reports cabled back from the New Zealand Base Depot in Egypt. Here, New Zealand staff met the hospital ships as they arrived and compiled the cables for New Zealand. Captain Norman Fitzherbert, the officer in charge of the New Zealand Records Section, wrote of the difficulties he had in compiling the casualty lists: 'The wounded are at once put on the nearest available ship and brought to Alexandria (48 hours steam). Immediately on arrival they are met by a number of motor ambulances and a Hospital train … The motor ambulances are used for distributing to the various hospitals in and around Alexandria. The train is filled and sent to the hospitals at Cairo and Zeitoun.

'Two or more ships have, after calling here, gone straight on to England with wounded cases.

'The first official intimation of casualties is from a list sent by medical officer in charge of each ship on arrival, this list in a great many cases not giving any particulars of wounded, and giving no information as to which hospital men are being sent. From this list my cable to you is made out. I am thus obliged to wait for the returns from the various hospitals before I can record the nature of the wound and the name of the hospital to which the man has been sent. This return I usually receive in the course of a few days or possibly a week.'[90]

Fitzherbert went on to stress that additional information on wounded would only be sent if the person's condition worsened.

All this information concerned only the wounded who had arrived in Egypt or who were known to have died of wounds on the voyage from Gallipoli. Lists of dead, other than the officers, had not been made out by the still disorganised battalions.

In New Zealand, there were already disquieting undercurrents. The first wounded to reach Egypt sent private cables home to inform parents and next of kin. In many cases cables were received from men not yet reported wounded, or cables mentioned other men killed and wounded who had not yet been reported in New Zealand. The Defence Department and the government were inundated with inquiries from anxious parents and relatives. On 4 May the Prime Minister reassured the country: 'You can assure the public that no news has come through with which they have not been made acquainted and I deprecate the mischievous rumours which have been put into circulation.'[91]

Massey promised that the Defence Department would announce casualties whenever the cables were received. First a telegram would be sent to the next of kin, and half an hour later the details would be released to the press: 'This system would be strictly adhered to and the public are warned not to believe reports from any other sources.'[92]

Major Frederick Stuckey. Died of wounds, 25 April 1915. *(NZ Herald)*[93]

MAJOR STUCKEY'S FATE.

NO TRACE DISCOVERED.

Efforts to discover the fate of Major F. Stuckey, who was reported on May 4 to have been seriously wounded, have not yet resulted in conclusive information. Major Stuckey was in command of the 6th, Hauraki, Company, and the anxiety of his friends has been increased by statements in letters written by members of that company, either that Major Stuckey was killed in action or died of wounds. A further inquiry was sent by a friend in Auckland to Colonel A. B. Charters, officer commanding the New Zealand base camp in Egypt. The following reply has been received :— "Major Stuckey reported wounded, but no trace in hospitals, Egypt, Malta, England, and can get absolutely no other information from front or elsewhere."

Although the officials at the base evidently have no knowledge of the present whereabouts of Major Stuckey, he has not been officially reported "missing." In fact, less that a fortnight ago, his mother, who resides in Nelson, was officially informed that he was "progressing favourably.

On 5 May, Massey spoke at Otorohanga, where there was widespread interest at an apparently disproportionate number of casualties among the Waikato officers. He referred to the current anxiety at the absence of a complete list of casualties. He read a cable that did little to reassure his audience. 'Only a few particulars as to the killed have yet been received. We are working at high pressure.'[94]

On the same day the national dailies reported that 'a conviction was secured against Isabella Margaret Morpeth of Picton Street', Auckland. She had sent a 'misleading telegram' contrary to the War Regulations Act of 1914. In it she had cabled her aunt, who had two nephews at the Dardanelles, 'Plugge and 700 New Zealanders killed', which she had overheard from a gentleman in the street. The Defence Department stated such prosecutions were necessary to 'stop a prevalent and most deplorable practice'.[95]

Each private cable and then the letters home became ripples in an increasingly disturbed pond. By mid-May the casualties published in New Zealand totalled 1162: 76 men killed or dead from wounds, four dead from disease, two missing and 1080 wounded. At Anzac Cove, New Zealand casualties were already double that figure.

Private cables continued to arrive and the growing demand for information could not be quelled. Almost every day items appeared reassuring people that everything possible was being done to tell them all the casualties: 'With reference to your telegram of May 2. I am informed that the lists of wounded who have arrived in Egypt are despatched duly when checked. No lists of the killed in action except the officers had

New Zealand's response. Pride, recruits and a surge of public patriotism. *(Wilson & Horton)*

THE LANDING.

A STIRRING STORY.

HOW THE AUSTRALASIANS GAINED A FOOTING AT THE DARDANELLES.

"NO FINER FEAT IN THE WAR."

OPERATIONS PROCEEDING SUCCESSFULLY.

FURTHER LIST OF NEW ZEALAND CASUALTIES.

Mr Asquith made a speech in the House of Commons describing the landing and subsequent operations of the Allies at the Dardanelles. He referred to the dash with which the Australians and New Zealanders carried a position and pushed the attack forward and said that operations were being continued and pressed on under highly satisfactory conditions. Mr Ashmead-Bartlett, who was an eye-witness of the landing of the Australasian forces, vividly describes the gallantry with which they captured and maintained positions in the face of incessant shrapnel fire. He expresses admiration of the courage of the wounded and says that there has been no finer feat in this war than the sudden landing in the dark and storming the heights, above all holding on while reinforcements were landing. A further list of casualties among the New Zealanders came to hand yesterday.

Ashmead Bartlett's despatches. Headlines, *The Lyttelton Times*, Saturday 8 May 1915.[96]

reached Egypt on May 5th. The lists of wounded are not cabled from the front owing to the difficulties but are made on the arrival of the ships.'[97]

On 19 May the Governor's assurance was given in a speech to St Johns Ambulance in Auckland: 'But I do want to dispel the idea that everything is not being done to give you the true "facts of the case".'[98]

The feeling grew that the casualties were so bad the government was holding the true figures back. In every district telegrams were arriving: 'We regret to inform you that Private … has been wounded in action at the Dardanelles.'

Parents anxiously waited for more news, and were assured by the government and the Defence Department that further details would be sent and that 'no news was good news'. This backfired when, for the first time, men previously reported wounded were now said to be missing.

Anguish was mixed with pride. On 8 May papers published Ashmead Bartlett's despatches giving a full account of the landings. It carried around the world the story of the landing in the dawn by the Australians and New Zealanders. It eclipsed the efforts of the other nations at Gallipoli. From now on the ANZAC legend had centre stage.

So, New Zealand believed that their brave sons landed with the Australians before the dawn of ANZAC Day. It is a legend that persists to this day. And it is legend. Godley wrote to Allen: 'In Ashmead Bartlett's letter which you read with such interest the words "New Zealand" and "New Zealanders" was not once used from start to finish by him. Fortunately before his letter was despatched, it fell into the hands of the Admiral's Chief of Staff, who is a friend of mine, and who inserted the words wherever necessary.'[99]

6

HANGING ON

It's a — failure, but we can't chuck it.
Fenwick diary

Yesterday was a day in a lifetime. The infantry, Australians and New Zealanders, suffered pretty heavily having no artillery to shell the enemies' guns although the fleet shelled them heavily. Shrapnel and snipers very active. A few casualties on beach. Felt pretty funky at first but am getting over it.'[1]

On 26 April, the sky paled and the sun rose above the still Turkish-held heights of Chunuk Bair. The dawn was greeted by the clink of pick and spade, and the crack of rifles once again rose to a crescendo. The bush-covered slopes above the bay looked like an overnight goldrush town. It had been raining, and ground sheets and greatcoats lay over bushes as men dug alongside or sprawled under them asleep. Everywhere was the debris of battle: packs open with the contents trodden into the mud scattered by men searching for food and water during the night, letters and papers fluttering on the beach, and all up the slopes the smoke from hundreds of billy fires as men had the first brew of the day.

In the gully above the cove, anxious staff officers of the ANZAC listened for the crump of Turkish artillery that would signal the beginnings of the Turkish counter-attack to drive them into the sea. Instead they heard the bark of two field howitzers of the 4th (Howitzer) Battery of the New Zealand Field Artillery (NZFA). Gunner J.D. Hutchison manned one of the guns. 'Got ashore by daybreak, leaving most of the horses and drivers on board. Dragged the guns into scrub just off the beach. Concealed them with scrub and built sandbag wall.'[2]

'The first round, fired at ten minutes to seven, was sent into the "blue" at a range of 3000 yards … and an involuntary cheer went up from the hillside at the welcome sound.'

It was music to the ears of the battle-weary men in the firing line.'[3] It was also the first time the Howitzer Battery gunners had ever fired live ammunition.

After the high hopes of the previous day, Godley and Bridges' divisions were now besieged in this tenuous beachhead on Turkish soil. Exhausted men dug in, and waited for the relief promised by Hunter-Weston's advance from the south. Godley wrote: 'We

Digging in below the Sphinx. The ANZAC perimeter looked like an overnight goldrush town. *(WF-002083-68-p8b, Charters Album, NAM Waiouru)*

Landing the guns, 26 April 1915. *(WF-002082-10, Deans Album, NAM Waiouru)*

are now just holding on, trying to reorganise and getting the dead-beat men replaced in the trenches by others not so done … The beach is like Margate! Crammed with stores, donkeys, mules, marines, Jew Mule Corps men, Australians, New Zealanders, Indians and all sorts.'[4]

All of the New Zealand Infantry were ashore as the last of the Wellington Infantry landed from the *Achaia.*[*]

George Bollinger was one of them. 'Am still standing by, rain has set in. The battle on shore never ceases and the ridge of the hills in front of us resembles the twinkling lights of a distant city for hundreds of yards with the flash from the Turkish rifles … 3.50 a.m. "Packs on!" was roared out. Torpedo destroyers are alongside to take us ashore. 9.40 a.m. On shore in the thick of it. The first casualty in our Coy was in my Section … Stray bullets were landing around us and suddenly Pte Tohill who was standing just in front of me dropped with a bullet through his shoulder. Immediately after Pte Swayne was shot in the forehead. It was a relief to get ashore.'[5]

It was a statement Bollinger would soon question. The Wellingtons joined the rest of their battalion and the Otagos at Plugge's Plateau overlooking the beach. 'Violently shelled all day and bullets were falling around and whistling by continuously. Everyone soon becomes accustomed to them however, except "Paddy" the regimental pet. Had six men killed and 30 wounded during the day. There is no flat land. Men are buried anywhere and the whole place is covered with graves, usually marked with a small cross of boards from biscuit boxes.'[6]

---

[*] Some 5100 New Zealanders had landed by 1 May 1915. The remaining 1200 New Zealanders on the transports, drivers, grooms and boatmen, returned with the transports carrying wounded to Egypt.

Above this narrow beach, 'already piled up with ammunition, water in tins, and tanks, stores, troops landing, dressing stations and wounded being re-embarked,'[7] Bridges, Godley and Birdwood established their Divisional and Corps headquarters. They were all crammed into the mouth of a narrow gully, cut as a step into the seaward face of Plugge's Plateau. It reflected the plight of their men around them. There were three headquarters of the corps, within 100 metres of each other, perhaps 100 metres from the beach, and no more than 700–1000 metres to the farthest point inland of their front line.

Perhaps never in history had 20,000 men been wedged in such a small area of inhospitable ground. The perimeter stretched like two arms of a triangle. The northern arm ran from the beach below Walker's Ridge, up its eroded clay slopes onto Russell's Top, then up First Ridge to Baby 700. Short of Baby 700 it joined the second arm as a dotted line of outposts at the head of Monash Gully. The second arm ran from the beach some 1400 metres south of ANZAC Cove up Bolton's Ridge, a finger spur on the seaward side of 400' (Lone Pine) Plateau, across the edge of the Plateau and along the crest of Second Ridge, ending in Dawson's position at Quinn's. It encompassed some 2500 metres of coastline, and followed a ragged perimeter along First and Second ridges of some 4000 metres from beach to beach. The farthest-advanced post at Quinn's was some 1200 metres from the sea.

The natural apex of this triangle was Baby 700 and this the Turks held. Without Baby 700 in Birdwood's possession, it seemed impossible to hold the beachhead. From Baby 700 the Turkish sniper could fire down the length of Monash Gully, the main communication way. Already snipers were infiltrating across The Nek and firing into the backs of men holding the posts along Second Ridge. From Baby 700 it was possible to see along the length of Second Ridge as far as the 400' Plateau. Down First Ridge, The Nek, along the length of Russell's Top and the top of Plugge's Plateau could also be seen. Everywhere in the ANZAC perimeter was overlooked.

They were also hemmed in on the coast. From the south at Gaba Tepe, Turkish observers could see the coastline along to the southern headland of ANZAC Cove. The northern headland, Ari Burnu, and part of the beach inside the cove were also visible. From the north at Nibrunesi Point the sweep of the beach south to Ari Burnu was open to Turkish observation and fire.

The ANZACs were trapped. That morning the Turkish commander, Mustafa Kemal, knew he had stopped the invader. It was now a matter of driving him into the sea.

'There is no going back a single step. It is our duty to save our country, and we must acquit ourselves honourably and nobly. I must remind all of you that to seek rest and comfort now is to deprive the nation of its rest and comfort for ever. I have no doubts of your courage. I know that until the enemy is hurled back into the sea not one of you will show signs of weakness.'[8]

Kemal's battalions were as exhausted and disorganised as their opponents. They, like the ANZACs, had been committed piecemeal all through 25 April and into the night. Savage unrecorded battles spluttered all along the perimeter, but while the ANZACs could not break out, Kemal's men also missed opportunities to break in —

A 4.5-inch howitzer of the 4th (Howitzer) Battery. New Zealand Field Artillery at the mouth of Howitzer Gully, above Anzac Cove. Initially, these were the only howitzers at Anzac and played an essential part in keeping the Turks out. Ammunition was in short supply and at times firing was restricted to two rounds per day. *(PAColl-0914-1-04-2, Alexander Turnbull Library)*

Approaching Anzac Cove, a steam pinnace, having dropped its strings of boats, moves out to make way for the next string coming in — a continual stream of troops being landed, and wounded being re-embarked. *(E.B. Paterson Collection — PAColl-0914-1, Morison Collection, Alexander Turnbull Library)*

the opposing forces leaned against each other like two punch-drunk fighters along the line of Second Ridge.

The Turks were unaware that Russell's Top was open to them, and a 300 metre advance here would bring them to the Sphinx and destroy the ANZAC line. Equally, in the south of the line, Bridges' exhausted Australians did not realise that the 400' Plateau was unoccupied. Had this been gained then the five finger spurs falling away to the south towards Gaba Tepe would have been under Australian control and Gaba Tepe itself would have been vulnerable.

On the left, the steep razorback spur of Walker's Ridge had been held overnight by Braund's 2nd Australian Battalion as well as New Zealand remnants of the first day's battle. They held the junction of Walker's Ridge where it linked up with Russell's Top, but Russell's Top itself was deserted; a gap lay between Braund and Pope's 16th Australian Battalion at the top of Monash Gully. Fighting above ANZAC Cove in late April 1915 would be similar to fighting today on the gorse- and scrub-covered slopes around Wellington Harbour and the Hutt. It 'was very thick and stood about 5ft high and was of a laurel leaf type very like "Tote" that is found in New Zealand.'[9] It was in such scrub that the ANZACs laid in their coffin trenches. They could see 10–20 metres, perhaps 60 metres in places where animal tracks ran down through the growth. Somewhere across the Plateau and over the gully from them was the ANZAC line on Second Ridge. No one knew where; to look was to court a sniper's bullet. All they could see, in the distance, was the crestline rising in the haze towards Chunuk Bair.

That morning Birdwood divided the line between Godley's NZ & A Division and Bridges' Australians. For the first time, Godley assumed command of his New Zealanders in battle. He was given the left flank from the beach up Walker's Ridge and the head of Monash Gully at Quinn's and Courtney's posts. Godley divided his front and gave Walker's New Zealand Infantry Brigade the responsibility for establishing outposts on the coast to protect the beach, and for garrisoning Walker's Ridge. Monash's 4th Australian Brigade would garrison Pope's and hold the head of Monash Gully at Quinn's and Courtney's. Godley conferred with Walker and determined that the Canterbury Battalion under Major A.E. Loach, the Second-in-Command who had succeeded Stewart, would reinforce Braund's men on Walker's Ridge. Already part of the Canterburys was garrisoning the lower slopes, and elements of the 12th Nelson Company had reached Braund's party during the night.

The scattered Aucklanders would be relieved and brought back onto Plugge's to reorganise, the Wellingtons would remain in reserve on Plugge's, less Brunt's Taranakis at Pope's, and the Otagos would be sent forward to link up between Braund's position and Pope's. On Walker's Ridge, Braund's men had fought themselves out. His tenacity on the night of 25–26th had ensured the survival of the ANZAC line. Now he and his men were asleep on their feet. Many of his officers and NCOs had been killed and wounded. During the night he had been everywhere and everything. He had rallied his thinning line and fought off the repeated Turkish probes with bayonet charges into the bush and constant fusillades of fire. For 24 hours, his men had met every Turkish advance with an advance of their own. They had held the line, but no action had been taken to dig in and consolidate the position. It was too much for tired men to dig, and Braund had not the subordinate commanders left to urge them. In the comparative quiet of the morning they slumped in their scrapes of earth 'weary to the point of exhaustion'. The Turks ceased to be important, and the sentries had to be continually prodded awake.

Brereton's Nelson Company had found his scouts, and joined Braund's party: 'We began to dig in where we were. The ground was very hard but our lives depended on it, and although we had only the entrenching tool, we got down slowly. We realised that picks and shovels are very important weapons to carry into action, almost as valuable as rifles ... I spent most of the night listening to the yarn of an Australian private who ... explained very shrewdly why they had lost so many men that day, putting it down to not digging enough cover and drawing fire by moving and talking too much.'[10]

A dangerous lethargy was evident all along the line. With so many officers and NCOs dead, the isolated ANZAC parties dozed as they kept watch. By contrast, Kemal's commanders deployed snipers to harass the ANZAC line and pushed men forward. The isolated outposts forward of the main ANZAC line on the inland slopes of Second Ridge were gradually eliminated by Turkish fire or withdrew as lack of water forced survivors to retire.

Men scrape 'coffin' holes on the ridges above Anzac Cove, and peer into the metre-high scrub that was gradually cut away by the constant stream of bullets. Harold Arthur McCoy, aged 44, of 1st Canterbury Company, is smoking the pipe. He was mortally wounded at Helles on 8 May 1915, and died two days later. *(Judge Gresson Collection – PAColl-3603-12, Alexander Turnbull Library)*

In the tangle of gullies at the head of Monash Gully, it was impossible to establish who was ANZAC and who was Turk. Pope's party on the spur at the head of Monash did not know Jacob was in front some 50 metres away on the next spur, and no doubt fired at their own men during the night of the 25th. It was the same at Quinn's; Dawson's men were fired on by Turks and ANZACs and the fire from the rear became so heavy he withdrew into the gully.

Here they met up with Jacob's party, which had also pulled back. It was Jacob who reoccupied Quinn's Post, taking Dawson's men with him while Dawson reported back to Plugge, his battalion commander.

The next niche in the crest south on Second Ridge was held by a party of New Zealanders. This was Major G. Mitchell and the 10th North Otagos. They had been sent forward in the early hours of the 26th and occupied this gap in the Australian line: 'During this and following nights, when the bayonets of the Turks shone in the moonlight from the scrub 20 yards from Courtney's Post, the Australian line at that point constantly charged or made feints of charging. But with two sides at such close quarters in the dark, nothing but the intensity of the fire can have prevented the Turks from streaming over the Australian posts, isolated and half-surrounded as they were on their narrow foothill at the valley's edge.'[11]

Warrant Officer Porteous, who won the Military Cross for his action at Courtney's, noted in his diary: 'Turkish guns bombarding our position from daylight until dark. Then after dark attacking by bayonet charges.' The 10th Otagos had 13 killed and 20 wounded. It was the Turkish snipers who were 'quite annoying'.[12]

Behind the lines, Plugge's Plateau was being developed as a last bastion to protect the beach if the perimeter should fall. It was here that Plugge's Aucklanders gathered: 'Sinel came in looking a wreck, mud-stained and with a twisted ankle and reports a frightful time where he was. Major Stuckey severely wounded is on the hospital ship; likewise Morpeth. Flower and Dodson are both dead … We are to stay in reserve today and endeavour to collect the Auckland Battalion which has been pretty hard hit … From all accounts there is about half of it left … All day Hauraki men have been coming in by ones and twos from all quarters. They have been mixed up with Australians and other battalions all over the place … '[13]

Lieutenant Colonel Arthur Plugge commanding the Auckland Battalion with his adjutant, in the trenches during the first days ashore. *(WW1 Photographic Collection A.A. Perry Negatives, Auckland War Memorial Museum)*

By Tuesday 27 April, Algie recorded that 99 men of the Haurakis had reported in, of the 227 that had landed.

The South Canterburys were also badly shaken and dispersed. Sergeant A.T. Morris joined them: 'Eventually I learnt that my company, or rather what was left of it, had assembled near the beach on the left flank, so away I went wondering how many I would find. Here and there I met one or two as I strode along. You should have heard the various greetings and inquiries concerning their pals. Yet it was awful. On my arrival about half a company left, eagerly looking forward for a pal who in most cases, did not turn up.'[14]

They talked of the events of 25 April and every word was praise for the Australians and the stretcher bearers: 'I don't know how they do it. Four of us carried a pal down from the trenches, and we were just dead beat, yet two of these chaps carried wounded all day.'[15]

Unknowingly, life within the perimeter was assuming a pattern that would make it unique. 'In a few days our clothes were in an extraordinary state of rips and tears. The seat of our pants looked as if we spent the time sliding down hill in a sitting

The Auckland Battalion crammed into the trenches during the first days ashore. 'From all accounts there is about half of it left.' *(WW1 Photographic Collection A.A. Perry Negatives, Auckland War Memorial Museum)*

position. Everyone was in the same state and senior officers went about with shirt tails showing.'[16]

Algie of the Hauraki's wrote: 'Our diet for the last three days has been bully beef, biscuit and water. We have not had a wash since we landed but Sinel and I managed to have a shave this morning using a tin lid for a glass. The Colonel caught us in the act and thought it a great joke.'[17] Water was so scarce that washing and shaving for the men were forgotten luxuries. All water had to be pumped ashore by barge and was strictly rationed, with sentries standing guard on the five tanks by the beach. 'Sometimes it runs short, three tanks being riddled by shrapnel by enemy. Almost every day mules get killed by shrapnel. Enemy have range of beach to a nicety and damned if we can locate them!'[18]

There were no safe areas. Snipers made all movement risky along Monash Gully, and shrapnel threatened to cut the lifeline over the beach by day as Fenwick noted: 'The firing is still incessant. Not five seconds interval between shots all day. At sunset we got our usual dose of shrapnel, and it was lively for a time. The beach is so crammed that it is marvellous we don't lose more. At night the whole hillside is lit up with tiny lights — fires and candles in dug-outs. The whole hill is riddled with "funk holes" dug by the men and this is the only thing that has saved us.'[19]

Lack of water, lack of space, monotony of food, all gave warnings of problems to come. Men risked shrapnel to bath in the sea, for already the local inhabitants had introduced themselves: 'We have fleas, lice and ticks now, and Capt Sinclair is fixing tubs of disinfectant on the beach for the men to soak their underclothes in. Our sanitary arrangements are fair. The whole hillside is a rabbit warren of dug-outs, and

Henderson and his donkey. This photograph was used as the model for Horace Moore-Jones' painting of John Simpson Kirkpatrick and his donkey, Murphy. Simpson evacuated wounded from the front line down Shrapnel Valley, and became a symbol of all the bravery of the stretcher-bearers. 'Has the bloke with the donk stopped one yet?' was the constant query. He did on 19 May 1915. Henderson was one of a number of New Zealanders at Anzac doing similar work. *(AG-577/023 – James Gardner Jackson, Hocken Library)*

it is quite impossible to use any part of the hill. I suggested that the only safe way was to use the water's edge at low tide, and this has been done. All the same, most men had constipation for the first few days, as the bowels refused to act under the nerve shock of shelling. A few cases of diarrhoea occurred but not true dysentery … The numbers of dead Turks are a menace as the smell is already getting very severe near the trenches. The sun is excessively hot after 12 and headaches are common. At nightfall the evenings are cold, cold enough to keep you awake.'[20]

Nightfall brought welcome relief. Turkish artillery fire stopped as observers could not see targets. 'Dawn and evening are wonderful times here in Gallipoli. In the evening the sun sinks golden behind Imbros Island, tinting its outline from hilltop to coastline a soft lemon tint, whilst all the sea and sky are a soft peaceful grey, or rather bluey-grey shade, swathed in peace and stillness, no ripple on the sea, and no cloud in the sky.'[21]

Braund's men on Walker's Ridge had no appreciation for such a dawn on 27 April. They craved sleep and relief. This day was going to see the next major crisis since the night of the landing. Kemal's 19th Division had been attacking piecemeal since the 25th. He had been reinforced with two fresh regiments and planned to drive the invaders into the sea. He would attack with two regiments from Baby 700 across The Nek and onto Braund's and the Canterbury line on Russell's Top and Walker's Ridge. If successful this would rip open the left of the ANZAC line, exposing the length of Second Ridge to Turkish fire from the rear.

'At daylight this morning a terrific artillery duel raged. The Turks put hundreds of shells onto our landing place … '[22] Braund's line came under pressure as the unseen Turks started firing from Baby 700 and infiltrating forward across The Nek. His reaction was as it had been for the previous two days — to charge and drive the enemy back. His men left their trenches and ran forward. Many were cut down, many went to ground to avoid the fire; men filtered back wounded or afraid. Braund, his command disintegrating around him, called for reinforcements.

Brigadier General Walker had established his headquarters on the centre slope of Walker's Ridge. He committed the Wellington Battalion from Plugge's Plateau to Braund's assistance. Malone, the Commanding Officer, recorded: 'Away we went. Arrived at the foot of the ridge, found General Walker and heard a roar for reinforcements coming down the hill … General Walker told us to send up a company at once, packs to be left at the bottom. 'I enquired what they were to do? where to go? and what was the position? I was told they would be met at the top and put right. So away they went.'[23]

The Wellington West Coast Company was sent first, followed after more cries for reinforcements by Hawke's Bay. The engineer Charles Saunders went with them: 'We started up the ridge following what might have been a big goat or sheep track, with scrub on either side and very steep in places … My, how I did perspire and pant, it was awful, and as we passed up a continuous stream of wounded were coming down. The wounded were carried in stretchers, which were very few, overcoats, waterproof ground sheets, anything in fact, and as we passed them we could hear, "Good lad, give the buggers one for me" or "Go for them, mate" … All the time we were passing back orders by word of mouth, such as, "Water for the trenches." "Water for machine guns at the double." "Reinforcements wanted." "Reinforcements at the double." "Ammunition at the double." "More reinforcements at the double." "At the double."

'No one will ever know what "Walker's Ridge" meant that bloody Tuesday unless he was there.'[24]

At the top they joined the Australian line and charged forward. All was confusion and despite the constant fire whipping through the bushes, very few Turks could be seen as Major Hart, Second-in-Command of the Wellingtons, described. 'Before the last men of the leading company were in the firing line, many of the first men were back again wounded … The bullets were falling on our position like water out of a hose and we had little protection as the Turks occupied other higher ridges on our left and on "our front".'[25]

Braund had advanced to where the plateau narrowed, and the 500 New Zealanders with the Australians were crowded into an area some 80–100 metres wide. They found themselves too densely packed and suffered needlessly from Turkish fire. George Bollinger was with them. 'On we rushed against a rain of bullets and our men began to drop before they fired a shot. We started to get mixed and were everywhere amongst the Australians. Our men were dropped in hundreds.'[26]

At the top no one had a clear idea what was happening and at the foot of Walker's Ridge an increasingly furious Malone objected to the piecemeal commitment of his battalion. He moved the remainder of his men about halfway up the ridge in reserve. To more yells for reinforcements, Malone went forward to find out the situation for himself. He met Colonel Braund on the top of the ridge.

'He didn't know and knew nothing. Had no defensive position and no plan, nothing but a murderous notion that the only thing to do was to plunge troops out of the neck of the ridge into the jungle beyond.

'The Turks were lying down, shooting down all the bits of track that led from the ridge inland … and dropping our men wholesale.'[27]

It was this confusion and constant firing that the men remembered most about this day. Dan Curham was one of the Wellington machine-gunners. 'An order came down, "Machine guns to the front!" We clambered up that hill puffing and panting, by the time we got to the top we were really breathless. And then because of our ignorance, and because we had been called up, the machine gun was taken right forward into the open among the scrub facing the Turks. Our officer was killed in the first few seconds, one sergeant was killed and the other was wounded, all within the space of a minute or two. Both corporals killed and the guns never came into action. We had to come back and leave the guns there with men being killed all around us.'[28]

The men forward on Russell's Top were soon lost from each other in the brush, hugging the ground to avoid the incessant firing. Towards the late afternoon, those on the left saw wave after wave of Turkish soldiers advancing over the seaward slopes of Battleship Hill and Baby 700. Nerves were at breaking point, and men started filtering back out of the firing line. Suddenly it became a rush, and men came tumbling back through the scrub. Saunders had brought his Engineers up to help the Infantry dig in: 'Suddenly crowds of infantry, New Zealanders and Australians, jumped in over the parapet of the trench onto the wounded, shouting, "Down the hill boys, the Turks are onto us in droves." Had there been a clear field to run I think perhaps I would have. I felt very nervous, but I could not picture myself going back down that hill and the Turks lying over the edge on top, picking us off like flies. Luckily we sappers were blocking the track … and the cries of the wounded all helped, so I shouted out: "You can't get down the hill for reinforcements coming up. We're the first of them." I got the sappers to "fix bayonets" and out of the trench we jumped. Those who had come in came back with us and we went for the Turks and drove them back at the point of the bayonet.'[29]

Men can also remember Braund standing in the path of those running back, threatening to put a bullet into them unless they turned round. The ANZAC line had almost gone, but the Navy at sea poured shell after shell onto the Turkish advance on the seaward slopes and drove them back.

Malone directed his rear companies forward to the junction of Walker's and Russell's Top to secure it. Majors R. Young and W.H. Cunningham of the Hawke's Bay and Wellington West Coast companies were ordered to establish a line and dig in. Bollinger was with the Hawke's Bay Company: 'We rallied together only 30–50 of us and put up a terrific fire against hundreds of Turks. We were cut off from our right and just waiting for the end to come. Private Thompson (Napier) here did worthy work. He mounted a machine gun under fire. We started to improve our trenches, at the same time keeping up a heavy fire. At dusk we dug in the machine gun. Dead and wounded were lying everywhere. At 8.00 p.m. trumpets were sounded right along the Turkish line and they rushed us. Although they got within 10–20 yards, our heavy fire, greatly assisted by the machine gun, kept them off. Every hour they came, chattering like a lot of coolies loading a coal boat.'[30]

That night Malone and Hart sited a line behind Braund's forward position, less exposed to Turkish fire. 'I went up with Hart and we divided up the ground held, sent for picks and shovels and the night was passed by all hands dig, dig, digging.'[31]

The Wellingtons had lost two officers killed and six wounded, 37 men killed and 164 wounded, a total of 209 casualties of the 450 men forward in the firing line. Hart himself was wounded as he supervised the digging. 'I was hit in the left thigh which put me out of action at about 9 o'clock.' He was carried down the ridge and along to the Cove; the next day he was loaded onto a transport, the *Derrflinger*, which would sail for Alexandria with 800 men tended by three doctors and no nurses. 'The ship was like a shambles. Wounded men were lying in every crook and corner, all still wearing their blood covered clothing … 28 men were buried at sea. A few who were hit in the head suffered intensely and groaned or screamed in agony the whole way across.'[32]

For Malone it had been a frustrating day. He reinforced Hart's line with a platoon of the Ruahines and refused Braund's request for more reinforcements to hold the forward line. 'Braund then said as I would not send him up more reinforcements he would have to retire to his first position. I told him that he ought never to have left it

Looking north towards the outposts and Suvla Bay in the distance. In the foreground is Mule Gully, above it the track up Walker's Ridge. The outposts are on the seaward side of the foothills beyond Walker's Ridge.

(009377, Alexander Turnbull Library)

Burying the dead on Russell's Top during the Armistice. Rhododendron Ridge is on the left skyline, Baby 700 in the centre. The Turkish front line at The Nek is beyond the large group of standing men. Taken from the ANZAC front trenches, this was the scene of the attacks on 27 April, 19 May and 7 August 1915.

(013A, AL0645, Stereo Glass Plate, Wingnut Archive)

… Col Braund then came to see me and on my asking why he had been doing as he had, said that the truth was he feared that if he didn't go on his men would run away. I said that was no reason to sacrifice aimlessly my men.'[33]

Malone reported the situation to Brigadier General Walker and asked that Braund's battalion be relieved and the position consolidated by the Wellington Battalion. He had his way, and the next morning: 'At 6.00 a.m. the Australians left. It was an enormous relief to see the last of them. I believe they are spasmodically brave and probably the best of them had been killed or wounded. They have been, I venture to think, badly handled and trained. Officers in most cases no good. I am thinking of asking for a Court Martial on Colonel Braund. It makes me mad when I think of my grand men being sacrificed by his incapacity and folly. He is, I believe, a brave chap, because he did not keep out of the racket. If he had, it would have been better for us.'[34]

Malone, here, is far too harsh, but it is the anger of a man who sees the weapon he has honed placed in someone else's hands and misused before he has a chance to test it. Godley must have had similar feelings on the day of the landing when the New Zealand Infantry passed to Bridges' command. Malone did not baulk at losses: 'I would not have minded losing the men, if only in a fair go, but to have them thrown away is heart breaking.'[35]

Braund's bravery was never in question, but the best of his leaders were dead, and his men were exhausted and poorly trained. In the attack the Australian battalions were without peer. But by temperament they did not settle easily to the defensive role, requiring patience and the steady development of defence work. 'They were there to kill Turks', not dig their way to Constantinople. Perhaps, because of Godley's rigorous training schemes in Egypt, or because since 25 April the New Zealanders had been used to hold the line, a distinction between the approach of Australians and New Zealanders was becoming evident.

'Now in the affairs of war there is also a difference between the New Zealander and Australian. The Australian resembles the Irishman — daring, desperate, and frequently reckless; the New Zealander resembles the Scot — equally daring, equally determined, but more canny and cautious. In brief, the New Zealander is more ready to weigh the issues and count the cost.'[36]

Birdwood himself became alarmed at the Australian attitude when forced back on the defensive. 'A-1 in attack but curiously callow and negligent in the defence.'[37] Unquestionably the New Zealanders adapted more quickly to holding and developing the defensive line. This may have been due to a number of factors. Bridges' 1st Australian Division had suffered close to 2000 casualties on the first day and were badly disorganised, but although loath to dig, nothing would dislodge them. This was not all; C.E.W. Bean wrote: 'There is a clear and interesting difference between the New Zealander and the Australian. The New Zealander regards the Turk much more kindly than our men. "Kind hearted beggars, the New Zealanders," said one of our chaps the other day. "A Turk snipes them and then they catch the beggar and take him by the hand and lead him down to the beach." Both New Zealanders and Australians have told me that they had orders from their subordinate commanders in

Bivvies on the slopes above Anzac Cove. 'I was brought up in the bush country of New Zealand — it didn't look that wild to me.' *(019A, AL0654, Stereo Glass Plate, Wingnut Archive)*

some cases to take no prisoners, in the first rush at any rate.' Bean was sceptical of this, but observed: 'But undoubtedly the New Zealander fights more with his gloves on than the Australian: the Australian when he fights, fights all in.'[38]

For both countries, it was their first experience of the terrible destruction that a high velocity bullet inflicted on human flesh. Rumours circulated of Turkish atrocities, and in the first days a fierce hatred grew, and few prisoners were taken.

These days of holding on revealed the amateur status of the ANZAC. In Egypt, training had been for a war of movement, attacks in formation over open desert. The anticipation of the landing in Turkey had envisaged the same rapid advance. Even now, when it became a state of siege, there was no sense of urgency, of digging in and trying to sap forward to link up the exposed and isolated forward outposts, or to gain more ground by entrenching. The value of the pick and shovel would be appreciated through bitter experience. But for the present, men hung on, seeing this as a temporary set-back; as rumours throughout the night spoke of a British advance from Helles, why dig when tomorrow your trenches might be miles behind you?

In such situations the strength and personality of the commander became important. Malone was such a personality in the aftermath of the Walker's Ridge battle. A stickler for organisation and discipline, he had been cursed by his men in Egypt. On Walker's Ridge he drove them equally hard. 'We go on digging under shell and rifle fire night and day, but thanks to our excellent digging our casualties get less.'[39]

The Wellington Regiment with New Zealand Engineers assisting dug forward onto Russell's Top and across the plateau until they overlooked Monash Gully and could support the position at Pope's as Charles Saunders recorded. 'It was dangerous work … as a shovel went up in the air to throw dirt out, it was pierced by a Turkish bullet … I got men, sappers in pairs in the end of each bit of trench, gave them their directions and they sapped towards another pair. One place, where there was a big break, four men had been in the firing line … and all four of them had been shot, three of them lay in the slight trough they had scratched out before being shot, and the fourth lay about three yards behind … probably where he had thrown himself when hit. I had to put one of my men in … He was a towny of mine and I was sure I was sending him to his death, and so was he, but it was his turn.'[40]

It was such men who earned Malone's admiration: 'They are all splendid. I cannot sufficiently express my admiration of them all. None better in the world.'[41] He drove them on but recognised the demands he was making and did everything to ease the strains the trench life imposed. 'Digging as usual. All water and food has to be carried

Lieutenant Colonel Malone of the Wellington Battalion on Walker's Ridge. 'The art of warfare is the cultivation of domestic virtues.' *(D.G.W. Malone)*

up 500 feet from the beach, nearly a mile up a steep track and the carriers are under snipers' fire all day. Now and then one gets shot. Still they go on grimly climbing, sweating, tripping, falling but no grousing or complaining.

'We have some mules helping now. If only we could get plenty and save the men, I would be glad. I am arranging every day to send some men to the beach for a swim and a few hours' spell from the trenches. Whenever one sits down, one goes to sleep without effort.'[42]

Men lived in a stupor of exhaustion and, in this state, spy mania flourished. Tired sentries jerking awake at the sound of someone approaching would shoot first. Braund himself would be killed in this manner.

The position of the ANZACs had been stabilised. Walker's Ridge was secure and the Canterbury Battalion had established three outposts along the beach to the north to protect this flank. They were established and dug by night, and although completely dominated by Turkish fire from the heights above during the day, they secured the coastal approach.

By the end of April, Birdwood's ANZAC Corps had 7500 casualties. Two brigades, each of two battalions, from the Royal Naval Division, had landed and reinforced Bridges' Australian Division. Turkish pressure noticeably slackened, for Kemal's men, after the failure of the attacks on 27 April, were now entrenching to block any breakout.

'The enemy's gunfire has practically ceased, his rifle fire is still active … The impression is that they have withdrawn the majority of the infantry and artillery which was engaging us, and have sent them to reinforce the troops opposing the 29th and French Division [in the] South. We are being actively contained by a small force. To prevent this, pressure on our side is essential.'[43]

Baby 700 was the key to the ANZAC situation. If this could be secured then the Turks would be forced back onto Third Ridge. This would give the besieged a much needed breathing space and allow them to go onto the offensive.

At present the line on Russell's Top overlooked the fork at the top of Monash Gully. The first prong, nearest to Russell's, was Pope's, where the Australians held on to 100 metres of the crest. Next to it was Deadman's Ridge, full of Turkish snipers, and then Quinn's Post on Second Ridge, now held by Captain Quinn of the 15th Australian Battalion.

Quinn's Post was reached by moving up the track in Monash Gully, past the foot of Pope's Hill then right up a small watercourse, screened from view from Deadman's Ridge by the scrub and shoulder of earth at the side of the watercourse. At the top was a line of disconnected rifle pits in the scrub, dug just on and just below the crest, some 10–20 metres from the Turk. It was a semi-circular basin cut into the side of Second Ridge, and the southern third of the semi-circle could be seen and fired upon from Deadman's. At Quinn's, the Second Ridge dipped down and was overlooked from higher ground from both sides. To the north was Baby 700 and its long forward slopes, soon known as the Chess- or Chequer-board, from the crisscross of Turkish trenches on it, and to the south the small rise of Courtney's Post and the opposite ground in Turkish hands both looked into the basin at Quinn's. At Quinn's, the existence of the

ANZAC line depended upon five metres of crestline, with behind it the sheer clay face of Monash Gully.

Both Turk and ANZAC realised how precarious the position was at Quinn's, and in the first week, Monash's Australians and New Zealand Engineers fought off continual attempts to throw the ANZAC line off Second Ridge. It was a flank suspended in air, overlooking the eastern arm of the head of Monash Gully. Although Pope's Hill could fire in support of it, to the professional army officer it was untenable. Yet it had to be held if the beachhead was to survive.

It was this situation that Godley was ordered to resolve. His NZ & A Division held the head of the valley. Birdwood tasked him to seize Baby 700. It was an operation beset by many difficulties: the men were tired after a week in the line. Canterbury, Wellington and Auckland had suffered heavily in the fighting of the past week, and it was the same in the 4th Australian Brigade. The critical posts of Pope's, Quinn's and Courtney's had faced a week of incessant firing and probing attacks.

Initially Birdwood considered an advance along the whole of the front, but this was abandoned when both Bridges and Walker objected on the grounds that co-ordination between the brigades on Second Ridge would be difficult. Walker had assumed command of the 1st Australian Brigade, on Johnston's return on 29 April. Also, Bridges' brigades were now too weak to both advance and hold the existing trench line. Godley's NZ & A Division were keen to mount an operation to seize Baby 700, and Birdwood accepted that the plan should focus on this feature.

It would be Godley's first operation with his division. He and his staff had a major divisional attack to plan, using both the New Zealand Infantry Brigade and the 4th Australian Brigade. In addition, a battalion of the Royal Marine Light Infantry (RMLI) was placed under his command as a reserve for the operation.

Details were issued in NZ & A Divisional Operation Order No. 4 on 2 May. The division was to seize Baby 700 and exploit forward and secure Mortar Ridge. It was a difficult operation. There were two approaches to Baby 700. One was across The Nek, running the gauntlet of fire from Battleship Hill, the slopes of Baby 700 itself, and from the Turkish line on Second Ridge. The other approach was out of the two gutters at the head of Monash Gully. This second course would involve men climbing out of the western fork of the gully behind Pope's, or out of the eastern fork at the foot of Quinn's. The problem here was Turkish observation and snipers who, from the ridge between Pope's and Quinn's at the head of Monash Gully, controlled the routes up the valley by day. Any large-scale movement in daylight would forewarn the Turks of an attack.

Godley appreciated these difficulties. He planned to mask the move into Monash Gully by attacking by night and suppressing the Turkish positions at the head of the gully with as intense an artillery preparation as the limited ammunition resources within the perimeter would allow. For 15 minutes all available guns of the Navy and the field and mountain batteries ashore would fire on the slopes of Baby 700, then, as his infantry advanced, this fire would lift onto the rear slopes and rifle and machine-gun fire would rake the parapets of the Turkish trenches. His two brigades would attack simultaneously and gain at night, by rifle and bayonet, the ground that Godley knew would be impossible to seize by day.

At 7.15 p.m. on 2 May the 16th Australian Battalion would assault from the foot of Quinn's and extend the line held on Quinn's onto slopes above Bloody Angle. The 13th Australian Battalion would then follow up and seize the inland slopes of Baby 700 up to the crest. At the same time the Otago Battalion would attack from behind Pope's Hill and seize the seaward slopes of Baby 700 from the crest to The Nek. The Canterbury Battalion would follow up this success by seizing from The Nek to No. 1 Outpost. It was a very ambitious operation to be carried out over restricted and difficult country by night. In his orders to his brigades, Godley stressed the need for close co-ordination and contact to be maintained between the New Zealand Infantry Brigade on the left flank and the 4th Australian Brigade on the right. Godley saw this as essential to the success of the operation.

The 15th Australian Battalion garrisoning Pope's were tasked with filling any gaps that existed between the Otagos and the 13th's. The Royal Marine Light Infantry battalion was positioned half on Russell's Top and half in Monash Gully to exploit success. 'The attack was timed to commence at 7.15 p.m., by which hour the Brigadier, New Zealand Infantry Brigade, had arranged that the Otago Battalion would be in Monash Gully ready to advance.'[44]

The attack failed — the Otagos were late. Private Ewen Pilling wrote: 'This day will never be forgotten by any of the original battalion. New Zealand's mistake — Otago's mistake — call it what you will, someone blundered.'[45]

Promptly at 7.10 the artillery of the warships, *Triumph*, *Dartmouth*, *Bacchante*, *Queen*, *Prince of Wales*, *London*, *Majestic* and *Canopus* lifted from Baby 700 onto its rear slopes and Battleship Hill. It had been the heaviest bombardment yet heard at ANZAC. Australians of Monash's Brigade, men of the 11th Battalion, clambered up the slopes of Bloody Angle and with a cheer went over the crest towards Baby 700. They were met by the enfilade fire of Turkish machine gun and rifles from Baby 700 and Second Ridge and suffered many casualties. As they charged, the supporting troops behind in Quinn's could be heard singing *Tipperary* and *Australia Will Be There*. The 11th was quickly followed by the 13th Battalion, who clambered up the slopes and extended beyond the 16th Battalion, seizing an abandoned Turkish forward trench on the base of Baby 700 at the start of the Chessboard. Despite the bravery of their advance the Australians did not gain their objectives, for as they advanced Turkish fire from their left cut them down — there was no sign of the Otagos.

Throughout the night the Australians grimly dug a shallow trench among the scrub some 100 metres beyond where they had started. The co-ordination so necessary to the success of Godley's plan had failed to materialise. At 7.15 p.m. the Otagos were still struggling in single file up Monash Gully, against the lines of wounded and the battalion of Royal Marines clustered in the valley amid the constant attention of Turkish snipers. Unlike Monash, neither Johnston, commanding the NZ Infantry Brigade, nor Moore, commanding the Otagos, appreciated the difficulty in moving the battalion up the valley and onto Pope's in time. There were two possible routes:

directly across The Nek, a distance of some 200 metres, or down from Otago's position on Walker's Ridge onto the beach, around through Anzac Cove and up Shrapnel Valley into Monash Gully, some 2600 metres. Moore wisely chose the second route.* However, his battalion did not start moving from Walker's Ridge until 4.45–5.15, and other than the company commanders, few Otagos such as Private W.N. Anderson were aware of what the night operations entailed. 'Sunday 2 May. Very ordinary day, but we have just received orders to move about 5 o'clock and make an attack … We had tea about 4.00 p.m., packed our valises in a side trench and proceeded to the beach where we were given potatoes, tea and ham … As we left the beach, General Godley, standing on the side of the track said to us: "Finish them off this time."'[46]

Private Peter Thompson was with the leading company, the 4th Otagos: 'Our way to our objective lay through the long winding gully known as Shrapnel or Suicide Gully. All through the gully snipers lay carefully concealed. At different points we had to rush the whole battalion past in batches of four or five men at a time. It took us some considerable time to get through and delayed us very considerably. We lost several men coming through. Before reaching the Australian trenches from where we were to advance, we had to scale a very steep face, in fact so steep, that a rope had to be employed to gain the top …'[47]

It would be 7.45 before the Otagos arrived at the foot of Pope's, where the Australians of the 15th Battalion grimly told them that they were late and that the Australians had already taken their objectives. They soon found this was not the case. Moore hurried his men up the clay slopes and into the trenches at Pope's. As can be imagined, tempers frayed among the officers, and the men sensed that the plans were already in disarray. It had been raining and the clay slopes leading to the trenches at Pope's were turning into a greasy slide as they scrambled up. At the top, the trenches allowed Moore to deploy only a platoon at a time. It was dark, and the ground ahead fell away into a saucer basin before climbing to the rising ground 100 metres away. Apart from firing on the right flank, nothing but scrub could be seen in front of the Otagos as the first platoon clambered on the parapet. It was now 8.45 p.m. The Otagos were one and a half hours late. Thompson recorded, 'On reaching the trenches we deployed to an interval of two paces and advanced on a column of platoons. We gained good ground and formed mass behind a small ridge.

'We took a breather and charged. Up till now not a shot had stirred from the Turkish trenches, but immediately we started to go in with the bayonet, the Turks opened with a hellish storm of lead from both machine gun and rifle. The whole place was a sheet of flame.'[48]

Forewarned by the Australian advance, the Turks were waiting — each platoon of the 4th Otagos was mowed down by fire, and only a handful reached the Turkish front lines. No one entered the Turkish trenches alive. The men manning the front lines on Russell's Top and Pope's could see the attack in the light of the Turkish illumination

---

* The route across Russell's Top towards The Nek was covered by a number of Turkish machine guns on a narrowing front which at The Nek was 30–50 metres wide.

Looking down from Courtney's Post onto the Brigade Headquarters area in Monash Gully. The defensive trench line, put in place in case the Turks break through, is clearly visible . The track and line of bivvies running at an angle to the top right of the photo lead to Pope's Hill. *(WF-002081-2A, P.R.M. Hanna Album, NAM Waiouru)*

Looking up Monash Gully. Deadman's Ridge is on the skyline to the right at the head of the gully, separated from Pope's Hill, which is on the left skyline. In the foreground are the sandbag barricades in the area of Brigade Headquarters. These were staggered at intervals up the route for the men to run between to avoid sniper fire from Deadman's Ridge. *(WF-002082-104, Deans Collection, NAM Waiouru)*

shells: 'The Turks were entrenched some 50–100 yards from the edge of the face of the gully and their machine guns swept the edges. Line after line of our men went up, some lines didn't take two paces over the crest when down they went to a man and on came another line.'[49]

In the 4th Otagos, Major R. Price, Company Commander, was killed. So were Spedding, his second-in-command, and Egglestone, one of the platoon commanders. Lieutenant J.L. Saunders, the only remaining officer of the company, found himself with a handful of men hugging the ground below the parapet of the forward Turkish trench. Ewen Pilling was one of these: 'Frank [Adamson] and I kept together and hailed each other till within a few yards of the Turks' trench. Here he failed to answer my call and I halted to find that I was alone in the Turkish lines. Immediately a machine gun opened fire on me and I lay down in a shallow hole while fire poured over me. I could feel the bullets sweeping across my body and over my hands. One took away part of the heel of my boot. As I lay there I must have fallen asleep.'[50]

Behind, in the forward trenches at Pope's, the wounded Moore committed his next company, the 8th Southlands. They attacked to the right of the 4th Otagos, and because of the ground also had to move forward platoon after platoon. Fire was hitting the trench parapet, and many men would not move forward. Fred Rogers was in 7 Platoon. 'Our officer was missing, and Colonel Moore said, "Advance your platoon!" and there was no reply. My Sergeant was laying on the left of me and I says, "Bill, you will have to take charge?" "Oh I am not going to take charge," says Bill. I said, "You got to!" So Bill gave a half-hearted "Advance No. 7 Platoon!" and we advanced slowly up the slope and the machine-gun fire was pretty hot, and there were dead Turks, pretty numerous, all lying about. They had been there a week and they were swollen and we were glad to take cover behind them.'[51]

Private Anderson captured the mood of the men. 'We went forward knowing that it had already failed. Broken up into a scattered mob by the shrubbery all we could do was go to earth and wait for reorganisation that never came.'[52]

Tired, dispirited and bewildered, men slumped into the scrub conscious only of the incessant noise, branches and twigs falling on them, Turkish flares above them, and a line of fire from the slope ahead. Private John Skinner 'caught up with two men out of No. 9 Platoon, and one of them was a devout Roman Catholic and he was praying aloud to the Holy Mother Mary that he'd get hit, a blighty one so that he could get out of it, and it wasn't long before he got his wish. He and his companion were killed and I had my rifle smashed in my hand, all with the same burst of fire.'[53]

By now Moore's last companies had edged forward. Major Moir, the battalion second-in-command, had gone with these and organised the men to dig a trench roughly in line with the 16th and 13th Australian battalions. It was on this line that the dispersed and bewildered elements of the Otagos withdrew and consolidated.

'When I woke up an hour and a half later the firing had ceased. I could hear Turks jabbering in the trench and I rolled back and set out to find my own lines. Again I listened and still could hear the Turks. I rolled back and then set out on my hands and knees in search of my own company. I came upon another trench and again I listened.

At first the voices seemed to be Turks but soon I was undeceived when I heard a loud "Damn!" I jumped up and yelled "Otago there!" At once seventy rifles were levelled at my head, but I was not long in reassuring the boys.'[54]

The Divisional Signallers under Captain Henry Edwards had run a line forward from the NZ & A Division Headquarters to Pope's and to Walker's Ridge, where Johnston was watching the battle from the Wellington trenches with Malone. A line was also laid from NZ Infantry Brigade Headquarters forward to Pope's, but this line was repeatedly cut.* Johnston lost contact with the Otagos at about 10.30 p.m., but the reports filtering through indicated that though the objectives set had not been gained, there were sufficient prospects to warrant reinforcing the attack. Plagued by uncertain communications, Johnston sent his staff captain, Alfred Morton, forward to find out what progress had been made. He reported to Colonel Moore, but was caught up as some of the 8th Southland Company broke; Morton led them back into the attack and was never seen again.

Godley believed The Nek to be now in Otago hands. He directed Johnston to send forward the Canterbury Regiment to link up with the Otagos. The leading Canterbury Company advanced up Russell's Top but returned with the news that The Nek was still Turkish. A second attempt was made and also failed. Finally, at 3.00 a.m., the battalion was once more ordered forward and after blundering into the western fork of Monash Gully, part of a Canterbury company under the Adjutant, Captain Critchley-Salmonson, reached Colonel Moore's position. Here Critchley-Salmonson was ordered to prolong the Otagos' left flank.

With 50 men, Critchley-Salmonson moved up the western arm of Monash Gully, climbing the slope and over the crest following the line of the Otagos' advance. 'By some miracle' he hit upon the left of the Otago line and set his men, now down to a party of five, to dig a continuation of the Otago trench. His party was joined by more Canterburys under Lieutenant Shepherd and they linked the Otago line back in an angle to where it fell away into the top of the gully.

Morning came, and with the light came Turkish fire on the exposed New Zealand and Australian positions. 'The man next to Salmonson, shot from the front, fell across him. Another, shot from the left rear, fell beside him. A rush of men occurred. "Otago is retreating," they cried.'[55] Some men of the Otagos could be seen running back over the crest into Monash Gully. Critchley-Salmonson, fired on from all directions, called out but could not make contact with anyone on his right flank and gave the order for his men to retire. The left flank gradually crumbled, and each of the three pockets in turn, Canterburys, Otagos, Monash's Australians, withdrew or were shot off the slopes. Engineers were with each brigade to assist with digging in. Sapper E.C. Clifton was attached to the 4th Australian Brigade: 'Our duty was supposed to be to see that the infantry got properly entrenched after advancing. We had to work up an awful

---

* Lance Corporal C.R.G. Bassett was one of three signallers who ran a telephone wire forward from the NZ Infantry Brigade headquarters on Walker's Ridge, across Russell's Top to Pope's Hill. All three were recommended for an award.

Major G.R. Pridham (later Lt Colonel), Royal Engineers, on Gallipoli reading the latest news while in command of the New Zealand Engineers. *(WF-002082-88, Deans Collection, NAM Waiouru)*

gully beyond description. More than half our lot are wounded and missing.

'The Australians lost terribly and the gully was an absolute deathtrap. We were only in the way and were sent out to be massacred. The Turks held the skyline and there seemed to be a bad want of co-operation between our guns, machine guns and infantry. The Australians were all shouting that our machine guns were all firing on them and whether true or not, the idea seemed to demoralise them for a time and when it was shouted that the Turks were advancing some actually began to move or run, but soon recovered. A firing line was gradually built up around the skyline. The edge was like a precipice and footholds had to be dug to give them a firing position. The poor chaps were mown down by machine gun and rifle fire ... Hunt was next to me and got hit in the leg and a bullet struck an entrenching tool I had, it would otherwise have gone through my arm. I was told off to get Crawford [shot through the arm] away. I had to pull him out of the trench under fire, and we had to slide down the loose earth to the bottom of the gully. It was an awful night.'[56]

It was obvious to all that the attack had gone terribly astray. However, at 3.00 a.m., as the Canterburys were attempting to reinforce the Otagos, Godley moved the reserve battalion of Royal Marine Light Infantry forward, and informed Monash that they were placed under his command and tasked him to ensure that the ground won by his brigade and the Otagos was held. The Royal Marine Light Infantry was committed up the valley in the Otagos' footsteps to reinforce the line.

Like the Otagos, they were held up by the congestion at the head of the valley. Dawn had arrived before they had cleared Monash Gully and as they tried to advance they met New Zealanders and Australians retiring. All was confusion added to by our artillery falling short and shells exploding among the Marines and the 16th Australian Battalion. Despite this, the Marines pushed forward to be fired at from The Nek and Turkish positions on Second Ridge. 'With much slaughter, they were driven again into the valley. For many days afterwards on the ugly bare shoulder at the top of Monash Valley, their dead lay like ants shrivelled by a fire, until a marine climbed out at night and pushed them down into the valley, where they were buried.'[57] The name Deadman's Ridge clung to this shoulder from that day.

Out on the slopes forward of the crest, isolated parties of Australians and New Zealanders still hung on, Fred Rogers among them. 'Morning came and I could hear them digging in behind, just prior to that Joe got smacked. He got smacked through

Fighting on the edge of a cliff: an Australian soldier loads his rifle at Pope's Hill, 26 April 1915. *(P05382-005-1, Australian War Memorial*

'The attack failed. New Zealand's mistake — Otago's mistake — call it what you will, someone blundered.' The dead in No Man's Land during the Armistice. *(022A, AL0645, Stereo Glass Plate, Wingnut Archive)*

the lung and through the back, enfilade fire across his chest … So I says, "Well I'll hop back and see what's doing." So I got back into a bit of a trench and it was that crowded you couldn't stand. Major Moir says, "Somebody will have to get out. There's too many of you." I says, "I was last in, I'll get out." I threw myself out of there and the bullets just flew dust all over me. I lay there for quite a while and Peter my mate with me yelled out to me, "What'll I do with Joe, Fred?" and I yelled out, "Take his personal effects and his identification disc." Peter was just a lad. "Ooh Fred," he says, "they're all covered in blood," he says, "I can't do it." "Well," I said, "You'd better leave him and come back, but take your time because otherwise you'll get killed.'"[58]

Peter got safely back, and they found themselves part of a small garrison of some 40 Otagos, under Major Moir and Captain Fleming of the 8th Southland Company. 'Swept by fire from the Turkish trenches, assailed by showers of bombs, confronted by the constant threat of being overwhelmed, cut off from all support and from supplies of food, water and ammunition and given up as lost, they grimly retained their hold on this advanced position for three days.'[59] Finally, on the night of 4–5 May, the ragged handful left withdrew onto Pope's, now garrisoned by the Auckland Battalion, and ran the gauntlet of being fired on in the belief that they were Turk.

There was the smell of failure at the head of Monash Gully on the morning of 3 May. Godley had gone forward with Tahu Rhodes, his ADC, and Aitken, his orderly. At the head of the gully below Deadman's, Australians and Marines were hopelessly intermixed, as Rhodes recalled. 'A hand-grenade was thrown over and exploded within a few yards of us and amongst some men of the Marine Brigade … several of them completely lost their heads and ran away down the hill as fast as possible. Luckily there were Australians in the trench and they hung on … Several bombs were thrown and the Gen. and I ran about rallying the men and taking them back to the trench … Aitken was killed.'[60]

By the afternoon Monash's men were back in their trenches. Apart from the scattered Otagos still forward and unable to move, no ground had been gained. Lieutenant Colonel Moore mustered the remnants of his battalion below Pope's Hill and moved them down to the beach.

Five officers and 60 men answered the roll but over the next days men came straggling in. No complete account exists of the losses suffered by Otago in this attack. The *War Diary* records five officers wounded, eight missing, 11 men killed, 174 wounded and 208 missing, leaving a strength of 365 out of the 800 who went into the attack. But in truth, the Otagos never knew how many were lost. Walk among the gravestones of Quinn's Post cemetery today and headstone after headstone records an Otago soldier killed in action 1–23 May 1915. It would be that long before the Otagos sorted themselves out. Each diary entry, each memory of a veteran such as Peter Thompson, is a record of friends lost: 'At the first roll call of my Regiment [4th Otago Company] only 57 out of 200 odd men answered, while in my platoon 14 out of 50 answered. In my section, 3 answered, leaving 5 unaccounted for.'[61] Pilling noted: 'Ryburn turned up safely but there is no word of Adamson. I am afraid he is lost. Both Childs and McQueen are away wounded and my cousin Lieutenant Egglestone is away wounded.'[62]

The Canterburys too were despondent. Frank Hardey thought it was 'a bad "smack up". We got pushed right off and had to retire, getting an awful gruelling going back. The stunt had been horribly bungled. What between misunderstandings, bad guides, and the reinforcements we had a real good scare. The reinforcements were English — RMLI — and they let us down in a most disappointing way. We have had reason now, on several occasions, to be bitterly disappointed in our brothers from England. We ask ourselves, "Where is the Army for which England for generations had such pride?" To France and mostly under the sod, and these volunteers from rural England, and from the huge mill towns, are a disappointment to us Colonials who have had the Army held up as an example and pattern incomparable.'[63]

The men were worn out and dispirited. Brereton saw them on the beach, 'deadly tired with eyes bloodshot and staring from the horror of the night, as well might be after such a bloody business where no amount of bravery or sacrifice gave any hope of success. Again, our maps were to blame, as on them the plans were made; but the ground proved entirely different.'[64]

But this time it was too easy to blame the maps and the Royal Marine Light Infantry or 'Run my lads Imshi' as they became known. It was New Zealand's mistake, and there were many, among the New Zealanders, who thought through the reasons for the failure. Lieutenant Colonel Malone, a witness to the attack from his forward trenches, wrote: 'In my opinion the plan was not good and doomed from the start. They tried to go in where the Turks had been attacking for days.'[65]

Dragging the dismantled 18-pounder guns of the 1st Battery, New Zealand Field Artillery, up Walker's Ridge on to Russell's Top. The 1st Battery covered the Australian line on 400 Plateau while the guns of the 2nd Battery covered Quinn's Post from Plugge's Plateau. *(WF-002363-12–1978-1949-12, W.A. Hampton Collection, NAM Waiouru)*

The men, too, analysed the failure. Corporal Charles Saunders of the Engineers, who witnessed the attack, noted: 'The attack was a dead failure … Perhaps it would have been an impossible feat in any case but I am certain the arrangements doomed it to failure from the start … This criticism is made without apology, it is just my idea, as a man who had to think for himself, and has had to fight his own battles in civil life … I was reporting the result of my reconnaissance up the gully on the left about 10.00 p.m. that night and I heard the officer in charge of the attack. Speaking through the phone to this effect, "tell them to dig in! dig, dig, dig, dig!" If he said dig once or rather shouted it, he did so from 10–12 times. I knew then that what I had feared, had happened; a lot of lives lost and no advancement. God! If he had seen that edge of the face of the side of the gully and our men like ninepins, he would have seen that it was hardly possible.'[66]

It was Godley, the Divisional Commander, Johnston, the New Zealand Brigade Commander, and Moore, Commanding Officer of the Otagos, who contributed most to the failure of 2 May. They failed to appreciate the difficulties that would be faced by the men at night in the tangle of scrub-covered gullies below Baby 700. At every level, reconnaissance was lacking. Johnston had only just returned. He had come back too early, for he was still not well. Naturally anxious to command his New Zealand Brigade in battle, Johnston relied on the knowledge of those who had been there since the landing. Moore was equally neglectful; he did not reconnoitre the route and the approaches to the objective from Pope's, but apparently confined himself to observing the ground with Johnston from Russell's Top. It was a rushed operation and the poor communications meant that once Moore's Otagos got behind, the plan fell apart. Monash's brigade did everything demanded of it, but Godley was asking too much. It was too ambitious a plan, with too many troops crammed into too narrow a piece of ground.

The New Zealanders did not show the dash of the Australians, and Godley and his divisional staff showed their inexperience in this, their first major operation. The Royal Marines should not have been committed, and became scapegoats for a failure that was due to inadequate planning. 'The throwing in of the Marines at daybreak to retrieve a battle already lost resulted only in the slaughter of many brave officers and men.'[67]

Godley never learned from this failure. Both Johnston and Moore were regular officers, and Godley's protégés. His report made no personal criticism and he qualified the extent of the defeat.* 'The net results as regards gain of ground was nil but it is believed that heavy casualties were inflicted upon the Turks, and that the operation was very valuable in demonstrating to them that our force was capable of determined offensive effort. It also had the effect of completely stopping the enemy's sharpshooting for several days.'[68]

---

* This loyalty to the 'Club' and the failure of commanders to criticise omissions by British Regular Officers was a feature of the campaign and became bitterly resented by the New Zealanders. Brigadier General Harold 'Hooky' Walker was the notable exception to this rule. When appointed Commander of the 1st Australian Division, he insisted on Australians being given command appointments and was ruthless with inefficient officers regardless of background.

He wrote to Allen: 'The battalion, I am sorry to say, suffered very heavy losses, but did extremely well. The whole operation relieved the pressure on us very much and it is reported that a great number of Turks were killed, in fact we have seen from the trenches great numbers of dead.'[69]

It was not a period when the men were told much at all, other than that an attack was to be made. Certainly they would not share in the distribution of the operation report. However, in the cramped conditions within the perimeter, the orderlies and signallers acted as a channel of rumour. For the first week men had little time to think, but now with the positions stabilised they could see there was obviously much going wrong and much that had not been planned for.

In spite of 1000 New Zealand casualties, nothing had been gained. The civilian-turned-soldier in the ANZAC ranks saw the reality, heard of the report and wondered if anything was being learned. Malone wrote in his diary on 4 May: 'I am getting sick of it. The war is a "joke war". Ever since August last we have been getting "notes" from the Front, all emphasising that Modern War is a question of (1) Artillery (2) Digging (3) Telephones (4) Periscopes. We are constantly told to read and digest. We do so. But when we want artillery to help us, phones and periscopes to enable us to work quickly and safely — we get almost nil results.

'Our howitzers are short of ammunition, our 18 pounders don't seem to be able to get into action, and the naval guns can't talk soldier gunnery.

'As to phones — after losing life after life, I got two small field phones cost near enough 25/- each [Malone purchased these out of Regimental funds]. They were old and worth about 5/-. Very soon one was taken away. As to periscopes — 4 per company were issued. Every man or two ought to have had one.

'If it were not so serious — the penalty — one could roar with laughter at the preach and no practice. As to digging, if we had to depend on others we should go short, but that we can do, but even then it is hard to get hold of the tools.

'The Briton is a muddler all right. Still he gets there. This is how we feel. If only some German "thoroughness" could be put into us. What a people we should be?'[70]

A sense of failure permeated throughout the ANZAC lines. Captain Aubrey Herbert, Intelligence Officer of the Division, echoed others: 'Our attack has failed, and we have had many casualties, probably not less than 1000. The wounded have been crying on the beach horribly … The complaint is old and bitter now. We insist that the Turks are Hottentots. We give them notice before we attack them. We tell them what we are going to do with their Capital. We attack them with an inadequate force of irregular troops without ammunition in the most impregnable part of their Empire. We ask for trouble all over the East by risking disaster here.'[71]

The ANZAC area was a prison and Baby 700 impregnable. The pressure was now on the ANZACs to see that the Turks did not break in through the half-open door between Pope's and Quinn's.

On 3 May 1915 New Zealand received the first official casualty lists. They shocked the country, but editorials claimed that the cost was slight against the achievements reported. The country took heart and recruiting soared. It would be a week later before the cables arrived detailing the officers dead, wounded and missing, and the men wounded from the Otago attack.

At the landing little hope was held for those captured by the Turks, but, as captured Turks stressed that prisoners were taken and well treated, both friends and families prayed for the word that their lost one was a prisoner.[72] Those on Gallipoli saw it as a faint hope at best. 'At nightfall we get the tally for the last 12 hours. How much N.Z. and Aust. have paid for the Empire: how many killed, wounded or sick. The Headquarters on the hill telephone their total losses and deducting from this the number of men attended in the beach hospitals we arrive at the number of dead and missing — better dead any day. A number of pathetic little bundles — identity disc, purse, pocket book etc. wrapped in dirty handkerchiefs — are handed into the AAG [Assistant Adjutant-General] whose task it is to compute our list of dead. Captain Morton has been missing for several days. He was such a delightful man, an artist all through. He was always pointing out the colours of sunsets and skies to me with a wonderful touch of description. I earnestly hope he did not lie watching the sun go down.'[73]

As news of the missing reached New Zealand, the American Consulate and the Red Cross were besieged with queries. They would wait months in fading hope. Not one of the Otagos missing in that attack was reported taken prisoner.[74]

In the south at Helles, Krithia and Achi Baba were still in Turkish hands. Evaluating his force's strength, Hamilton decided to plump for Helles as the place of the next major thrust. Here, as at Anzac, he desperately needed reinforcements to make good his losses. The Helles front appeared to offer advantages lacking at Anzac: easier country, better communications, better chance of co-operation with the Navy as his army advanced, and perhaps most important of all, a staff and a division that Hamilton and his staff trusted most. This was his regular 29th Division under General Hunter-Weston, and the French Force. Hamilton would agree that the ANZACs had done well for irregular troops, but the terrain and the apparent demoralisation on the night of the landing left a question mark over the ANZACs' abilities to achieve any more at Gaba Tepe. Kitchener and Hamilton's concern was Achi Baba. This, they believed, was the vital ground dominating the Narrows.* It was in the south at Helles that the issue must be pressed to a conclusion. On 4 May Kitchener cabled to Hamilton: 'I hope the 5th will see you strong enough to press on to Achi Baba anyway, as delay will allow the Turks to bring up more reinforcements and to make preparations for your reception. The Australians and New Zealanders will have had reinforcements from Egypt by then, and … could spare you a good many men for the advance.'[75]

Birdwood had told Hamilton after 2 May, that, despite his losses, he had straightened out his line 'and feels safer now and is pretty happy! He is sure he can hold his own against anything except thirst.'[76]

---

* Achi Baba did not dominate the Narrows. It was masked by the rugged Kilid Bahr Plateau north of Achi Baba. This had to be won if Hamilton's army was to control the Narrows. It was a much more formidable obstacle than Achi Baba, although, as history shows, Achi Baba was obstacle enough.

Hamilton directed Birdwood to cease offensive operations at Anzac, concentrate on holding on, earmark two of his best infantry brigades and hold them ready to be sent as reinforcements for the Helles offensive. Birdwood asked both Bridges and Godley to select their most effective brigade. They chose the strongest of those available. Godley selected the NZ Infantry Brigade, 2443 strong, Bridges the 2nd Australian Brigade, 2568 in strength. Also despatched from Anzac were five artillery batteries, including the 3rd Battery NZFA still on board the transports, for there was no room to fit them into the Anzac beachhead, and on the night of 4 May the artillery sailed south.

On the night of 5 May, Hamilton ordered the two brigades to Helles. The men were relieved in the trenches by battalions of the Naval Division. They marched to the cove and linked up with the bearer sub-divisions of the field ambulances. No one seemed to know what was afoot, but the best rumour was that the NZ Infantry was 'to go as garrison for the time being, to Chanak which has fallen. This is to give them a rest.'[77]

In the Auckland Battalion, Private Frank McKenzie recorded in his diary: 'Evening 5 May. Embarked tonight after two days and nights without sleep. Kept on barges in bitter cold. Brian Willis got a spent bullet in the lung on our barge and we put him off

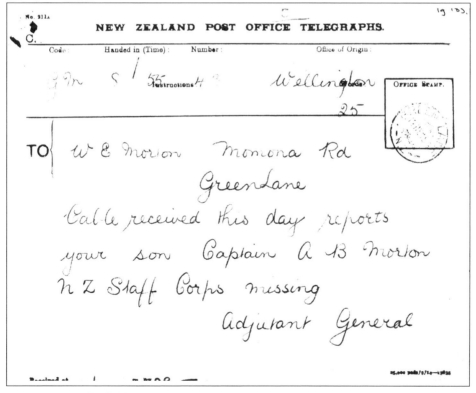

Morton telegram. *(Alexander Turnbull Library)*

Anzac graves on Walker's Ridge. The one on the right is that of Captain A.C. Bluck. The one on the left is Warrant Officer Class I Joseph Marr, both of the Auckland Mounted Rifles. They were sniped and killed on 18 May 1915 and buried alongside one another. Both were blown out of their graves by Turkish artillery fire and had to be re-buried. *(WF-002082-65, Deans Collection, NAM Waiouru)*

into the launch … We are going some ten miles down to help the Tommies and we expect another smack up. These Turks are game fighters. They stick to it like glue and don't mind dying. What is left of the Auckland Battalion is packed like sardines in a hold of a destroyer, which took us off the barges. The men are all worn and weary and nerve wracked, but fairly cheerful. We long for a quiet rest, but we long more still to get the Turks in the open as they got us that first Sunday. There will be a reckoning then.'[78]

As they sailed south, rumour grew on rumour. The men enjoyed the hot cocoa and rum that the destroyer crews liberally dispensed, and for the moment were content to let tomorrow take care of itself.

More New Zealanders were on the way. Birdwood had asked for reinforcements from the Mounted Rifles brigades still in Egypt. He wanted them as individual reinforcements to build up the strength of his depleted infantry battalions. Maxwell, Commander in Chief Egypt, however, acceded to the wishes of the commanders of the Mounted Rifles and Light Horse brigades in Egypt. Russell and Chauvel had no wish for their brigades and regiments to be broken up. They wanted action at Gallipoli but they wanted to fight in their own regiments, even if as dismounted rifles. Maxwell accepted this, and although Hamilton had asked for 1000 men, he sent 3000, consisting of the two brigades — the 1st Australian Light Horse and the New Zealand Mounted Rifles brigades, complete with their signallers and ambulances.

The Australian Bear and the New Zealand Kiwi after the Turk.

'At 2 o'clock we [the officers] had to parade before the Brigadier [Russell] to receive the usual criticism. He also informed us that we would be leaving for the front in a few days, which caused great excitement, but he further added that we would be going without our horses, and I must honestly say that this announcement rather knocked our hats in … Whilst we are delighted at getting to the front, and showing what we are made of we are keenly disappointed at leaving our dear old horses behind, for the trouble is we may never see them again.'[79]

After a week of frantic activity they left for the front, and sailed on 9 May: 'We marched out at 11.15 p.m. for Palais de Kouhba, our first march with full packs up. It wasn't the game it is cracked up to be, but we got through very cheerfully.'[80]

Ahead of them lay Anzac, now officially known by that name. Lieutenant Colonel Fenwick, DADMS of Godley's division, bitterly wrote: 'Total to date 5000 (approximately) casualties, about three men per yard of ground gained. An order came out naming this bay Anzac Bay, after NZ & Australian Divisions. It does not matter what it is called. Perhaps it will be some day known as Bloody Beach Bay. God knows we have paid heavily for it.'[81]

7

HELLES

A young wounded officer of the 29th Division said it was worth ten years of tennis to see the Australians and New Zealanders go in.[1]

At Helles, on 8 May 1915 it was a lovely spring morning. This was the third day of the offensive to seize Achi Baba. Hamilton, Commander in Chief, had come ashore and taken a vantage point on Hill 114 to observe the battle. As he and his staff took position, the day and the view made the prospect of war seem remote: 'The grassy slopes that crown the cliffs are carpeted with flowers. The azure sky is cloudless, the air is fragrant with the scent of wild thyme. In front, behind a smiling valley studded with cypress and patches of young corn, the ground rises gently to the village of Krithia; standing amidst clumps of mulberry and oak; and thence more steeply to a frowning ridge beyond, its highest point like the hump of a camel's back. Away to the right, edged with a ribbon of silvery sand, lie the sapphire fields of Troy. On the left, a mile out in the Aegean, a few warships lie motionless, like giants asleep, their gaunt outlines mirrored in a satin sea; while behind them in the tender haze of the horizon, is the delicately pencilled outline of snowcapped Samothrace. As far as the eye can reach there is no sign of movement; the world seems bathed in sleep. Only high on the shoulder of Achi Baba — the goal of the British troops — a field of scarlet poppies intrudes a restless note.'[2]

At 10.15 the illusion was broken as the warships at sea and the hidden artillery on the beaches and fields around Hamilton's position on Hill 114 started to pound the slopes of Achi Baba and the suspected Turkish line, south of Krithia.

This bombardment continued for 15 minutes, and as it ceased long lines of soldiers could be seen rising from the trenches and advancing over the gentle slope of the centre spur between the scattered copses of mulberry and oak. Despite the shrapnel, the spaced lines of infantry moved steadily towards the white vertical pencil in the distance that was the Krithia mosque. This was the New Zealand Infantry Brigade, their task to seize Krithia.

They were four battalions of infantry, numbering 2500, against an estimated nine battalions of Turks. It was the climax of two days of battle. Now Hunter-Weston,

Commanding the British 29th Division, asked one brigade to succeed where his division had failed. Turkish machine guns and artillery had stopped the British offensive; it had been the same on the right flank where the French had failed to take the much more formidable obstacle of the strongly entrenched Kereves Spur. On the first day of the battle, artillery ammunition had been so scarce in the British batteries that Turkish officers interrogated afterwards were unaware that there had been a bombardment. Regardless of this, Hunter-Weston believed in daylight assaults covered by artillery and then 'trust our bayonets once we get in'. Before the battle Hamilton saw 'that it would be good tactics, seeing shell shortage is our weakness, to make use of the half hour before dawn to close with the enemy and fight it out on their ground. To cross the danger zone ... by night and overthrow the enemy in the grey dawn.'[3]

However, Hamilton allowed his subordinate to persuade him otherwise. Hunter-Weston argued that a night advance was too difficult for his troops, as too many officers and NCOs had been lost since the landing. Night offered too great a risk of confusion and loss of control. On each of the first two days of battle, 6th and 7th, at the same hour, his brigades had advanced in broad daylight and been cut down before reaching the Turkish lines. Now on the third day and at the same hour, but with even less artillery ammunition, Hunter-Weston asked the NZ Infantry Brigade to capture Krithia and open the way to Achi Baba. Nothing in the plan had changed, a night advance was not considered, and in reply to Hamilton's directive that the attack be pressed with 'the utmost vigour', Hunter-Weston's imagination was providing only more of the same.

Until 8 May Helles had been a pleasant change for the two brigades. Both had been included in a composite division under the command of Major General Paris of the Royal Naval Division. They were part of Hamilton's Reserve, but Hamilton had given Hunter-Weston control of the battle and permission to use them at his direction. All this was unknown to the New Zealanders as they dug 'funk holes' and watched the sights in the olive groves above V Beach. The sound and sight of battle in the distance on the 6th and 7th appeared to be as battles should be fought: straight from one's imagination or out of *Boys Own*, with figures advancing in the distance, the distant puffs of shrapnel, the various uniforms of the staff on horseback, it was a far cry from the madness of the Anzac landscape. New Zealanders such as Lieutenant Colonel Malone at last felt the war was being fought as they had trained for it in Egypt. 'It is a relief to get in where war is being waged scientifically ...'[4]

'We are now enjoying a splendid rest and watching our fellows slowly driving the enemy back ... it is grand to see the advance after our uphill fight among the hills and cliffs ... There are Imperial and French troops here and they knew the game thoroughly.'[5]

No one, officers or men, had any real knowledge of what was intended for the New Zealand Brigade. Everyone had faith that now they were part of a well-planned affair which would soon link with the ANZAC positions further up the coast.

After a pleasant night on the 6th and an equally restful day on the 7th, the New

New Zealand Infantry resting and playing cards among the olive groves at Cape Helles before the attack on 8 May 1915. *(Judge Gresson Collection – 23 August – PAColl-3604, Alexander Turnbull Library)*

Colonel F.E. 'Earl' Johnston commanding the New Zealand Infantry Brigade, smoking a cigarette with his Headquarters staff. The Brigade Major, Major Temperley, sits with his head turned towards camera.

(WF-002083-49-p3d, Charters Album, NAM Waiouru)

The reserve trenches at Helles, 1000 metres behind the front line. It was from such trenches that the New Zealanders advanced on 8 May 1915, many not knowing that their own troops were in front of them.

(WF-003520-12, F.W. Watson Collection, Puke Ariki)

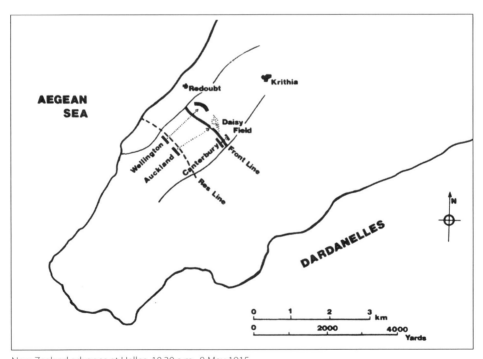

New Zealand advance at Helles, 10.30 a.m., 8 May 1915.

Zealanders moved forward to the reserve trenches of the 88th British Brigade of Hunter-Weston's 29th Division and were placed under his command. That evening at 11.25 p.m. General Hunter-Weston issued a warning order to his brigades for the following day's operations. 'The advance will be resumed at 10.30 tomorrow. The New Zealand Brigade will be prepared to move through the 88th Brigade at that hour. 87th Brigade will be the left of the advance. 88th Brigade will be in reserve in their present position. The Indian Brigade and Composite Naval Brigade will maintain their present positions.'[6]*

However, 87th Brigade on the left had been held up for the last two days by machine guns above Gully Ravine. Hunter-Weston agreed that this brigade would confine itself to locating these machine guns and establishing a series of posts on the eastern rim of the ravine to protect the left flank of the NZ Brigade as it advanced up Krithia Spur. The 2nd Australian Brigade remained in reserve.

Though the warning order was issued late in the evening of the 7th, there is no record of it being passed to the New Zealand battalions. That night was spent moving into the reserve trenches of the forward brigades of 29th Division. The battalions had moved up Gully Ravine in the dark. It had been a confused march, with the soldiers not being sure where they were going and what they were to do. Morning found the Wellington and Auckland battalions in the reserve trenches, some 800 metres behind the front line. The Canterbury and Otago battalions were still some distance further back.

This was the position at 8.55 a.m. when Colonel Earl Johnston received written orders for the day's operations. He moved forward to a ruined hut behind his two forward battalions and called in his commanding officers. His orders were brief. The brigade was to capture Krithia Village, and the attack would be carried out along Krithia Spur with Wellington on the left, Auckland in the centre and Canterbury on the right. Otago, the weakest, would remain in reserve. Zero Hour, to start the attack, was 10.30, and at 10.15 there would be 15 minutes of artillery fire on the known Turkish positions.

It was 10.10 a.m. when Johnston finished. The start time of 10.30 left the COs (Commanding Officer) of the battalions 20 minutes to brief their men and get them into position. It was not enough and in the rush things went wrong. Colonel Brown of the Canterburys hurried back and briefed his company commanders, who included Major C.B. Brereton commanding 12th Nelson Company. '"The battalion will attack from the front line trenches at 10.30 a.m. precisely; 12th Company will lead." Then he smiled and added, "and I am sorry, gentlemen, that I cannot give you any further information." It was indeed a meagre order … we knew nothing, not even how far it was to the front line.'[7]

---

*   There was reluctance to use Cox's 29th Indian Brigade because they included Moslem troops, and until victory was assured there were doubts held about their performance — see Hamilton, *Gallipoli Diary. Vol. 1*, p.193; and Bean, *The Story of Anzac*, Vol. II, p.8.

If the company commanders knew little of the detail for the attack, the men knew even less. They were told to move forward, and forward they went. They rose to their feet and in long lines among the low corn, platoon by platoon, company by company, the men swished forward, 12 paces apart, heavily laden with packs and rifles carried at the trail as Lance Corporal E.P. Williams of the Canterbury Battalion detailed: 'The advance was made in artillery formation — a fact that saved us from much loss on account of the shrapnel that was fired against us … The bullets were now falling around us, and at one spot, where the valley narrowed into a kind of defile, through which a creek with a bed of yielding mud was the only available track, some of our fellows were shot … we were a target for the enemy machine guns and advanced at the double … I found myself hampered with ammunition and it seemed an age before I could cross the open space confronting us and gain the shelter afforded by banks and a stack of stores.'[8]

Under shrapnel fire the Canterburys moved past the reserve trenches occupied by the Wellington and Auckland battalions and the leading companies halted behind the front trenches of the 88th Brigade, 800 metres ahead.

Nothing could be seen of the Turkish lines and many of the Canterburys did not realise that there were friendly troops in front of them until they reached the front trenches occupied by the 'Dubsters' — an amalgamation of the Dublin Fusiliers and Munster Fusiliers, both of whom had suffered heavily in the River Clyde landing at V Beach.

At 10.30 the Wellingtons and Aucklanders advanced. Brown held his battalion back until the others advanced up with him. George Bollinger was with the Wellingtons. 'We advanced this morning in extended order. Our company covered 100 yards frontage and went forward in eight lines. I was in the fourth line. Immediately we moved off the enemy dressed the country with shrapnel and machine gun fire but the New Zealand Army never faltered. Shrapnel was bursting amongst us all the way. We advanced right through our regulars and formed a new position 400 yards ahead.'[9]

All battalions suffered casualties in reaching the front line, but it was beyond the front line that they struck the brunt of the Turkish fire. On the left the Wellingtons suffered heavy losses to enfilade fire from Gully Spur — the hidden machine guns that 87th Brigade still could not find and suppress. They dug in some 300 metres ahead of the old front line. In the centre, Auckland advanced across open patches of clover between the scattered copses of trees that made up Fir Tree Wood. Among the advancing infantry was Frank McKenzie: 'Bullets and casualties thick. I wondered why I was not hit as they whistled everywhere … reached some brush and scattered bushes … as we got nearer we crept on our stomachs inches at a time … We crawled for about an hour and men were hit everywhere. Major Dawson was hit in the back. We couldn't get any further and couldn't retire. I scratched a little hole in the bushes and lay for about nearly six hours and bullets hit everywhere …

'I am not religious, I did not like Church Parades when weary from working parties. But in times of mortal danger one prays for help from our Saviour. When the attack was spent I looked in a daze for the long lines of soldiers to my right and left who started in the assault. I saw only Major Dawson, Sergeant Commons and two others going on. So I flopped down and began to scrabble a depression in the rock hard soil with my useless entrenching tool … As I scrabbled a bullet hit the rocky soil under my tummy — whang! I went on scrabbling — whang! A bullet cut the straps on the pack on my back. In imagination I could see the Turk slipping back the bolts of his rifle for a third bullet (in between the other two). I found myself singing a hymn. As I scrabbled I found myself singing the first line "Hide me, Oh my Saviour hide" — whang, under my tummy — "Till the storm of life be past" — whang, through the straps, slowly waiting for the third bullet — "Hide me O my Saviour hide" and slower and almost silent — "Till the storm of life be past." I lay from 11.00 a.m. till dark, blisters burning the legs upturned below the shorts, parched with thirst, a full water bottle on my hip, dead afraid even to move in case that third bullet came.'[10]

With heavy casualties from unseen snipers and machine guns, the Aucklanders withdrew to the edge of the woods and dug in. Sergeant Joe Gasparich was one. 'I had an entrenching tool and we dug down — at first we had to lie on our bellies and scratch, every time we threw earth up we got a shower of bullets because Jacko, we found out afterwards, was lined up along a ridge well above us looking down on us.'[11]

It was the same on the right flank. Colonel Brown held back his battalion, but finally at 10.50 a.m. he gave Brereton the word to advance with his 12th Nelson Company: 'The 12th Nelson Company will attack in lines of platoons extended as far as possible, platoons at 150 yards distance; objective prominent brown house in front. 'An officer asked how far the attack was to go, and I told him, "As far as you can get!" He did his best to carry out the order but was killed about 200 yards ahead.'[12]

It was obvious that speed was the only way that men could get across the open fields to a hollow some 150 metres ahead, which could provide some shelter. As Brereton gave the order to advance, the men leapt to their feet and doubled forward: 'For two hundred yards we sprinted, thinking oddly how beautiful the poppies and daisies were, then from sheer exhaustion we rushed to ground in a slight depression and lay there panting. We had kept about ten yards apart but soon the spaces were filled by those of our mates who managed to get so far.'[13]

Brereton watched his men falling in the bright sunshine. 'I was starting with the last platoon, but I had not gone ten yards before I felt the terrible pain of a bullet through the top of my head and as I fell I could see in imagination, but very vividly, great flames rushing out of my head. It crossed my mind instantly, "Serve you damned well right for ordering men into such a fire".'[14]*

Like the other two battalions, the Canterburys were pinned down 100 metres forward of the front trenches. The New Zealand attack had been halted. On the left the Wellingtons had made the most ground — perhaps some 300 metres. In the centre the Aucklanders had retired back onto the fringes of the wood, almost onto the front British trenches. On the right in the Canterbury Battalion some of the Nelson Company clung to a hollow 100 metres ahead of where they had started. With them is Cecil Malthus.

---

* Brereton would recover and serve again in France.

'Hugging the ground in frantic terror we began to dig blindly with our puny entrenching tools, but soon the four men nearest me were lying, one dead, two with broken legs, and the other badly wounded in the shoulder. A sledgehammer blow on the foot made me turn with a feeling of positive relief that I had met my fate, but it was a mere graze and hardly bled.

'Another bullet passed through my coat, and a third ripped along two feet of my rifle sling. Then the wounded man on my right got a bullet through the head that ended his troubles. And still without remission the air was full of hissing bullets and screaming shells. After an hour the fire slackened, but we continued working feverishly, in the cruel pain of sheer weariness, until each man, including the wounded, had a shallow pit to lie in. By then it was neatly two o'clock in the afternoon and I devoured a tin of bully beef and fell asleep for awhile.'[15]

Hunter-Weston's plan for the third day had failed. No Turk had been seen, and soldiers were still not sure where the enemy was or how far away he was entrenched. They sprawled exhausted in their trench scrapes, listening to the crack of bullets overhead and the cries of the wounded lying helpless in the fields behind them under the hot midday sun.

At 3.00 p.m. Hunter-Weston ordered the New Zealand Brigade to repeat its attack at 5.30 p.m. The brigade would attack as before, alone and in daylight. The Otago Battalion in reserve was to come forward and assist the Auckland Battalion, which had suffered the heaviest casualties. The Third Reinforcements that had just arrived from Anzac that morning would be placed in support. Colonel Johnston received and passed these orders on to his battalion commanders. Reaction was adamant. A further unsupported advance would see the battalions destroyed with no possible benefit. Johnston protested to headquarters 29th Division but was told that the instructions issued to him were to stand.

Hamilton had witnessed the failure of the morning's attack. He knew that the French on the left had made no progress. Johnston's protests against the likely destruction of the New Zealand Brigade had also been passed on to him. 'There was an opinion in some quarters that we had done all we could, but I resolved firmly to make one more attempt. At 4.00 o'clock I issued orders that the whole line, reinforced by the Australians, should on the stroke of 5.30 fix bayonets and storm Achi Baba.'[16] The attack would be supported by all available artillery and naval support firing for 15 minutes from 5.15.

In the New Zealand lines, the Otagos came forward in the later afternoon, in open formation and under fire. The 4th Otago and 8th Southland companies moved forward in support of the Auckland Battalion facing Fir Tree Wood, and the remaining two companies, the 10th North Otago and 14th South Otago, were brought up to support the Wellington Battalion on the left. Lieutenant Colonel Malone brought up his Ruahine Company, which had not taken part in the morning's advance. The orders for the afternoon advance were as brief as those of the morning. Malone queried them with his Brigade Commander.

'At 5.30 — in spite of my pointing out that unless the troops on my flank came up and went forward, we couldn't — we were ordered to: "Fix bayonets — Go right thro — No shilly shally." Colonel F.E. Johnston thus giving me the order! I pointed out that for troops at varying distances from 0 to 1400 to 1500 yards to start an attack at the same instance — didn't give [my] people [the Wellington Battalion — being the only battalion that had gained any fresh ground] a chance in the face of enfilade machine guns and rifle fire not to mention about artillery fire and all against an invisible foe — I was sat on and was practically told I was more bother than I was worth!'[17]

It was a repeat of the morning's shambles. All along the line the word to advance was given, and 'men rose, fell, ran, rushed on in waves, broke, recoiled, crumbled away and disappeared.'[18]

The 2nd Australian Infantry Brigade were ordered to attack on the New Zealanders' right. They, like the New Zealanders that morning, were given 25 minutes' notice. 'The most that could be done was to rip out an older to move at once in fighting column …' They advanced up level with the forward New Zealanders, suffered heavily and were forced to ground. 'They set us an impossible task.'[19]

No additional ground was gained. In the centre the Auckland Battalion, supported by the Otagos, charged across open ground, the 'Daisy Patch', and were cut to pieces, Joe Gasparich is one of them. 'No sooner had the word been given to us when up jumped a whole mob of the Auckland Battalion on my right — and they yelled their heads off: "Come on you buggers!" — and there they went. When I went away first I made a vow to myself. I said that if ever I get into an attack in open country and we're going to rush the enemy, I'm going over in the first wave because I looked at it this way — whoever the enemy is, he won't be expecting it at the precise moment we make the charge and once we start he will be looking for it every second … So I hopped up. Grabbed my tunic and pulled it on. The web equipment over my shoulder loose, my rifle and bayonet and I ran. These other fellows were more than halfway across the "Daisy Patch" and I chased them … with the bullets whizzing all around me. I came across to a dry watercourse and the fellows had lined up along this and formed a firing line.

'There was Jacko, and I could see him, right along the ridge, he was entrenched. There he was absolutely as safe as houses — we were stonkered — it was madness for us to take that! But, blow me down, if a Turkish officer did not get out of his trench up on the ridge, a couple of hundred yards away. He must have been overexcited or something. He wanted to win his way to heaven two or three times I think. He had a sword, of all things, and he waved his sword round his head. Well that was too much for me. I thought if he can stand up and do those things, I can. So I stood up and took a steady bead on the gentleman and squeezed the trigger and just as I did so I got a whale of a bang in the elbow, so my rifle dropped to the ground and I grabbed my arm and my hand felt hot and I looked down and there was blood squirting out.

'I slithered down out of the fire and on the bank at the side was Captain Bartlett, wounded, lying in the scrub, bandaged up, and I remember saying to him: "Sir, this is a sheer waste of good men," I said. "I'm going back, I'm going to take the risk and go back and see what I can do to stop this senseless waste of life." So I took off my web equipment and I set off at the gallop and the ground was jumping and the bushes

Soldiers of the Canterbury Battalion hastily dug in at Cape Helles before the attack on 8 May 1915. *(WF-002663-10, Canterbury Infantry Officer's Album, NAM Waiouru)*

were swaying and it sounded as if I was running through a swarm of bees on the move, and I ran into a gap that had been cut by some Pommies who were down behind us. I was bone dry and I wanted a drink, and they didn't have any water. But they had the rum ration, so they gave me a good solid swig of rum — and I would have taken on anybody!'[20]

Every battalion had its Daisy Patch, and those that succeeded in running forward unscathed found cover. Behind them the following waves of men were cut down and eventually refused to move forward. The Auckland and Otagos grimly held on to the fringes of the wood but were pulled back after dark. 'We retired over the open area — the Daisy Patch — where the dead and survivors lay among the poppies and daisies, the cries and moans followed us in our retreat.'[21]

The day's fighting had seen the brigade suffer over 835 casualties. In the Auckland Battalion, only two officers were unwounded, and the battalion was reduced to 268 men.

New Zealanders as a body experienced what the Otagos had suffered on the Bloody Sunday of 2 May. The men were puzzled and bitter. After the months of hard training in Egypt during which the professional Imperial officer and soldier had been held up as an ideal, here they were fighting with them, but where was the professionalism? A private soldier of the Otagos wrote: 'Our work last night was of a most unsatisfactory nature, and blame is attachable in some quarter. We were pushed forward in a most

The 15th North Auckland Company, Auckland Battalion, moving forward in the attack on Krithia, 8 May 1915. 'We were pushed forward in a most disorganised state ... We were given no direction or objective and all our men were not able to take a position when they got up.' *(WF-003520-04, F.W. Watson Collection, Puke Ariki, New Plymouth)*

disorganised state … We were given no direction or objective and all our men were not able to take a position when they got up. The position seemed too crowded … The whole of the NZ Brigade was fearfully mixed up … It is a pity that the advance was made under such conditions because it does not increase the fighting power of our men to whom great credit is due for the discipline that exists. They go forward whenever they are ordered although they know that in many cases they are walking to their death.'[22]

The stoicism and initiative of the New Zealanders under fire earned the admiration and praise of the staff watching the attacks. That was scant consolation to the men and officers taking part. By the evening of 8 May, after 14 days on the Peninsula, the New Zealand Brigade had suffered over 2000 casualties. On the first day, the Auckland and Canterbury companies from the *Lutzow* had suffered more casualties than New Zealanders had experienced in three years of the Boer War. Wellington had lost heavily on 27 April, Otago had lost half its strength on 2–3 May. Through all that struggle at Anzac there had been no time to think of the casualties, no time to think about the planning and purpose of the campaign. Men were tired and concentrated on getting through each day. There was a feeling that things had gone wrong, but among the men the most common remark was, 'What will they think about this at home?'[23]

There was the feeling in the ranks that even though the whole thing might be a bloody failure, soldiers had to see it through. Otherwise how would they face those back home in New Zealand? Now, on 8 May, the New Zealand Brigade had been destroyed as a fighting machine.

It was reduced to 1700 men and, like the 2nd Australian Brigade, had been uselessly thrown away on two quickly forgotten Balaclavas. Plugge of the Auckland Battalion had been wounded. Brown was the third CO of the Canterburys. Moore of the Otagos and Malone of the Wellingtons were the only remaining original COs of the Brigade. Malone's Wellingtons, at half strength, were the strongest of the four battalions. His casualties since the landing had been 80 killed, 350 wounded, 42 missing and 42 sick in hospital — 514 out of 937 that came ashore. Malone was emphatic about the reasons for the failure: 'By a night advance I am quite satisfied we could have gained the same ground if not more, with probably no loss at all! Such is the scheme of war as preached by people who are supposed to know better. "C'est magnifique, mais ce n'est pas la guerre." That is my criticism of this war in these parts … I am quite satisfied that the New Zealand officer has absolutely nothing to learn from the imported man and that active service has taught the latter nothing.'[24]

In all quarters the New Zealanders found there was an unthinking rigidity in the approach of many of the Imperial officers that did not allow for the conditions they met on the Peninsula. For these officers, orders were orders, regardless. The New Zealanders grew bitter also when, after repeated failure, the same officers suggested that 'regular' soldiers would have succeeded in the same circumstances.

This bitterness was to grow in the weeks ahead. While New Zealanders had no illusions about the job to be done and the likely cost, they now started to question the ability of their commanders. They held the forward trenches at Helles until relieved on the night of the 8th, digging and resting by day, clearing the dead and wounded by night. Dysentery started to spread, and confidence waned. A soldier of the Wellingtons wrote: '10th May — Still in the trenches, a quiet day, my nerves gone, feel miserable, been hoping a bullet gets me.'[25]

Malone noted in his diary that the losses of the Otago and Auckland battalions had been so severe that both were demoralised and unfit for operations. Lieutenant Algie was one of the few surviving Auckland officers; his battalion could muster 268 men out of the original 1000, while their share of the 3rd Reinforcements brought their strength up to just 468. 'Our company went in 120 strong and came out with 55 men. A terrible price to pay. The casualty list of our officers is now 26 and only 4 of us are now left. Sinel and I in the 6th, Ward in the 16th and Major Bayly in the 15th.'[26] Bayly was killed by a stray bullet as the battalion embarked to return to Anzac.

The losses in officers and NCOs had a crippling effect. Strong leadership was needed to rebuild the spirits of the shattered battalions. In some cases there was blind resentment by Main Body survivors towards the new reinforcements. 'The reinforcements have arrived and they sicken me. There are none of our officers left to see about promotion for the survivors. F.H.J., who has another section now, gets no promotion while cowards who asked to be left at the base in Egypt and who have seen no fighting retain their rank.'[27]

Men grew outwardly callous and unless they happened to meet a close friend

Anzac Cove. This beach was the lifeline to the besieged inside the Anzac perimeter under artillery fire from north and south. Shipping movement by day became impossible. Watson's Pier, to the right of the barges, was built using a naval shell of the *Goeben* as a pile driver. Boxes of stores have been stacked along the pier to protect working parties from shrapnel fire. *(WF-002415-8, Norman Annabell Album, NAM Waiouru)*

On the beach at Anzac Cove, looking north to Ari Burnu headland. The space is crammed with stores and men. *(O15A, AL0645, Stereo Glass Plate, Wingnut Archive)*

among the reinforcements, a gulf existed between the survivors and new arrivals. Privately, in their diaries, the main body men cried for missing friends. 'I haven't had the heart to write in this lately. One feels fearfully lonely with only one pal left.'[28]

The originals from the landing realised that this was not another Boer War. It was not going to be 12 months and then home to be feted as a hero. It would be attack after attack after attack. The casualties suffered so far made men realise that death or maiming was the likely outcome. Lieutenant Colonel Fenwick wrote: 'One man looked at me this morning and said, "They say we shall have to hold this place for three months, Sir?" I said, "Oh, perhaps less than that." He looked down this beach where the pretty shrapnel clouds were floating, "Then I expect it will be only our reinforcements who will be here then."'[29]

The 3rd Battery NZA was one of the batteries supporting the New Zealanders at Helles on 8 May. It remained at Helles until the middle of August when it sailed for Anzac. Among men of this battery too, entries are a record of Turkish shelling and casualties: 'While helping Moonie to dig his dug-out, Gunner Richardson was unfortunate to stop a bullet in the side, he died within half an hour, just as the doctor arrived … We have got used to this now and apart from being sorry that another of our mates has had to leave us, these scenes affect us but little. His wound is bound, his disc taken off, his uniform placed over him after all papers etc. have been taken out, he

The Royal Marine Light Infantry (RMLI) moving along North Beach to occupy the outposts. The outline of Plugge's Plateau is on the skyline. *(WF-002270-17, Alexander Orr Collection, Wairarapa Archive)*

is then wrapped up in his blanket and pinned in. He lies just a little way off the main track along the cliff for all to see. The Minister arrives, we were fortunate in being able to get one on this occasion, we desert the guns for a few minutes and crawl along to the shallow grave dug earlier in the day by volunteers, to pay our respects to the dead. We have to lie or sit under cover so that the enemy may not "spot" us and let fly. We gather round the grave, his own puttees are used to lower him into his last resting place. The Chaplain speaks, all's over.'[30]

In the line south of Krithia the New Zealanders dug in and improved their meagre gains: 'Tuesday 11th May. Joyful news this morning. We heard we are going to be relieved from trenches tonight. 8.00 p.m. We are now going out of trenches. Manchester Territorials taking our place ...'[31]

The New Zealanders were relieved by the 42nd Territorial (Manchester) Division: '[It was] in the middle of a very wet night and I was sorry for those boys. Most of them seemed to be only 17 or 18 years old, and physically they were not of a very high standard compared to we Colonials. I can remember the Sergeant Major dumping these poor young chaps, some of them crying, in our trench, and even though we were glad to get out of it, I was sorry for them.'[32]

It was a night that, as George Bollinger recalled, put the final seal on their Helles experience: 'Oh what misery ... we had to trudge 5 miles to beach. The night was pitch and torrents of rain came down. We arrived at beach about 3.00 a.m. this morning and lay down in the rain. Dogged tired we slept. At 8.00 a.m. we moved a mile inland. It has rained all day and everything is miserable. Dysentery has set in and men are generally done up.'[33]

Helles was a stalemate, Kiithia and Achi Baba as far away as ever. Hamilton wrote: 'We are now on our last legs. The beautiful battalions of the 25th April are wasted skeletons now; shadows of what they had been.'[34]

The New Zealanders now in reserve provided working parties at Helles: 'Since then we were wharf building and road making on the beach, until we got to hot thieving from the ASC [Army Service Corps] stores ... We've had a rough time, an experience to live through, and wonder that such things can be, but we must take things as we find them, and hope that we'll have the good fortune to get through alive.'[35]

8

THE SIEGE OF ANZAC

Practically we are like a rat in a trap. The rat cannot get out and the owner of the trap does not like putting his hand in, and can only annoy the rat by pushing things through the bars. Unquestionably we are held up. What good we are doing I can't say; perhaps the War Office can, but NZ is losing good men for some reason or other.[1]

Anzac was a tiny, foreign and besieged foothold on Turkey. Its shape had been determined by the failure of the attacks in May, and it was to remain unchanged until the beginning of the August offensive. Birdwood's ANZACs held two ridges on an inhospitable coast. On land they were always overshadowed and under fire from higher ground, and at sea, their only source of communication and supply, they were under fire from both flanks. In the north, guns in the Anafarta area and Suvla could fire at any shipping moving into Anzac by day. In the south, the batteries in the olive groves inland of Gaba Tepe could fire on to the southern arm of Anzac Cove at Hell Spit and reach inside the cove itself, bursting shrapnel over the beach at the north end of the cove. All the beleaguered garrison could do was to hold on and wait for the forces at Helles to break out and link up with them.

Within the Anzac lines everyone, such as Lieutenant Colonel Fenwick, was aware that the landings had failed and the Turks held the upper hand: 'The official *Guide Book* says "bears, hyenas and other wild animals inhabit this place". We have seen no bears or hyenas and are trying to push the other wild animals back to Constantinople. The trouble is we have bitten off more than we can chew and we know it. I blame Winston Churchill for the loss of our boys. The job is too big for anything under 100,000 men and we are about 40,000 effective.'[2]

The move of the New Zealand Infantry Brigade to Helles on the night of 5 May left Godley's NZ & A Division a New Zealand one in name only. New Zealanders remained in his headquarters, and in the artillery, engineers, signallers and medical staff, but the division's share of the ANZAC front line was now held by two half brigades, each two battalions strong, from Major-General Paris's Naval Division and the 4th Australian Infantry Brigade under Colonel John Monash.

The ANZAC front was divided into four sections, Nos 3 and 4 being in Godley's area. Monash's brigade held No. 3 Section, the vital head of Monash Gully, from the line on Second Ridge of Courtney's, Quinn's and the gap across the head of the gully to Pope's Hill. It was reinforced by two battalions of Brigadier General Trotman's Naval Brigade. Trotman, as the senior officer, commanded No. 3 Section. On his left was No. 4 Section; the line on Russell's Top, Walker's Ridge and the Outposts was held by Brigadier General Mercer's Royal Marine Light Infantry Brigade. Birdwood had told Hamilton he was confident he could hold Anzac and he had indicated that the attack of 2–3 May, though it had failed in its objectives, 'had straightened out his line on the left.'[3] He professed to being 'pretty happy' but privately he had doubts. Bean records Birdwood as saying, 'I shall be a little anxious while I have to rely on the 4th Australians and Naval battalions.'[4]

Both the naval brigades had been shaken by their experiences in the attacks on 2–3 May, when they had been committed to a hopeless cause with no directions and been severely mauled. Now holding the line on Russell's Top and supporting the Australians at Pope's and Quinn's, they could see their mummified dead 'like shrivelled ants' covering the slopes of Deadman's Ridge, and heaped in untidy piles at the foot of Bloody Angle. They also suffered from the scorn of both the Australians and New Zealanders, who, in searching for reasons for the failure, fixed upon the chaotic withdrawal of the Royal Marine Light Infantry as the principal cause. Charles Saunders was working with Mercer's Brigade on Walker's Ridge: 'I don't go much on the Naval Division. Several have shot their toes off while cleaning their rifles … They are a lot of boys.'[5]

The 4th Australian Infantry Brigade had also been weakened by the failure of 2 May and its morale was low. Among the Australian brigades it had the reputation of a 'bad' brigade, and Monash, though he would win fame as a corps commander, did not have a grip on the situation within his brigade. Personal rivalries soured relationships between his battalions, and their standards of training and discipline were poor. Individual bravery was never in question but the conditions in Monash's sector gave cause for concern. Bean visited them in late May at Quinn's. 'The poor old 4th certainly has the worst bit of country to hold … It is easily the worst place in our line. The fire trench is shallow, the parapets very low — and they look very thin, and the tunnels through which you grope from one trench to another are simply a rabbit burrow — you can scarcely get through some of them. In one trench there is an archway left to avoid enfilading fire … It is not four foot — scarcely three foot thick; but in it is a dead Turk. His boot and fingers of one hand stick out from the roof as you squeeze your way under … The men were fine breezy chaps, but they were far more amateurish and casual than any of the lines we had so far gone through.'[6]

Because manpower was so reduced all available men held the front-line trenches by night. The inner-line trenches of Plugge's Plateau were deserted by day and manned by parties from the beach through the darkness.

The original scattered line of trench scrapes had been joined into a front line, but on Birdwood's insistence, this front line at Quinn's and Courtney's had remained shallow enough for the men to jump out if the Turks attacked. Birdwood feared that too deep a trench, particularly with the limited fields of fire available, would see the garrison trapped and destroyed. Supports to the front line were held below the crest, but here they were subject to any bombs that missed the front trenches and rolled down the rear slope.

Because of the closeness of the Turkish trenches, the supports and the front line had always to be on alert, ready to fix bayonets and rush forward to reinforce the front trench, or drive the Turk out if it should be taken. Godley and Birdwood were both conscious that a successful advance by the Turks in No. 3 or No. 4 sections would inevitably mean disaster at Anzac. Should Quinn's Post fall, then the tenuous communication way up Monash Gully would be completely open to Turkish fire and impossible to use. Already Turkish observation and sniping by day and night was taking a steady toll on fatigue parties as they laboured up the valley with boxes of ammunition and bully beef and kerosene tins of water. The fall of Quinn's would see the gradual unravelling of the line on Second Ridge, as Courtney's and Steele's posts would then inevitably fall. Equally, a 200 metre advance by the Turks on Russell's Top would have the same effect. The Turk would be able to fire into the rear of the ANZAC line on Second Ridge.

This constant threat of attack from an enemy a 'biscuit throw away' led to a tension and pressure on the soldier not evident on any other front in the First World War. One company of the battalion held the front trenches, another company occupied the support trenches some 5–10 metres to the rear. In reserve, in any dead ground on the rearward slopes, the remaining companies dug and carried by day and slept at night dressed and fully equipped.

It was with relief that Birdwood and Godley welcomed the New Zealand Mounteds and the Australian Light Horse in early May. 'Thank God, you have come' was Birdwood's greeting to Mackesy, CO of the Auckland Mounted Rifles. Their view of Anzac quickly dispelled hopes of a rapid advance for the Mounted Rifles. They too marvelled at the efforts of the Australians in seizing a foothold on the first day and quietly endured the good-natured chaffing of the gaunt exhausted men as they clambered up to the positions on Walker's Ridge and Russell's Top to relieve the Royal Marine Light Infantry Brigade. Charles Saunders was one who welcomed them. 'We sappers made up for our infantry being absent I can tell you. A lot of us were at our bivouac half way up Walker's Ridge, when the Mounteds passed us on foot with improvised packs and equipment. How they laboured up the hill that broiling hot day. As they passed us we greeted them with cries of "Where are your spurs?" "Lend us a curry comb?" "What Ho! The elite without their nags!"'[7]

The rough terrain, the tiny foothold of land and the ragged, worn men with lined faces and sunken eyes whose response to questions were curt grunts, and who replied to cheerful greetings with: 'You'd think it was our birthday!', made the reinforcements determined to show that if infantry could win these hills, then the Mounteds would hold them against any number of Turks.

The regiments spent their first night bivouacked on the slopes below Walker's

Ridge. 'Mine like the majority was none too comfortable. Selected in darkness mine was upon a one in one slope and I had to brace my feet against a tree stem to keep myself in position. Where we were, in the donga surrounded by cliffs of clay, the continuous rattle of the rifles made a terrific din and at times we could scarcely hear ourselves speak. It worried us little as the old hands told us that most of the fire passed overhead and out to sea.'[8]

Both the New Zealand Mounted Rifles and the 1st Australian Light Horse Brigade were placed under Godley's command in the NZ & A Division area. The New Zealand Mounted Rifles took over No. 4 Section from the Royal Marine Light Infantry, who were glad to see the last of Anzac. Russell commanded this section while Chauvel replaced Trotman's Naval Brigade and assumed command of No. 3 Section. Trooper Kenneth Stevens was with the Auckland Mounted Rifles: 'As darkness fell we relieved a battalion of the Royal Marine Light Infantry. The pollution in the air was most pronounced and unpleasant. The enemy kept up a hail of bullets streaming over our trenches all night. When daylight came we started to look with periscopes, made from pieces of looking glasses on sticks about eighteen inches long, for the cause of the polluted air and found there were numerous dead Turks and New Zealanders in No Man's Land between the Turkish and our trenches which were about forty yards apart.'[9]

One of Stevens' trench mates, a Boer War veteran named Bill Callaghan, took the periscope and peered through it at the clusters of New Zealand dead lying forward on Russell's Top. He turned and passed it to Stevens saying: 'If their mothers could see them this war would end today.'

'In less than twelve hours with the bullets crashing around the trench all night, in the polluted air and one look over in No Man's Land in daylight, all the glamour in war for me was lost.'[10]

Under Russell's energetic direction, the Mounteds consolidated their position on Russell's Top and sapped out into No Man's Land towards the Turkish front line. Tunnels were dug at right angles out towards The Nek, then these were broken through and the tunnel entrances connected in a continuous line. It was hard work and made more unpleasant by the dead. If they were in reach they were hooked into the trench, rolled into a ground sheet and carried through for burial, but the stench of the dead and the attendant flies by day were part of the price of holding the front line.

The Canterbury Mounted Rifles manned the outposts and the lower slopes of Walker's Ridge, with the Auckland Mounted Rifles on the left of Russell's Top facing The Nek, and the Wellington Mounted Rifles on the right overlooking the top of Monash Gully towards the Chessboard and Deadman's Ridge. Next to them, across Monash Gully, the Light Horse occupied Pope's.

'It is very like Paekakariki. We are near the top of the hill … Below us is a beautiful bay [which] the Turks are constantly shelling and from our position above we can watch the men bathing and the shells bursting within 50 yards of them … Below us the bay, with a lovely calm sunlit sea, beyond two large islands, one very much like Kapiti.'[11]

On the left of the line, the Canterbury Mounted Rifles were holding the outposts. These three positions denied Turkish infiltration along the beach but were dominated by the Sari Bair Range and the foothills along the coast above them. Each outpost had started as a smattering of shell scrapes, where movement was impossible by day, but now each in turn was developed into a small fortress, cut off by day but capable of matching Turkish fire. When the Mounteds arrived they found the Naval Brigade and the Marines had surrendered the initiative to the Turks. Turkish snipers had driven the naval garrison deep into the trenches, careless movement meant death, every loophole had been zeroed in on by snipers, and at night the Turks showed their mastery in handling the machine gun by spraying the top of the sandbags with fire, ripping the sandbags and killing any of the sentries peering over the parapet.

The Mounteds slowly wrestled this mastery from the Turk, and accepted the challenge offered by the broken foothills stretching north below the Sari Bair Range towards the open cultivated areas of the Suvla Plain. Major Percy Overton, the second-in-command of the Canterbury Mounteds, co-ordinated the patrolling programme. On 16 May he wrote: 'The country here is very hilly and is broken with deep gullies, the sides of which are very steep and covered with dwarf oak and scrub holly but will suit us down to the ground as it is what we are accustomed to. I am assisting General Birdwood's staff by reconnoitring.'[12]

It was country similar to the high-country runs and scree slopes of inland Canterbury. On the 14th a party of the 10th Squadron Canterbury Mounted Rifles under Major George Hutton sailed north in the destroyer HMS *Usk*, landed at Suvla Bay, 'and mustered the point, Nibrunesi, for observers, found none but got four wild sheep'.[13]

From their arrival, the Mounteds made the foothills and plains to the north their own. Overton had earned a reputation as a scout in the Boer War and he consolidated that reputation at Anzac.

'I have been out on two occasions on reconnaissance outside our outposts and through the Turkish lines. The first time I took Corporal Denton and we had a great day together and gained a lot of valuable information for which General Godley thanked me. The last time I was out for two nights and a day and I took Trooper M. McInnes and Corporal Young. We had a most exciting and interesting time dodging Turkish outposts. I was able from what I saw of the country to make a map and gain much information as to the movements of the Turks, and would not have missed the experience for worlds.'[14]

Hemmed in by Baby 700 on the obvious route to the vital heights of Chunuk Bair and 971, the left flank offered the best way out of the impasse. The Turkish commanders appeared to have considered the terrain too rugged for a major advance. From the Turkish perspective it was the ANZACs who were pinned against the sea, and the isolated ANZAC outposts were to prevent the Turks breaking in rather than being a way for the ANZACs to break out.

Overton's reconnaissance showed that the valleys or deres leading up towards the heights bordering the coast offered routes for infantry. Turkish observation posts on the foothills would have to be captured, but his reports confirmed a drift in thinking that was already evident among officers of the NZ & A Division.

Captain Robert Guthrie, Regimental Medical Officer of the Canterbury Mounted Rifles. He stands on the parapet of the Mounteds' trench on Russell's Top during the Armistice, 24 May 1915. The Sphinx is in the background. *(WF-002082-27, Deans Collection, NAM Waiouru)*

'If their mothers could see them this war would end today.' New Zealand dead in the trenches at Gallipoli.

(WF-002077-12, F.M. and W.R. Pyle Collection, NAM Waiouru)

Malone was one who had thought of the possibilities on this flank. After the failure at Helles he discussed its possibilities with Lieutenant Colonel George Richardson NZSC, a New Zealand regular officer. Richardson had been at Staff College in England at the outbreak of war, and had been appointed AA & QMG (the principal administrative officer of the division) in General Paris's Royal Naval Division headquarters. Encouraged by Richardson's response, Malone discussed the plan with Paris and promised to bring it up with his superiors at Anzac. 'If I were GOC [General Officer Commanding a division] I should make a good defensive line on the ground we have gained, make it impregnable, then garrison it with the weakest troops. Except a few take all the best troops north to Gaba Tepe or Anzac Bay, as I believe is the right name of our landing place N[orth] of here.

'Then prepare a plan of attack on Hill 971 from Nibrunesi Pt. Get every available man of war to come up and at night take position at sea commanding 971 and line thence to 224 D5 [Baby 700] which is the crest of the Ridge. A frontage of about 2800 yards … Then march up, say three divisions, say 45,000 men, to take up position to attack …

'Everything and everybody in position by night and attack commenced at dawn … At dawn the troops now at Anzac Bay to make a feint and so engage Turks now facing them.

'Aerial reconnaissance would show, I believe, that the Turks have not really fortified the NW slope of the position to be attacked. The crest gained. Dig in. Bring up guns etc. and prepare for a further advance either immediately or next day to Mai Tepe and thence to Kilia Tepe on the straits. This would cut the Turks' communications.

'At present it is stalemate and attack direct on Achi Baba or 971 must be slow and costly … Manoeuvre is the antidote to entrenchment.

'I hope to be able to get GHQ [General Headquarters] to consider such a plan, if one is not already under way.'[15]

This prospect was already being considered at Anzac. Overton's reconnaissance had convinced Brigadier General Russell and Powles, his brigade major, that the way out was through the unguarded ridges and valleys to the north. They spoke to Godley, and Braithwaite, his GSO1 (General Staff Officer), noted in his diary on 15 May: 'Everything tends to the belief that we ought to open and extend our frontage, and possibly move forward to take 224 D5 [Baby 700] via the North valleys on our left flank.'[16]

Godley briefed Birdwood, who was enthusiastic and directed that further patrolling be conducted. On 27 May, Overton sent three patrols to establish the routes to the main ridge. Lieutenant Allan Finlayson led a patrol up Sazli Dere, but was fired on and forced to return. Captain N.E Hastings worked his patrol past Turkish outposts in Chailak Dere and reached the point where the valley climbed to the apex of Rhododendron Ridge, but a Turkish picquet forced him back. Overton patrolled up the Aghyl Dere and followed the southern branch towards Chunuk Bair. He reported that the outposts appeared to be manned only at night and the Turks apparently believed the rugged nature of the country would prevent operations in this area. By the end of May, Godley, Birdwood and Skeen, Birdwood's chief of staff, were working on a plan similar to that contemplated by Malone.

'The Great Sap', which was dug from the northern headland of Anzac Cove north along the coast to the outposts manned by the New Zealand Mounted Rifles. The Maori Contingent would widen it to 1.5 metres by the beginning of August. *(WF-002082-84, Deans Collection, NAM Waiouru)*

On 30 May, Birdwood briefed Hamilton. His plan envisaged a feint towards Gaba Tepe in the south, simultaneously with a night advance north through the foothills to seize Chunuk Bair. The highest point, 971, was excluded because Overton had discovered a steep impassable chasm that separated the features of Chunuk Bair and Hill Q to the south from 971 in the north.* Birdwood was well aware of the difficulties: 'A night attack will involve a certain number of troops losing their way. This, however, is not a matter of consequence, as they will know they all have to press upwards.'[17]

The attack would need to be carried out as quickly as possible. Birdwood hoped for June. He wanted another 3000–4000 reinforcements and saw Cox's 29th Indian Brigade as perfect for the task, since 'it is ideal country for Gurkhas.' He would use the New Zealand Mounted Rifles as the spearhead, for they knew the ground and were already itching to end the deadly monotony of trench life at Anzac.

Hamilton was impressed. Operations at Helles were expensive in men and Achi Baba was as remote a prospect as ever. But Hamilton needed men to ensure success. He cabled Kitchener asking for two corps totalling four new divisions. For three weeks there was no answer. The Dardanelles stalemate had resulted in a crisis within the British government — and for most of May the higher direction of the war languished. In Britain, Churchill was replaced at the Admiralty and a coalition government was established. The Dardanelles Committee was formed to decide policy but it was not until 7 June that the committee met to consider the question of sending support to the Dardanelles. They gave Hamilton his reinforcements. Three divisions of the New Army would be despatched, the last arriving by the middle of July. Hamilton was cautioned: 'While steadily pressing the enemy, there seems to be no reason for running any premature risks in the meantime.'[18]

It was a little late for such advice. At Hunter-Weston's request, Hamilton had agreed to further operations at Helles on 28 May and 4 June. The latter effort was particularly well planned, with troops going into battle for the first time knowing what their objectives were, and how they were to achieve them. It came close to success, and with the Turkish front penetrated and crumbling, Hunter-Weston, with 18 battalions of British and French troops in reserve, had to choose between reinforcing success or reinforcing the flank where the attack had broken down. His choice was to reinforce the tenuous flank and everything previously won was lost in the Turkish counter-attacks. The forces at Helles were now exhausted. Hamilton had no choice but to delay any further operations until late July. Birdwood's plan would have to wait.

In early May, there were immediate and pressing problems within the Anzac perimeter. 'The Turks have a very strong position slightly above us and we have not enough men by half to shift them. I am sure they have two armies, one for fighting and one for digging, as their fire is ever so much heavier than ours and also for every shovel full of earth that we pitched up, they pitched up three and man for man, our Colonials were better and stronger men.'[19]

---

* The seizing of 971 would later be included in the final plan, but unquestionably Overton's original assessment of the difficulties imposed by the country was correct.

The Turks, under Kemal's inspired leadership, threatened to dig the ANZACs off the Peninsula. Line after line of brown earth crept down the slopes of Baby 700 and onto the Chessboard. They burrowed forward at The Nek, at Quinn's and on the Lone Pine Plateau. The ANZACs were left hanging on to the rim along Second Ridge. Turkish fire now dominated the main artery up Monash Gully, as Percy Fenwick described: 'Have just got back from the Valley of Death, otherwise called Monash's Valley after Col. Monash … At the south end of our beach is a steep bluff which the enemy are particular fond of shelling. You have to cross this bluff climbing over it by steps cut in the clay, and go down the other side into the valley. If the Turks shell you while you are crossing your chances of being unhit are about equal to one's chances of winning Tattersall's sweep. As soon as you strike the valley all your chances are quadrupled. The valley is really pretty, a deep cleft between high hills covered with vivid green scrub. A narrow road winds through this. The first thing one notices is the number of stretchers with wounded passing down to the beach … The whole valley roars and cracks with echoing shot — howitzer, shell, maxim, rifle and grenades. Overshot bullets sing gaily overhead and everyone seems inclined to hurry. Half a mile up a good well has been sunk giving 400 gallons a day. A few more yards and we were stopped by an Australian Colonel who advised us not to pass Suicide's Corner. He told us he had seen 14 men shot as they tried to rush past the turning. Three were caught in 10 seconds. All this in the last 4 hours … The Engineers have built traverses of sandbags and put a man with a red flag to warn you to keep under cover, but there is a hundred deadly yards over which you and death race for stakes …'[20]

It was the same on the beach. Shelling was making landing of stores and men by day increasingly risky. It had forced Godley's headquarters to move further up the slopes of Plugge's Plateau onto 'Godley's Terrace'. On every side was depressing evidence of growing Turkish superiority. Lieutenant Colonel W.G. Braithwaite, GSO1 of the NZ & A Division recorded in his diary: 'The Turks continue their relentless fire by day and night. Shelling still continues. The Army Corps Commander Lieut[enant] General WR. Birdwood was wounded yesterday in the head whilst visiting Quinn's Post and today, Major General Bridges, Commanding the 1st Australian Division has been rather badly hit in the thigh by a sharpshooter while going up Monash Gully.' Birdwood was only slightly concussed but Bridges died of his wounds. Walker replaced him as Commander 1st Australian Division. 'Periscopes are running short and there is a shortage of looking glasses, as the ships from which they were taken have also scattered to the four winds.'[21]

Fear of submarines had driven the large fleet of transports that had been anchored off Anzac back to the harbours of Imbros and Lemnos. Except for three warships, the two old battleships *London* and *Triumph* and a cruiser, a hospital ship and a few barges and tugs, the seas were deserted. The armies at Helles and Anzac were on their own.

On 18 May, aerial reconnaissance indicated an imminent major Turkish offensive at Anzac. In the late afternoon of that day, artillery fire was heavy and a Turkish warship in the Narrows fired 48 shells over the Peninsula, damaging Courtney's Post and wrecking the dressing station in Monash Gully, as Charles Saunders described:

'We engineers had to "stand by" as all the trenches were full of infantry. What a noise there was with each shot fired by either side echoing down the ravine; our Indian Mountain guns and 18 pounders on top of Walker's Ridge gave the Turks' trenches socks!'[22]

Mustafa Kemal, commanding the 19th Division, had been placed under the orders of Essad Pasha in the Anzac Area. Essad's forces now numbered 42,000 infantry against an ANZAC strength of 17,356 men with 12,540 rifles and 43 guns. This included the 2nd Australian Infantry Brigade, which had returned from Helles on 16 May. It was held in reserve.

At midnight there was a burst of fire from the Turkish trenches and the Mounteds on Russell's Top and Walker's Ridge 'stood to' and manned their trenches. Rum was issued to all ranks. Bill East was in the Wellington Mounted Rifles. 'We were told to stand to — expecting an attack by the Turks and next thing I knew there was a sergeant alongside me. He said, "Come on. Hold out your pannikin, where is it?

'I found my pannikin, held it out and he just about

Bringing down a stretcher case to the New Zealand Field Ambulance dressing station at the foot of Walker's Ridge. *(WF-002447-71, A.V. Short Collection, NAM Waiouru)*

half filled it with rum. I said to the joker alongside me, "Here what's this stuff?" He says rum, he says, get it into you, it'll do you good, so I took a sip of it and just about coughed and couldn't get my breath or anything else. However, I made the attempt and I swallowed the lot, and that was the end of me because I didn't know anything more about the attack or anything else. It was all over by eleven o'clock the next morning and I was just coming to life with the sun beaming in on me. That was my first experience of a fight.'[23]

In the Auckland Mounted Rifles' trenches facing The Nek on Russell's Top, two saps had been dug at right angles from the existing front line to close the gap between the Mounteds and the Turkish trenches. They had not been completed, and on 19 May they were merely two big ditches with no parapet or firing step and not wide enough for two men with webbing and rifle to pass each other. Two squadrons were holding the front line and the new saps — 3rd Auckland held the left, 4th Waikatos the right. The 11th North Auckland Mounted Rifles were in support back in the maze of communication trenches in a dip at the rear of the plateau. Their position gave neither observation not field of fire.

Private Fred Palmer was manning the Wellington Infantry machine gun sited by Wallingford on the left flank. It could fire along the left sap and the old front line. 'The faces just got larger and larger in the dawn until you could see the brass buckles on their belts and I tapped the gun and they were wiped away.'[24]

At a range of 10–20 metres the Mounteds opened fire and the Turks advancing in line were shot down or went to ground. 'It was murder ... the worst moment in my life.'[25]

All along the Anzac front line the fighting continued until sunrise. On Russell's Top, Turks poured through the gap into the centre between the two forward saps. In both saps the Mounteds stood, kneeled, lay out in the open or wedged themselves with a boot into the earth wall, firing at each wave as they passed. There were no bombs or flares — it was bullet, rifle butt and bayonet.

In the right sap, Lieutenant C. James and the Whakatane Troop were posted as garrison. Their orders were to hold for 20 minutes at all costs. At 3.30 a.m., as the Turkish attack started, James and his men clambered into the open, opening fire on the Turks running past them at 3–4 metres' range. Within minutes James was dead and two thirds of his troop were casualties, but throughout the fight reserves came forward, first from 4th Squadron and then from 11th Squadron, and the sap was held.

Sergeant John Wilder was on the right flank in the 9th Squadron Wellington East Coast Mounted Rifles. 'In five trenches we had a fairly warm time this

An Auckland Battalion machine-gun team firing a Maxim gun on Russell's Top. *(WW1 Photographic Collection A.A. Perry Negatives, Auckland War Memorial Museum)*

morning. Turks charged our left wing [Auckland] and we gave them a pretty fair smashing. They also attacked on the right [Australia]. Altogether they lost 2000 men during the day, our casualties only amounted to 150 for the same time. Our troop got a lot of good shooting.'[26]

As day broke, scattered parties of Turks were still being ordered forward. In the trenches adrenalin was high. Men were jostling each other for a position on the firing step, swearing as bolts jammed and barrels burnt. Others stood calmly on the parapet picking off any movement. The Commanding Officer of the Aucklands, 'German Joe' Mackesy, was one of these. An order came to cease fire, saying that Australians were in front. Men remember Mackesy shouting, 'Australians be damned, ask where that order came from?'[27] The firing continued.

The attacks were heaviest along the Australian front line, but apart from Courtney's Post, where Turks briefly entered the front trenches, the line held. Dead and dying Turks lay in great numbers in No Man's Land.*

The Turkish commanders discovered what the ANZACs had learnt at such great cost on 2 and 8 May at Helles. Bravery alone was no defence against strong

---

* Pte A. Jacka, 14th Australian Battalion, would win a VC for his actions at Courtney's Post.

entrenchments and well-sited machine guns. In particular the machine guns sited by Major Jessie Wallingford and Captain John Rose of the NZSC and machine gun officers of the NZ Infantry Brigade and 4th Australian Brigade respectively, made the most vulnerable point, Quinn's Post, secure against attack. Godley had recruited these officers from the Musketry School at Hythe to train the New Zealand forces. He was one of the first to recognise the advantages of pooled or 'brigaded' machine guns and, acting on Wallingford's advice, the NZ & A machine guns transformed the situation between the isolated posts at the head of Monash Gully. The technique was also adopted by the 1st Australian Division. Godley 'asked permission to place two machine guns at Steeles' on the left of the area belonging to the 1st Australian Division'. Godley explained 'that each unit could often be best defended by its neighbours, and asked that officers of each division might visit adjoining posts of the other in order to arrange for mutual support.'[28] Eleven machine guns coveted the head of Monash Gully and it was this crossfire that wrought such devastation on the Turkish attack.

The extent of the Turkish losses was not at first appreciated until a member of Birdwood's staff came forward and looked over the parapet. A counter-attack was ordered but by now the opportunity had gone, as the Turks were back in their trenches and reorganising.

Clutha McKenzie was one of the 6th Manawatu Squadron ordered forward for the

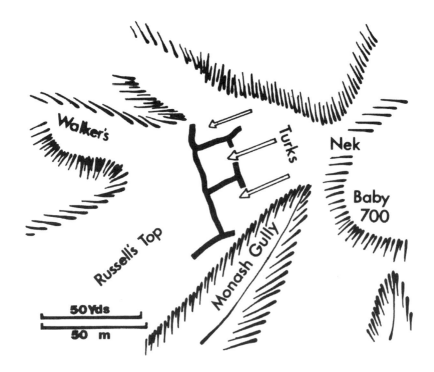

The Turkish attack, 19 May 1915.

counter-attack: 'At 1.00 p.m. our troop went into No. 4 Sap. Our troop was ordered to get over the parapet and lie down. Here we lay in the hot sun, with the dead of three weeks' past battles around, waiting the order to charge. There was a terrific fusillading all along the line and after half an hour we were recalled as it was expected that the enemy would charge us. We waited for them but they did not come and fusillading gradually slackened. So we withdrew and the attack was abandoned. Had we made the charge they consider that few of us, if any, would have come back, so terrific was the fire on account of which the attack was given up. Machine guns would have mown us down. Godley several times ordered us to move but our Brigadier refused.'[29]

Rod McCandlish was in the same squadron. 'Prepared to make an attack on Turk trenches. Was ordered out of sap and lay under heavy fire. Hell to pay over it.'[30] Both Meldrum, Commanding Officer of the Wellington Mounteds, and Mackesy, Commanding Officer of the Auckland Mounteds, objected to such a counter-attack. Finally, Russell appeared to have convinced Godley that the attempt could not succeed. This action had important repercussions. As the diaries show, the men were quick to blame Godley and when Mackesy, a noted horseman, returned to Egypt to advise on an outbreak of strangles among the horses, his men saw this as a direct consequence of his refusal to counter-attack. It was a curious situation. Godley demonstrated that he understood the power of the machine gun in the defence. Yet he failed to take into account the fact that the Turks possessed the same defensive power. He was prepared to launch an unsupported squadron across The Nek in daylight at the strongest sector of the Turks' defences. It was the same ground over which a division of Turks had just failed. Incidents like this would occur again in June and in August. It was more than a case of just not crediting the Turk with the same ability as the ANZAC. It appeared that Godley could not or would not question a directive given him by Birdwood, even when the inevitable delay in ANZAC Headquarters' learning of the situation meant the opportunity had long passed. In such situations Godley would privately detach himself from the consequences and accept the order without demur. This eventually destroyed the New Zealanders' trust in Godley as a commander.

The front trenches, already unpleasant with the smell of dead, were now unbearable, as these bodies had been disturbed and augmented with hundreds more: 'With a hook on the end of a stick we collected as many Turks as we could reach from our trenches. One we hauled in had lain less than a yard from our parapet and he hardly hit the bottom of our trench before he threw his hands up and pleaded for mercy. There was a not a scratch on him and he was the cause of the only laugh we had on that day of sad and sordid events. He became a prisoner instead of having a rope put around his neck and dragged along the bottom of our trench to the huge trench grave we dug for Turks.'[31]

That afternoon, informal armistices occurred as both sides were conscious of the agony of the wounded in the hot sun. But generally these were brief, as both sides feared further attacks. Most of the wounded died, neglected between the lines. The attack demoralised the Turk, and it also brought about a change of heart among the ANZACs. The Turk had been painted as a cruel foe. Little mercy was expected for anyone who fell into his hands. A grudging respect had developed for his bravery

Lieutenant C. James, 4th Waikato Squadron. 'Hold for 20 minutes at all costs.' *(NZ Herald)*

and skills as sniper, bomber and machine gunner. In these arts he had forced the ANZACs to strive to meet his standards. Before 19 May, the Turk had been impersonal, a movement behind the parapet, a figure in the distance, a shadow behind a loophole. Now they had seen him advance and die, face to face. He was human too, a fellow sufferer.

The attack sped up the return of the New Zealand Infantry Brigade from Helles. After absorbing the Third Reinforcements of 839, the brigade numbered 2700 strong instead of 4055. Already it had suffered over 2000 casualties. Frank Hardey in the Canterbury Battalion watched from the ship. 'Arrived at Anzac, however, we knew at once we were back. As we lay out waiting for the steam boats and lighter we watched. Right round our circle of hills we could hear the unremitting crack of rifle fire. Sometimes we could distinguish the "twin cylinder motor bike noise" made by machine guns. Bullets started pinging round us as we transferred into the tugs; someone got killed, several wounded ... Indeed, we realised we were back home again!'[32]

The infantry went into reserve and quartered in gullies off the beach and Shrapnel Gully, known as 'Rest' and 'Reserve' gullies. 'Rest' at Anzac was a misnomer. Unlike Helles, where labour corps unloaded stores, all the work at Anzac was carried out by troops resting from the front lines. Private Ben Smart, of the Wellington Battalion, 19 years old, was one of the Third Reinforcements: 'On fatigues this morning making a mule track up this gully to bring up stores but we have to carry all water up by hand in kerosene tins and I may say the job nearly succeeds in breaking our hearts.'[33]

It certainly broke their health. There was no rest for anyone at Anzac. 'We made roads, dug saps, and any pick and shovel work that was going. Sometimes we would work all night to work unobserved.'[34]

The flies and heat made sleep during the day impossible and the men were always on call to reinforce the line. Everything had to be carted to the front line by men and mule, and in many areas it was too risky to take mules. Every day and night long lines of fatigues would trudge from the beach 1000–1500 metres up Walker's Ridge or along Shrapnel Gully. Charles Saunders described the back-breaking work of fatigues.

'The actual fighting at Anzac was easiest of all. The fatigue work was enormous, colossal. Imagine a man with two kerosene tins full of water tied together with a belt and slung over the shoulder climbing for half a mile up these grades, slipping back, up and on again, the heat of the sun terrible, bullets and shells everywhere, and as often happened, a bullet and shrapnel hitting the tins and bursting it and the priceless fluid running away just as he had scrambled almost to the top. Nothing for it but to go all the way down again for some more. No I think everyone who was at Anzac will agree with me that the hardest fighting done there was by the water and rations fatigue.'[35]

On 24 May an armistice was arranged to bury the dead. Front lines were fully manned, men tensely watching for any signs of treachery. It was unnaturally quiet, with the chance for a swim and shave uninterrupted by shrapnel, a chance to look up mates in other units or visit the front line: 'Saw everyone strolling around. It reminded me of half time at a big football match.'[36]

For those burying the dead or policing the armistice arrangements, such as Lieutenant Colonel Fenwick, it was a horrible experience: 'May 24th. The most ghastly day. This morning I was ordered to act as delineating officer for the burial of the dead. The Turks had asked for an armistice and it had been arranged that no firing should take place between 7.30 a.m. and 4.30 p.m. today. At 6.00 a.m. I and my orderly, Crawford Watson, left with Col. Skeen and others and went along the beach towards Gaba Tepe. 50 men, carrying white flags, followed. The

P. M. Hanna sniping in the trenches. *(WF-002081-1, P.M. Hanna Album, NAM Waiouru)*

battleships fired till 7.10 a.m. and at 7.20 we crossed our wire entanglements on the beach. Raining heavily. I got the loan of a dead or missing man's overcoat and was all right.

'We were met by some Turkish officers who arrived on horseback followed by very fine looking Turks, carrying Red Crescent and white flags. One of the officers was a German doctor. We were introduced by our interpreters and moved up the hillside in two long lines. Every hundred yards or so we stationed a man with a white flag, and opposite to him the Turks posted one of their men. We clambered through dripping bushes, with beautiful poppies and flowers, reaching the top wet through. From here we could see, over to our right flank, rough high hills covered with dense, waist-high scrub, and occasional open patches of cultivated land. At the top of the second hill, we halted for a slight argument as to our route. The Turks wanted to keep up toward our trench, but Col. Skeen refused so we kept straight down a steep narrow cleft between. Here we heard two wounded men crying for help, and found one with a fractured leg. I gave him cyanide and borax and he touched his forehead and breast. The Turkish Medico was a charming gentleman and we talked in French. Coming over the crest of the hill, I found the first New Zealander, lying on his face. Poor lad! A few yards climb brought us onto a plateau, and a most awful sight was here. The Turkish dead lay so thick that it was almost impossible to pass without treading on the bodies.

Stacks of supplies, loaded barges and tenders at Anzac Cove. Looking south to Hell Spit with the headland of Gaba Tepe in the middle distance. *(WDF-002447-79, A.V. Short Collection, Wairarapa Archive)*

Turkish prisoners under guard at Brigadier-General Russell's headquarters on Russell's Top. He was human too — a fellow sufferer. *(WF-002363-19-1978-1949-20, W.A. Hampton Collection, NAM Waiouru)*

'The awful destructive power of high explosives was very evident. Huge holes surrounded by circles of corpses, blown to pieces. One body was cut clean in half; the upper half I could not see, it was some distance away. One shell had apparently fallen and set fire to a bush, as a dead man lay charred to the bone. Everywhere one looked lay dead, swollen, black, hideous, and over all, a nauseating stench that nearly made one vomit. We exchanged cigarettes with the other officers frequently and the senior Turkish medico gave me two pieces of scented wool to put in my nostrils. Further along the plateau, the distance between the trenches narrowed. We kept very carefully in the centre. The narrowest place was not 17 feet apart.

'In this trench lay 4 dead Turks, head to heel, blocking it. We stopped our men. I found an officer's sword and a bugle, and kicked it towards our trench and asked a corporal to deliver it to Col. Beeston when he was relieved.

'Our men and the Turks peered over the sandbags and all seemed pleased at the chance of seeing each other without the fear of immediate death as the price of curiosity. At one place a curious sight fascinated me.

'In one charge 5 or 6 Turks had reached our trench and died with their heads on our sandbags. From here a long file of dead reached back to the front of the Turks' trench.

'At another place a dead T officer lay close to out trench face down, grasping his revolver. We passed on until we stood on the plateau at the head of Monash's Valley — the Valley of Death.

'From here we looked down that awful cut between the mountains. We could see the widening road, crossed by sandbag traverses to prevent the snipers killing the men as they marched up. Here we parted from the Turks. They went to the right and we descended the side of the cliff, and up again. In this manner neither side had the advantage of seeing the other's trenches. In a steep cut I found a NZ Officer, head down. I got his identity disc.

'Meantime, we found 2 dead snipers and then 8 or 9 more, hidden in holes. How many lives they took before they had died, no one knows. At least 50. We climbed up through deep, narrow, winding trenches, emerged on the plateau again and met the Turks. Again there was a mass of dead Turks. From here the land was flatter and we moved on through a welter of corpses.

'Behind us, for at least two miles, we could see our burial parties working furiously. In some cases the dead actually formed part of the trench wall. It was a terrible sight to see arms and legs sticking out of the sand, underneath the sandbags. The final stage was opposite the extreme left flank. There was a narrow path, absolutely blocked with dead, also a swathe of men who had fallen face down as if on parade — victims to our machine guns. The brink of the precipice was thick with bushes and every few yards we found dead. Here I saw 2 NZ Officers; one was Grant. Our journey took from 7.30 to 12.30. Col. Ryan came up here and after superintending the interment, I left, feeling deadly ill. I got back via the wonderful trenches of the left flank, and found Guthrie, Blair, and Findlay, who gave me tea. Padre Bush King was here. Padre Luxford had been busy on the plateau reading hasty services over our dead. I only saw about 10 of ours but, at a very moderate estimate, I saw 2000 dead Turks.

'The Turkish officers were charming. The Germans were rude and dictatorial and accused us of digging trenches. I lost my temper (and my German) and told them the corpses were so decomposed they could not be lifted and our men were merely digging pits to put the awful things into. He was a swine, this particular German. The Turkish medico was extremely nice. We exchanged cigarettes and I said to him I hoped after the war we should smoke a cigarette — I cut short suddenly, for I was going to say "in Constantinople", but he smiled and bowed and it was all right. I pray God I may never see such an awful sight again. I got back deadly sick and got phenacetin and brandy and lay down. I shall certainly have eternal nightmares. If this is war, I trust NZ will never be fool enough to forget that to avoid war one must be too strong to invite war.'[37]

For both sides it was the chance to examine the opposing lines. 'It was here, as we were climbing up our trench that we saw General Birdwood, General Godley, Col. Monash, Onslow, and the staff who had been quite frankly walking along the front of our trenches reconnoitring.'[38] Certainly Turkish sentries at Deadman's could view the length of Monash Gully. It was evident to all that an advance of 10 metres at Quinn's would pull on a thread that would unravel the front line.

On 25 May any elation still evident after 19 May was dismissed by the sinking of the HMS *Triumph*. Godley and Birdwood were with Overton in a mine sweeper reconnoitring the coast. They were looking at the *Triumph*, stationary off Anzac Cove, 'when we suddenly saw her hit about midships … In fifteen minutes, she had turned turtle, and lay bottom uppermost, like a great red whale … She is a great loss to us … and we feel we have quite lost an old friend.'[39]

The Navy was 'now out of it' and more than ever the ANZACs felt themselves a

Anzac Cove. 'Indeed we realised we were back home again.' A ruined barge is being used for firewood and trench supports; the hospital area is in the right foreground. *(019A, AI0645, Stereo Glass Plate, Wingnut Archive)*

force besieged. 'General Godley looks ill tonight. I think like all of us he had a shock when the *Triumph* was sunk … The men are horribly bitter against Winston Churchill. They say we are sent here with no guns, little ammunition, no aeroplanes, and the whole adventure is a betrayal. Their language is blasphemous but deadly earnest.'[40]

Turkish activity increased immediately after the armistice. North of Anzac new trenches could be seen on the ridge from Baby 700 to Chunuk Bair and there was more activity among Turkish outposts along the foothills. This was probably in response to the Mounteds' patrolling. The Turks dug a small outpost on the spur inland from No. 2 Outpost. Russell got Godley's permission to capture and garrison it. This was carried out on the night of 28 May by 1 Canterbury Yeomanry Cavalry Squadron of the Canterbury Mounted Rifles led by Major Percy Acton-Adams. They were relieved the same night by Major Charles Dick and his 6th Manawatu Squadron of the Wellington Mounteds, who moved forward with picks and shovels to develop the post. Rod McCandlish was one of them: 'Fell in 7.30, 200 rounds and 24 hours ration. Canterbury took Turk trench and we dug in under fire. Chamberlain hit. Fast and furious work, very bad digging. Very bad position. Fired on from all sides.'[41] They could be seen by the Turks on the Table Top and Rhododendron Ridge inland. Steep gullies allowed Turks to infiltrate either side of the position and the Mounteds back in No. 2 Outpost could give little support. They remained pinned down under fire all day during 29 May.

That night Dick's squadron was relieved by 100 men of Major Selwyn Chambers' 9th Wellington East Coast Squadron. John Wilder was one of the troop sergeants: 'We went out and took the trench the Canterbury chaps had taken. It was regular

An Armistice was arranged. A blindfolded Turkish officer, Major Kemal Ohri from General Essad Pasha's Staff, is escorted into Anzac to discuss terms for burying the dead. *(003A, AL0645, Stereo Glass Plate, Wingnut Archive)*

Burying the dead, 24 May 1915. 'Saw everyone strolling around. It reminded me of half time at a big football match.' Turkish soldier with Red Crescent marking the dividing line between Anzac and Turkish work parties during the Armistice with Baby 700 in background. *(WF-002270-18, Alexander Orr Collection, Wairarapa Archive)*

hell for the 24 hours that we were there, we hardly had a moment's peace. We were absolutely surrounded by Turks who were just beneath us under the cliff with covering fire on the other side of the gully. The Turks were almost close enough to touch, but the covering fire kept us down and they just threw in bombs as they liked.

'The only thing to do was to pick them up and throw them back at the enemy. They were all time fuses. I saw one chap throw back four in no time. They (the Turks) did try shortening the fuses, but after a few had burst in their own hands they went back to the long fuses again.

'Things were much the same all night and next day except that in daylight we had to keep much lower as they could enfilade our trenches from anywhere pretty well; our orders being to hang onto the trench, there we had to stay. I don't think we could have got out had we wanted to … we only had 96 men to start with and we lost about 31 killed and wounded.'[42]

On the night of 30 May, the post was finally relieved: 'About 5.00 p.m. on Sunday evening the Turks sapped under one corner of our trench and blew it up, and the fire being too hot to build it up again we had to retire to the first two corners and build barricades. When this happened and the Turks got in at the other end we thought it was all up …

'Canterbury and the rest of our own Regiment fought their way in to us at 10.00 p.m. Sunday evening and guarded the track whilst we carried our wounded down the hill to the stretchers, which was an awful job, but they all got through safely. We eventually got to our bivvies at 12.00 p.m. dead beat, but they had some hot tea waiting for us.'[43]

It had taken the Wellington Mounted Rifles and two squadrons of the Canterburys to relieve Chambers' men. Major George Hutton's 10th Squadron of the Canterburys tried to re-establish the position 'but before we could do anything the Turks became rather pushing and took up all our attention. I had just got into the trench when Sgt Berryman was hit alongside me and I got one through the hat that slightly stunned me.'[44]

Hutton withdrew, after first personally returning to rescue a wounded man. They fought their way back to the beach: 'They were a solid mass of men, rear ones pushed the front ones, they didn't fire a shot at us much to my surprise. They charged continuously shouting, "Allah! Allah!", but they stopped shouting when we opened fire.'[45]

At daybreak on 1 June, No. 3 Outpost was in Turkish hands and being entrenched. Bodies of the New Zealand dead had been stripped and thrown over the parapet, and the naked body of a sergeant lay face down sprawled head first over the forward edge. The casualties to the New Zealand Mounted Rifles were 26 killed, including three officers, and 65 wounded. The securing of an isolated trench by a squadron on the night of the 28th had developed into a hard-fought battle over three days, which involved the entire New Zealand Mounteds Brigade. A new No. 3 Post was established just to the north of No. 2, and the position that had been lost became 'Old No. 3'.

During the night battle of 30 May, Brigadier General Russell had given Meldrum of the Wellington Mounteds permission to abandon the post. Godley, on learning of this, opposed it and insisted that the post be held at all costs. Russell continued to urge that the post be abandoned and Godley referred the decision to Birdwood, who gave permission to withdraw.

The action was to increase Turkish activity in the foothills north of Anzac. It convinced Kemal, whose 19th Division held the Sari Bair Ridge, that if he could send a regiment down through the foothills to retake Old No. 3 Outpost, the ANZACs in turn could send troops up onto the high ground. Kemal urged a larger garrison on this flank but his superiors were unconvinced. Nevertheless, 'the hilltops in the broken country on our left front are now being lined with trenches in all directions, their number increasing daily'.[46]

Major Percy Overton believed that the foothills to the north were now 'so carefully picqueted by the Turks that the first movement of troops in that direction will at once be detected… I am now of the opinion that any attack made by us on 971 and "Q" [Chunuk Bair] is doomed to fail as the element of surprise will be lacking.'[47] Birdwood and his staff were more optimistic but he ordered that no further activities other than patrols were to be undertaken on this flank.

In late May there was activity all along the line, for on 29 May the vulnerability of Quinn's was tested. For days, miners among the Western Australians garrisoning Quinn's reported hearing evidence of Turkish digging. This was largely discounted, though some counter-measures were taken. On the morning of 29 May, the Western

View from Russell's Top across Monash Gully towards Second Ridge, with bivvies behind Pope's Hill on left in foreground. The bowl that is Quinn's Post is at the top of the track at the base of the spur leading down from Pope's. The zig-zag track leading up to Courtney's Post can be seen on the right. *(WF-002270-08, Alexander Orr Album, Wairarapa Archive)*

Men of the Otago Mounted Rifles clear terraces at No.2 Outpost. The Great Sap winds along the base of the foothills, with Walker's Ridge, The Sphinx and the Razor Back linking to Plugge's Plateau. The Ari Burnu spur descends down to the sea at the northern end of Anzac Cove. *(Alan Lawson Collection – PA1-o-1312, Alexander Turnbull Library)*

Australians reported that a Turkish mine was underneath and about to blow. It did and Turks occupied part of Quinn's. Charles Saunders watched the battle from Popes. 'We were in the thick of it at Pope's Hill, but Quinn's Post had a rougher time and were driven out of their trenches. The Turks occupied our trenches there and were driven out by a very stubborn counter-attack … whatever has been written about the Australians I am certain nothing they did surpassed what I saw that grey morning at Quinn's Post … Silhouetted on the skyline were four Australians with rifles at the fire position, bayonets fixed, firing at swarms of Turks over on the plateau, some matter of 10 yards from them … I could see them firing and pulling the bolt back for the next cartridge and firing again, until one was hit and down he dropped and rolled down the steep slope like a log — down went another soon after, and he also rolled down amongst the men below gathered for the counter-attack … Soon after the third man was hit and rolled down. The fourth man fired 5 times whilst he was alone in that terrible position and then he calmly turned round and slid down amongst his comrades unharmed.'[48]

Quinn of the Post was killed but the position was regained. Monash's brigade were 'so done that they had to be relieved.' The Canterbury Battalion got the job and Frank Hardey was one of them. 'We marched single file all the way through an 8 ft deep sap, and emerged at last into Monash Valley. They were still fighting like hell up at Quinn's and several of our men were killed by strays and snipers. That night we [the Canterbury Battalion] took over. Thus then we were at last on Quinn's — the most hated and feared post on the line.'[49]

9

SUMMER

Whilst seated one day in my dugout,
Weary and ill at ease,
I saw a gunner carefully,
Scanning his sunburnt knees;
I asked him why he was searching,
And what he was looking for,
But his only reply was a long-drawn sigh
As he quietly killed one more.

Am. Park, *The ANZAC Book*

On 1 June 1915, the NZ Infantry Brigade relieved Monash's 4th Australians in No. 3 Section at the head of Monash Gully. Pope's Hill would continue to be held by the 1st Australian Light Horse Brigade under Chauvel, who as senior man was Section Commander. The New Zealanders would man the line on Second Ridge, at Quinn's and Courtney's posts. The Wellingtons held Courtney's, the Canterburys Quinn's. The Aucklands and the Otagos would remain in reserve, the Aucklands relieving the Canterburys at Quinn's, the Otagos the Wellingtons at Courtney's. Each battalion would spend eight days at the post before relief.

The battalions had been 'resting' since their return from Helles. They were sick of digging roads and trenches and of the constant demands of carrying rations, water and ammunition up to the forward trenches. All were keen to get back into the front line — it promised to be easier. 'On Fatigues. Not in the trenches yet … Hope we shall have a go in the trenches soon.'[1]

The feeling was shared by their commanders, such as Malone of the Wellingtons: 'We started relieving the Australian 4th Brigade (Infantry) yesterday. I am to command what is known as Courtney's Post and will be under Colonel Chauvel. Taranaki went over today. I and the remainder of the battalion go tomorrow. Glad to be at steady fighting work again. It is getting very slow.'[2]

Quinn's was the northernmost post on Second Ridge. It was a small basin gully with a double line of trenches dug into 10 metres of crest around the basin lip. It was overlooked from both the north and the south by Turkish trenches: the Chessboard (the slopes of Baby 700) to the north, and the high ground of German Officers' Trench and Johnston's Jolly to the south. Its existence depended on the machine-gun fire from Pope's across Monash Gully and from Courtney's Post on higher ground to the south of it. It could do little to defend itself. The Turks had almost dug the ANZACs off the crest; their nearest trenches had sapped to within four to six metres of the front line at Quinn's and subjected the garrison to a constant stream of grenades, and rifle and machine-gun fire. As the Turkish line was only a 15-second dash away, the front and support trenches on and immediately below the crest were always crowded to repel an attack. Casualties were heavy, and 24 hours at Quinn's was all most men could stand. Birdwood had initially forbidden deep trenches there lest the men be trapped if the Turks attacked. This order had been rescinded after 19 May, but any trench improvements had been destroyed in the fighting on 29 May. The engineers including Charles Saunders went forward to assist the infantry.

'Had breakfast at 5.00 a.m. (bully and biscuit), loaded up our gear and started off for Quinn's Post, the "death trap" of the ANZAC line … I shall never forget the sight of that place — mangled bodies of our own men and Turks everywhere — rifles twisted and misshapen by bombs as were the bodies — corrugated iron sheets just like huge nutmeg scrapers with bullet and bomb holes — the ground itself worse than after any flood or storm — to look at it, made one sad — it seemed wounded and bleeding in its own way — the whole of the trenches full of flies and vermin and blood stains.'[3]

Since 29 May the Turks had had ascendancy at Quinn's. All the loopholes had to be closed because of Turkish sniper fire. Any periscope lifted above the sandbag parapet would be smashed by a bullet. Parts of the front trenches had collapsed and the Turks had occupied mine craters just beyond and erected blockhouses in them. Quinn's was divided into six sectors, each of which held a garrison of 30–40 men. Sectors 1 and 2 connected with Courtney's Post on rising ground to the south and were relatively secure. Sectors 3 and 4 were in the centre. It was at No. 3 that men climbed up faggot-bound steps from the gully below and entered the post. This was between narrow sandbagged walls 'encrusted with blood' from the dead and wounded. These centre sectors were most feared, because here the Turks had sapped to within four to six metres. In No. 4 a barricaded sap ran from Quinn's to the Turkish line and the listening post in the sap was just two metres from the Turkish post.

Nos 5 and 6 ran north around the edge of the lip until No. 6 ended abruptly above the edge of the eastern arm of Monash Gully. It looked directly across to Deadman's Ridge, a haven of Turkish snipers who wrought havoc on the traffic up Monash and the unwary in the rear of Quinn's.

Now it was the Canterburys' turn: 'No sooner did we fill the trenches than the Turks opened up with rifles and bomb fire which has lasted without ceasing for the whole of two days and nights.'[4]

It was a war of grenades — something the ANZACs had never seen before the Walker's Ridge battle. The Turks were well equipped with a manufactured, cricket-ball-shaped grenade of German pattern. The ANZACs were forced to improvise, and

The bomb factory. It was placed centrally in the triangle formed by the headquarters of the two divisions and that of the ANZAC Corps — and about 100 metres away from each. *(H10291-2, Australian War Memorial)*

Looking through a loophole at Quinn's. The Turkish line is the opposite line of sandbags. On the right is a communication trench dug during one of the raids on the Turks. A body can be seen on the skyline to the right of the picture. *(WF-002415-65, Norman Annabell Album, NAM Waiouru)*

a bomb factory was established on the beach. Gunner Norman Hassell of the NZ Field Artillery was one of the workers. 'My duties at the bomb factory were simple in the extreme and consisted of making exceptionally crude bombs out of whatever material was available. These bombs consisted of a jam tin or cigarette tin packed full of spent cartridge cases, nails, bullets, or like articles with a plug of gelignite stuck in the centre into which a fuse and detonator was fixed, the lid being then tied down with any odd bits of wire or string we could pick up. To keep up our supply of "packing" we took it in turns going up the front line trenches and spending the day picking up all the spent cartridges fired by our infantry chaps and filling sugar sacks with them which we would carry back with us …'[5]

There were never enough bombs. Lieutenant J.L. Anderson of Godley's headquarters ran the factory, and it was 'going in great style … and instead of turning out about 100 to 140 we can now make 400 but supplies are running short …'[6]

The attack of 29 May had exhausted the ANZAC supply, but the Turks never seemed to be short. 'All in all, it can be easily understood that no man entered Quinn's without reluctance and foreboding. Luckily the Turks often made the fuses of their bombs too long, so that they lay fizzing for as much as two seconds, before exploding, and we generally had time to throw an overcoat over them or dodge round a corner of the trench.'[7]

The bombing was at its worst in No. 4 sector, particularly in the listening post closest to the Turkish lines. Watches here broke the strongest of men. Cecil Malthus recalled: 'I remember in particular a slightly wounded man who ran out streaming with blood and roaring at the top of his voice. He was badly shell shocked, though that term was not yet familiar, and he had to be transferred to the ambulance corps down on the beach, where he lasted another couple of months. If hitherto I had any zeal for the business, the sickening terror of those tense watches dispelled it. To lie cowering in the darkness of that cramped and evil-smelling pit, and watch a big bomb sputtering among the corpses just against our loophole, while waiting for the burst, was an experience that no man could endure unmoved.'[8]

Conditions at Courtney's were not as bad. It was one post on Second Ridge that overlooked the Turkish line, but the post was cramped and little development had been done. Malone was not impressed — 'a very higgledy piggledy show'. The men of his battalion were more descriptive, as George Bollinger wrote: 'We are terribly cramped here and are like flies hanging onto a wall. The dead are buried all amongst us and there is not an atom of shade from the burning sun. Burrowing, etc has laid the hillside bare. At present it is a query whether we will blow the Turks up before they blow us up.'[9]

As at Quinn's, 'Courtney's Post hangs by its eyebrows on the edge of a steep gully … When we first took over it was a sort of rabble ground, scrambling, unformed, loose tracks and bivouacs scraped out, here, there and everywhere on the hillside so that Colonel Malone said that getting the men out was like digging periwinkles out of their shell.'[10]

Each of the posts had a commander who would stay there while the battalions of the brigade rotated through in turn, the battalion commanders coming under the post commander for orders. As he had done at Walker's Ridge, Malone set immediately to organise Courtney's Post. His appointment was Post Commander and he would stay at Courtney's as the Wellingtons and Otagos took turn about as garrison.

'I put Major Cunningham in charge of my battalion and began to take hold as O/C [Officer Commanding] Post. Built a new HQrs bivouac and propose to retrace the ground to make room for the men. I put all the Machine Gun men in one place … There is a lot of work to be done remodelling, but we will get it done soon. The men are keen.'[11]

His battalion wrested the ascendancy from the Turks and the closed loopholes were reopened. Malone's instructions to his battalion were bomb for bomb and bullet for bullet. 'Interviewed Col. Chauvel as to alteration in position — sandbags, periscopic rifles, flares, bombs, tools etc. — and asked for extra supplies to have store in hand. He was very nice and agreed to everything.'[12]

Lieutenant T.P. 'Army' Grace, noted rifle shot and commander of the sniping parties at the head of Monash Valley. *(NZ Herald)*

Dramatic changes were effected in days. Trenches were deepened and roofed over, terraces were levelled, and Turkish snipers were attacked. 'We have told off a special sniping party to deal with some snipers who have, ever since the landing, practically commanded the valley … and have killed and wounded a large number of men including Gen. Bridges.'[13]

Malone directed one of his officers, Lieutenant T.P. 'Army' Grace, a noted rifle shot, to pick the best men in the battalion and clean out the enemy snipers. The men operated in pairs, one observing and the other firing. 'Today we bagged two of the snipers and have quite altered the atmosphere. Yesterday six men, Australians, were wounded within the hour. Today no casualties, except the two Turks killed. Moreover the Turks in trenches in front of us are learning that there is a change.'[14]

In a matter of days the situation changed in the New Zealand posts on Second Ridge. For the first time since the landing, the ANZACs seized the control of No Man's Land from the Turks. The snipers stalked their Turkish opponents as they had deer and pigs in New Zealand. Private Jimmy Swan was one whose exploits were legend in the Wellington Battalion: 'We have good sport and I reckon I got quite a number. We are out on the hillside concealed in bushes and when we see a hillside darkened we know a Turk is looking out and we snipe away … When they find us out we conceal ourselves on another point and so on … we have them now [that] they are frightened to look through a crack in the sandbags … I have been having a duel with a sniper this

Fatigue party moving up the Walker's Ridge track, with the Sphinx in the background. *(WF-002447-48, A.V. Short Collection, Wairarapa Archive)*

morning, he has been trying to stop me from shooting at a machine gun but I stopped him first, I can see him kicking and struggling in the bushes 400 yards away.'[15]

Chauvel, the Commander of No. 3 Section of the ANZAC line, recognised the success of Malone's scheme and appointed Grace to be in charge of snipers throughout the section. 'Grace's snipers, posted throughout the valley, placed a barrier as impenetrable as any earthwork between the traffic in Monash Valley and the Turks whose trenches overlooked it. Thenceforward, provided the snipers were first warned, even a convoy of mules could go to the supply depot near the head of the gully at midday, without a shot being fired at it.'[16]

They were an elite band. Harvey Johns was one of them: 'You got that good, you could shoot the left eye out of a fly ... If we could find loopholes, we'd shoot at the top of the loophole to bring the stuff down by tearing the sandbags and loosening the earth and so enlarging the hole, and I am afraid that once or twice we split the end of our shot, so that when it hit, it would branch out and make a mess of the loophole ... but when our officer found we were splitting, and making Dum Dum bullets, he sailed into us properly.'[17]

Eventually orders came out from the New Zealand Brigade 'that this practice was to cease as there was always the danger of such a bullet hitting a man ... It is contrary to the rules of the Geneva Convention to use them and we fight under these rules and always try to fight fair.'[18]

A sniper with his spotter from the Maori Contingent at No.1 Outpost. *(Album 382, p.14 n6, Auckland War Memorial Museum)*

Chauvel, Godley and Birdwood were constantly visiting Quinn's and Courtney's in early June. They were impressed by Malone's work at Courtney's. Brown of the Canterburys had little time to commence the same improvements at Quinn's. From the time of occupying the post his battalion was committed to restoring the damage caused by the Turkish attack in late May.

On 1 June, two New Zealand sappers, Lance Corporal Frank Fear and Sapper Edgar Hodges, crept out from Quinn's and destroyed a blockhouse that the Turks had built in a mine crater blown on 29 May. They crawled to the blind side of the blockhouse, clearing the roof, while the Turks were firing continuously from loopholes on the other side. After 35 minutes' work they placed a 12–pound charge of gun cotton, lit the fuse, holding the match inside a haversack to mask the flame, then leapt back into Quinn's four to five metres away. There was an explosion and the New Zealanders crawled back and found 'a mass of broken beams and tumbled earth, amidst which lay the enemy dead.'[19] Both were awarded the Distinguised Conduct Medal (DCM).

On 3 June, Birdwood received notice of an attack at Helles. Hamilton requested a feint at Anzac to prevent reinforcements being drawn south. The New Zealanders would attack from Quinn's and seize the trenches opposite in Turkish Quinn's, while the Australians to the south would attack German Officers' Trench and silence the machine guns that fired along the front of the Turkish trenches and which had defeated the previous raids.

That same day, Birdwood was informed that 4 June was the date of the Helles attack, and Hamilton's obsessive regard for secrecy meant that the earliest the Anzac feint could be conducted was the night of 4–5 June. Lieutenant Colonel C.H.J. Brown issued detailed orders and called for volunteers. Despite the optimism painted in the regimental histories, men were reluctant, as Frank McKenzie explained: 'They called for volunteers to storm a trench, so joined in, twenty-five wanted from company. Only four, including Hall, Jones and myself at first, but later made up to fourteen when Frazer explained it did not mean certain death.'[20]

Fifty men from each of the Auckland and Canterbury battalions were selected. Norman Hardey was one who chose not to go: 'I picked it for a disaster right away, and stood down from what I considered straight suicide. I'm not very heroic, I'm afraid, over taking a choice of that sort. My platoon was occupying the trenches on No. 3 section from where our chaps set out. The show started with a bombardment by our artillery and supporting fire from Walker's Ridge. The noise was hell let loose with the appearance of a glorious firework show. The shells from Sykes' Battery came whizzing straight at us like greased lightning and burst with a bright glare just beyond us over the Turkish trenches. Then quietness and our chaps had got there. They got there so quickly that the Turks were taken unaware and many were shot and bayoneted before they could even get on their feet. They took the trench after a sharp struggle and frantically commenced to make it secure. Imagine the job they had! A honeycomb network of trenches; they had taken 50 yards of one trench and they had to try and close up all communication trenches and tunnels and block in the ends of the piece they had taken with sandbags.

'Meantime the machine guns on the Lone Pine gave them hell. The trench was filled with dead and wounded Turks who had to be heaved over the parapet. Besides, they had taken three score prisoners and these had to be sent back over the fire-swept zone. We took them over and sent them down to the prison camp. Meanwhile a sap had been cut from No. 3 out to the captured trench, and picks, shovels, ammunition, and as many bombs as possible were sent up. Our own dead and wounded had to be got out. Dead to be thrown over the top, wounded dragged through the newly cut tunnel into No. 3. Picture in a space of trench (the captured bit) big enough for 50 men the scene of confusion — about 30 chaps with rifles replying to the Turks, as many more men a working parry trying to make the place secure, the wounded to remove, the prisoners to get away, communications to be kept up — and all amidst the cries of the wounded and the uproar of battle. Ernie Frazer got killed that night; he showed great gallantry.

'They got tolerably secure by dawn and the Turks seemed scared off. False hopes! At four o'clock they set on to us. Up every communication trench they came with literally hundreds of bombs. They caused awful slaughter; the machine gun fire kept down the heads of our defenders. They held the inferno till 5.00 a.m. and then returned. The bravery of our chaps was prodigious, but they had been sent to do the impossible. When at last they gave back, the bombing was awful and our own supply was not anything like sufficient to cope with the Turkish attacks. The dying and dead were left. Cases of ammunition and stacks of sandbags were left for Johnny Turk. When the last of them retired through our line we on No. 3 began to get it too, the bombs dropping around pretty briskly, because our sappers had cut a sap right through from our No. 3 blockhouse into the captured trench, so the Turks had a protected way down which to come in safety after they had retaken the trench. They came well armed with bombs, and presently we had to retire out of No. 3 and No. 2. It was a mighty queer sight. Driven from our trenches by the bombs, we dropped back and took up positions commanding the skyline. Each man fixed his bayonet and took up a fire position, waiting and praying that Johnny Turk would come on to push home his advantage. His bombs came in scores. They must have come right up to our trenches along the sap but ventured no further. They use a bomb like a cricket ball — a fine thing for the job. When the Turks succeeded in throwing them far enough to clear the crest of the hill, they would roll down amongst us. They started pelting them to land on our road and they were rolling down and bursting around headquarters. It was an awful time. Acting Lieut. Col. Brown was hit and looking awfully grim, was carried away. Our Chief gone! The divisions 1, 2, 3, 4, 5 and 6 were the sections (each under an officer) into which Quinn's was subdivided. Presently they quietened off and our engineers crept up to see what damage had been done to our trenches. They reported they would have them fit for us by the afternoon. In the meantime we put in a few observers just merely to warn us against attack. We got a hasty meal the Quarter-Master had brought up and were allotted back to the trenches. We went in feeling mighty queer. Massey had No. 3 post. He directly supervised 3B whilst I took 3A, under him …

'What a night of suspense! No one to sleep — stand to arms all night — everyone, although they felt the strain, realised the responsibility — no speaking, except in whispers — no noise — all eager listening in suspense. Where Massey was, the gaping tunnel ran right into the Turk trench. It was roughly boarded up. We could hear the Turk shovels and they could hear ours working. I wonder if they were in suspense like we were? Next morning at 9.00 a.m. we were relieved. Thank God, nothing had happened! We were so worn out and our nerves were like fiddle-strings.'[21]

The results of this raid were far reaching. As a demonstration it failed, for lines of Turkish reinforcements could be seen moving south. The greatest effect was on the morale of the men: 'This is the fifth time we have taken those trenches, the fifth time we have been driven back, and, each time, the Turks are given a new lease of life. Our loss in morale is tremendous. The Turks are always cocky and impertinent after each attack for days. I cannot understand for the life of me, why it should take five attacks to prove we cannot hold them after we have taken them … Very bad generalship, I reckon, as we lose so much by the fruitless attempts, both in casualties and morale. Our infantry came back at daylight, or rather what was left of them — big strong bushmen and miners from Westland NZ — shaking and trembling like little children.'[22]

The ANZAC headquarters was also concerned and issued a memorandum on 6 June: 'Cases have recently occurred in both divisions in which the rifles and ammunition of dead and wounded men have not been brought back to our trenches … The mere fact of leaving them behind allows the enemy to suppose that we have retired disorganised and demoralised and gives him an opportunity of regaining his morale …

'Should by any chance arms or ammunition be abandoned close to our line it is up to the Divisional Commander concerned to consider what can be done to recover these on the first possible occasion.'[23]

Not surprisingly, Godley took this as a criticism of his New Zealanders' performance on the night of 4 June. He ordered another raid from Quinn's on the night of 7 June and tasked it with 'recovering material, arms, ammunition and tools etc. lost during the sortie of the 4/5th June and also to destroy the Turks fire trench in front of the centre of [Quinn's] Post.'[24]

The raid was to be carried out by the Aucklanders, led by Lieutenant Colonel R. Young. The Canterburys, now commanded by Lieutenant Colonel J.G. 'Jacky' Hughes, who replaced Lieutenant Colonel C.J. Brown, were reserve. They assaulted at 10.30 p.m., and in spite of heavy fire, seized some 20 metres of trench. Barricades were erected but by 2.00 a.m. these had been driven in and the parties forced to retire. 'No demolitions were carried out and no stores were brought back with the exception of one rifle and one loophole.'[25]

On 4 June Godley wrote to his wife: 'I am sitting in my dugout, writing and thinking of you and waiting for one of these horrible sorties to take place. Quinn's Post … is our most advanced post and juts out in front of all the others … the Turk trenches are only about 10 yards off and all day and all night mining and counter-mining, bombing and sharp-shooting, go on without ceasing … the ground is becoming so broken up with mines and the whole place so untenable for us, that we have to go out tonight to take the trenches opposite … My division landed 8543 strong and has had

Reading the mail from home: an *Otago Witness* is carefully read at Courtney's Post.
(WW1 Photographic Collection A.A. Perry Negatives, Auckland War Memorial Museum)

Lieutenant Colonel John Gethin 'Jacky' Hughes, NZSC, DSO, Commanding Officer of the Canterbury Battalion. *(WF-002082-83, Deans Collection, NAM Waiouru)*

4332 casualties: more than 50 percent … Johnston, Pinwill and Fenwick have all been rather seedy with diarrhoea … but how I hate it all, though one is very proud to command such splendid men as these are.'[26]

This was a side of the man his New Zealanders never saw. All they witnessed was another fruitless raid that had been anticipated by the Turks, and more casualties, all for some picks and shovels. The Canterbury and Auckland Battalions were both badly shaken and men were cracking.

'This has been a day of great misery. We have been in the trenches for the past eleven days and have during that time taken part in three attacks, besides at all times being harassed by the bomb attacks of the enemy. Everybody is showing the utmost limit of fatigue, but as we lie upon the slopes of Quinn's Post with the sun pouring a blistering heat upon us, there is small chance of sleep. A plague far greater than the heat is the myriad flies which settle upon our faces, arms and bared knees, stinging and irritating … I suppose they are more truly hated than the little dark men over yonder.'[27]

Hatred grew against the men who ordered the raids. Bobby Young, the commanding officer of the Aucklanders, received his share. Private William Newell had recently arrived with the Fourth Reinforcements, and his diary captures the mood of the Auckland Battalion: '19th June … Inlying picquet later was inspected by Col. Young who the old hands call the Dugout King, and shouted to him, "Get back to your dugout or you might get hurt." I do not think a lot of him. Feeling a bit sick.'[28]

The entry may be an overstatement but undoubtedly the men were angry. They were doing everything asked of them, but they saw their lives as being thrown away to no purpose. The brunt of their anger focused on Godley, whom they saw as the principal culprit. He was an easy man to blame. Both he and Birdwood paid regular visits to the trenches: 'General Birdwood was round today and spoke to us all. He is a real decent soldier and we all like him.'[29]

Godley, by contrast, would move through impassively, asking no questions, offering no greetings, and the men would watch him pass. 'He never said "gidday boys" to us or anything else or asked how far away the Turk was or asked for a periscope to look over the top … and I thought it was a pretty poor performance …'[30]

In every war, men moan about the 'bludgers' at headquarters, and Anzac was no different. But the headquarters at Anzac were less isolated from the front lines than headquarters in any other theatre in this war. On Russell's Top, Russell's headquarters was 20–30 metres behind the support trenches. At Quinn's, the NZ Brigade headquarters was at the foot of the post, perhaps 100 metres from the front line. Godley's and Birdwood's headquarters were 100 metres apart and less than 1000 metres from the front. Yet to the men, they lived in a different world.

The staff of the headquarters on the beach lived under the illusion that they shared the same conditions and were attuned to the problems but this was not always the case. They certainly ran the constant risk of shrapnel, and 'it is the first time that the headquarters staff of an Army Corps has been so close to the trenches and so exposed to the continuous range of enemy guns.'[31] But most of the headquarters' staff never realised the rigours of life in the forward trenches. Many of them saw those trenches only on the day of the armistice. 'At 1.30 this afternoon, Staff Sgt Ward came to my dugout and took my photo together with 2–3 others of the staff. After this we went with the camera to the trenches on the left flank and was more than surprised at the work entailed in modern trench warfare.'[32] Headquarters staff did not endure the fatigues, the sentry duty, and the constant aching for sleep. Equally important, they ate better than the men.

'This perhaps sounds very strange on "active" service but I have had visitors every day this week. Some to breakfast, others to tea and one or two to supper. A lot of my

Anzac in June–July was one enormous hospital; men were evacuated by the boatload daily. *(33990, Alexander Turnbull Library)*

The Signals Office of Godley's NZ & A Division Headquarters on Godley's Terrace, above Anzac Cove. A line was laid to brigade and battalion headquarters and to the artillery batteries. *(WF-002082-93, Deans Collection, NAM Waiouru)*

friends have been very poorly indeed with the heat etc. and the two corporals from Gen. Headquarters (Sir Ian Hamilton's) come over to our Head Qtrs every day from Imbros and they purchase tomatoes, milk, eggs, sauce and bring me their daily ration of fresh meat. This is more than I can eat myself so I invite numerous friends into my luxurious premises to dine etc. I have a fireplace close by and cook anything from porridge, Blancmange, etc. to my success of the season, omelette with a lettuce "Ally Sloper" … My favourite dish for a light and easy tea is Fran's Old Breakfast Dish — eggs with a little milk added — the bread dipped in to soak well, then brown to a beautiful oak shade and served up hot with a little sugar or pepper and salt according to taste. Grilled chops are exceedingly successful …'[33]

Luxuries like this were never seen by the men in the front line. If they were lucky and knew a mate on the beach at headquarters, in the medics, or in the artillery, they might get the chance to drop in and have a brew 'with milk and sugar', but the soldiers in the front line were more conscious of what they did not have, as Frank Hardey complained. 'Right through the piece we have every kind of drawback to contend with. We were always short of bombs. If the miners cut a mine under the Turkish trenches we wouldn't be allowed sufficient gun cotton to make it worth while. If we were building a road they would not give the engineers blasting charges to cut through a cutting; instead 500 men would work in relays night and day … If an artillery observer sighted a good object and phoned it down to his guns the message would come back, "Sorry no ammunition, they won't allow us any more until tomorrow".

'… Great things were always expected of us and often good work was done, but how lamentable after precious lives were lost and good work marred by the fact we had not been provided with the very best of facilities for carrying the venture through to a successful conclusion.'[34]

'They', the faceless few who are always blamed by the hard-pressed many, became the bludgers' on the beach.

The attitude was not restricted to the men. Commanding officers of the New Zealand Infantry were unhappy with Brigade Headquarters, divisional staff officers with Corps Headquarters, and everyone appeared unhappy with Hamilton's staff, even if they respected Sir Ian Hamilton himself. Lieutenant John Anderson on Godley's Divisional Headquarters wrote: 'It is a crying shame that a tottering Empire like the Turks have bombs, guns and every appliance. While we, the strongest and richest

Empire, send out an expedition like this, under-manned, under-armed and only half equipped, with very little knowledge of the country and a staff that keeps 60 miles away … In the six weeks here we have only had three visits from any of them … they can have very little first hand knowledge of the whole situation. By the way this is not only my opinion.'[35]

Godley's division was not a happy one. Monash's Brigade was racked by ill-feeling and disputes between his battalion commanders. The same friction became increasingly evident between Colonel Earl Johnston and his staff of the New Zealand Infantry Brigade, and his battalion commanders. It grew during the long hot summer months at Anzac. There was also tension between some of Godley's Imperial officers and their New Zealand counterparts. Many New Zealanders were becoming increasingly angry at what they saw as the patronising arrogance of a few British officers. It was an anger that increased after their experiences at Helles. "Almost as good as a regular" was the highest praise they could expect, yet all they had witnessed was poor planning and the blind obedience to orders seen to be doomed in advance. Anyhow after this show, the Government won't import junior subalterns at big salaries to teach us our job.'[36]

Colonial commonsense was often discounted by the British professionals. Lieutenant Colonel Fenwick experienced this when he questioned the landing of reinforcements at Anzac Cove during daylight when the Turkish shrapnel was so effective: 'I was speaking of this to a senior officer, and he smiled the usual smile we bestow on infants. "Well, no one was hit, don't you know, so what's the harm?" I suggested that if it was advisable to land guns in night time, it was equally advisable to land men. He explained that was mere ignorance on my part. "We don't want the Turks to know we have landed the guns, and we don't mind them knowing we have landed the men. Besides you see, we must run risks." "Lord only knows why," I said. "If the men are wanted why risk losing them?"

"O, it does not matter losing a few," was the answer. "It matters a terrible lot to certain obscure people in New Zealand who happen to care for those few," I said.'[37]

Engineers and men of the Maori Contingent working at the mine entrances under Quinn's Post. *(WF-002363-17-1978-1949-18, W.A. Hampton Slide Collection, NAM Waiouru)*

Japanese mortar at Courtney's Post, a gift from the Japanese government, but its ammunition had to be strictly rationed.
(WW1 Photographic Collection A.A. Perry Negatives, Auckland War Memorial Museum)

Malone's relationship with his brigade commander, Colonel Earl Johnston, and the brigade major, Major Temperley, had grown increasingly strained and reached breaking point in June and July: ' … but my officers as well as my men have all turned up trumps. I am sorry to say I don't get on well with my Brigadier (Col. F.E. Johnston) and our Brigade Major (Temperley). They think I am a nuisance because I have an opinion of my own and do not slavishly toady to them. All the worse for me. If I want telephones, machine guns, work done, water, things for my men I will not take no for an answer, and keep on until I get what I want. But that is not the way of what we call the "Imperial Army". There, apparently the junior officers always take no for an answer. Because I insisted on having the Brigadier's refusal, to give me certain men for special work, referred to the General for his decision, I was called "extremely insubordinate". I insisted and had the matter out before the General and told him straight that the Brigadier seemed to try and thwart me wherever he could and didn't treat me fairly and that I had got to the point of asking to be relieved of my command in the brigade and to be given another job. The General was very nice, as he can be, since then the Brigadier has been a different man altogether. Temperley is no good. But I do my job without fear and do not ask for favours. My battalion is absolutely the best here, bar none … Yet not one word of encouragement, praise or thanks has the Brigadier or his staff ever given us. They seem to dislike our success. Some people say that is what is wrong with us. The Brigade as a brigade has not distinguished itself— my battalion as a battalion has.'[38]

By 9 June Godley recognised that it was imperative to relieve the exhausted Auckland and Canterbury battalions at Quinn's. Although the Wellingtons were in the line at Courtney's, they were ordered to replace the garrison. They did so on 9 June and the former garrison went off 'as though they were leaving a death trap. They were cowed and dreaded being in the position.'[39] Malone relished the challenge: 'Such a dirty dilapidated unorganised post. Still I like work and will revel in straightening things up … Quite a length of fire trench unoccupied owing to the bombthrowing superiority of Turks. No place for the men to fall in. The local reserve is posted too far away, and yet there is at present no ground prepared, on which they could be comfortably put. I selected a new HQ shelter for myself and gave orders that every rifle shot and bomb from the Turks was to be promptly returned at least two fold. We can and will beat them at their own game.'[40]

While Malone relished the challenge, his men saw little to look forward to. George Bollinger wrote: 'We moved into Quinn's Post at 8 o'clock this morning. In places our trenches touch the Turks and consequently all trenches are made bombproof. One would never credit miles of enemy divided only by a narrow bank of earth; is it a wonder men break down? The heat is intense; flies swarm the trenches in millions. The stench from the bodies of our men lying on trenches in front is choking and nearly unbearable. The world outside has great confidence in their men but I often wonder if they realise, or try to realise what a hell the firing line is and know that every man desires and cannot help desiring immediate peace.'[41]

Apart from a three-day spell on Imbros, Malone would remain at Quinn's from

9 June until 5 August. His work at Quinn's demonstrated all his strengths as a commander. He was a man one could not be neutral about; he was either loved or hated and even those who hated him had to grant his abilities grudging recognition. Temperley wrote: 'Colonel Malone was a picturesque rugged figure, a typical old New Zealand pioneer with a powerful jaw and an appearance of great strength and determination. He had a forcible character, almost incredible tenacity of purpose and power to impose his will upon his subordinates … His heart was in order, method, good organisation, sanitation … His battalion was splendidly drilled and disciplined … it was Malone's battalion and every man in it breathed the spirit of Malone …'[42]

It was this tenacity of purpose that imposed order amidst disorder at Quinn's. Malone became landlord and Quinn's was recognised as Wellington Property. Although other battalions would spend time in the line there, they had to leave the position in the same condition in which they found it. C.E.W. Bean visited it with two other journalists on 18 July: 'Yesterday I took Nevinson up to Quinn's and Malcolm Ross also. Quinn's was absolutely transformed since my last visit. It is laid out in terraces, each with a shed on them with an iron roof, well sandbagged, under which the supports sleep. We had tea with Col. Malone … on a little terrace in front of his dugout. "The art of warfare," he said, "is the cultivation of the domestic virtues." If he had roses he would plant them there. The trenches are well bomb proofed. We have steel loopholes, and two m[achine] g[un] emplacements — and the loopholes are level with the ground.'[43]

A Turkish shell bursting on Russell's Top, seen from Quinn's Post with Malone's terraces in the foreground. The sandbagged trench-line on Pope's Hill immediately across from Quinn's is clearly visible. The skyline on the right and the area to the right of Pope's is held by the Turks. *(H16897-2, Australian War Memorial)*

Transformation at Quinn's Post. Malone's terraces and shelters in the gully, immediately behind the front line. The sandbag parapets on the left of the terraces were erected to protect men from sniper fire from Deadman's Ridge, on the left of the picture. The two communication trenches to the front line are above the terraces, and mines are being dug at the top and bottom of the earth chute. *(Gallipoli Photo Group – March Hillard Collection, Archives New Zealand)*

Malone outlined his 'domestic virtues' to his wife: "'Inspiring the men with confidence — cleaning one's boots and shaving daily, bathe even in a pint of water, keeping calm no matter what the racket or noise. Getting and keeping everything as near normal as possible. No pigging it — no letting things slide — no "near enough because it is War we are at". At the same time the utmost preparation to meet every possible contingency to the best of one's ability. The insisting that every man and officer constantly asks himself— If such and such a thing happens what will I do, and answering and men knowing the answers to the questions.'[44]

The photos show the revolution at Quinn's. Trenches were deepened and covered with beams, sandbags and corrugated iron; loopholes were opened all the way along the line. Machine guns were installed behind other concealed loopholes, to fire only if the Turks attacked. Because of the nearness of the edge to the front line, Turkish grenades had rolled down to kill and wound men in the gully behind Quinn's. Chicken wire was now stretched on poles along the front line so that grenades would strike the wire and bounce back.

Men in reserve gathered rubbish daily, cooking was centralised, and the strictest standards of sanitation were enforced. 'The only space available for latrines was on the slope exposed to snipers, thus necessitating the construction of sandbagged protection. Later on we were forced to tunnel through a knoll about 30 ft in order to use a small protected hollow on the other side for latrines.'[45]

Vic Nicholson of the Wellingtons remembered Colonel Malone's daily ritual of bathing in a pint of water outside his dugout at Quinn's and once parading and berating his battalion to: 'be like cats … cats always cover up what they do and always go back to the one place … unlike [his men] who soil the ground everywhere.'[46]

To achieve these standards Malone drove his men hard. 'He worked us to death sometimes, even when we came out for a spell in the trenches and were supposed to have a little rest near the beach. We were worked building tracks, hauling stuff up, sometimes guns, sometimes ammunition and he worked us.'[47]

But he also earned their respect and trust. 'On our part we promptly realised that there was sound commonsense in everything the "old man" did. He was one of the few commanding officers who really thought about war. His ideas were original and practical — all directed either to increasing the comfort and wellbeing of the men or to improve their fighting capacity and security.'[48]

The fight at Anzac was also waged underground. Since May, volunteers with mining experience had been formed into gangs under the direction of engineers such as Charles Saunders to thwart the threat of Turkish mining to the posts on Second Ridge. Shafts were driven into the eastern side of Monash Gully between 6–12 metres below the crest towards the Turkish line. 'Started 50 miners, all experienced men at mining — volunteers called for from the Infantry. Got our levels and started three drives 5' x 5' and 30 ft below our trenches. Very easy place to mine as we just drive in from the face below our trenches. The drives were connected up half way between our firing line and the Turks, then drove listening galleries Y shaped off the main drive and the tips of the arms of the Y's 15 ft apart … If the enemy drove a gallery in between our Y's they were never farther away from our listeners than 7 ft.'[49]

From late May until the evacuation in December, it was mine and counter-mine. H.V. Howe was an Australian corporal on the mining gang at Quinn's: 'Our mining gangs were probably as expert a lot of miners as could be found anywhere in the world — we knew our jobs, and we worked like Trojans. We were as anxious to get out of those mine tunnels before the Turks blew them in on us as the authorities were to get the tunnels completed. We worked at a terrific pace in ground as hard as concrete — every inch had to be taken out with picks and shovels — no explosives were permitted. The tunnels were approximately six feet high, and two feet six wide — the smallest area in which a man could effectively swing a pick. Each gang was expected to drive twelve feet in an eight hour shift. Four men to a gang, each took an hour on the pick, an hour filling sandbags with dirt broken down by the picker, and two hours carrying the bags out and emptying them. It was the hardest labour on the peninsula.'[50]

Men resting from the line would assist in carting the dirt away from the shafts and soon it was possible to identify each post on Second Ridge by the scar of raw earth and clay that marked the rear of each of the posts. Every man who served at Gallipoli can remember the sounds of tunnelling under his feet and the ever-present fear of a mine being ignited and blowing the post to oblivion.

'Quinn's was such a restless place. If they weren't bombing us they were mining underneath … To stop the bombs we put up wire netting on poles … so the bombs would hit the wire netting and bounce back into No Man's Land and burst there … We were so close, we could hear [the Turks] coughing or talking, and then when we did try to go to sleep … thud, thud of picks and shovels working a few feet under your head and you never knew, you know … our engineers dug in from the back of the hill … and then the Turks would tunnel … sometimes they met and that meant panic …'[51]

In the end some men could not face the trenches. Saunders had such a man who 'had been on the water fatigues since the landing — he didn't like the trenches. He complained about being always on the water. I took him up to the trenches with me praying for a bomb to land near us but not too near! Soon one did and one couldn't see (him) for dust disappearing round a traverse — mind one couldn't have seen me for the same reason — I didn't see him until I got back to the bivouac; he told me he was quite satisfied to carry water. He did two men's work on the water — and was one of the most useful men I had on that account.'[52]

With mining as with everything else, improvisation was the key to success. 'In fact one had just to belong to the HHM (Helping Hand Mission) if one wanted any gear for one's job and must wait an opportunity and take whatever one saw.'[53] This was particularly so in the front line. There never seemed to be timber, corrugated iron or sandbags available to improve the trenches, though the dugouts on the beach seemed to have plenty. Wire netting screens were wanted at Quinn's. They were set at a 60° angle on the parapet — and bombs hitting the netting bounced back and exploded harmlessly. The authorities could not provide, but when netting was seen in a stores dump on the beach, a party of troops would be sent under an officer waving a grubby piece of paper and they would 'purloin the lot'. Timber and corrugated iron would find its way forward in a similar fashion.

Despite the improvements no-one could forget it was war, and both the strain on the men and the living conditions were turning Anzac into an enormous hospital.

'The flies are becoming an awful nuisance. The air is full of them — blow flies and the small house fly. So many unburied bodies around, so many unsanitary latrines and general dirtiness. This is not a clean army in its ways and even actual washing is very difficult. We are on half a gallon of water a day again. And corned beef and salt bacon makes one very thirsty, quite apart from the heat.'[54]

The monotony of the diet and the lack of rest guaranteed that if a man had a weakness, his spell at Anzac would find it and break him. Nineteen-year old Private Ben Smart was in the Wellington Battalion. 'We went into the firing line at 4.00 p.m. and do 24 hours in the firing line, 24 hours in the reserve trenches, and 48 hours in reserve which is practically resting … During the day we do a half hour's observation with the periscope every 2 hours. At night we go on for one hour's observation at a time by looking over the top of the trenches every minute or two. This is pretty risky work. We have to keep an extra watch at dawn because this is when troops may be expected to attack … The trenches are only 25 to 30 yards apart here. In front of our trenches are a few dead bodies which have been lying out here for some time, and every time a bullet hits one of them which is pretty frequently, they let out a terrible stench.'[55]

Food was abundant but monotonous. On the beach the Army Service Corps turned food supplies into miniature fortresses to protect themselves from the constant shrapnel: 'thousands of cases of bully beef, mounds of cheese, hundreds and hundreds of sides of bacon, and castles made of Huntley and Palmer's aggressively nourishing biscuits'. Bully beef was salty and stringy; the cheese smelt and ran like yellow lava in the heat. The bacon was the same as the beef, although it made excellent 'slush' lamps for the bivvies. It was a diet that demanded water, but water was rationed to half a gallon a man per day.

The biscuits were an epic in themselves. They were best used by the tinful in lieu of sandbags, and when the scanty supplies of paper ran out, men wrote home on the indestructible biscuit. 'These biscuits were not of the household variety, but were great big affairs four inches square and as hard as a rock. The only way to eat them was to break pieces off the corners and keep them in the mouth until they were soft enough to chew.'[56] Men pounded them into a porridge, or threw them at the Turks, who 'sometimes throw them back.'[57]

The lack of any fresh fruit or vegetables saw the onset of malnutrition, gum sores, and boils that the heat and dirt turned septic. The same happened with any cut or scratch; men's knees and elbows became covered with sores. The Anzac Headquarters did not initially see such matters as a problem. It was over to the men or their battalions to improve the diet. A similar view was expressed by Bauchop of the Otago Mounted Rifles. They were the last of the mounteds to arrive, and occupied No. 3 Post. Bauchop praised the quantity and quality of the food as far superior to that of the Boer War. This may have been true, but that war had been a war of movement. At Anzac, troops were confined to an increasingly rotten and unsanitary area from which there was no escape and no relief. 'Friday 11 June was a notable day, as on it we received our first issue of bread since landing nearly two months ago.'[58]

In June a bakery was established on Imbros and men at Anzac started to receive bread. 'When the bread boat arrived from Imbros, each loaf was cut into two pieces and apportioned out, each man's piece being all he would get for another ten days.'[59]

Any change in diet warranted an entry in the diary, for they were few and far between. 'In our rations we had bread and 8 ozs jam each. Things are looking up. Dysentery has been very prevalent here all along and I have been pretty bad with it the last few days.'[60] Dysentery became a daily entry and a part of Anzac life: 'They gave us a great surprise today — we were issued with 1 and 3/4 eggs. There was some argument about the 3/4's.'[61]

There were no canteens at Anzac where troops could buy 'pickles, sauces, dried or tinned fruits, tinned milk, sweet biscuits, chocolate or margarine.'[62] Birdwood did not see this as necessary. It was only after repeated requests from both divisions that some effort was made. The New Zealand Infantry Brigade *War Diary* of 3 June requested battalion representatives to report to the beach to purchase canteen stores. They did, but as the diary notes, only mineral water was available.

So in the confined space at Anzac, two worlds continued to exist. There was the world of headquarters and the beach area, where men could bathe daily, have first

Quinn's Post from Pope's Hill with the front line trench on Pope's in the foreground, looking across the the terraces. The pickets on the skyline mark the line of the chicken wire fence built to stop Turkish grenades rolling down on the terraces. The communication trench on the right leads to the front trench and Courtney's Post. *(H15389-1, Australian War Memorial)*.

Engineers building Watson's Pier at Anzac Cove using an 11-inch shell from the German battlcruiser, SMS *Goeben* as a pile-driver. *(WF-002298-34, Russell Family)*

call on supplies landed and improve their diet by trading souvenirs or purchasing foodstuffs from sailors on the barges, who ran a prosperous black market. 'Sapper … came back from Lemnos and brought me a dozen eggs and Abbey and I settled them at one gulp — it was great. The naval men get eggs and condensed milk from Imbros and retail it on the beaches at 3/- a dozen and 3/- a tin. They only pay 1/- for each so they make money.'[63]

There was also that world inhabited by the soldier in the trenches. It was November before canteen stores began to arrive in any quantity. A large shipment came in the week of the evacuation, when it was too late for the men to benefit, and most of these stores were destroyed or left for the Turks, although each man had his pay debited for his portion to reimburse regimental funds.

Such comforts meant a lot to the men, but their importance and the difference they made to living at Anzac was not always appreciated, even by the most concerned of officers. On 14 July, Private Ben Smart of the Wellingtons was asked 'if I would be batman to Lt. Col. W.G. Malone, O.C. Wellington Infy Battalion and at present officer in charge of Quinn's Post and I accepted the job as I am pretty well knocked up … Had a good night's rest and today made a spring cleaning of the Colonel's "bivvy". He has a lovely place and when inside it one could not realise they were only a few yards behind the firing line. I manage to get a bit better tucker here, always milk and sugar in the tea, rice and treacle, beans and potatoes etc. It is vastly different from the company.'[64]

The flies swarmed in the heat and fed on the dead, the latrines and the rubbish. 'Flies, they flew in and out of your mouth, over the top of you and you couldn't drink your tea and you couldn't even stew a bit of stew that flies wouldn't get into you, and every bush you touched buzzed with flies.'[65]

It was impossible to arrest the spread of sickness, as the men in the trenches had no means of keeping clean 'and water is worth its weight in gold … and our singlets want a wash badly but the longer you wear them the warmer they get! Those little crayfish are keeping most of us company.'[66] Everyone was lousy; many caught the parasite on the troopships coming to Lemnos or in trenches once occupied by the Turks. On the beach you would see men, naked, bending over a singlet and shorts searching for lice. 'The boys used to use a candle to run up the seams of their trousers and sizzle them off. You never was a soldier unless you were lousy.'[67]

Inoculations for typhoid prevented an epidemic that would have wasted this army 20 years before, but men were falling sick in their hundreds, and thousands had to be evacuated with dysentery and abdominal disorders. Despite this the troops endured, spent each day surviving, and lived for letters from home and a chance to yarn with their mates about New Zealand, of hunting and fishing, of oysters and a good feed, of the beaches, of the farm, and 'of clean girls in summer dresses'.

'Sunday: Came out in gully at 8 for 24 hours rest. Got NZ mail and put the day in reading two *Guardians*, which I got, about a dozen times.'[68] Mail from home kept them sane, though religion too played its part as Ben Smart recorded. 'We had two voluntary Church services today taken by a Presbyterian Chaplain, the first services we have had in a long while. At the morning service we had the hymns *Fight the Good*

The Mounteds cooking on the terraces below Walker's Ridge; Troopers Cruickshanks, Diamond, R. Fullerton-Smith and Pringle. *(Album 238, p.18 n4, Auckland War Memorial Museum)*

Fight and *Eternal Father Strong to Save*. At the evening we had *O God our Help in Ages Past*, *Onward Christian Soldiers* and *Through the Night of Doubt and Sorrow*. Of course after each service we sang the National Anthem. Today we received a parcel each personally addressed to us, from the Wellington Committee of the Countess of Liverpool's Patriotic Fund. Each parcel contained a pencil, rubber, white handkerchief, 1 cake soap, 2 pairs socks and a card wishing us "Kia Ora".'[69]

'But I must get this letter finished … We went to Communion (everyone who is there does) and sang hymns. Some of the Maoris were there too and sang with great vigour and said their prayers aloud in Maori, while a little way off some pious Indians, Mohammedans, were flattening themselves out towards the sun and invoking the same "Allah" as the Turks. Altogether it was a strange setting for Mass and it had a distinct spirit of its own pervading it throughout as it always does when everyone is on the edge of things.'[70]

For many, the long letters they had sent in Egypt were now reduced to the Field Service postcards and scraps of paper on which they wrote home in indelible pencil. Many shielded those in New Zealand from the realities of life at Anzac, but it was hard to stop pessimism creeping through. 'If Bill and I go under, Mother is not to be bossed by anybody, not even her own family, and see that she enjoys life all she can, bless her. I grow prouder of her every day I live and may I always do.'[71]

By June and the arrival of the Fourth Reinforcements there were few left of the Main Body men. Those who remained were gaunt, physically and spiritually fine-drawn. Two thousand Fourths arrived, including 250 men for each of the infantry battalions. With these the New Zealand Infantry Brigade now numbered 3190 out of an establishment of 4055. Since the landing, 6313 infantry of the brigade had come ashore; now fewer than half remained. Even the reinforcements were not immune: New Zealanders were being evacuated at an average of 40–50 men a day. Men would return from hospital — 'June 27 Sunday again and we have Childs back with us' — only to break down again, 'July 16 — Childs was again carried away on a stretcher, yesterday, quite a wreck with enteric and dysentery. He returned too soon and should have had a longer rest after his wound.'[72]*

Sickness was now taking as many men as bullets and shrapnel had in April and May. Sergeant George Bollinger was one of these: 'Saturday 26th June, We came out of the trenches at 9.00 a.m. after 24 hours of misery — flies, and heat in the day, and want of sleep at night.'[73] The next day his cry could have been echoed by every man at Anzac: 'Sometimes I wonder if England is bankrupt for troops. We are doing 96 hours a week without sleep in the trenches and beyond that doing fatigues.' On 29 June he was carried out to the beach on a stretcher and placed in the field hospital, 'but as I was getting worse they decided to send me to the hospital ship.'[74]

Russell received 420 men of the Fourth Reinforcements. This brought his brigade up to 1212 out of 1541, with a further 500 in the Otago Mounted Rifles. His brigade had been ashore less than a month but had already suffered over 700 casualties, the majority being sick and wounded.

By the beginning of June, New Zealanders killed and wounded numbered 2635. Almost as many again had been evacuated with sickness. Godley saw his force rapidly disappearing. 'Our wounded are beginning to come back already but at our present rate of wastage, we want far more reinforcements than are provided for, and I hope whatever extra men you send will come in the form of reinforcements.'[75]

Anzac in June and July was the monotony and uncertainty of trench warfare. Artillery, though limited by ammunition on both sides, attempted to destroy the trenches, and death or injury came by sniper's bullet, shrapnel pellet, or gassing and asphyxiation in a collapsed trench or mine shaft. Frank McKenzie in the Auckland Battalion wrote: 'A bomb woodened thirteen of our fellows one day, including one of our officers, who however was incapable, and makes way for a better man. The Turks put some beautiful "Black Marias" in our valley behind last night, seven in all, in the crowded road and bivouacs, but not one was touched. But again they landed on the trench where tea was being served, and the Sergeant with the dipper and eleven out of the queue got it badly. Just luck you see.'[76]

Artillery was important to both sides, as Jimmy Swan recorded. 'We have the Turk's guns sorted out to a tick here. In the morning one gun, we call it "Christian Awake", comes over the beach onto a certain patch and as a rule the boys are very careful as regards cover until she starts and stops … then we knock about anyhow until her next period of fire, she never seems to alter it. Then we have "Gentle Annie", "Hell Fire

* Sgt H.P. Childs died on the hospital ship.

Sgt H.P.J. Childs. 'He returned too soon.' *(NZ Herald)*

Mack", "Jack Johnston" and the "Slug". This one never fires until tea time or after.'[77]

Within the Anzac perimeter it was an artilleryman's nightmare. There was not enough space to lay out the guns properly, and what areas there were meant dragging the guns up the steep cliffs onto the plateaus that were open to Turkish fire. Another four-gun battery of the New Zealand Field Artillery arrived with the Fourth Reinforcements, bringing the New Zealand Artillery Brigade up to four batteries of 18 pounders, one of which was at Helles. There was also the invaluable 4.5–inch 4th howitzer battery. Each battery generally had a very limited arc and could fire at close range in support of only one section of the front line. The 2nd Battery NZFA [New Zealand Field Artillery] , or 'Syke's Battery, could fire in support of Quinn's Post, and ammunition was hoarded to meet any Turkish attack.

The 2nd Battery played an important part in defeating the Turkish attack on 29 May. Firing started at 2.30 a.m., 'and from then on until 8.30 a.m. we pumped in the shells. It was glorious … Meanwhile Turks' artillery fire was landing shells all over us, rattling bullets up against the shield and could hear the thud as they hit the sandbags of emplacement.

'Noise so great that it took four men to pass down Roger's orders from the telephone observing station. Fired about 550 rounds from 3 guns, some of the time only 2 guns, No. 1 gun being out of action for a while … Batt[ery] from Gaba Tepe enfiladed us with heavy fire but a destroyer came right in and belted Hades … two Aust 3rd Brigade artillerymen were about 4 yards in front of our No. 2 gun repairing telephone wire. We called to them several times to get out of it but they would not and just ducked down whenever we fired. As our guns were just clearing the crest in front of us it was most risky for them, especially as No. 2 gun had two premature bursts at the muzzle … sure enough No. 2 gun had another premature … I went over to give a hand and found both of them riddled.'[78]

To the men in the trenches, a swim at the beach was one of their rare pleasures: 'We had our swim during the afternoon and how we did enjoy it. It is a rather weird experience swimming with the shrapnel bursting all around one, and yet one would rather do that than go without the only means of getting a wash … I used to dive down and get a handful of sand from the bottom and rub it over my skin, face as well.'[79] 'On any afternoon the beach looks just like a holiday resort except that bathing suits are not the fashion.'[80] Towards the end of July sniping and shrapnel became so serious that many abandoned swimming by day, and those close to the beach bathed at night. However, many were prepared to take the risk. 'I went in for a swim —

again I got into shelling and one shrapnel shell killed two fellows right alongside of me as we swam for the shore. Several were wounded and I helped one get in who had two pellets through his right arm and one in his right shoulder. Poor devil, he was grateful. One of those who was killed was hit with a percussion cap right between the shoulder blades. It was horrible.'[81]

On 29 June, the Turks made their last serious attack on the Anzac perimeter. Once again the main threat was across The Nek and down Russell's Top against trenches now manned by the Australian Light Horse. It was a repeat of 19 May, and the power of machine guns and shrapnel again frustrated human courage. 'In front of Quinn's, they only managed to get out of their trenches and when fired at went back into them again … I went into the sniper's post on the left of Quinn's today to see the Turks lying dead on the parapet along Walker's Ridge.'[82]

The New Zealand Maori Contingent, 477 strong, arrived at Anzac on 3 July. They were attached to the New Zealand Mounted Rifles Brigade and were sent to No. 1 Outpost, which became known as the 'Maori Pa'. Godley wrote to Allen about the Maoris: 'I had a communication the other day asking for their strength and if they required any special diet. I replied … that I hoped that during their stay here there would be sufficient Turks taken prisoner or killed to go round.'[83]

A picture for the folks at home. Two Auckland soldiers look at the camera, while behind them a sniper with periscope rifle and his spotter engage the Turks. *(WW1 Photographic Collection A.A. Perry Negatives, Auckland War Memorial Museum)*

The Maoris were put to work enlarging the sap from the base of Walker's out to No. 2 Outpost so that it would be wide enough to take mules. The garrison found 'rest' more and more arduous as terraces were levelled, roads dug and water tanks brought ashore. It was evident that something was afoot. This 'something' was Birdwood's left hook, but as the work increased grave concern was voiced by brigades at the condition of the men. In late July one of the brigade commanders sounded out his RMOs [Regimental Medical Officers]. Their opinion was: 'The general health of the troops and their physical condition is below normal and is getting progressively worse.' The principal symptoms were 'gastric derangement, bronchial afflictions, loss of weight, rapid pulse, dilation of the heart'. The causes were irregular rest and meals, poor diet, 'heat, dust and flies'. The RMOs stated that no improvement in sanitation was possible unless they moved to fresh ground.[84]

The sickness rate had brought a demand for drugs used in the treatment of stomach ailments and dysentery. Extra supplies were requested. Hamilton's staff responded with 'a tabulated statement giving comparisons in figures of the drugs consumed by our Corps and the Army at Helles which showed that our consumption in drugs was greater than that of the Armies in the South in fact, nearly double, in the case of some drugs'. The answer as far as Hamilton's headquarters were concerned, was 'more care would have to be exercised in the issue of these drugs'.[85]

The paper war had to be won before more drugs became available. Fenwick visited Hamilton's administrative headquarters on the *Aragon*. 'This seemed full of Generals and Admirals. I found a medical officer who assured me that officially my existence was unknown to him. I told him we needed disinfectants and other things and he explained to me that he was not responsible for the supply of this. I could not quite understand what he was but retired quite convinced in the multitude of governors there is chaos … No one seems to care a rap whether our men are dying or not. I heard one officer breathe a sigh of thankfulness. "That's good news," he said. I asked what? "Twenty cases of soda water have come safely for the top dogs," and all care seemed to fade away.'[86]

The sick list was so great that orders were passed demanding that every man possible be kept at Anzac. Charles Saunders sent his best friend to the doctor: 'Abbey came back very wroth. The Captain told him he was malingering. I went straight to the Colonel and told him to come and see Abbey. He was lying in his dugout, as sick as a dog, just racked with retching and suffering with dysentery also. The Colonel gave orders for the Doctor to send him away — and I helped him to the beach and put him aboard a barge for the hospital ship … The Doctor had orders to send away as few men as possible but it puzzles me that a man holding Captain's rank can so blindly follow the letter of an order, when his experience tells him it is wrong.'[87]

The best seat in the house: a six-seater with a view over Anzac Cove. *(J03659-1, Australian War Memorial)*

Graves among the bivvies at No. 3 Outpost. Trooper Ernest Ruapekapeka Gripp, killed in action, 30 May 1915. His brother Harris died of wounds at Malta on 28 August 1915. Behind his grave is Trooper Fred Coates, also killed on 30 May in the fighting for Old No .3 Outpost. Coates was regarded as one of the outstanding scouts in the Wellington Mounteds. *(J.C. Read Collection – PAColl-1655, Alexander Turnbull Library)*

Summary discipline at Anzac. The CQMS of 15th North Auckland Company appears before Captain Colvin Algie on a charge of 'pinching our rum'. The Company Sergeant Major (CSM) and escorts are present as Captain Algie reads the charge. *(Price Family)*

More positive steps were taken: the battalions longest in the line were rested for three to five days on Imbros in preparation for the coming offensive. Ewen Pilling went with the Otago Battalion: 'It is wonderful to be able to sit, walk, lie down, or stretch oneself without fear of hostile bullet or shell. Like most here I am very tired. One only begins to realise how tired one is after a short spell and I could do with a longer rest ... Out of the original officers and non-commissioned officers in our regiment we have only one officer and three corporals remaining. The faces of the regiment have also changed. Many gaps have been filled ... My promotion first to Corporal and later, to Sergeant, in each case filled a gap. Those at home may think these promotions out here are a reward for a special piece of work. That is not so. One's old ambitions and childish visions of winning a VC [Victoria Cross] or some other distinction, fade away under such active service conditions as we have experienced here. We put little value on decorations now, and will be satisfied if we do our work and get back home alive.'[88]

Throughout the summer, as the men weakened discipline was tightened to maintain standards. There was a steady stream of courts martial, mainly for insubordination, theft and similar offences. Lectures were given: 'June 18 — Lecture by Capt Cross this afternoon on "Discipline" mainly about the heavy punishment one can be given on active service.'[89]

Men tormented by heat and flies took a risk swearing in front of an officer. The Wellingtons were particularly strict on this and on 27 June, Private Smart recorded: 'Pte S.C. Adams sentenced to 14 Days' Field Punishment for excessive swearing.'[90]

It was an accomplished man who could be drunk at ANZAC but Private Littlejohn of the Canterburys managed, and received field punishment for his efforts.

On 5 July, Routine Orders published: 'At Cape Helles on May 5 Pte T. Davies 1st Royal Munster Fusiliers was ordered to be shot for cowardice in the face of the enemy by quitting his post but on July 3 this sentence was commuted to one of 10 years' penal servitude.'[91] No sentence of death was carried out against a New Zealander at Gallipoli, though during the war 28 New Zealanders were sentenced to death, and five executed, all in France.

Veterans of the Wellington Battalion remember Private J.R. 'Jack' Dunn, a member of the machine-gun section, being sentenced to death for sleeping at his post. It happened in late July at Quinn's Post. A photo exists showing the sentence being read out to the battalion on 5 August. The prisoner under sentence stands in front of his

No. 1 Outpost: 'Maori Pa', home of the Maori Contingent. *(Album 212, p.5 n2, Auckland War Memorial Museum)*

fellows, bare headed, guarded by two escorts with fixed bayonets. The sentence was remitted on medical grounds as Dunn had not been relieved from sentry duty at the proper time. He continued to serve on the Peninsula and was killed three days later on 8 August.[*] Perhaps this was never intended to be more than a warning to men now so worn and tired that 'you were dead from your feet up, and at night time when you were standing to, you would sell your soul for an hour's sleep.'[92]

The Anzac Garrison was now hard at work developing roads and accommodation within the perimeter for the next offensive. This was to be the left hook through the northern foothills that had been planned in May but was delayed because of lack of men. Malone, who was one of the first to consider it, now had doubts. On 19 June he wrote to Lieutenant Colonel Richardson at Helles: 'It's a bit late for that turning movement or rather it will be much more difficult — where a month ago the door was wide open, it is now shut with more or less a division of Turks and lines of entrenchments. In front of here, tier on tier of trenches which, being on the forward slope, ought to be untenable, but artillery or ammunition is scarce.'[93]

The men too were aware that something was going on: 'Our first intimation of a shift was scented out by chaps going bathing. They saw that the ammunition being unloaded was all Mark 7. Thousands of boxes of this mark were being unloaded from

---

[*] See Christopher Pugsley, *On the Fringe of Hell: New Zealanders and Military Discipline in the First World War*, Hodder & Stoughton, Auckland, 1991; and Pat White, *Gallipoli: in Search of a Family Story*, Red Roofs, Wairarapa, 2005.

Quinn's Post, a sentence of death. Private J.R. Dunn of the Wellington Battallion is sentenced to death for sleeping at his post. On medical recommendation the sentence was revoked and Private Dunn was released. The prisoner is standing bare-headed in the foreground, in front of the man with fixed bayonet. An officer is reading the finding of the court martial to the assembled battalion. *(Auckland War Memorial Museum)*

the barges, taken to the extreme left and stowed away. Mark 7 has a much higher muzzle velocity than Mark 6 which we use, and is only suitable for the more modern rifle with which Kitchener's New Army are armed. Another ominous sign was that all the Army Service stores, Ordnance Depot, Field Ambulance, Dressing Stations etc. on the beach were transferred from the care of ANZAC to the Tommies. This clearly spelled a move, and speculation was rife as to what they were up to and what they'd do with us. We honestly thought we were being relieved.'[94]

10

THE BATTLE FOR CHUNUK BAIR

They came from safety of their own free will
To lay their young men's beauty, strong men's powers
Under the hard roots of the foreign flowers
Having beheld the Narrows from the Hill.[1]

If I were asked to give a description of the colour of the earth on
Chunuk Bair on the 9th or 10th of August, I would say it was a dull
browny red— and that was blood. Just dried blood.[2]

'We are about to move out soon, round left flank … No movement all day 6th and go out on night with rest of Brigade to take Chunuk Bair in a big combined movement against 971, Koja Chemen Tepe.

'We are pleased to be moving, but the men are rundown and the reinforcement men are in a big majority, so I am not too sanguine about what we can do.'[3]

Birdwood's plan had grown enormously from that contemplated in May. Three months of fruitless and costly hammering at Helles had worn down the British 8th Corps as well as two French divisions in the south, so now Birdwood's ANZAC Corps would play the primary role in the centre of the Peninsula. Increased by 25,000 men, the Corps would break out of the ANZAC foothold. Godley's NZ & A Division, reinforced by a further division of Kitchener's New Army, would make a left hook to the north and seize the high ground of the Sari Bair Range.

This would happen in two stages. Russell's Mounted Rifles, with the Maoris and a British brigade, would open the door by seizing the foothills in a silent night attack. That same night, two columns would advance up the deres. On the left, a two-brigade column of Cox's 29th Indian Brigade and Monash's 4th Australians would seize 971, or Koja Chemen Tepe, and Hill Q, and on the right Johnston's New Zealand Infantry would capture Chunuk Bair. It was estimated it would take six hours to reach the crests in the dark, but dawn would find them secure on the heights. These moves

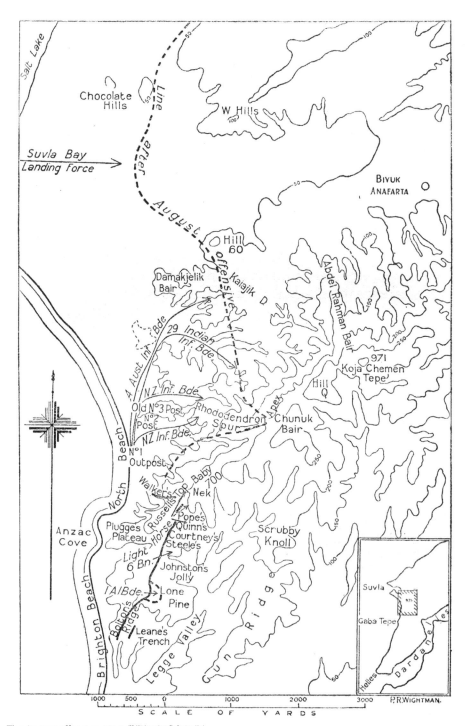

The August offensive, 1915. *(P.R. Wightman, Lucas, The Empire at War)*

would be supported by the landing of a fresh corps, the 9th Corps, under General Stopford at Suvla.

Made up of Kitchener's New Army Divisions, this corps would advance across the Suvla Plain, take the high area north of the Anafarta Gap and link up with the ANZACs on the vital ground. The operation was to be supported by an elaborate series of feints — at Helles, with another push toward Achi Baba, and at Anzac by Walker's 1st Australian Division, who would thrust south-east across the 400 Plateau at Lone Pine, as if aiming for Gaba Tepe. This was planned for the evening before to draw Turkish reinforcements down onto the south of the ANZAC position and away from Chunuk Bair.

To assist the assault onto Chunuk Bair, there would be a thrust across The Nek towards Baby 700 — the traditional field of slaughter. This would only occur with the final thrust by Johnston's New Zealanders onto the crest of Chunuk Bair. To do otherwise, as all acknowledged, would be suicide. The thrust would be made by the 3rd Australian Light Horse Brigade, newly arrived and eager for action.

It was a highly ambitious plan and placed great demands on the tired troops and weakened staffs of the ANZAC divisions. The best of Godley's staff had gone, sick and wounded, and now Godley would have resources, almost equivalent to a corps, to be co-ordinated by his divisional staff. It was too much to expect. Their only experience had been the disastrous 2 May attack, although Godley appeared to have every confidence: 'You will soon know that we are preparing hard for a good push, which will I hope, land us overlooking the Straits. I am to attack the big ridge, Koja Chemen Tepe — Chunuk Bair, which has been dominating us all this time. In addition to my own Division, I have under my command the greater part of the 13th Division under fat old Shaw of the Sherwood Foresters.'[4]*

All through the nights of early August the soldiers of Shaw's New Army 13th (Western) Division were smuggled ashore. Transports crept in with no lights, disembarked their troops and were gone by daylight, leaving the sea deserted except for monitors and destroyers bombarding the coast. 'About 30,000 troops landed at this position last three days. Gurkhas, Tommies etc. Everything ready for advance.'[5]

The news was received with mixed feelings among Godley's men. The Mounteds, the last to have arrived, looked forward to getting out of the trenches. Sergeant Wilder of the Wellington Mounteds wrote on 4 August: 'Persistent rumours are going round that we are going to advance. It's about time we did something.'[6]

The infantry of the Main Body was less enthusiastic. 'Rumours of big left flank movement. Fellows getting worn out, and going away sick. Feeling sick and "fed up" myself.'[7] The summer heat of July had taken its toll; Russell's Mounteds, including Bauchop's Otago Mounted Rifles and the Maori Contingent, numbered 1900 instead of 2500. The infantry numbered 2800 out of 4000. On the evening of 5 August Russell's Mounteds gathered at No. 3 Outpost, the home of Bauchop's Otago Mounteds.

---

* Godley was not being too uncharitable. Major General Shaw weighed close to 20 stone (127 kilos) and found both the climate and terrain especially trying.

Johnston's Infantry filed out from the posts on Second Ridge and moved down to the beach and along the sap beyond Walker's Ridge. Ormond Burton, a stretcher bearer, watched them pass: 'Battalions that had landed a thousand strong and had received the 3rd and 4th reinforcements were now down to four or five hundred men. I knew very many in the Auckland Battalion and stood for a long while greeting my friends. Most were thin and tired. The mile of march had exhausted them. They were shadows only of the men who had left Egypt so short a while before … They passed on in the growing darkness to "Happy Valley".'[8]

The infantry lay in Happy Valley, resting in the scrub while officers moved to No. 2 and No. 3 outposts to reconnoitre the ground with binoculars from the forward trenches. Men prepared for battle. Each man was to attack in 'light order' carrying 200 rounds of ammunition, two days' iron rations (bully beef and biscuits), first field dressing, two sandbags, rifle and bayonet.

Bombing parties were organised, four men to each platoon. 'We work in fours, one thrower, one assistant and two carriers …'[9] Each carried six jam-tin bombs. On the afternoon of the 5th every man had been issued with three pieces of white calico 'to be sewn on the right shoulder at the back and one each on the back of the upper arm.' This was to identify the ANZAC and British troops in the night advance.

Half in hope, half in fear, the exhausted men drew on their spiritual reserves and awaited the advance. Sick men in hospital begged doctors to let them out so that they could be with their mates. Everyone sensed from the activity that this was the big one. Those lucky enough to survive unscathed since the beginning pondered on their chances. In the bivvies the night before the move to Happy Valley, concerts and sing-alongs were held. Songs were wistful and conjured up thoughts of home. Letters were posted, some with a premonition of death. Malone wrote: 'I expect to go thro alright, but dear wife, if anything happens to me you must not grieve too much — there are our dear children to be brought up — You know how I love and have loved you … I am prepared for death and I hope that God will have forgiven me all my sins.'[10]

In the gully north of Walker's, men had to lie low by day, tunics inside out so that the patches would not show, to avoid being seen by Turkish aircraft. Frank Hardey of the Canterbury Battalion wrote: 'We were in direct line for the Turkish artillery to smack us up but by keeping hidden we remained all the next day unmolested … We rested all day, cleaning our arms, getting a bit of extra sleep and feeding up. How wonderfully fresh and sweet was the heather-laden breeze out here in the open spaces. We were right away from the stench of dead bodies and decaying refuse. How silent and serene, with no firing or battle noises to mar Nature's beauties. But it was the calm preceding the storm.'[11]

Within the ANZAC perimeter the gunners were preparing. Godley's New Zealand Artillery had been reorganised into two brigades. 'Lt Col. (G.N.) Johnston is now full Colonel, Symonds and Sykes Lt Colonels. First brigade is 1st and 3rd batteries and the other howitzer battery which should be in Egypt by now. Second Brigade is 2nd Battery, us (4th Howitzer Battery) and 4th 18 pdr. battery also now in Egypt.' On the 6th the gunners were 'busy all morning bringing up ammunition till we had 400 rounds per gun stowed handy, and all afternoon fusing this lot. The big work started at 4.30 p.m. No. 1 gun fired steadily 4.30 p.m. till 9.30 p.m. when we (No. 2) joined in.'[12]

After artillery and naval fire, the first of the feints went in at Lone Pine. It was an operation that had been strongly opposed by Walker, the Australian Divisional Commander, but on Birdwood's insistence he determined to give his 1st Australian Brigade, the attacking force, every chance of success. Underground tunnels led forward to an underground line 70 metres from the Turkish line. It was here that the first wave of attackers waited. The 1st Battery New Zealand Field Artillery was one of the batteries firing in support of the attack.

Bombardier Arthur Currey was a member of a forward observing party in this front line: 'Our battery was to smash down the barbed wire in front of the Turkish trenches at all costs. At 4.30 p.m. on 6 August all guns were to bombard Lone Pine until 5.30 p.m. and then the 1st Brigade of Australian Infantry were to charge … At 4.30 all guns opened fire … I was watching the effect when a Turkish shell topped our sandbags, smashed my periscope and knocked it out of my hands. As I stooped to pick it up another shell smashed into our station and blew our wall to pieces … Our trenches were full of gay Infantry waiting to charge … two men next to me were knocked out but I still missed injury.'[13]

At 5.30 the Australians clambered from the trenches and scrambled towards the Turkish front line. There was a frozen moment as the line faltered. They had discovered that the Turkish line was timbered over. Some fired then leapt down through gaps torn in the timber roof, others ran onto the uncovered support lines.

'The fight lasted four days and nights. I was over in the captured trenches early next morning and things were a mess. Some of the trenches were blocked with our wounded, in others the dead Turks lay four deep and we had to walk on top of them. It took several days to clear the trenches and our dead on top had to be left there.' Currey was running messages and 'in trying to get back to our old trenches I got blocked in a tunnel with a lot of our wounded. There were all sorts of wounds, one fellow was shot in the neck and with protruding eyes was gasping for breath. One had his jaw shot away … Another young fellow was shot in the thigh and was pleased to think he had got off so lightly. They had been wounded eighteen hours and were still unable to be carried to our own lines.'[14]

Lone Pine was a subterranean battle that burned, smouldered and erupted again throughout the days of the August offensive. Turks and Australians killed one another in dark stinking pits blocked with bodies. One had to look to Verdun and the struggles in the cellars and tunnels of Fort Douaumont and Vaux to find a comparison with the horror and human endurance of both sides in the battle at the Pine. Seven Victoria Crosses were awarded there, one to Captain Alfred Shout, a New Zealander serving with the 1st Australian Battalion, for his action on 9 August 1915. He died from wounds received from a bomb bursting in his hand on 11 August 1915. The feint cost the 1st Australian Division over 2000 men, and the Turks 5000. Walker had achieved his goal. 'It drew upon itself the whole of the immediate Turkish reserves,'[15] and for three days monopolised the attention of the Turkish commanders. The situation was ripe for the left hook to the north of Anzac.

The Mounteds were well prepared for their role in the foothills. Brigadier General Andrew Russell had gone through the detail of the operation with his regiments to make sure everyone knew his job. Sick men with enough strength to hold a rifle relieved the fit men in the trenches and everyone waited for nightfall. John Wilder of the Wellington Mounteds wrote: 'It's going to be pretty warm, it will be one of the biggest affairs in history … We attack, as far as we know, about 10 o'clock tonight. If things go well we'll give the Turks a horrible shock.'[16]

Russell had allotted the following tasks to his regiments: Canterbury and Otago were to go for Bauchop's Hill, a Turkish-held hill just north of No. 3 Post, which ran from the sea plain up on the north of Chailak Dere. Auckland was to take Old No. 3 Post, which had been lost at the end of May. This was inland on the same spur as No. 2 and No. 3 outposts and since May had been turned into a strong position by the Turks with wire and electrically detonated mines guarding the approaches. Wellington was to take the Table Top, inland from old No. 3 Post, and also Destroyer Ridge, just south of Old No. 3. Table Top overlooked Chailak Dere and Sazli Dere, while Destroyer Ridge overlooked the approach up Sazli Dere to Table Top. These were the routes forward for Johnston's infantry onto Rhododendron Ridge and Chunuk Bair. The Maori Contingent was in reserve apart from 50 men with the Canterburys and 50 with the Otagos to bolster the numbers. It was to be a silent attack with no firing — only the bayonet, and if necessary the bomb, were to be used.

To the north again, Brigadier General Travers with two battalions of his 40th Infantry Brigade of the New Army, the 5th Wiltshires and the 4th South Wales Borderers, would seize the lightly held Damakjelik Bair, the low foothills north of Bauchop Hill between which ran the Aghyl Dere, the route of the left Assault Column towards 971 and Hill Q. At 8.30 p.m. the Mounteds started filing out along the deres towards their objectives. For some weeks past a destroyer had been sailing in close to the coast and punctually at 9.00 p.m. bombarding Old No. 3 Outpost illuminated in the beam of her searchlight. It was the same tonight. The bombardment hid the sound of the Auckland Mounteds arriving at the foot of the hill from 9.00 p.m. They formed up with two squadrons forward, 11th North Auckland on the left, 3rd Auckland on the right, and 4th Waikato in the rear. Then, with the bombardment still going on, they made their way up the slope. K.M. Stevens was the sergeant under Lieutenant Harry Mackesy, who commanded the bombing squad in the 11th North Auckland Squadron.

'When the destroyer ceased firing Harry Mackesy and the bombing squad scrambled up the cliff face … half the squad went with Harry and I, with the other half, went straight ahead to cut the Turks off at the rear … In the pitch black darkness I fell into the first trench on top of the cliff and then ran on falling across two narrow trenches, but I did not stop until I reached the high ground on the far side of [Old] No. 3 Outpost.'[17]

The Turk manning the switchboard to fire the mines was bayoneted before he could detonate the charges, and the Turks sheltering in the rear of the post were bombed and bayoneted as they fled towards the Table Top and dispersed into the deres. By

Auckland Mounteds in the captured Turkish trenches at Old No. 3 Outpost. *(C Athol Williams Collection – PAColl-0184, Alexander Turnbull Library)*

10.00 p.m. the post had been taken, 100 Turks were dead and a few were prisoners. Auckland's losses were seven dead, including Mackesy, who died from his wounds, and 15 wounded. Stevens found himself alone: 'There were rifle fire and bombs exploding back where Harry and his party went, and shortly after I heard men scuttling through the scrub up the hill, but I did not know whether they were friends or foes. I lay low as I was not game to go back or I may be shot for a Turk.' He lay there until he heard infantry filing past and then, knowing he was safe, crawled into some thick scrub and slept, 'enjoying a blessing which had been denied us since landing — pure, fresh air'.[18]

At 9.30 p.m. the Wellington Mounteds moved along the Sazli Dere past the Auckland Mounteds. Major Dick's 6th Manawatu led the regiment and seized Destroyer Hill at bayonet point. His men then piqueted either side of the dere, and the remaining two squadrons passed through, led by Commanding Officer Lieutenant Colonel W. Meldrum, later known as 'Fix Bayonets Bill'. 'At the foot of the Table Top we found a barbed wire fence erected right across the Dere. Thus, to save noise, we went round in single file and came to where it was intended to start the attack up the hill. There was no moon and the night was dark but it could be seen that a mass of scrub and dwarf trees ran for some distance up the slope. As it would prove very difficult, and certainly noisy, to go through this, after a few minutes' discussion with the Squadron Leaders Majors Elmslie and Chambers, I altered the plan of attack and decided to penetrate right up to the blind end of the dere, where a ridge running from Old No. 3 Post joined on to the north west end of Table Top, to scale the ridge near the junction and to make the attack on Table Top from behind its right shoulder. This did not take long and we went on up the Dere. Hereabouts we had a very awkward five minutes. We realised that any moment we might be fired on either from the trenches on Table Top above us on the right or from the Ridge [from old No. 3 Outpost] on the left. But the darkness was all in our favour. But suddenly when we were halfway along the Dere an incendiary bomb went off on top of the Ridge about 100 yards behind us on the left and set fire to some scrub.

'Word was sent back along the line to lie down. For fully five minutes the scrub blazed, lighting up both the Ridge and Table Top. We expected any moment to be seen but the low bushes along the side of the Ridge must have thrown a shadow across the Dere which kept us out of sight.

'As the fire died down we rose and moved forward again until we reached the blind eye of the Dere.

'Here we halted for a few minutes to select a route and still in single file we started to climb up the steep face. Major Elmslie led, using an entrenching tool to cut steps where needed.

'The hillside here was of dry clean earth, free from stones and no sound was made by the falling earth as the steps were cut. On getting over the top of the Ridge, a halt was made until some 20 men had assembled.

'With bayonets fixed these went on up the hill to the trench at the rear of Table Top. A small Turkish outpost was overpowered and silenced.'[19]

Meldrum's men had captured the steepest and most difficult of the Mounteds' objectives. It was all but deserted, the garrison presumably having gone forward to assist in the battle for Old No. 3 Outpost, from which firing could still be heard, and Destroyer Ridge. Meldrum records the Table Top being taken at 5 minutes to 11. Signal parties laying telephone wire moved with each of the regiments and at 12.30 a.m. Russell's headquarters were told that Table Top had been captured. The Wellington Mounteds' casualties numbered four killed and nine wounded. 'From then on till daylight digging went on. The piquets were meantime kept busy. From time to time parties of Turks, either retiring from Old No. 3 Post and Destroyer Ridge or coming forward to occupy the trenches were captured and brought within our lines. By morning we had 150 prisoners in hand.'[20]

For Russell's headquarters at No. 2 Post, it was a time of watching into the darkness and waiting. Captain King NZSC was Russell's staff captain. 'We heard a lot of firing going on by Bauchop's Hill, so concluded Canterbury and Otago had also arrived, but had evidently run into something pretty solid from the row going on — also from the fact that the Turks over the way opened up with a 75 mm gun and a 6 inch bomb thrower which starred peppering the hill we were on.'[21]

A platoon of Maori was attached to both the Canterbury and Otago mounteds. Peter Tahitahi was in one of these, and advanced with the combined South Island Mounteds in the attack on the Turkish positions: 'There were dead Turks in the trenches, some of them were half dead, just laying there— you could feel it when you tramped on them — breathing. We just turned the bayonet with the rifle round and finished them off.'[22]

To the north the Otagos seized Bauchop's Hill and the Canterburys took Walden's Point, an extension of Bauchop's towards the coast. It was a grim dour battle in the dark. Arthur Bauchop was mortally wounded towards dawn, and 'Old John' Findley, the Canterbury's commanding officer, was wounded as the South Island Mounteds progressed up the slopes, marking their path with their dead. The Otago Mounted Rifles lost 34 men killed and 65 wounded out of an approximate strength of 350. All that was heard was the crack of rifles and tapping of Turkish machine guns and then, faintly in the distance, cheers from the slopes, and the flashes of the Turkish fire receding up the hills. The door was open. Russell and his men had secured the foothills. Today it is a forgotten epic, yet C.E.W. Bean described it as 'This magnificent feat of arms, the brilliance of which was never surpassed, if indeed equalled, during the campaign.'[23]

Despite the brilliance of the Mounteds' success, the New Zealanders were falling behind the timings laid down for them to be on Chunuk Bair in the dawn. Bauchop's Hill was to be captured by 11.00 p.m. It was not until 1.10 a.m. that it was reported cleared. There was still time, but the infantry had the steepest country to negotiate.

Johnston had given orders to his infantry commanding officers in Happy Valley on 5 August. It was planned that the Otago, Wellington and Auckland battalions would move along the Main Sap to No. 2 Outpost and then up Chailak Dere in that order, followed by a Field Company of Engineers and the 26th Indian Mountain Battery. They would move through the dere and on to Rhododendron Ridge. Johnston tasked the Otago Battalion with securing Rhododendron Ridge facing Chunuk Bair. The Wellingtons following up would secure and piquet Cheshire Ridge overlooking the Aghyl Dere and a road that climbed up to a stone enclosure on the ridge below Chunuk Bair known as 'The Farm'. The Canterburys would move separately from the remainder of the brigade up Sazli Dere and were to secure the southern edge of Rhododendron Ridge facing Battleship Hill. Auckland would remain in reserve.

Once this had been achieved the brigade would seize Chunuk Bair with two battalions: the Wellington Infantry on the left and the Otago Infantry on the right. The Otagos were to start moving up Chailak Dere at 10.30, by which time it was anticipated that the Mounteds would be clear of the dere and the way open for the infantry. The Canterbury Battalion would move off at the same time up Sazli Dere. Malone for one had his doubts.

'I do feel the preparation, as regards to our brigade anyway, is not thorough.

'The Brigadier [Johnston] will not get down to bed rock. He seems to think that night attack and the taking of entrenched positions without artillery preparation is like "kissing one's hand". Yesterday he burst forth, "If there's any hitch I shall go right up and take the place myself." All, as it were, in a minute and on his own! He says, "There's to be no delay." He is an extraordinary man.

'If it were not so serious it would be laughable. So far as I am concerned, the men, my brave gallant men, shall have the best fighting chance I can give them or that can be got. No airy plunging and disregard of the rules and chances.'[24]

There was little unity among the commanders of the New Zealand Infantry Brigade. It was evident that Johnston and Temperley were unhappy with Malone. In Temperley's eyes Malone 'was not a man of many ideas, but the few he had, he retained with inflexible resolution … He was no tactician; he was not even greatly interested in tactics,' and as far as Temperley was concerned he was not a good leader 'for he never had a grip of the military situation.'[25]*

Hughes, Commanding Officer of the Canterburys, was regarded with equal suspicion. Young was Malone's protégé, so it is easy to see why both Johnston and Temperley entrusted Moore, a British Regular Officer, and his Otago Battalion with leading the brigade.

At 10.30 the Otagos, led by the 10th North Otagos commanded by Major Frank Statham, moved up Chailak Dere. They were immediately held up by barbed wire and small parties of Turks bypassed in the Mounteds' advance. Private Anderson was a member of the bombing party at the head of the 10th North Otago Company:

'We slowly and quietly pushed on till entering a deep gully. I was with an advanced segment who lost contact with the main body. The Lieutenant in command sent Phillips and me back to get in touch with the others. We contacted Colonel Moore and told him of our position. I expected he would have given us some sort of word to take back but he seemed to think it was of no importance. After some further delay,

---

* Ironically, in an age when few professional officers read into the theory of warfare, as a territorial officer, Lt Col. Malone had in fact conducted a deep and wide-ranging study.

away on our left there came the sound of "Hip Hip Hurray" the only time I ever heard cheering at a success. Colonel Moore remarked that they all seemed to have gained their objectives except us.'[26]

It was 3.00 a.m. before Moore got his now scattered battalion onto the Table Top, where he met up with Meldrum and the Wellington Mounteds. Major Statham had moved through an hour before across a narrow saddle that linked the Table Top to the broad western end of Rhododendron Ridge. It was about 4.00 a.m. with dawn rapidly approaching when Moore, with about one third of his battalion, linked up with the 8th Southlands and 10th North Otagos moving with Statham.

Conscious of the delays, Johnston pushed Malone's Wellingtons past the Otagos up Chailak Dere. Behind them all was confusion as the waiting infantry blocked the sap below No. 2 Outpost and the mouth of the dere. 'Well it was what we, in a joke, called a concertina march — moving and stopping —moving and stopping; oh, it was deadly. Sometimes we would get long enough to sit down and sometimes we wouldn't.'[27]

So they trudged and shambled into the night, with bloodrimmed eyes and tired curses as they stumbled into one another. At each halt, men fell asleep or wordlessly collapsed as stray bullets from the battles in the foothills around them took a steady toll.

The Canterbury Infantry Battalion moved out to go up Sazli Dere but found their way blocked by troops waiting in the Main Sap. 'At out appointed hour we set out. We found Auckland halted in the sap, but as we had to reach our objective at an appointed time our OC (Lieutenant Colonel Hughes) pushed on. The result was a jam, and before we knew what had happened all hands were stuck fast. This necessitated a sorting out … This first mishap hindered us about two hours and night time was awfully precious. Eventually we swung into our particular gully [Sazli Dere] in good order, the battalion moving in column of fours, our company leading. We were being guided by a scout on whose knowledge of the country everything depended. By this time we were free of our outposts, and were moving towards the enemy's country. The sensation was somewhat uncanny … We marched right to the head of the gully, where we were checked by a cliff that rose perpendicular before us. It was then that the guide made the discovery that we were lost. A nice lookout! Due to deliver an attack at a prearranged time, and here we were bushed in the enemy's country!'[28]

Unknown to Hughes and the Canterbury Infantry, they had followed Meldrum's Wellingtons' route and were now below the cliff face scaled by the Mounteds onto Table Top some hours before. 'The scouting parties we had dispatched returned with no solution to our difficulty, so we about turned and retraced our steps along the way we had come.

'The long snakelike line wended its way back amidst a silence one could almost feel. Thro' creek beds, up steps cut in the rock by the Turks, slipping and scrambling. Presently someone slipped and fell dropping a shovel with a noisy clatter. The noise rang clear in the stillness, the line involuntarily paused and listened. Immediately from the right hand arose a jabbering we realised was Turkish. We had run into an outpost. But for once fortune smiled upon us. An NZMR patrol had been stalking this particular outpost and just as the Turks discovered us, they themselves were discovered.'[29]

The Mounteds mopped up the Turkish outpost and directed the Canterbury Infantry up the cliff face onto the Table Top. 'What a climb! ... The OC MR directed our Col. to Rhododendron and we felt at last we were on our way. Grey dawn was in the skies when yet another discovery was made ... it was found that only two platoons of the Second Company were in touch with us. The rest of the battalion was missing.'[30]

The battalion had become split when it had retraced its steps. The bulk of the Canterburys ended up back at the start point in the main communication sap. It was dawn before the two platoons from Second Company joined the Otagos on the western spur of Rhododendron Ridge.

The Wellington Infantry made better progress. As dawn broke the battalion had almost reached the head of the Chailak Dere, at the junction of Cheshire and Rhododendron Ridges. This junction of the two ridges offered about a hectare of ground which was concealed from the Sari Bair Ridge above and became known as the Apex. Malone reported back to Johnston:

7th August

OC NZ Inf Bde
    I am occupying a position nearly at the head of the gully. As it is day and I am not sure of my position, I am lining the crest of the surrounding ridges to ensure reasonable safety. I am reconnoitring forward and will act on further knowledge and report.

                                         W.G. Malone
                                            Lt Col.[31]

Later, Malone discovered that his piquets were deployed along the ridge that his orders had told him to secure. His battalion at least was in position to assault up Rhododendron Ridge onto the heights of Chunuk Bair, silent and above them some 500 metres away. No one knows for sure what happened next in the New Zealand Infantry Brigade. The story as passed down is a patchwork quilt of gaps, contradictions and generalisations.

It was already 4.30 a.m., the time for the feint to be launched across The Nek by the Light Horse back in the old ANZAC position. Brigade headquarters was following up the Wellingtons, with the Auckland Battalion behind them. By the time the Wellingtons, in single file, had cleared Chailak Dere and the brigade headquarters had joined Malone on the Apex, it must have been close to 6.00 a.m. They were well behind schedule and instead of assaulting the hill before dawn, it would now have to be a daylight attack.

C.E.W. Bean states that Temperley, the brigade major, accepted that the Otagos and Canterburys were dispersed and not in position but appears to have recommended that the Auckland and Wellington battalions attack the hill. 'But Malone of the

Wellingtons, the most forcible of the New Zealand Commanders, was against the attempt.'[32]

Malone had carried out the initial task set his battalion by Johnston and had piqueted the ridge. The next phase was to be the assault on Chunuk Bair. What we can be sure of is that Malone would have stuck to the principle that 'my men shall have the best fighting chance I can give them ... No airy plunging ...'[33]

It is on this evidence that history has labelled Malone the principal reason the New Zealand Infantry paused before Chunuk Bair. Brigadier General Johnston was by nature impulsive, and this may have been in Godley's mind when he tasked his brigade. However, Temperley's memoirs, written after his briefing of C.E.W. Bean on the events of August 1915, show that Johnston was not fit to command the brigade on the morning of 7 August. His stay on the Peninsula had been punctuated with illness, and in his exhausted state, he now had a crucial decision to make.

It should have been a simple decision. Birdwood had briefed all the brigadiers and commanding officers on 5 August, emphasising that regardless of any delays to any part of either assaulting column, the issue must be pressed by whoever remained and the heights seized and held.

Temperley described Johnston as 'a capable tactician with a good eye for country ... if he erred at all, he erred on the side of recklessness and inability to weigh the situation calmly ... his loyalty to the views of his superiors in the field was complete and unswerving whatever his own personal opinions might be ...'[34] The New Zealand Infantry had experienced all these attributes, often to their cost, in the months at Anzac, but now sickness had taken its toll on Johnston, as Temperley recorded. 'Though his fighting spirit remained as high as ever, he was now no longer in a condition to exercise command efficiently. He was always rather inarticulate and found difficulty in expressing his ideas in a way that others could understand ... As his Staff Officer I had learnt to know the working of his mind and to interpret him. This had become much accentuated since the battle started, he sat for hours in absolute silence, he was frequently barely coherent and his judgement and mind were obviously clouded.'[35]*

Temperley's account provided the substance for both Bean's and North's accounts on the experiences of the New Zealand Brigade in August. In the 1920s he enlarged on them and wrote in his memoirs that he advised Johnston to delay the attack on 7 August. 'We were alone and unsupported, having thrust deep into the enemy's position without any knowledge of what had occurred to our right or left. Prudence seemed to dictate a pause, particularly as any movement from the Apex at once produced a storm of rifle and machine gun fire from the crest. Accordingly I wrote a message to Divisional Headquarters saying where we were and how we were disposed but that "in view of the fact that we were absolutely unsupported on our right or left and could see no sign of movement of any troops we deemed it prudent to remain here and await a

---

* In the 1930s Temperly told Major W. Gentry, NZSC, that Johnston had been drinking rum from his water bottle throughout the night march, and by morning was drunk. (Author interview with Major General Sir William Gentry.)

further advance on the part of the Indian Brigade." [Brigadier General] Johnston … approved of this message and it was despatched.'[36]

This is corroborated by Johnston's account written in a letter to his brother after the battle; 'and from what I could see none of the other columns had got away from the beach, and as there was no point in assaulting the Chunuk Bair trenches on our own, I rang up the Division.'*

By now it was 8.00 a.m. and, as Bean stated, 'a deplorable delay had already occurred.'[37]

During this delay the tired infantry had slumped into the scrub and taken the opportunity to have 'breakfast', sucking pebbles to moisten dry mouths, carefully rinsing and wiping lips with a hint of water from their precious water bottles. They looked morosely at their hard dry biscuits and tinned salty beef, and shuddered in the light of what promised to be another clear, relentlessly hot day.

There had been little progress to the left or right. Earlier that morning on the right, back in the old ANZAC perimeter, men of the 3rd Australian Light Horse Brigade had filed into the forward trenches on Russell's Top. The attack was to start at 4.30 a.m., the same time as the first scouts of the Wellingtons reached the Apex. The Turkish trenches at The Nek were 30 metres away, protected by a criss-cross of fire from Turkish machine guns on Baby 700, The Nek and the Chessboard.[38] It was originally planned as a converging attack with the New Zealanders driving down from Chunuk Bair towards Baby 700 from the rear. However, the plan had been changed to an attack simultaneous with the final New Zealand thrust onto Chunuk Bair. That morning Birdwood and his chief of staff, Skeen, pictured from progress reports the New Zealanders struggling up the slopes towards their goal and ordered the attack to take place. '"It is not the Light Horse I am anxious about," said Skeen, "I think they will be all right. What I hope is that they will help the New Zealanders."'[39]

Artillery bombarded Baby 700 and Turkish Quinn's throughout the night. At 4.30 a.m. 'the artillery bombardment ceased, and three minutes later our chaps charged and were met with a regular hailstorm of bullets.'**

Turks must have been very strongly entrenched. Their rifle fire exceeded in volume anything yet heard on plateau. We all said, "Poor devils who have to charge thro that."'[40]

On the Table Top across the Sazli Dere from The Nek and Russell's Top, the Wellington Mounteds were helpless spectators to the slaughter. 'I saw the whole thing from the Table Top and don't want to see another sight like it. They were fairly mown down by machine guns.'[41]

The Light Horse attacked in four waves. It should have been stopped after the destruction of the first, but the Australian brigade commander on Russell's Top insisted the attack continue. The same fate was shared by the second and third waves and when the order finally went out to stop the fourth line attacking, it was garbled

---

* Brigadier-General F.E. Johnston to Guy Johnston, Lemnos dated 14 October 1915. Riddiford family.

** It appears the Light Horse had failed to synchronise watches with the artillery. The three minute delay allowed Turkish supports to reinforce the trenches.

Looking towards Chunuk Bair from the western slope of Rhododendron Ridge. In the middle distance is the slight rise where Cheshire Ridge joins Rhododendron Ridge at the Apex. Masses of troops are sheltering behind this cover. *(WF-002363-31-1978-1949-32, W.A. Hampton Collection, NAM Waiouru)*

and part of that line attacked also. Only dead men fell across the Turkish parapet. The 8th and 10th Light Horse regiments had 300 men each; the 8th lost 154 killed and 80 wounded, the 10th lost 80 killed and 58 wounded.

The attack was suicidal and should never have been ordered. Birdwood and the Australian staff of the 3rd Australian Light Horse Brigade must bear the brunt of the blame. But it was Godley whom the Australians identified as the villain, and The Nek was renamed by the men 'Godley's abattoir'.[42] In fact, if blame is accorded for the New Zealand delays and failures to move below Chunuk Bair on that morning of 7 August, then The Nek should more correctly carry Johnston's and Temperley's names.

To the north, Travers' 40th Infantry Brigade had seized Damakjelik Bair, but the brigades of Cox's left Assaulting Column had made little progress. In this, the least explored country, Overton acted as scout for Monash's 4th Australian Brigade. He accepted a local guide's advice and took a shortcut towards the Aghyl Dere and the way to 971. It was a disastrous decision and Monash's brigade became bushed and exhausted. At dawn they were still two kilometres short of their goal, held up in the foothills by Turkish snipers and the difficulties of the ground.

In this move Cox's 29th Indian Brigade became separated from Monash's 4th Australians. Overton returned to lead the Indians forward and was killed by a sniper at dawn on 7 August. He had led them to the head of the Aghyl Dere and below what he thought was the Indian Brigade's objective of Hill Q. But he was wrong, and when the leading battalion of the 10th Gurkhas climbed the tangle of slopes out of the valley, they found themselves with the New Zealand Brigade on Rhododendron Ridge.

One of the two 4.5-inch howitzers of 4th Battery, NZ Field Artillery, that provided essential fire support to the New Zealand attack on Chunuk Bair. It was a shell from one of these guns that most likely killed Lt Col. Malone on the evening of 8 August 1915. *(WF-002077-37, F.M. and W. Pyle Collection, NAM Waiouru)*

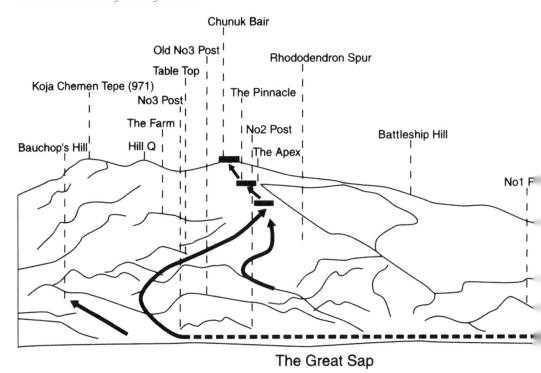

Panorama of the August offensive.

Johnston's New Zealanders on the Apex were closest to the goals set for that morning. Godley had received Johnston's signal recommending delay but at 9.30 a.m. replied, 'Attack at once.' Temperley pressed Johnston to ignore the order and urged further delay. By now it was already too late, and a priceless opportunity had been lost.

While the New Zealanders had vacillated from 6.00 a.m. onwards below Chunuk Bair, the crest itself had been almost deserted. It was held by an artillery battery protected by 20 infantry men. Overnight two regiments of the Turkish 9th Division had been rushed north to reinforce Lone Pine. They were commanded by a German officer, Colonel Hans Kannengiesser. Arriving at Anzac, he was directed to take his troops towards Chunuk Bair. Kannengiesser rode ahead with two staff officers and climbed Chunuk Bair from the valley to the east.

At 6.00 a.m. he reached the summit and saw Suvla Bay crowded with shipping and a British battery crossing the dry salt lake. He found a battery in pits to the east of the summit and the battery commander asleep. He woke the commander and directed him to fire at Suvla Bay. Below them, Rhododendron Ridge appeared deserted.

'Suddenly the enemy infantry actually appeared in front of us at about 500 yards range. The English approached slowly, in single file, splendidly equipped and with white arm bands on their left arms, apparently very tired, and were crossing a hillside to our flank, emerging in continually increasing numbers from the valley below. I immediately sent an order to my infantry. This was for the twenty strong artillery — covering platoon — instantly to open fire. I received this answer. "We can only commence to fire when we receive an order from our battalion commander."

'This was too much for me altogether. I ran to the spot and threw myself among the troops who were lying in a small trench. What I said I cannot recollect, but they began to open fire and almost immediately the English lay down without answering

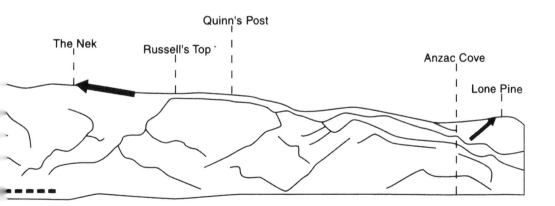

283

our fire or apparently moving in any other way. They gave me the impression that they were glad to be spared further climbing.'[43]

It was these 20 men who produced the storm of 'rifle and machine gun fire from the crest' to which Temperley referred. Kannengiesser was joined after 8.00 a.m. by two companies of the 72nd (Arab) Regiment of Kemal's 19th Division, who had been sent from the Turkish lines opposite Anzac to piquet Battleship Hill. Then the first battalion of his regiments arrived at 9.00 a.m. Kannengiesser himself was wounded by machine-gun fire from the Apex at this time.

Johnston brushed off Temperley's protestations and ordered the Auckland Battalion to attack, supported by the 10th Gurkhas, who agreed to co-operate with the New Zealand Brigade. Artillery fire was organised and the Auckland Battalion brought forward into cover provided by the Apex to form up for the attack. Zero hour was 11.00 a.m.

The Apex offered a frontage of 60 metres from the battalion to advance from. In front of this was an equally narrow saddle climbing to a small pinnacle 100 metres ahead. Here there was an unoccupied Turkish trench. Chunuk Bair was a further 400 metres beyond. Lieutenant Colonel Young of the Auckland Battalion, on receiving his orders, had gone forward to reconnoitre the ground. He found that any movement forward of the Apex now drew intense fire from the increasing number of Turks lining Chunuk Bair and the ridges either side. The frontage of attack was so narrow that his battalion would be forced to attack platoon by platoon, with the 10th Gurkhas following behind. He came back to Johnston and strongly recommended delaying the attack until nightfall.[44]

Young was supported by Wallingford, the brigade machine gun officer, who requested more time to bring all the brigade's machine guns forward onto the Apex to cover the attack.[45] However, Johnston would brook no further delay. He wanted to make amends for his earlier hesitancy, and with the irrational irritability of a sick man insisted that the attack be launched on time.

The Apex was coming under increasingly heavy fire and all morning men had been hit. Private O.W. Howe was in the Auckland Battalion: 'Well, we moved up towards the top of the hill a little after 10.30 … the majority of us were absolutely done up — myself included. We halted a few hundred yards from the top for a breather — made a line and were told that we were to make a bayonet charge. We had to go over the first trench and take and occupy the second one [on Chunuk Bair]. The order was given to get "ready" and then charge from where we were. I understood that we had to go to the top of the hill and charge from there, and so did all the other boys … Immediately we started … the fire commenced from the Turks — we were all surprised and all unconsciously stopped.'[46]

The leading platoon of the 6th Haurakis baulked at crossing the crest forward of the Apex. Major Sam Grant NZSC, who arrived with the 4th Reinforcements, took over the lead and yelled for the men to 'come on'. 'And we went. Some of the poor fellows will never go again. We hadn't gone 10 yards when a fellow was shot dead alongside of me. I just glanced at him and went on. I had three breathers on the way to the first trench. We did not go past it. 26 of our company reached the trench.'[47]

Captain Colvin Algie commanded the 15th North Auckland Company, which was next to follow the 6th Haurakis: 'And of course directly we appeared over the crest the machine guns opened on us and mowed us down. We went forward in lines of platoons about 25 yards apart … A gully halfway gave us a spell as we were all pumped, then on again. Our fellows kept dropping as we went but a number reached the trench. When I got in I found I was the senior, Major Grant and Sinel, the Colonel and Adjutant being missing … only 2 picks and 1 shovel reached the trench. It was very shallow and unprotected and in most places exposed to Turkish fire. We mustered 106 and 5 officers and were packed like sardines. We daren't stand up so digging in was very slow. Every time a shovelful of earth went over it drew shells from a mountain gun so it was decidedly interesting. Water was "non est" and we were right out of touch with our rear and no hope of communicating until dark. I sent a message back by a volunteer who got safely through. The Colonel [Young] came in at dusk having been just in rear of us during the afternoon.'[48]

The Auckland Battalion had advanced 100 metres along the length of a narrow ridge from one knoll to the next. It was a repeat of the slaughter of the Light Horse at The Nek. Some 300 men fell dead or wounded. Grant was mortally wounded. The survivors either stayed at the Apex or crouched in a shallow Turkish trench some 45 centimetres deep that cut across the narrow pinnacle slightly above the saddle of land leading to Chunuk Bair. To move was to die. Between them, groaning and crying in the sun, lay half the battalion. Snipers fired at any movement and the wounded who survived provided a muted chorus all through the day and into the night.

The Gurkhas, trying to follow the Auckland Battalion, had veered to the left off the crest of the ridge, ending in the Aghyl Dere below, and had lost touch with the brigade. Throughout the attack Brigadier General Johnston 'stood on the crest of Rhododendron Ridge cheering his men on. [He] had to be removed almost by force' by his staff, during which Second Lieutenant Cazalet was mortally wounded while dragging him down in cover.[49] It appears Johnston now directed the Wellington Infantry Battalion to make another attempt, and ordered that half the Canterbury Infantry move forward to the Apex to support this renewed attack.

Malone refused. In the crowded conditions on the Apex there was no privacy and Malone's discussion with his brigadier and brigade major took place among the men. Charlie Clark the bushman, a corporal in the Wellington Infantry, was one of these. 'So Wellington Battalion was called to go up … So these two colonels and Colonel Malone had a big row over it … Malone said … "My men are not going over in daylight — but they'll go over at night time and they'll take that hill." So he said, "Wellington Battalion come away from the ridge," and so we did. Colonel Malone said, "I will take the risk and any punishment. These men are nor going until I order them to go. I'm not going to send them over to commit suicide."'[50]*

---

* This is supported by an entry in the diary of Malone's batman, Pte Ben Smart: 'At 11.00 a.m. Gurkhas and Hawke's Bay Company, Wellington Regiment, both tried to advance but had to come back to the top of the Apex.' See also, Ferguson, *History of the Canterbury Regiment*, p.61.

The New Zealand Brigade was being torn apart by Turkish fire on the exposed slopes of Rhododendron Ridge as its commanders were tearing any sense of unity apart at the Apex. The promise of the Mounteds' success remained unfulfilled, the Otagos were once again reorganising and dispirited, the Canterburys were split, the Aucklanders decimated. Only Malone's Wellingtons, thanks to his intervention, were intact. Johnston reported the failure of the attempt to take Chunuk Bair, and Godley agreed to delay any further attempt until nightfall.

The agony of that day was not yet over. The Canterburys, now joined by some of their missing men, came under heavy fire on Rhododendron Ridge, Frank Hardey among them. 'We dug like hell … From Walker's Ridge to the Hills running round Suvla Bay, the naval shells were bursting … Presently, in spite of the bombardment, a machine gun came into action and found us out. One moment I was speaking with Mr Lawry as to the direction of our trench, next minute he was smothered in blood from his arm. The bullets were clipping the bushes like a scythe as Major Cribb passed. Soon I saw him helped back … dying … The man working pick to my shovel was shot dead. It was the hottest corner we had been in for some time.'[51]

The Canterburys suffered 107 casualties that day from rifle and machine-gun fire, and when Lieutenant Colonel Hughes was ordered to bring up half the battalion to support the Wellington assault, he brought forward three officers and 50 men. The Otagos further up the ridge suffered the same fate. Men dug in under steady fire, including Private Anderson: 'Odd ones were becoming casualties when on the face of one man facing me there suddenly appeared a mark the size of a sixpence exactly between the eyes. Blood spurted over me as he fell. Saying to myself, "bullets now or shrapnel later" I went on with the job.'[52] Minutes later Anderson was hit through the right arm and right leg by a single bullet.

To the north at Suvla, Major General Stopford's 9th Corps of Kitchener's New Army was landing. By midday on 7 August the best part of two divisions was ashore. Turkish opposition was negligible, and the Corps' objectives were deserted. In most cases, Stopford's men simply had to walk forward and occupy them. Of particular concern was the W Hills at the entrance to the Anafarta Gap. From here, Turkish artillery fired into the ANZAC perimeter and also onto the exposed slopes of Rhododendron Ridge. However, there was virtually no British activity; 3000 Turks, thinly spread, waited for the British force to advance.

Godley, in his headquarters at No. 3 Outpost, planned for another attempt before dawn on 8 August. He bolstered his assaulting columns with reserve battalions from Shaw's 13th Division. On the left Monash's 4th Australians were to make a further attempt to seize 971. In the centre Cox's 29th Indian Brigade, reinforced by the 39th New Army Brigade, would seize Hill Q. Johnston's New Zealanders were reinforced by two New Army battalions, the 7th Gloucesters and the 8th Welch Pioneers, and Russell's Mounted Rifles were directed to send forward the Auckland Mounted Rifles and the Maori Contingent as a reserve. They left from forward of Table Top at 1.30 a.m. and reached the Apex at 3.00 a.m. on 8 August.

The Wellingtons spent the first half of that same night digging in, and then they slept. At 1.00 a.m. Johnston issued orders to his brigade. They were to attack at 4.15 a.m. The Gloucesters and Wellingtons were in the first line, followed by the 8th Welch and Otagos in the second, with the Auckland Mounted Rifles and Maoris on Table Top as the third line in reserve.[53]

Artillery would fire on the crest from 3.30 a.m. until 4.15 a.m. Malone had already directed his scouts to patrol forward. They were led by Private Jimmy Swan. 'Being Regimental Scout I was told off to try and find out their next line of trenches, taking two more with me starting out at 10 o'clock. Being very dark we slowly made our way, up the next ridge at a rate of about a chain every 5 minutes, watching and listening. I discovered the trench … and was back and reported about 11.30 being dog tired. I lay down and was no sooner down than I was asleep. I was woken up at 1 o'clock to observe the artillery fire, that is, put their shots into the trench as near as I could judge them. That done I sat up with the outpost watching the bombardment.'[54]

At 3.00 a.m. the Wellington officers and company sergeant-majors went along the lines of dozing forms, shaking them awake. Malone had no illusions about the likely consequences of the day: '3.00 a.m. Col. Malone woke me up and said the Brigade was going to take 971 and he was going to lead our battalion. He gave me an address of his wife to write to in case he got hit. I think he thought he would pass out as he shook hands with me before he went over and said "Goodbye".'[55] Forty-six men of the Wellingtons remained on the Apex as machine gunners, stretcher bearers and runners.

Wallingford was determined to give this attack every possible support and 12 Maxim guns of the brigade lined the crest of the Apex and the slopes of Cheshire Ridge. Gun numbers One and Two were positioned by the guns while their reliefs and ammunition carriers stayed back in the dead ground, ready to move forward with ammunition or replace a man if he was hit.

The Wellingtons checked webbing, fixed bayonets and, in shirt sleeve order, shook out in formation. 'Chunuk Bair was just a mass of flame from exploding shells — every shell from the warships, from the batteries at Anzac itself just concentrated on that.' In the Wellingtons the Hawke's Bay Company led, 'as always', with the Wellington West Coast Company on the left. On the word, 'we did the first 200–300 yards at a lick — then down to a walk'.[56]

The narrowness of the frontage forced the two leading companies to advance two platoons up, with each platoon in fours. In the dark, a solid mass, 16 men across, moved forward, over the dead and wounded from the Auckland charge, through the Auckland-held trench on the Pinnacle, and towards Chunuk Bair. The two remaining companies of the Wellingtons, Taranaki and Ruahine, followed behind. It was impossible to form two battalions up as Johnston's orders had detailed, so the 7th Gloucesters had to wait until the Wellingtons had cleared the Apex before their first two companies could follow on. They too moved in a dense mass with platoons, two up, in columns of fours.

As the Wellingtons advanced they spread out, with Jimmy Swan in the lead. 'We skirmished up the top gradually opening out into a fan shape abut 100 yards across and rising and closing in onto a peak or narrow neck on top about 60 yards across then falling away on the down slope each side. We were advancing up … I bent down, ran about six or seven paces and looked over and sure enough I saw the trench with heads sticking up like rabbits.'[57]

Charlie Clark was with the Hawke's Bays in the lead. 'We walked over — we walked right up to the Hill and there wasn't a shot fired. Wasn't a shot fired until we got halfway up on the top and the shells were still coming. We sat down and waited. When the last shell came we charged that hill. The Turks, there were pretty few of them there, they scooted, and there was one old fellow there — he had a beard — about 70 — he pulled his rifle on us … The poor old joker, somebody shot him.'[58]

After months of fighting, Chunuk Bair, the goal of the Covering Force on the first day, had at last been taken. It was almost empty, occupied only by a machine-gun crew commanded by a German petty officer from the *Goeben*.*

Other small parties of Turks rapidly withdrew to the shouts of the leading wave of Wellingtons. Chunuk Bair, the attackers found, was two crests with a saddle between, some 200 metres in length. To the east, the ground sloped away quite steeply before flattening out into a step that contained some empty howitzer pits. Beyond these it fell away again into the valley. It was an amphitheatre, the arms of which were Hill Q and 971 to the north, and the junction of Su Yahtaga, or Third Ridge, to the south.

As it became light, the Wellingtons could see in the centre across the valley containing the north-south road and the village of Boghali and over the southern shoulder of Su Yahtaga, the straits of the Dardanelles — the Narrows. 'Some chaps had a glimpse of the sea and all the country in between and we knew perfectly well that this hill was the key to victory or defeat on the Peninsula.'[59]

It was quickly apparent that there could be no further advance to the east down into the amphitheatre before its arms on either side had been secured. That was beyond the Wellingtons' resources, so, as directed, Malone secured the crests of Chunuk Bair. He based his defence on the existing Turkish trench running along the crest. This was a straight ditch, some half a metre to a metre deep.

It seemed a miracle that the crests had been won so cheaply. Artillery fire in the night had wounded the Turkish commander and his men had deserted the hill. However, Hill Q to the north was still held by elements of the 4th Turkish Division. Malone's battalion had crossed before daylight unscathed but, as dawn came, from 4.30 onwards the route from the Apex along Rhododendron Ridge to the summit came under increasingly heavy artillery and machine-gun fire from the direction of Hill Q.

As with everything about this battle, Malone's siting of his defences is surrounded

---

* In 1914, the German battle cruiser *Goeben* and the light cruiser *Breslau* eluded the British Mediterranean Fleet and sailed through the Dardanelles to Constantinople. Both ships and crew passed into the Turkish navy, giving Turkey naval supremacy in the Black Sea and contributing to her entry into the war on the side of the Central Powers on 29 October 1914. *The Encyclopedia of Military History*, Dupuy and Dupuy, p.944.

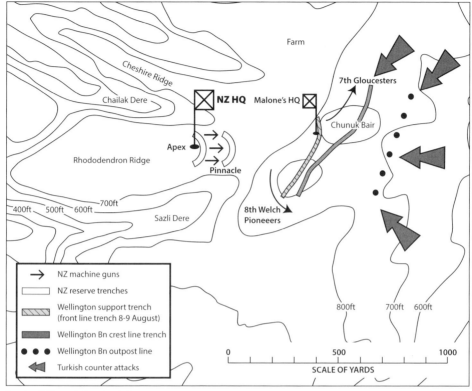

Battle of Chunuk Bair, 8–10 August 1915.

by controversy. In his orders at 1.00 a.m., Johnston had directed Malone's battalion to secure the crest from Chunuk Bair south to where it fell away towards Battleship Hill. The 7th Gloucesters were to come up on the Wellingtons' left and hold the crest to the north, facing Hill Q. The second line — the 8th Welch Pioneers and the Otago Infantry — would then exploit forward of this firm base, the 8th Welch Pioneers pushing forward onto the arm of Su Yatagha, which was the top of Third Ridge, the Otagos exploiting towards Hill Q. Johnston stressed that the Wellingtons were to hold the entry point onto the crest where the saddle linking the Pinnacle to Rhododendron Ridge joined the main Sari Bair Ridge, some 50 metres south of the highest point of Chunuk Bair.

A pamphlet had been issued in July at Anzac extolling the virtues of digging in on the reverse side of a crest and not on the forward slopes, as previously taught. This was due to the weight of artillery fire that had been experienced on the Western Front. Battalions dug in on the forward slopes could be seen and fired on by the enemy's artillery observers. Malone had read the pamphlet and discussed it with Temperley, the brigade major: 'I pointed out to him that he must not apply the very hasty lessons from another theatre of war to Gallipoli and that this idea was largely due to the great weight of German artillery … the Turks were inferior in artillery to ourselves.

This image was taken at dawn on the Apex on 8 August 1915. New Zealand Infantry Brigade machine guns are on the slope on the skyline, firing towards Hill Q. The man on the right is the machine gun officer of the Wellington Battalion, Lieutenant Allan Preston, captured in this picture a few moments before he was wounded in the neck. He won the Military Cross in France but was later killed. On the left are the rear companies of 7th Gloucesters, waiting to go forward. Two New Zealand Maxim guns can be seen on the skyline. *(WF-002363-32-1978-1949-33, W.A. Hampton Slide Collection, NAM Waiouru)*

Furthermore this particular battle was being fought above all to get commanding ground and observation and that it would be madness having gained the crest of the Sari Bair, to dig in below it and allow the Turks to concentrate for counter-attack and push us off again.'[60]

Lieutenant Colonel Malone accepted Temperley's points, but Temperley was unconvinced: 'Knowing as I did the obstinacy of the man, I was profoundly uneasy because I felt sure that whatever he said to me, he would be found digging in on the reverse slope when the time came.'[61]

The time had come and Malone's men were on Chunuk Bair. According to Temperley, who was one of the few surviving officers and, as brigade major, drafted the official report, Malone dug in on the reverse slope and wasted 'two priceless hours in undisturbed possession of Chunuk Bair'.[62] The tenor of this was accepted by Godley and Hamilton. It has become part of the ANZAC myth, accepted by Bean in *The Story of ANZAC* and by John North in *Gallipoli — The Fading Vision*. According to Temperley's account, Malone threw away the advantages of holding the crest and doomed the enterprise. 'The cost in blood was not light; the ultimate cost to the Empire and the cause for which the Allies fought no-one can measure.'[63]

There was little trust and less faith among the leaders of the New Zealand Brigade in those August days and Malone would be falsely condemned, first by Temperley and then by history. Certainly, in the advance up the slopes that morning, Malone was concerned with the problem of reverse or forward trenches in his defence of the hill. Ernest Harston was his adjutant: 'During the advance I was alongside [Lieutenant Colonel Malone] ... when he said this was still worrying him and he decided that two companies should occupy the forward slope and two the reverse slope, and that saps should be put through as quickly as possible from one to the other.'[64]

On the top this plan was at once put into effect. The leading companies of Wellington West Coast and Hawke's Bay[*] were detailed to occupy the existing Turkish trench on the crest line and the remaining two companies dug a support line 30 metres to the rear. Outposts were detailed to move forward down the ridge to the east to warn of any Turkish approach, and a section of ten men was deployed forward from each platoon, making a line of eight section strength piquets, one from each of the eight platoons in the two companies holding the crest line. Charlie Clark and his section formed one of the Hawke's Bay outposts: 'We went out and we went down about 2 chain I suppose ... into the valley ... and there were the gunpits there ... they were howitzer gunpits and the howitzer guns was taken away ... I forget how many men there were, it must have been 9 to 10 or 11, there might have been 12, but we decided we were going to have a game of cards — playing poker — with two men on view [sentry] and we were happy, quite happy ... it's a strange thing when a person is going into battle — they lose that fear. We were playing cards when the Turks made their attack — we never saw them coming.'[65]

Sergeant Harvey Johns was also on outpost duty that day. He was causing alarm and despondency among the transport elements behind the Turkish line by sniping at the traffic he could see moving in the valley to the east:

'I could see this transport way down the road. Well that's good enough for shooting and I tried myself out and I had about six shots at it. I must have been getting onto it, because they got in round the brow of a hill and stopped there and then I decided I had better get back to the men and all of a sudden on my left flank a Turk came out and lay down and started firing at me, then I had to back move the whole time while I fired at him. Then another one came out, and another and another until I had about 6 men firing at me, while I am back moving. My only chance is to fire for number one, fire for number six, back to number three, number four, make the fire erratic and that's the only way I got back and I got back to report it to the officer. I said, "They are coming over ... now Mr Jardine." [66]

On the ridge the companies were frantically digging in. It was light at 4.30 a.m. and by 5.00 a.m. the haze that is a feature of the Peninsula's climate cleared sufficiently for the Turks on Hill Q to see the activity on Chunuk Bair. From this time Malone's men came under increasingly heavy fire. Rather than a 'priceless two hours' the Wellingtons

---

[*] Not Taranaki as stated by Bean.

had had perhaps half an hour of relatively undisturbed digging on a 'hilltop, [which] is only a hilltop because it has resisted the elements for many years and it was impossible to dig trenches in the hard clay in the time we had at out disposal'.[67] Each man carried two sandbags, which he filled and stacked in front of the shallow trench.

The 7th Gloucesters, following up the Wellingtons across the ridge, got their leading companies across unscathed but the rear companies were met with heavy fire. There was already a trickle of New Zealand wounded going back. Jimmy Swan was one of these, having been shot through the right elbow. 'The Tommies are coming up … along a narrow ridge in a column four or five deep, the Turks are bowling them over thick as bees … I run along the ridge and double them off it into cover on the other side which will take them up to where they are wanted. Going down a little on the other side I reach cover carrying no more extra lead, tell the officer the position of the country and I hear him yelling to the men to double over the ridge in skirmishing order.'[68]

The 7th Gloucesters came forward on the Wellingtons' left and occupied the continuation of the forward trench on the northern crest of Chunuk Bair facing Hill Q. One of their companies also dug a support line, continuing that of the Wellingtons. The 8th Welch Pioneers behind the Gloucesters were not so lucky. They were cut to pieces and those who got across huddled in a leaderless mob in dead ground where Rhododendron Ridge joined the main ridge 60–70 metres below the crest line. They were eventually led by some of their officers to the right of the Wellington line on Chunuk Bair.

Already in the dawn, three battalions had made their way forward. The Wellingtons were complete and digging in, while the Gloucesters had at least half their battalion in position and were starting to dig in on the Wellingtons' left on the main crest of Chunuk Bair. The 8th Welch Pioneers had lost all semblance of organisation and those who had reached the ridge huddled for protection while some 60–80 were led forward on the right of the

The rear companies of the Gloucesters under fire. They are advancing from the Apex towards Chunuk Bair, 8 August 1915. *(WF-002363-27-1978-1949-28, W.A. Hampton Slide Collection, NAM Waiouru)*

Wellington line. Fire from Hill Q and Battleship Hill now prevented any further reinforcement.

Temperley's criticism both of failing to occupy the crest and of time lost is unfounded. If there was delay, it was the brigade's failure to send line parties forward once it was evident that the Wellingtons were on the ridge. There were no staff from brigade headquarters on Chunuk Bair and no communication with brigade. From the beginning of that day, Malone would co-ordinate the defence of the hilltop as the two raw Kitchener New Army battalions crumbled on the flanks.

On the left of the line, the Gloucesters never had a chance to dig in. Almost at once, fire from Hill Q killed the officers and non-commissioned officers rallying the men, and soldiers started to leave the firing line, seeking shelter below the crest. Nowhere were the trenches more than waist deep. Artillery from Anzac landed initially on the crest, but once the yellow and red identification flags had been seen, fire crept forward into the bowl of the amphitheatre and Wallingford's guns kept flaying the slopes of Hill Q and Battleship Hill. However, the ground allowed the Turks to mass at either flank, first from Hill Q and then Battleship Hill. Turkish reinforcements heading for Lone Pine were diverted to Chunuk Bair.

In the Turkish lines surrounding Anzac, alarm grew at the increasing signs of battle on the heights behind them. The stray bullets falling into their rear trenches and the activities of snipers such as Harvey Johns that morning had started rumours of defeat along Bomba Sirte (Second Ridge) and Gun Ridge (Third Ridge). Temperley, for all his bias, suggests what might have been: 'The New Zealand Infantry Brigade … was for 48 hours … at the throat of the Turkish Empire and had support been forth coming at the right time and place and had certain events turned out differently, the Turkish Army would have been beaten, Constantinople would have fallen and the war might have been shortened by two years.'[69]

It did not happen, but certainly the Turkish grip on the Dardanelles was threatened that morning of 8 August and the Turks reacted strongly. Fire cut the link from the Apex to Chunuk Bair. Turkish snipers along the line of hills overlooking Rhododendron Ridge harried all movement from the Table Top to the Apex. The way up the deres became clogged with dead mules and men as rifle and machine guns sniped away at the exposed places on the climb. Any Turkish units to hand were thrown piecemeal, and in increasing strength, at the Wellington and Gloucester lines on the crest.

This was the situation as Harvey Johns scrambled back to the Hawke's Bay lines: 'Things from then on started to move … about 50 Turks on the left flank were attacking our left flank. But this time at least half a dozen Turks had got over to our right flank and got behind a hedge and they were pumping away at us and having quite a glorious time. They were hard to see, and the only way you could detect them was by the shaking of the leaves as they fired and that was the only place you could fire at, making allowances for the distance between the point of his rifle to where the man would be …

'Mr Jardine said, "Come on then boys, we will have to get stuck in [and dig in further]." We had no time for that. So they dropped their picks and shovels and grabbed their rifles, it was so quick, it was just as well they did.'[70]

Charlie Clark, his card game rudely interrupted, was leading his section at speed back up to the crest. 'Our two sentries came charging in, they said the Turks are coming through on the flanks. We looked up and we seen a lot of our fellows coming back and we just hopped across that flat … It was always a joke after that; I led them out but by God I led them in too, so I did, I wasn't wasting time. On the top I flopped right in where Lieutenant Jardine was and the Turks had … followed us right in, because I had just got down … when he said well you can prepare to charge and I thought, "Well this is it." I was never too keen on a bayonet charge I don't mind admitting. I seen one or two bayoneted and I didn't like it … If I were faced with a joker coming at me with a bayonet I'd have shot him straight away.'[71]

The forward line of Hawke's Bay and Wellington West Coast came under fire from both flanks. Initially this fire was on the left from Hill Q and as it grew the Gloucesters on the northern crest broke under the pressure and retired back on the support line. Attempts to lead them back failed. The Wellingtons alone held the crest of Chunuk Bair.

On the right towards Battleship Hill, fire was increasing in the forward line. Charlie Clark remembers looking around him at the nearest Wellingtons and finding that the ten or so nearest were all dead or wounded: 'I didn't know where these bullets were coming from …' The soldier next to Clark was hit and he could see a Turk visible from the waist up firing into the trench, 'so I pulled my rifle over … and I hit him in the face and that put me off, but just as I hit him … somebody hit me with a sledgehammer and that's just exactly what it felt like … I hadn't been back with Jardine five minutes … when I was shot.'[72]

The slope of the ground east of the crest meant that Turks could creep up until they were 10–20 metres away before being visible. This and the fire from Hill Q along the line of the ridge decimated the forward line.

'The rifle fire was just intense. It was just a sheet of bullets going over, almost at ground level, and our field of fire was a man coming up the hill here, and his head is the first thing that comes into view … and our first targets was heads and there seemed to be thousands of them and the targets got bigger as the Turks came up the hill, and by the time they were fully in sight … they were within 20 feet.'[73]

The shallow trench was a mass of bodies. Harvey Johns further along remembers firing to either flank at a range of 60–80 metres on the right and about 60 metres on the left. 'The trench hardly counted, the earth was up in front and it gave you cover from fire. As a matter of fact, there was a dead Turk in front of me, he would be about a 12-stone man and I got hold of him with one hand and just pulled him over and put him in front of two of us and used him for cover … I got wounded about that time and got out but I should have thought there might have been 100 [in the front line] but then they packed an English Regiment on top of us and there was really hardly room for them to squeeze in …'[74]

From 6.30 a.m. the forward trench fought an increasingly lone battle against the Turks, who pressed the dwindling numbers from both front and flanks. The wounded filtered back through the supports and eventually survivors came dribbling back in ones and twos through the Turkish fire that now swept the forward trench and the ground in the rear, which was littered with bodies.

Afterwards, survivors talked about the VCs that should have been won that day. One who was mentioned was the unknown soldier who kept up a lone battle in the forward trench long after all other sounds of resistance had ceased from the crest — someone, perhaps like Private R.J. Davis, who after three years of Turkish captivity recounted his tale of the final fight in the forward line: 'Our newly captured trench was very narrow, and only about three feet deep. There was barely room for the troops to move at all in the trench, as we were packed very close together. About ten minutes after getting into the trench, we noticed a big mass of men advancing towards us from the left flank of Hill 971, at a distance of between five and six hundred yards. Immediately we opened fire, but someone called out that we were firing on Ghurkha troops. It was impossible to see from whom the order came and so as they were advancing from enemy territory, we took no notice of the order and continued to fire until they disappeared in a small gully, not to appear again until they were within from 10 to 15 yards all along the trench.

'Owing to the narrowness and shallowness of our trench we were nearly all exposed from the waist up to the rifle fire of the Turks. Directly in front of me was a small rising in the ground which shielded me from direct frontal fire, and made it necessary for me to fire a little to my left at a distance of not more than ten yards. One of our men was hit on the enemy side of our trench and was unable to get back himself, so I was able to pull him back into the trench unconscious. At such a short range and being outnumbered I soon noticed that there were very few of our men left firing.

'A Taranaki man named Surgenor was the only man left firing besides myself at the end of about half an hour. Besides the rifle fire of the enemy they threw bombs in all along the trench, and their machine guns which were situated on either flank were able to enfilade our position. Private Surgenor was hit in the head somewhere, but kept on firing with his face streaming with blood, until he got another hit in the head, which dazed him for a time, and knocked him back in the trench. This time I thought he was killed, but he partly came to soon after, and loaded rifles for me to fire. At that time I was using three rifles and each was burning hot. Owing to a traverse on my left I was not able to see how many were left, but the firing had practically died away there. On the right of my position I was able to see about thirty yards of trench in which all our men were wounded or dead. The time I was actually firing is very hard to gauge, but I think it was well over an hour before I was hit by a bullet on the right elbow while firing. It knocked me back into the trench on top of a dead sergeant. Private Surgenor bound my wound up, and we waited for the Turks to take possession of the trench, wondering whether our reinforcements would arrive before that time.

'About half an hour after I was hit, the Turks put in their first appearance in the trench on my extreme right. After throwing bombs into the trench to ensure against a ruse, three men made their appearance first and bayoneted every New Zealander they came to or else used the butts of their rifles. It was soon my turn and the foremost Turk

The trenches of the Apex, in the foreground, with the Pinnacle at the top of the clay spur with the northern crest of Chunuk Bair on the skyline. The New Zealand trenches originally ran from the crest to the right and beyond the photo's edge. For most of the battle they fought in a trench line just this side of the crest line. Photo taken in 1919. *(Field-Dodgson Collection – PA1-o-169, Alexander Turnbull Library)*

thrust at me four times with his bayonet, and each time I was able to grab it with my left hand, and thrust it away. The fifth time I was not quick enough and he drove his bayonet through my left arm. I was then at his mercy, but instead of using the bayonet, he loaded his rifle and pointing at me, was about to pull the trigger, when a crowd of Turks came in and someone in charge gave him an order for he stood up on the trench and fired towards our second line. Soon after that my captors made motions for me to get over the trench and I was taken prisoner.'[75]

Twenty-one New Zealanders were captured in the battle for Chunuk Bair, including 14 from the Wellington Infantry Regiment. All were wounded, and most were men who had manned the outposts or the crest line. William Surgenor was with Davie when the order came to retire back on the support line: 'Every man in the trench was killed or wounded including myself. I was hit in the mouth and leg … The Turks got into the trench and bayoneted or clubbed every man wounded except myself and Davis[sic].'[76] For the prisoners taken that day, the long agony of captivity was beginning. (See Appendix I.)

The support lines on the western slope below the crest of Chunuk Bair now took up the struggle. Not all the crest had been lost; the support line had been angled to take advantage of the ground and on the right it ran along the top of the ridge at the junction of the southern crest of Chunuk Bair and Su Yahtaga or Third Ridge. Here the Wellingtons still hung on to the crest line for most of the day. The Turks had at least 100 metres of open ground to cover and the line was better protected from fire from Hill Q. It would be late afternoon before the Wellingtons were driven back onto the seaward slopes on this flank.

'It was the fire from Hill Q that did the damage. It enfiladed the whole position. The Turks had a clear field of fire not only along the crest but also along the forward slope and over a considerable part of the reverse slope. In a very short time, probably about 8.00 a.m., we had been pretty well wiped out. We had no telephones and were not sure whether reports sent back by the wounded had reached brigade headquarters.'[77] Harston made his way back onto the saddle leading back to the Pinnacle on Rhododendron Ridge. Here he met up with a signal party, most probably led by Corporal Cyril Bassett, making its way forward. 'I found a signaller with a telephone and asked for reinforcements to be sent up from reserve and for the naval fire to be directed over the hill instead of into us, both of which were done eventually. I had the greatest difficulty however, in persuading Brigade Headquarters that the casualties were as heavy as I have said, but eventually this point was settled. I went back to the hill and the fight went on till night fell and we had repulsed a whole series of Turkish counter-attacks through the whole day.'[78]

The two New Army battalions had already been reduced to 60 men of the Gloucesters under a sergeant major and interspersed among the Wellington line. Their commanding officer, Lieutenant Colonel Jordon of the Gloucesters, positioned himself with Malone in his trench, near the junction of the saddle from Rhododendron Ridge with Chunuk Bair. The 8th Welch Pioneers were reduced to 30 men fighting on under one of their majors. These were the troops fighting in the line; large numbers of men had left the line and spent the day sheltering with the wounded behind the hill.

In a 'nightmare' of a day two Turkish regiments were committed to throw the enemy off the crest of Chunuk Bair. Charge was met with bayonet charge, every surviving officer wielding a rifle and bayonet. The narrow trenches were clogged with dead and wounded. Those wounded who could move crawled back into the top of the gully at the head of the Sazli Dere near the saddle where there was some protection from Turkish fire. But there was no protection from the blazing sun. Gradually the top of the gully filled with hundreds of wounded, and the slopes behind the Wellington trenches were littered with dead and dying, many being wounded again and again as the Turks resorted to grenading the New Zealand line from the shelter of the crest.

Charlie Clark, wounded in both legs, with a gaping hole in his calf and the bone smashed, crawled out of the firing line. In the early morning of the 8th, he and others dragged themselves down into the triangle of shelter below Malone's headquarters. On the way he met Harvey Johns, also wounded; together they went into shelter:

'There were about 300 wounded lying in the gully … we lay there in the sun … each man looked after himself … and you would speak to a man, one of your own men and later on you would get no reply, they were dying, dying out as the day went on.'[79]

On the Apex, Brigade Headquarters, the Otagos, and remnants of the Auckland

Infantry were subject to constant shell, rifle and sniper fire. Efforts were made to reinforce the Wellington line, and the Maoris and Auckland Mounteds were offered to help Malone's beleaguered band. Wallingford's machine guns on the Apex stopped any advance from either flank, but there were no guns on the hill, so two of the Wellingtons' guns were sent forward. Dan Curham commanded one of the guns: 'Well then word came down at daylight for machine guns to go up to Chunuk Bair. We leaped out of our trench. I was carrying [the barrel of] a gun and it was steep and hard going and there was a little bit of fighting at the top of the Hill, not much. It was fairly quiet and we got a little distance from the Apex when we were really into a hail of bullets from 971 … they spotted us. We were sixteen there, at least, two guns, and they began to fall and we couldn't run … with the load we had and the other men were carrying boxes of ammunition and it was a deadly volley, the ground just spurted up with dust around our feet and we tried to get through this great volley of bullets. Men fell all over the place. I just saw them fall, men I had been sleeping with and … fighting with and … from our own town lying there and we couldn't stop, we had to go on … What happened to the other gun I don't know, but I went on and found myself alone … I got to the top of the hill with a gun and I was the only one that got there. Couldn't use the gun, no tripod and no ammunition and there was a terrific fight

The New Zealand stretcher station at Chailak Dere. It could take three days for a wounded man to travel the 1500 metres to the beach. *(NAM Waiouru)*

going on because the Turks had reinforced and come back and although they couldn't dislodge our chaps they were creeping up the reverse side of the hill … and lobbing bombs over … Well I stayed up there all day and I couldn't do a thing and men were being wounded and killed all over the place and I spent till dark that night there, and you can imagine the appalling time it was.'[80]

The Apex, the saddle and the hill were a shambles of bodies and equipment, and through this two parties of signallers, one under Sapper B.L. Dignan and one under Corporal Cyril Bassett of the Divisional Signals Company, attempted to establish communications by telephone line with Malone's headquarters on the crest. Line had been laid between Godley's headquarters at No. 2 Outpost and Johnston on the Apex. It was not until morning that two line-laying parties made their way from the Apex towards Chunuk Bair. Sapper Dignan led one of these: 'Bassett started with one party and I with another. Bassett had an hour's start but was held up by a man of his being hit and by the Ak. Mtd Rifles (who were held up just over the crest by … snipers) using his phone.' In fact this was Harston, the Wellington adjutant, giving the first report to Johnston of the situation on the hill. 'Whittaker, Birkett and I went on and got into a gully the other side safely enough. Our wire gave out about 100 yards down the hill from Wgton HQ so I took a message up and reported and then when I got back Bassett … arrived with his party and some more wire so we made a duplicate [line] and Birkett and I took the line on to Wgton HQ.

'They stopped the Turks and then the Turks started massing somewhere and just then the phone went bung. Col. Malone had an important message to go through about this massing so I took it leaving Birkett to take the phone. I sent the operators up while Bassett repaired the line.

'Meanwhile the two operators [Whittaker and Edwards] had gone up and Bassett & Birkett came back onto the spot where the Ak. Mtd Rifles had been and mended the wire under fire and stayed out till early next morning.

'Total result of all this is that Bassett, Birkett, Whittaker, Edwards, McDermott and I had our names taken by the … Brigade Major. The six was eventually reduced to three with special for Bass as he was mentioned before.' (Cpl. C.R. Bassett had been recommended for his efforts during the Otago attack on 2 May 1915.)[81]

On the hill the wounded cried for water, the living scrabbled through the webbing and pockets of the dead for ammunition, and the dwindling band made charge after charge to the crest to repel the Turkish bomb throwers. The New Zealanders' bombs were soon exhausted, while the Turks could approach the crest unseen to throw theirs. Each time they did so, Malone led his Wellingtons forward in short bayonet charges to drive them back.

'It wasn't long before what there was of the trench, it was only about three feet deep in the first place. It wasn't long before the dead and wounded were so piled in the trench that we were standing on them and we only had coverage up very little above our knees. And there was this continual thought of the wounded. What can we do for them? But no one could do anything. No one.'

At 9.00 a.m. the Auckland Mounted Rifles followed by the Maori Contingent

Surviving members of the Wellington Machine Gun detachment on the Apex: nearest camera is Ted Becker, Oscar Solvander firing the Maxim gun, Shaw and Dickson. *(WF-002363-28 -1978-1949-27, W.A. Hampton Collection, National Army Museum)*

moved forward to reinforce the summit. The Maoris, like the Gurkhas before them, were driven by fire down the slopes into the Aghyl Dere below the Farm. They would fight there for the rest of the battle. The Auckland Mounteds followed the path taken by the Wellingtons, Gloucesters and Welch before them, hugging the dead ground below the Apex to the left across the saddle and up the slopes. It was a journey that took most of the day. 'We lined up, about ten men at a time and ran across a bullet swept area towards Chunuk Bair. George McKenzie was killed in the line in front of me... Shrapnel seemed to be bursting everywhere amongst us. A dead man named Carter, Auckland Infantry Battalion, whose identification disc I had a look at, had been killed the day before and I was lying alongside him and I pushed him on higher ground and got under him for shelter. Sandy McKay and Sgt "Boukau" McKay of Waipu were killed close to me … Eventually we were glad to move up over Rhododendron Ridge by crawling through the prickly scrub under enemy fire and then down into an eroded gully with steep sides and then up the floor of it to within one hundred yards of the top of Chunuk Bair.'[82]

The Auckland Mounteds fought on the right, where the crest was still in the Wellingtons' hands. 'Our firing line was about 100 yards from the Turks across a narrow tableland. There were no trenches and the thin scrub was the only shelter for most of the men, but there was a shallow depression where a few, mostly wounded, sheltered.'[83]

It was in the centre where the Wellington line was below the crest that the fighting was at its fiercest and Ken Stevens of the Auckland Mounteds witnessed the driving spirit of the New Zealand defence. 'There I saw the bravest man I ever saw, Colonel Malone who was doing the jobs from Lance Corporal to Brigadier General.'[84]

The slope was covered with wounded, and as the Aucklanders moved up they met men they knew. Charlie Clark, lying among the wounded in the gully, saw them come through. 'One of them was Lieutenant Henderson. He belonged to a family that I knew from childhood … I stopped him and we shook hands and his last words to me were "Is my brother Jack with you?" I said, "No … He left about four days previous on a hospital boat" … Well he says, "Thank God for that."'[85]

Joining the line, men threw bombs or anything in reach back at the Turks. It was a battle that raged all day and abated only at nightfall. Vic Nicolson was in the thick of it: 'It was just a mad whirl as far as I'm concerned, it's just a mad whirl but I can hear this in the background, I can hear this very, very clearly, I heard it then and I can hear it at times today; "Get the bastard before he gets you."'[86]

'Twice it looked very bad so with Colonel M [alone] we joined the lads in front. I had my revolver and a handful of cartridges and Col. M. seized up a rifle and bayonet as we went.

'The Wellingtons seemed to rise up each time from nowhere and the Turks were hurled back. In the first of these attacks the bayonet on Col. M's rifle was twisted by a bullet, so after this he kept it with him; as he said it was lucky.'[87]

The men clinging to the slopes of Chunuk Bair represented the only success that day. Inaction continued at Suvla, and Monash and his men were pinned down by exhaustion and the Turks a mile to the north, while below the New Zealanders Cox's column of Indians were jammed in the gullies of Chailak and Aghyl Dere. One battalion alone, the 6th Gurkhas under Major Allanson, fought their way through and established themselves on the slopes beneath the saddle that linked Chunuk Bair and Hill Q.

That afternoon of the 8th Godley called a conference at Johnston's headquarters on the Apex. It was a divisional conference to map out the activities for the next day. It was vital to exploit the successes gained by Malone and expand the hold on Chunuk Bair. 'With this in view and after consultations with Birdwood, who placed his last reserves at my disposal, and with Sir Ian Hamilton, who came over from Mudros, I made the following plan for the night of the 8th. The attempt on Hill 971 was to be abandoned, in view of the difficulties of the ground, and the heavy casualties of the Australians. Cox was to renew his attack on Hill Q with the 39th and Indian Brigades; Brigadier General Baldwin with the 38th Brigade from reserve, was to advance under cover of the position held on Chunuk Bair and, swinging to his left, occupy the crest [the northern crest of Chunuk Bair] between it and Hill Q.'[88]

The Wellingtons and Auckland Mounted Rifles would be reinforced by the Otago Battalion and Wellington Mounted Rifles. Once Baldwin had passed through they were to exploit towards Battleship Hill. These were ambitious plans, but success, if it was to come, demanded that the foothold on Chunuk Bair be enlarged.

The conference was to decide how that would be done, and in particular what route Baldwin's brigade would take to secure Hill Q in the main attack. It seemed that there was only one possible route, which led from the firm base established on the Apex, up the tortuous path on Rhododendron Ridge across the saddle and out of the Wellingtons' position on the crest. It would be difficult, and the crowded condition of the deres and paths choked with carrier parties, wounded, and tired, frightened soldiers waiting to be directed forward, emphasised the magnitude of the task. Godley had told Baldwin that this route along Rhododendron Ridge appeared the best and that 'I would meet him at the Apex to see the ground for myself, and confirm my view.'[89]

Temperley recorded: 'At the last moment General Godley was unable to come but we were informed that a General Staff Officer would be sent to explain his views. No Staff Officer ever arrived. Indeed no Divisional or Corps Staff Officer of any kind ever came to see the situation at our Headquarters throughout the battle.'[90]

This omission had disastrous consequences. Godley was held up by a telephone conversation with General Cox, so Brigadier General Johnston, obviously unfit, chaired the conference. Johnston told Baldwin that the shortest route was up the Chailak Dere, across Cheshire Ridge, then up through the Farm to Hill Q. This was over steep and unreconnoitred country. Temperley had already discussed routes with Baldwin's brigade major and had recommended attacking towards Hill Q from the position on Chunuk Bair. He put this forward as a better alternative: 'Colonel Johnston was in no mood to listen to me and rejected it at once. He then took General Baldwin to a point where they could overlook the ground over which he was to cross and there and then the decision was finally made.'[91]

This decision made it impossible for Baldwin's brigade to assault Hill Q before daylight on the 9th. That evening the firing on the crest died away and Meldrum's Wellington Mounteds and Moore's Otagos relieved the survivors on Chunuk Bair. Malone was dead. Artillery fire had been falling on the position all day. Red and yellow marker flags had been placed marking his forward positions 'but, like everything else, they had been shot away by the end of the afternoon'.[92]

A shell, almost certainly from the New Zealand 4.5 inch howitzers firing from within the ANZAC perimeter, burst above Malone's headquarters trench 'about 5.00 p.m. Swish swish came the shrapnel and all except two in our little trench were killed or wounded. Col. Jordan (Commanding Officer of the 7th Gloucesters) got a bullet through the mouth ... Col. M[alone] was killed the other side of me ... he collapsed into the Adjutant's [Harston] or Cunningham's arms [Wellington Second in Command].'[93]

Harston the adjutant would be one of the three Wellington officers to walk off the hill: 'I have always believed it was the destroyer as I saw her swing broadside on and the puffs of smoke from the gun as she fired.'[94] Certainly the ships offshore were supporting the battle, but their shells were directed well clear of the New Zealand positions on the crest at Hill Q and Battleship Hill, only the New Zealand howitzers were directly supporting the Chunuk Bair battle.

The New Zealand howitzers had played an essential role in defeating the stream of Turkish counter-attacks. Shells had fallen either side of the crest all day, but mainly at Turkish expense and the change in atmospherics as dusk approached impacted on the flight of the projectiles. Malone's death was an understandable consequence of a confused struggle at close quarters on such a narrow ridge where the distance between the two sides was 50–60 metres with the crest between. The New Zealand defenders knew that the supporting artillery fire was critical to their survival and accepted the realities that they would lose men because of it.

At 10.30 p.m. the Otago and Wellington Mounteds reinforced the front line below the crest of Chunuk Bair. It had not been intended to relieve the garrison but nothing else was possible: 'Of the 760 of the Wellington Battalion who had captured the height that morning, there came out only 70 unwounded or slightly wounded men ... Their uniforms were torn, their knees broken. They had had no water since morning; they could talk only in whispers; their eyes were sunken; their knees trembled; some broke down and cried like children.'[95]

Turkish fire had died away at nightfall and the reinforcing of the Wellington line was conducted with an ease that suggests what could have been achieved had Baldwin's brigade followed through on the same path and exploited north towards Hill Q. The Otago Infantry Battalion, 400 strong, with two squadrons, the 2nd Wellington West Coast and the 6th Manawatus of the Wellington Mounted Rifles, making up a total of 583 men, now garrisoned the hill. That same night below them in the deres to the north, Baldwin's 38th Brigade got lost. Temperley watched them pass. 'They had spent the whole day in great heat, appalling delays, without a meal ... all incredibly thirsty and not acclimatised ... to the conditions on Gallipoli ... The men looked willing enough but they seemed very young and immature and terribly tired.'[96]

Baldwin's lost column spent the night tracing and retracing its steps in the deres. Dawn found his leading troops still well short of the summit, labouring their way up to the ledge on the slopes below the Farm. It meant the failure of Godley's plan for 9 August. Time and troops were running out: 'I have never ceased to regret that I did not stick to my original intention of going to see the ground for myself. I feel sure that I should have insisted on the advance [of Baldwin's brigade] being made by the high ground, and it is possible that it might have succeeded.'[97]

On the 8th it was evident to all that Malone's achievements on Chunuk Bair offered enormous prospects if they could be exploited by the soldiers of the Empire struggling up the slopes. It was a soldier's battle — the Indians, Gurkhas, ANZACs and the raw soldiers of Britain were stolidly dying to meet their commanders' directions. It was the commanders, and Godley in particular, who failed to show the touch, the insight, that marked a capable tactician. Not even brilliance was required; the bravery of their soldiers only needed a commander to show sound judgement at the right time. There was no lack of this among the Turks. Mustafa Kemal would be given command of the Turkish divisions on this front and at once moved to the sound of the guns. He would counter-attack Suvla, consolidate the position there and then move to Chunuk Bair.

Godley moved his headquarters to the base of Rhododendron Ridge, at No. 3 Outpost, and stayed there for this battle. Not once did he move forward and only on 9 August did he leave his headquarters and observe the struggle from the deck of a destroyer off the coast. This curious detachment created a vacuum in command and in this Johnston became the de facto divisional commander. The result was that Baldwin's column became committed to an avenue of approach that would inevitably mean a daylight assault and failure.

Unquestionably, Godley's span of command was too large in this battle, but many of the problems were of his own making. He made poor use of Shaw's 13th Divisional Headquarters, and at the same time overloaded Johnston's Brigade Headquarters with up to 11 different battalions and regiments. First Malone, then Meldrum, became de facto brigade commanders controlling the elements of the brigade on Chunuk Bair. Johnston, or when the former was incapacited by a combination of illness and drink, Temperley, became the de facto divisional commander. Godley was a bystander.

Already on the night of 7 August there were indications that Godley and his staff were swamped by the number of formations and the scope of objectives to be co-ordinated by his division.

Bean recorded the following conversation at Godley's headquarters on the evening of 6th August. Godley said to Pinwill: '"Can I tell Army Corps that both the brigades have cleared this place?" Pinwill didn't seem to know, but said he'd find out. Presently he reported Monash's stretcher bearers just passing. "Then I can say both Brigades are past here?" said Godley. "No, no Sir, the Indian Brigade is only arriving." "What, are they behind Monash? Good God!" "But that was the order they were told to go in, Sir."' Bean noted this 'seemed rather an elementary part of the attack for Godley to have forgotten.'[98]

It was evident to all that by 8 August what happened with Johnston's New Zealanders would determine the success or failure of Hamilton's hopes and Birdwood's plans. Godley, from his action, does not really appear to have grasped this at the time. He allowed himself to be waylaid by Cox's queries when the situation demanded the priority for his attention was Chunuk Bair. There were enough indications on the 7th and 8th of Johnston's difficulties. Godley should have moved to the sound of the guns and positioned himself on the Apex. It was the commander's role to impart his will and direction to his brigadiers at that conference. Godley's moment of greatness was to have been Chunuk Bair — but he missed it.

The failure would confirm what the New Zealanders and Australians had felt ever since the landing. Godley was a mouthpiece for the ANZAC Corps commander's directives: what Birdwood asked for, Godley did, from the counter-attack of 19 May to the series of attacks from Quinn's.

Godley had Johnston's attributes: 'his loyalty to the views of his superiors in the field was complete and unswerving whatever his own personal opinions might be'.[99] Nowhere did he show a sense of what could be achieved in that terrain or an understanding of the condition and limits of his men. They came to believe that they were pawns, and condemned Godley for it. Godley's forté was as a trainer and administrator. It was to his New Zealanders' cost that he could not match his undoubted ability as a trainer with an appreciation of what was possible in battle. We would suffer dearly for it; had Major General Walker commanded the New Zealand and Australian Division in this offensive, it is likely that Chunuk Bair would have been one of the epic successes of the war. Godley was a product of his time and his New Zealanders outgrew him as they outgrew many of the conventions and shibboleths of Empire that they had accepted without question before Gallipoli.

But now, on the evening of the 8th, Malone was dead and the Wellingtons had been reduced to a shattered handful of men. It was the Otagos and the Wellington Mounteds who would continue the struggle. Ewen Pilling wrote: 'At 8.00 p.m. Sergeant Allen of No. 1 platoon lined up his men and led the way at a slow double over the ridge. I followed with mine, followed by the remaining platoons of Fourth Company, then the other Otago companies until the whole battalion was over.

'We swung round the edge of the hill in file. Wounded men on the way back told us how badly help was needed in the firing line. We passed a donga where 200 men were crowded together [most likely Gloucesters and Welch] with their sergeant sheltering like a flock of sheep. These directed us to where Wellington was to be found. In the darkness it was difficult to tell where to go. By this time our men's hearts were hardened, and it was well it was so, for the ground ten yards back from the trenches was covered with our own wounded and dead, and every now and then in the darkness we tramped on one before we knew he was there. From all sides came cries for "water" and "stretcher bearer" mingled with moans of agony.'[100]

The Wellington line was found to be a double line of 'barely waist deep holes' manned by a few wounded. Lieutenant Colonel Meldrum commanded the line. 'Colonel Moore was wounded almost immediately and retired leaving me in charge of the post. There was a lot to be done. The trenches were narrow and shallow and we were soon all at work — Otago on the right and left flanks and Wellington [Mounted Rifles] in the centre. We dug in until daylight.'[101]

Little could be done for the wounded; Rhododendron Ridge was littered with hundreds. The 16 stretcher bearers in each battalion toiled on, often in desperation, reserving their stretchers for the men of their own regiment. Forward on Chunuk Bair little could be done for those who had crawled into shelter at the head of Sazli Dere below the crest. That night, and indeed on every night of the battle, priority was given to getting men, water and ammunition forward.

'No officer, NCO or man is to fall out to assist to the rear a wounded man. To do this is a serious military offence. Stretcher parties will follow all columns and will attend to the wounded.

'Stretcher parties are not to block or interfere with the forward movement of troops. They are not to make use of any Communication Trench or Sap till all movement of fighting troops through it has ceased for the night.'[102]

Colonel N. Manders, Assistant Director of Medical Services to Godley's division, had made every effort to see that wounded would be cared for and evacuated promptly, but the narrow ridges destroyed his plans. It was the troops in the firing line who did what they could: 'I had taken two water bottles up the hill and did what little I could among some of them. The first one lay in a four inch hollow evidently scooped out by himself … He asked me if there was any hope of stretcher bearers that night, I had to tell him "No" … I told him his only hope lay in whether he could possibly struggle down himself. So he said "Help me to my feet then." I raised him and held him for a while to allow the giddiness to pass, but … he collapsed and I had to lay him down again. A bullet had … entered his chest and gone through his back. There was a big hole in his back and as I laid him down the air sighed and I could hear the bones grit. Another voice was calling for water and I left him.'[103]

On Chunuk Bair, men in agony prayed for death. Vic Nicolson later pondered, 'I know stories that we shot some of them, I don't know whether that happened, personally I never had to face up to that one. And yet no doubt it would have been a mercy, a blessing to some people to have been shot, by their own men.'[104]

Harvey Johns was lying alongside Charlie Clark. 'It came to night fall and I said to a mate of mine, "Well I am getting the hell out of this, one way or other, somehow" … so the two of us started to crawl and we would be getting helped by bullets and shrapnel, but we stuck it out and made the 300 yards back … we got in about midnight.'[105] They crawled out of the gully onto the saddle and up the slope towards the Pinnacle and the trench held by the Auckland Battalion.

Towards the top they became separated: 'I flopped over and lay there on a track and a man fell over me. "Who are you?" "I am a New Zealander, a wounded man trying to get back." It was Colonel Young, Commanding Officer of the Aucklands, who had been Company Commander of the Hawke's Bay Company. He said he would get some of the Fifth Reinforcements who had just arrived to take me back and he directed two English stretcher bearers to place me on the stretcher and he went off into the darkness to get some of the Fifth Reinforcements to help carry me back. These fellows just waited for him to go, and then turned me over and tipped me out, and off they went. Colonel Young came back just then and said, "Where's the stretcher … Why didn't you stop them?" I said, "How could I stop them in my condition?"'[106]

The few available stretcher bearers sometimes devoted themselves to assisting the men of their own regiment at grim cost to the many that received no assistance. Clark was carried to a dressing station where his wound had iodine poured into it and was bandaged. It would take him three days to travel the 1500 metres from the Apex to the Clearing Station below No. 2 Outpost.

Ormond Burton was one of the stretcher bearers clearing the wounded from the Apex. 'In the darkness we reached the Regimental Aid Post. Bullets were smashing into the stiff scrub everywhere like the heavy drops of a thunder shower. Heavy and continuous firing went on all night … We took up the stretchers that were waiting and went down the dere. For the next few days we were up and down with little rest. Chailak Dere was a dangerous highway and sometimes a desperately crowded one. On the high slopes it took six men to get a stretcher down. Four men were needed for the long hard carry to the Casualty Clearing Station near the beach but usually only two were available. Turkish shrapnel searched the ravine and the bullets fell everywhere. Snipers were busy at every exposed bend. As we went there was an unending line of mules laden with water and ammunition going up — and every kind of carrying party.'[107]

Engineers had sunk bores for water in the Chailak Dere to relieve the desperate needs of the troops, as Burton recorded. 'Not quite so far down as the well, in a gap … was a ghastly shambles. Some three hundred desperately wounded men had somehow congregated there — how no one seemed to know. No one appeared to be responsible for them. Their wounds were uncared for and in the heat some were in a shocking state. They had no food and no water except what was given to them by passers-by. Many were hit a second and third time as they lay helplessly. We reported all this to our own officers but they seemed helpless to get anything done. Many died there — some able to see the hospital ships with their green bands and red crosses no distance out to sea. On one trip I gave my water bottle to a Turkish officer lying there with four or five of his men about him. He gave every drop to his men and took not a mouthful for himself. I saw nothing more dreadful during the whole war than the suffering of those forgotten men.'[108]

The wounded lay and died in the deres and at the overcrowded Casualty Clearing Station on the beach. Shelling during the day made evacuation impossible and the crowds of wounded grew until they stretched from No. 2 Outpost back towards the original ANZAC perimeter, about a kilometre to the south, following the line of the Great Sap, dug to connect with the outposts. Colonel Manders, Godley's ADMS, who had worked so hard to make sure that this battle would not see the tragedy of the wounded at the landing repeated, was conscious of failure and knew that all his medical resources were exhausted. He wrote in his private diary, 'The lines of communication have broken down' and 'completed 31 years service — only one more'.[109] The next day he was dead, killed by a random bullet as he stood with Godley at No. 3 Outpost.

Men who had to pass, and could do nothing, raged at their plight. Aubrey Herbert, the Divisional Intelligence Officer, was one: 'I stumbled upon poor AC [a school fellow] who had been wounded about 3.00 a.m. the day before, and had laid in the sun on the sand all the previous day. He recognised me and asked me to help him, but was light headed. There were fifty-six others with him … It was awful having to pass them. A lot of them called out, "We are being murdered."'[110]

It was into this scene that 1900 men of the 5th New Zealand Reinforcements landed and were at once committed forward to assist their regiments. Moving along the Great Sap, they assembled below No. 2 Outpost. Among them was Leonard Hart of the Otagos: 'We were under the shelter of a small hill at this point and thought ourselves safe. The stray bullets from the Turkish trenches were coming right over the hill and falling right in front of us. But our officers, who were as green as what we were regarding the "ways of war" had not counted on shrapnel or snipers, and we paid heavily for it. It was while we were having our dinner that the first big losses occurred. Some Turkish snipers … opened rapid fire on us and men began to fall in all directions.'[111]

The Auckland and Wellington reinforcements were sent up Rhododendron Ridge while the Canterburys and Otagos were sent to drag a battery of guns out to No. 2 Outpost from the original ANZAC perimeter. Many were shot as they dragged the guns parallel to the sap. 'A lieutenant of our company named Hunt who was in charge of our party was shot through the chest and I heard that he died while being taken aboard a hospital ship.'

Frank Hunt did not die. 'A sledgehammer like blow on the chest — a pellet of lead into the right lung near the heart and oblivion for me. Later I came to life on the beach near the cove in great pain and wondering how and when I had reached hell — utterly lonely and helpless. Bursting shells all around, confusion all round too. War at its worst!'[112]

Eventually the 5ths reinforced the New Zealanders at the Apex. 'The events of the next few days I have not a very clear recollection of, except that it was little else but blazing away at the Turkish trenches to keep them quiet. We all learnt what real hunger and thirst are like. The quart of water which we had in our water bottles when we left the beach was all most of us had for two days.'[113]

The climax to the battle for Chunuk Bair was 9 August. It was Godley's last attempt to enlarge his hold on the crest. Hamilton had more men to offer but Birdwood, with Godley's concurrence, refused. Congestion in Chailak Dere and on Rhododendron Ridge was such that he could not supply water to the men he had. Lack of water was crippling the efforts of Godley's men.

On the left, men of Cox's Indian Brigade, supported by the 39th New Army Brigade, were clinging to the slopes of the ridge, just 150 metres short of the top below the saddle that linked Hill Q and Chunuk Bair. It would be another dawn attack after an artillery bombardment by all available guns; Allanson's 6th Gurkhas, who had spent the night of 8/9 August clinging to the slopes above the Farm, would charge the Hill. This charge was to support Baldwin's attack, but there was no sign of Baldwin's brigade.

It was 5.23 and Allanson's men went straight for the top: 'For about ten minutes we fought hand to hand, we bit and fisted, and used rifles and pistols as clubs, blood was flying about like spray from a hairwash bottle.'[114] The few Turks holding the saddle withdrew, and Allanson and his Gurkhas saw the Narrows as had the New Zealanders before them. It was now that Baldwin's brigade should have attacked through the New Zealand lines on Chunuk Bair. This would have given Godley's force the ground it so desperately needed. But it was not to be. Baldwin's men were stuck below the Farm and the New Zealanders were using all their energy to hold what Malone had won.

Allanson's men had no time to consolidate, for almost immediately artillery shells landed among them, the Gurkhas ran, and the Turks reoccupied the crest. This shelling was part of Godley's support for the renewed attacks on the heights. It also burst among the New Zealanders who had been fighting off Turkish counter-attacks since 4.00 a.m. It hit the trenches on the left of the line, 'killing the gallant Major Statham, together with his brother beside him as well as Sergeant Major Porteous and six or seven men'.[115] It had the same effect on the New Zealanders as it had on Allanson's men. Part of the line fell back with the wounded: 'Poor old Hughie Pringle was killed, his throat ripped by a piece of it, and presently there came groping past us Clutha McKenzie blinded, young Mell Bull his jaw smashed and another unrecognisable.'[116]

It was Meldrum who rallied the men: 'It was a very critical moment for the Turks were very close up. Major Elmslie was close by me at the time in the centre and while Captain Kelsall and I ran out to turn back the men who were retiring, he called on one of his troops to follow him and led them up to the trench that had been vacated. He fell just as he reached the trench, but picking himself up, quickly dived over the parapet, the men following.

'As he got up so quickly I thought he had only stumbled and it was not until the Turkish attack had been broken … that I heard that he had been fatally wounded.'[117]

The casualty clearing station on the flat below No. 2 Outpost, 7 August 1915. Shrapnel and sniper fire made evacuation by day impossible. The lines of wounded would eventually reach back to Anzac Cove.

(Gill Denniston Collection – PA1-0-863, Alexander Turnbull Library)

By early morning Meldrum had lost half of the men garrisoning the hill. The scattered line of trenches filled with dead and wounded, and the men scraped another line behind it, often using the bodies for cover. Friends kept each other there and fought alongside each other, regardless of who was left in command. They held the weaker with them too: 'A — suddenly cried, "Come on boys, retire!" I turned on him, "You cow, I'll put a bullet into you" … He knew that it was meant and subsided.'[118]

Meldrum requested reinforcements and at midday 50 soldiers of the 6th Loyal North Lancashires reached his position from the Apex. During the day they fought off attacks from the front and from the flanks. 'The bombs did us the most harm. The Turks swung them in long woollen socks and they came hurtling through the air for some 30 or 40 yards, rolling into our trenches and exploding there. Many men were wounded. Some jumped behind the trench and lay or knelt behind the parapet … we fought them all along the trench line.'[119]

Three regiments of Turks had been decimated in attempts to remove the New Zealand line. They were fully stretched, and there was mounting concern among the Turkish command. They knew that if Chunuk Bair was lost, the Turkish line holding the ANZAC perimeter would have to withdraw from Second Ridge, and Third Ridge would become as vulnerable as Quinn's Post on Second Ridge had been in early May.

The New Zealanders were equally exhausted but the foothold remained: 'If only Abdul had known how few were left … but there, he didn't and possibly he was as exhausted as ourselves for New Zealanders had not died for nothing. In the little neighbouring trench over which no Turk had come alive, the only sign of life among the many there, was the stump of an arm which now and then waved feebly for help and a voice called "New Zealand" to four listeners who could give or get no aid for him.'[120]

That evening the New Zealanders still held the trenches. Meldrum got his tired men to dig in and by nightfall trenches had been deepened and machine guns positioned on each flank. Were it not for his lack of numbers and the exhaustion of his men, Meldrum was confident he could hold Chunuk Bair's seaward slopes. The Otagos had lost 17 officers and 309 men. The Wellington Mounteds had 73 left out of 193. Johnston's brigade and the elements of Russell's Mounteds that had reinforced it had no more men to offer. For 36 hours they had held the slopes of Chunuk Bair, and now they were spent. Godley decided to consolidate. Shaw's 13th Division would assume command of operations from the Farm south, Cox's 29th Indian Brigade would command north of the Farm. The New Zealanders on the Apex, the Aucklanders at the Pinnacle, and Meldrum's men on Chunuk Bair would be relieved and withdrawn to Chailak Dere to reorganise.

Two new Army battalions would replace the New Zealanders. The 6th Loyal North Lancashires, already in position on the Apex, would be one of these, and the 5th Wiltshires, one of the battalions in Baldwin's brigade, the other. The latter battalion was exhausted, and when it was learnt that it could not reach the hill until 1.00 a.m. on 10 August, Johnston asked permission to use the 6th Leinster Battalion that was already at the Apex in reserve. Godley refused as he was determined to hold one fresh battalion in reserve.

Despite all that had been achieved by the New Zealanders, Temperley saw the opportunity to correct what he saw as Malone's errors on the hill. 'The Colonel of the North Lancashire battalion was a regular officer. I explained to him the unfortunate situation of the trenches on Chunuk Bair and he decided to push saps out from the existing trench and so gradually construct a new trench line of which he fully appreciated the importance.'[121]

It appears typical of the man that he discounted what Malone and Meldrum had achieved and that he imagined a regular officer would naturally succeed where he believed the New Zealanders had failed. At 8.00 p.m. the relief began. The 6th Loyal North Lancashires relieved Meldrum's men and occupied the narrow ring of trenches below the crest. Meldrum told his successor that while he was confident that the position could be held, more trenches needed to be dug before the inevitable Turkish counter-attacks at daylight as the two relieving British battalions had twice as many men as Meldrum's garrison. Meldrum's New Zealand machine guns were left in position, and his best scouts remained to brief and assist the British battalions. Despite this advice, little was done. (Behind them on the Pinnacle the 6th Leinsters relieved the Auckland Battalion in a position the Aucklanders had fortified and where they had dug a communication trench back towards the Apex as well as one down the side of the spur towards the Farm.) It was not until 2.00 a.m. on the 10th that the exhausted and inexperienced Wiltshires were led up to the summit to join the 6th Loyal North Lancashires. Wounded still littered the ground behind the trenches, and instead of digging in, tired men were allowed to pile arms and sleep in the open at the head of the gully near the saddle, where the wounded had collected over the two days of battle. New Zealand patrols had already established that the Turks were massing to attack and had briefed the incoming commanding officer on what to expect.*

Beyond the crest, Mustafa Kemal was gathering every available man to remove this cancer from the Turkish line. He had three or four regiments, including the last Turkish reserves on the Peninsula. At dawn, with bayonets fixed, they swept over the crest of Chunuk Bair in four waves. By now the supply of Turkish grenades was exhausted and Meldrum's scouts forward with the British believed the attack lacked the intensity of that of the previous day. Any determined defence might have held, but the 6th Loyal North Lancashires did not resist but broke and ran, as did the Wiltshires below them. Only the few New Zealanders forward showed any fight. Panic spread and the Leinsters at the Pinnacle also fled. Kemal's counter-attack threatened the entire line.

Wallingford's New Zealand machine guns were still on the Apex. Dan Curham's gun had been cleaned and Curham was test firing it.

'I was firing not up to the hill where our fellows had gone, but to 971 [in reality Hill Q, as 971 is obscured from Rhododendron Ridge] ... an adjoining hill that was

---

* Lt J.E. Cuthill of the Otagos took a patrol forward on the night of 9/10 August and confirmed the Turks were massing for an attack. Meldrum briefed his successor accordingly, and emphasised the need for both British battalions to dig in. The Wiltshire's failure to do so reflected the raw inexperience and lack of urgency of its officers.

connected by a ridge and you could see the dust where the bullets hit and it was tat! tat! tat! … until I knew the gun was in good order and I was still fingering it and looking at the hill and I saw a most amazing sight. A great mass of Turks coming over the hill … I had my gun trained on the very spot and all I had to do was press the trigger and, of course, they fell all over the place.'[122]

The Navy and the artillery at Anzac joined in and broke Kemal's lines into fragments, but the British forces had been thrown off the crest. The exhausted New Zealanders were thrown pell mell back up to the Apex to hold what they had won. The Pinnacle was lost and the Apex was threatened, and panic spread. Men — New Zealand, British and Indian — ran down the track from the line. Wallingford, always the man for the crisis, stood pistol in hand, firing at those that fled, rallying them and turning them back.

All along the line men had reached breaking point, Kitchener's New Army battalions particularly so. Temperley records: 'On August 10th I saw 300 or 400 of them running forward to the Turks with their hands up. To save a disaster of the first magnitude and to prevent the whole front collapsing I gave orders to the machine guns of our Brigade to open fire upon them and at some cost in life the movement was checked and they ran back to their lines.'[123]

The New Zealand Infantry resting in Chailak Dere were rushed forward to hold the Apex, Frank McKenzie among them. 'Major Hume and No. 4 Platoon were last of [the] 3rd [Auckland Company] and had not yet gone down the hill to rest, so Major Hume raced us up to the crest to fill the gap. Major killed before we reached crest. We lay down and blazed point blank and after about an hour their attack ceased and they lost fearfully. But beside the Major, out of the 27 of my platoon only nine came out unhit and most of these had a scratch. I got my radius bone laid bare by a bullet and one through my mess tin, strapped on the small of the back. Cursed heartily because it didn't take a splinter off the bone and give me a spell away from the scrap.'[124]

Every available man was needed to hold the line and Sir Ian Hamilton, in recognition of what the New Zealanders had achieved, ordered them to hold the Apex 'forever'. It was an honour that they were well prepared to forego. Physically spent they dug in and held on 'with dead all around us … All the boys were singing out for water … Things seem to be getting worse every day.'[125]

Godley wrote of the battle to his wife: 'It was within an ace of coming off, but it didn't and it can't be helped. The troops did all that could be expected of them. Both of the New Zealand Brigades and the Indian Brigade were easily the best. Monash's lot of Australians were very good up to a certain point, but not quite good enough and the New Kitchener Battalions were really tried too high for the first time … I am of course, very disappointed not to have got the ridge, but I have got a good deal and I think Birdwood realises and thinks we could have hardly done more. It has been a fine command, but the casualties are horrible and the difficulties of getting the wounded out of that awful country have been ghastly.'[126]

Godley also wrote to Allen, praising the bravery of his officers and men. 'Russell's conduct of his attack was of a very high order and Johnston's operations were most excellently conducted, both handled their brigades to my entire satisfaction.'[127] But failure of any nature suggests that blame should be attached to some quarter. The whispers had already started as to why Chunuk Bair had been lost. Sir Ian Hamilton noted for 10 August: 'Now — Chunuk Bair has gone! … Trenches badly sited, they say, and the Turks able to form close by in dead ground.'[128]

Hamilton enlarged on this likely cause of failure in his despatches. Malone was named as responsible for siting the trenches, and in the body of the report Hamilton wrote: 'Also many officers are of the opinion that they had not been well sited in the first instance. On the South African system, the main line was withdrawn some 25 yards from the crest instead of being actually on the crestline itself, and there were not even lookout posts along the summit … here we were faced by regulars taught to attack in mass with bayonet or bomb. And the power of collecting overwhelming numbers at very close quarters rested with whichever side held the true skyline in force.'[129]

There was no one to dispute this; the surviving Wellington officers were wounded and gone, and indeed had no knowledge of the slur. Temperley drafted the report of the Infantry Brigade's operation and it was accepted by his superiors. It was also accepted by many New Zealanders, for the majority of the New Zealanders who fought on Chunuk Bair were on the rear slopes in trenches sighted below the crest. They had no knowledge of what had been, accepting in the urgency of battle the situation as they found it. Only the Turks and the now dead Wellingtons knew that it was impossible for either side to hold the crest. Malone's bravery would be praised, but his competence quietly questioned. Historians of the campaign accepted that he committed his troops to the rearward slopes and surrendered the crest. Today few realise that it was New Zealanders who first saw the Narrows from Chunuk Bair, for both Godley's report and Hamilton's despatches accorded Allanson's Gurkhas this honour.

Inevitably, the news filtered to the men. 'The beach was the source of all the news on the Peninsula. Info leaked from the Corps and Div HQ per medium of signallers and batmen. They gave the troops the news as freely as any sensational newspaper … a signaller friend on Corps Headquarters spread the news through our battalion that the Corps Commander had said the New Zealanders had been thrown off Chunuk Bair because they hadn't tried to dig in on the forward slope of the hill. From the same source came the story that the Australian Fourth Brigade attack had failed because "it wasn't pushed with sufficient vigour". The reports angered our troops at the time … anything savouring of criticism of the line troops by headquarters aroused very bitter feeling after the August fighting died down and the troops realised the operation had failed.'[130]

The battle-weary New Zealanders were bitter that, after all their efforts, the ground had been lost and their wounded left to die on the Turkish-held slopes. The suspicion of blame fanned this bitterness into anger towards their divisional commander, Godley. Walker publicly signalled the bravery of his Australians with seven VCs awarded for the battle at Lone Pine. In Godley's area of operations only one was awarded, to Cyril Bassett, for his work on the slopes below Chunuk Bair. Others were recommended, but not awarded: Allanson of the 6th Gurkhas was one, and Meldrum recommended Major Elmslie of the Wellington Mounteds, who died on Chunuk Bair and whose body his men carried down from the heights that night to bury alongside that of Major Chambers at Old No. 3 Outpost. A niggardly Godley decided to make a single recommendation and the inevitable comparison with the seven Australian awards suggested Australian success and New Zealand failure.

The belief grew that Godley would not hear of recommendations for VCs to officers as they were only doing their job, and by the end of August the men were prepared to believe anything of their commander. The New Zealanders saw the mediocre rewarded and the dead blamed. They laughed bitterly at Johnston's 'excellently conducted' operations and spoke of the VCs that should have been awarded: 'Richard Warden, the great scout of the Auckland Battalion, killed on Chunuk Bair — the unknown soldier who was the heart and soul of the Wellington forward trench on Chunuk; Major Wallingford MC the hero of Anzac, and Fielden Taylor, the chaplain.'[131]

It was Cyril Bassett who epitomised the feelings of the New Zealanders after Chunuk Bair. To the end of his life, this shy man tried to keep his VC a secret, even to his children. 'All my mates ever got were wooden crosses.'

On 20 August the New Zealand Infantry Brigade's fighting strength was recorded in the *War Diary* as 850 men.

Casualties in the New Zealand
Infantry Brigade from 6–14 August were:

Approximate Strength 5th August		2800
5th Reinforcements arrived during the battle		1000
		3800

	Killed	Wounded	Missing	
Brigade Headquarters	1	9	1	
Auckland Battalion	63	229	28	
Canterbury Battalion	67	268	11	
Otago Battalion	51	214	63	
Wellington Battalion	107	311	291	
	289	1031	394	1714 casualties

NZ Infantry Strength 20th August	850*

Losses in the New Zealand Mounted Rifles Brigade
from 6–12 August were:

Approximate Strength 5th August	1900
5th Reinforcements	500
	2400

	Killed	Wounded	Missing	
NZ Mounted Brigade Headquarters		5		
Auckland Mounted Rifles	57	144	27	
Canterbury Mounted Rifles	24	63		
Wellington Mounted Rifles	26	105	15	
Otago Mounted Rifles	28	84	7	
Maori Contingent	16	84	4	
	151	485	53	689

Most of the missing were lying on the slopes of Chunuk Bair.

Today, three monuments command the eye on the twin peaks of Chunuk Bair. On the southern peak stands the Turkish memorial to Kemal's feat in throwing back the British forces off the crest on 10 August 1915. The inscription acknowledges this as the turning point in the campaign. Further along, on the high point of Chunuk Bair, is the New Zealand memorial. On its base is inscribed:

In honour of
the soldiers
of the
New Zealand
Expeditionary Force
8th August
1915
From the Uttermost
Ends of the Earth.

Next to it is a bronze statue of Kemal Ataturk representing the moment he orders the counterattack that wins the battle for the heights. On a stone plinth above the cemetery are recorded the names of 852 New Zealand dead who fell in the battle for Chunuk Bair and who have no known graves. There are ten gravestones in the Chunuk Bair cemetery, including one for a boy of 17.[**] From this cemetery the waters of the Dardanelles can be clearly seen.

The Turkish crest line trench occupied by Malone has gone, and in its place are a network of defences built by the Turks after August. Pines now clothe the heights, but on the seaward slopes, walk 30 metres down towards Rhododendron Ridge and the line of ragged scrapes that marks Malone and Meldrum's trench line can still be seen

---

[*] Lt J.E. Cuthill of the Otagos took a patrol forward on the night of 9/10 August and confirmed the Turks were massing for an attack. Meldrum briefed his successor accordingly, and emphasised the need for both British battalions to dig in. The Wiltshire's failure to do so reflected the raw inexperience and lack of urgency of its officers.

[**] 19/1950 Pte Martin Andrew Persson, WIB, KIA 8/8/15, aged 17.

on either side of the track. If you clear away the pine needles that fill them, the debris of battle is still evident: particularly shrapnel ball and bone.

The soldiers who fought on Chunuk Bair performed one of the outstanding feats of arms in New Zealand history. It was a soldier's battle. 'There was no power of command; in the nature of things there could not be; but every man on that ridge knew that the thin line of New Zealand men was holding wide the door to victory … How men were to die on Chunuk was determined largely by how men and women lived on the farms and in the towns of New Zealand.'[132]

Victory is a big word, and it is unlikely that most New Zealanders who fought on Chunuk Bair saw their hilltop as the door to victory in the campaign. Certainly some would have seen its importance, but for many it was just another hill that had to be taken, but for those who stood on it as dawn broke on 8 August they knew that there were no hills of any importance between them and the Straits in the distance. It was also important because, once the hill had been won, there were moments aplenty when it could have been lost again. Some unwounded men left the line on Chunuk Bair. It could be said that for the men, fighting isolated and outnumbered, this was a sensible option to take. But most did not take that option, for the New Zealander fought on Chunuk Bair as he had lived. It was another struggle, like breaking in the land or clearing the bush. He fought in the same way he once played rugby, completely professional despite his amateur status.

On Chunuk Bair, New Zealand soldiers gave up their amateur status and found an identity as fighting men. For an army 'is also a mirror of its own society and its values, in some places and at some times an agent of national pride or a bulwark against national fears, or perhaps even the last symbol of the nation itself.'[133]

On Chunuk Bair we demonstrated our nationhood to the world for the first time in a manner that we in New Zealand have only just begun to appreciate. It would be seen again on the Somme in 1916 and 1918, at Messines and Passchendaele in 1917. It would also become the hallmark of Freyberg's New Zealanders in the Second World War.

'But the way men died on Chunuk is shaping the deeds yet to be done by the generations still unborn … When the August fighting died down there was no longer any question but that New Zealanders had commenced to realise themselves as a nation.'[134]

Perhaps if we have a Day and a Dawn Service that is uniquely ours it should be this day — the day we 'beheld the Narrows from the hill'.

11

HILL 60

So all day long the noise of battle rolled
Among the mountains by the … sea
Until King Arthur's table, man by man,
Had fallen in Lyonesse about their Lord.

Alfred, Lord Tennyson, 'Morte d'Arthur'

The agony of August was not yet over for Godley's New Zealanders. Sir Ian Hamilton was determined to make one last effort. Stopford, the commander of the 9th Corps, had been replaced, and the 9th Corps, reinforced by the 29th Division from Helles and the newly arrived Yeomanry Division from Egypt, operating as dismounted infantry, would make another attempt to seize the Scimitar and W Hills from across the Suvla Plain.

'We should command the plateau between the two Anafartas; knock out the enemy's guns and observation posts commanding Suvla Bay, and should easily be able thence to work ourselves into a position whence we will enfilade the rear of the Sari Bair Ridgeand begin to get a strangle grip over the Turkish communications to the southwards.'[1]

The ANZACs were to play a minor role in this attack. They were to seize Hill 60, or Kaiajik Aghala, a tiny knoll at the base of 'Flat Hill', a spur running down from 971 on the Sari Bair Range. Included in the task was the seizure of two wells at the Hill's base to ease the water problem at Anzac. The capture of Hill 60 would secure the right flank of the 9th Corps' attack on W Hills. It would also secure the access between the British forces at Suvla and the new Anzac perimeter, by enlarging the junction which, although a kilometre deep from the sea coast, was open to Turkish sniper fire from Hill 60.

Ironically, on 8 August water parties from Monash's 4th Australians had sauntered over Hill 60 looking for the wells marked on the map at the northern base of the hill. However, since 9–10 August it had been occupied and entrenched by the Turks.

From the ANZAC lines on Damakjelik Bair, glimpses of the raw clay of the Turkish trenches could be seen among the dense prickly scrub on the forward slope and crest of the hill. In between the two forces was the open gully of the Kaiajik Dere. It was planned that at 3.00 p.m. on 21 August, simultaneously with the 9th Corps' attack, the ANZAC Force would seize Hill 60. The Indian Brigade would attack on the left, the New Zealand Mounted Rifles in the centre and 4th Australian Brigade on the right. Brigadier General Cox of the 29th Indian Brigade would command the operation.

The 29th Indian Brigade and the Connaught Rangers were to seize the two wells to the north of Hill 60. The Canterbury and Otago Mounted Rifles would seize Hill 60 and the 4th Australians would take the spur just above the Hill 60 knoll.

The elements of the New Zealand Mounted Rifles and the 4th Australian Brigade numbered in total less than a full strength infantry battalion. The exertions of August and the increase in sickness after the struggle meant that units existed in name only. The Otagos and Canterbury Mounteds together numbered 400 fit men and the 4th Australian Brigade totalled 500 men. Fitness too was now measured in terms of a man's ability to stand and carry a rifle rather than fitness to fight.

Little was known about Turkish strength on Hill 60 but all available artillery would support Cox's attack. On 21 August this was changed. A shortage of artillery meant that priority was now given to bombarding the Turkish positions in front of 9th Corps, and only when this was complete would fire shift to support the attack

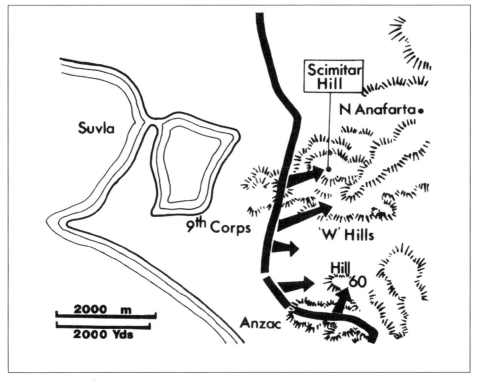

Projected advance from Suvla and Anzac, 21 August 1915.

on Hill 60. Because of this the start time was postponed until 3.30 p.m., 30 minutes after the assault by 9th Corps. This change in timings made the need for the attack questionable, as its original purpose had been to secure the right flank as 9th Corps attacked — not after the attack.

To the infantry waiting in the trenches on Damakjelik Bair, it seemed that very few of the shells landed in the Turkish positions on Hill 60. Certainly the Turks, seeing the Suvla Bay advance, were alert and expecting an attack. As the New Zealanders charged forward they were met by intense, accurate Turkish fire. Lieutenant Gordon Harper noticed his sergeant, George Ferguson, cracking jokes with the men as they waited for the artillery to lift. 'His body was the first we had to jump over as we left the parapet. His South African ribbons were still on his breast.'[2] Though the New Zealand howitzers had caused heavy casualties in the Turkish trenches, the attacking waves of the Canterbury and Otago Mounteds suffered heavily.

Trooper Edward Templar took part in the assault: 'In the morning General Godley came up and told us he wanted us to take a Turkish trench out on the left that afternoon. There was 43 of us left out of the 8th South Canterbury Mounteds … We had to cross two gullies where it was safe to stop for a spell. Then we had to plough through a stretch of scrub, then open going in full view of the Turks.'[3]

The Mounteds seized 100 metres of trench at the southern base of the knoll. 'Some

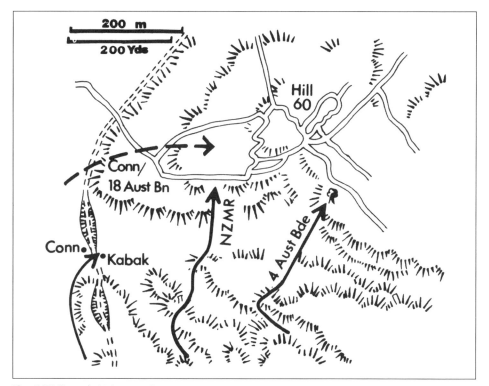

The ANZAC attack, 21 August 1915.

of us got there. We had a roll call the next morning, 18 of us. Our one officer was killed plus the Sergeant Major, and there wasn't one with a stripe among us. However, there were some Southland Mounteds further along the trench and we attached ourselves to them. Luckily we had Robin Harper there with a machine gun. There was an elderly major with the Otago boys and when the Turks counter-attacked that night he sent word along that we were not to fire a shot until he gave the order. I think the old boy had one too many swigs at the rum jar and he was going to take all these Turks as prisoners. However, at last Robin Harper let fly with his machine gun. Then we all let fly and those we didn't hit vanished in the dark. The first one that Robin bowled over was so close that the blast of the machine gun set his clothes on fire.'[4]

It was a grotesque close-quarter trench battle; the men were fine-drawn, gaunt, with nerves on a knife edge. They were dressed in brimless forage hats, cut-down trousers and boots, no socks and in many cases no shirts — just brown grimy bodies, shaven-headed, walking skeletons fighting over bodies sprawled in the saps, with rifle butt, bayonet or bomb. The Turks as always were well provided with bombs and it was against the constant tide of Turkish bombers edging their way back along the trenches from the high ground that the New Zealanders blocked the access with sandbag barriers and hung on.

On either flank, although the Connaught Rangers had seized the wells, both the Indian Brigade and 4th Australians had suffered heavy casualties in assaulting across the open ground and had been forced to take cover short of the Turkish trenches. Each effort to reach the New Zealanders that afternoon added to the sprawled bodies. The Australians fell first and then the 10th Hampshires, the reserve battalion, as they tried to join them.

Fire from bursting shells set alight the dead scrub, much of which had been chopped down for Turkish bivouacs. Among it lay wounded Australians and Hampshires. Survivors sheltering from the Turkish fire could only watch in helpless horror as the flames reached the bodies of the dead and wounded, 'ignited their clothing and exploded their bombs and rifle ammunition and thus pieces of burning cloth or wood were flung to other ridges starting more fires. Any wounded man who so much as stirred to crawl out of reach of the flames was instantly shot by the Turks.'[5]

At 4 o'clock Russell had asked the 29th Indian Brigade for assistance on the left flank. Shortly after, the Connaught Rangers, who had taken the wells at the northern base of the hill, could be seen swarming across the seaward side of the hill and across the front of the trench held by the New Zealanders. Had bravery been enough it would have succeeded, but like equally brave charges before it, such as by the Light Horse at The Nek and the Auckland Battalion at the Apex, this one withered under the Turkish fire, suffered heavy losses, and gained nothing.

After this, remnants of the Connaughts were led along the trench line held by the New Zealanders and established a link between the position on Hill 60 and the Indian Brigade on the plain. Only a toehold had been won on Hill 60. The Turks still held the crest and Russell realised from reports received that his troops could do no more. 'Have captured about 120 yards enemy trench and one enemy machine gun which we are using against Turks but cannot push on. Men exhausted.'[6]

The Mounted Rifles at the Outpost in late August before the attack on Hill 60. *(Album 382, p.15 n4, Auckland War Memorial Museum)*

After dark Brigadier General Russell of the New Zealand Mounted Brigade had gone forward and found his men holding two detached lines of the Kaiajik Aghala. On his left the Indian Brigade held the plain at right angles to that gained by his men. If he had had fresh troops, the Indian position on the plain would have been the ideal base for an attack to seize the summit of Hill 60. Russell and his superior, Cox, believed it was necessary to seize the summit before daylight and requested a fresh battalion to carry out the task.

Godley had recently been reinforced by the 5th Australian Infantry Brigade, the first formation of the 2nd Australian Division to arrive on Gallipoli. Godley had no wish to commit any of this raw and inexperienced brigade to battle. However, on receiving Russell's request, he released the 18th Western Australian Battalion to support the attack. About dawn, after stumbling through the dark in the belief that they were going to occupy some trenches, the commanding officer and company commanders were briefed by candlelight by Russell's brigade major, Powles. This was the first they knew of the attack.

Powles then led the battalion forward in person to the start line on the edge of a sunken road. No time had been allowed to tell the men anything at all about the operation. They were to go in with rifle and bayonet. At dawn, company after company charged the hill and, like the Connaught Rangers before them, suffered heavy casualties from machine-gun fire. In spite of this the Australians seized the continuation of the trench held by the New Zealanders, but lacking bombs they were grenaded out of it by Turkish reinforcements bombing their way down the trench line. The Turks forced the remnants of the battalion back, until they were holding doggedly to a 50 metre stretch on the New Zealanders' left. The knoll remained in Turkish hands. Casualties in the 18th Battalion numbered 11 officers and 372 men out of 750. Over half of these were killed.

Desperately short of men, Brigadier General Russell, in committing the 18th Battalion, repeated the same errors that had destroyed the Royal Marine Light Infantry on 2 May below Baby 700. Of the 4000 men committed to this minor operation, 1300 were casualties. Of the 400 New Zealand Mounteds, 209 were dead or wounded. The gains were minimal. Cox's Indians and the Connaught Rangers had seized the two wells on the plain, while on Hill 60 the Connaughts, the New Zealand Mounteds and the Australians held 200 metres of trench. These were the only successes in the battle. On the plain to the north, 9th Corps had been thrown back onto its start line with heavy casualties and nothing to show.

Hamilton recorded: 'Suvla gone wrong again. ANZAC right … The Indian Brigade have seized the well at Kabak Kuyu, and that fine soldier, Russell, fixed himself into Kaiajik Aghala and is holding on there tooth and nail.'[7]

It was Hamilton's only success. The few survivors of the Otagos and Canterburys held Hill 60 and engineers linked the trenches there with the lines on Damakjelik Bair. Sergeant J. Wilson led one of the parties strengthening the line: 'At 7.00 p.m. we went out in front of Turkish trenches and put out trench wire and trip wires to prevent Turks from creeping up in the dark and throwing bombs into our trenches. We had a covering party of Gurkhas out in front. They lay on the ground in front of us in dead silence and we nudged them along as we progressed with the wiring. We were not

A machine gunner of the New Zealand Mounteds, carrying the barrel of a Maxim gun, doubles forward over open ground covered by Turkish snipers during the August offensive. *(WF-002415-27, Annabell Album, NAM Waiouru)*

attacked and had to stretch the wires over the dead bodies of Australians and Turkish troops. I had to peg some trench wire right across the charred corpse of an Australian. There were dozens of bodies, mostly Australians, and as they had been lying there for nearly a week, it was like a charnel house and the stench was awful. There was also the dead body of a German officer right in front of the trench. It took us until 10.30 p.m. to finish, when we went back with the Gurkhas, and joined them in a drink of tea and some of their chapatees, made of ground rice, curry, etc and baked very thin. Quite good.'[8]

The battle for Hill 60 was not over. The crest was still in Turkish hands, and this minor operation to secure the flank of a now failed attack gained a momentum of its own. It was now seen as even more important to gain the knoll to ensure the security of the junction between Suvla and Anzac.

On 23 August, the Auckland and Wellington Mounteds relieved the Canterburys and Otagos. There was to be another effort to seize the hill. Major George King NZSC now commanded the Auckland Mounted Rifles: 'On 25th we got orders from Gen. Cox who commands this Section (No. 5) to attack the rest of Hill 60 on the night of 26th. Our Bde [Brigade] was to find 300 men (which was all the fit men we had) and we were to be assisted by the 18th Australian Battalion and the Connaught Rangers (K's Army) so we spent all afternoon having a good look at the position from every available place, and trying to locate all the Turk trenches.'[9]

Finding sufficient numbers to make the assault was Russell's main concern. Because of the maze of trenches on the summit he was determined to use those units who had been involved on 21 August and knew the ground. Sickness had taken such a toll that small detachments of fit men had to be made up from every unit into brigade groups.

Reinforcements had made up the mounteds once again into some semblance of fighting strength. Trooper J.W. Watson of the Auckland Mounted Rifles made a series of terse entries in his diary: 'Went out to Hill 60. Fifth Mounted Reinforcements arrived from Egypt. Squadron up to 72 men' [out of 150]. The next day it was, 'Getting shrapnel all day and bombs at night. Things are very lively', and on the day before the attack, 'As usual the old men [Main Body] are worn out. I'm still doing well but getting very thin.'[10]

Auckland could muster 60 fit men for the attack, Canterbury 90, Otago 50, and Wellington 100, a total of 300 out of 2000. They were commanded by the Boer War veteran, Major James Whyte, NZSC, of the Wellington Mounted Rifles. The recently promoted Major King was second in command for the operation.

As long as there was a 'stunt' on involving their mates, men were determined to stay and not be evacuated with the large numbers of sick. Sergeant John Wilder wrote: 'August 21 Saturday — Took quinine, rum and whisky before turning in last night and felt a different man this morning, thank heavens! Was lucky to escape the Doctor yesterday, he sent a big lot away — I don't want to go.'[11]

The attack would be carried out by three groups; on the left flank, a detachment of Connaught Rangers that would be 250 strong, in the centre the New Zealand Mounteds, 300 strong, and on the right the 4th Australian Brigade, 350 strong,

Body of a Turkish soldier on the trench edge, Hill 60. *(Gill Denniston Collection — PA1-o-863, Alexander Turnbull Library)*

including 100 men from the 18th Australian Battalion. The New Zealand Mounteds in the centre had as their reserve 100 more men of the 18th Australian Battalion. Russell wished to attack by night, and this view was shared by Monash and the other ANZAC officers. However, Brigadier General Cox determined on a daylight assault after an hour's artillery barrage, the bombardment starting at 4.00 p.m., with the troops attacking Hill 60 from three sides at 5.00 p.m. on 27 August.

Godley spoke to the Mounteds before the attack. Sergeant Wilder recorded: 'He was full of praise and soft soap, but it did not go down too well.'[12] The troops were under no illusions as to the job to be done. What they wanted to hear was that the artillery would be on time, and that they had the ammunition, grenades, and men to make the attack properly.[13]

The day of the 27th was spent in preparation. Sergeant Wilder wrote: 'August 27 Friday — We go for a flutter this afternoon. Just missed a trip to Alexandria, Colonel would not let me go, sent McKiver instead.'[14] This is the last entry in his diary. He, like many others, died that day.

Trooper J.F. Rudd was a reinforcement with the Canterbury Mounted Rifles and attached to the machine-gun section. He went forward into the trenches and recalled being told of the attack. He spent the afternoon preparing and cleaning ammunition and loading it into belts for the machine gun. 'Spent the afternoon doing it and when I'd finished I was sitting thinking. Jack Bendon, a very young chap came up in front of me. I thought he was trying to tell me something — he was as white as a sheet. Jack said, "I'm going to be killed this afternoon." I said, "A lot of us will be killed." Just as we went over he fell beside me dead. Ah, Hill 60!'[15]

Stretcher bearers from Otago Mounted Rifles with casualty. *(Gill Denniston Collection – PA1-o-863, Alexander Turnbull Library)*

Detailed maps of the Turkish trench system were issued to the attacking troops and objectives were laid down for each of the three forces involved. However, all the private soldiers knew, such as Trooper Bill East, was that they were going to attack a Turkish trench: 'We were told we were going to make an attack on the Turkish trenches ahead and we had been given the signal to charge. I was behind Major Taylor, Bruiser Taylor we called him, and he was carrying his sword. I do not think he was supposed to. When the word came to charge, Bruiser pulled out his sword and yelled out the word "Charge" and then next thing I knew he was flat on his face — he had been shot through the head — I could see he was dead. I didn't know whether to go back or to go forwards. I was right behind him. So I went forward and all the rest were coming with me across an open piece of ground. We were just anybody's mutton, and we ended up in the first of the Turkish trenches … We were firing as quick as we could, lined up in the trench, one alongside the other, and I was talking to a chap from the Canterbury Mounted Rifles, and I said, "What sort of an outfit's this?" He said, "Well, it isn't nearly as bad as Chunuk Bair." I said, "It's bad enough, isn't it!" Next thing I knew there was a blast from this gun which sprayed us with pellets which I got in the lung. I had to drag myself away — I felt myself getting weaker and weaker so I dropped everything and made my way to get out of it. Everybody was bumping past to get past in the trench.'[16]

The first line of Canterbury and Auckland Mounteds had gained their trench. They came under fire from the network of trenches beyond towards the crest and they threw out the dead and debris of battle. They were joined by the second line of Wellingtons and Otagos, who assisted the first line in consolidating their hold on the trench and then charged forward to secure the next trench line some 40 metres away. Each of the trenches was choked with Turkish dead and wounded. What followed was typical of the battles in France, with small parties of New Zealanders bombing their way forward around the angles in each of the trenches, and using bayonet, rifle butt and bullet as they fought their way through the maze towards the crest.

On the left, the Connaught Rangers were keeping pace with the New Zealand advance, but on the right, the trenches opposing the 4th Australian Brigade had been missed by the preliminary artillery bombardment. All the bombardment had done was warn the Turks opposite that an attack was coming. 'While the men in the advanced trench awaited the order to charge, hostile rifle and machine gun fire was tearing the parapet above the heads.'[17] When they charged the Australian line was swept away, two thirds being killed and wounded.

As the fighting went on into the night, the Connaught Rangers were thrown back on the left, and gradually Russell committed all his reserves to hold the crest. The men of the 18th Australian Battalion were used first, followed by the 9th and 10th Light Horse over 28–29 August. They fought themselves to a standstill until they had linked with the New Zealand position on the lip of that slight mound overlooking the plain and consolidated the position.

It was an inferno that consumed the last fighting strength of Godley's New Zealand Mounted Rifles and the 4th Australian Brigade. Those not fighting were too sick and manned the trenches. Those fighting were killed, wounded, or exhausted to the point where they too joined the sick. Regimental stretcher bearers made superhuman efforts to ensure that the wounded would not join the stiffened bodies beside the trenches or covered with blankets at the dressing stations that lined the route.

Padres like Dore, Grant and Luxford were selfless in their administering to the men. There was no room for differences of religion; care was given to everyone. The padres paid the price. Chaplain Major William Grant was one of these. On 28 August he went forward into the trenches on Hill 60 looking for wounded. 'The trench was full of wounded Turks whose wounds he dressed. Presently voices were heard down the trench and the Chaplain's companion said: "I think there must be Turks in the trench." The Chaplain answered: "Well, we'll go a little further, and see if we can reach them." The Chaplain crept forward to a bend in the trench. Suddenly there was a report, and the Chaplain fell forward.'[18]

Father Dore, the Roman Catholic chaplain to the brigade, attached to the Auckland Mounteds, was also shot when tending the wounded in the Aghyl Dere. Shot through the spine, he would normally have died as being too critical to move from any of the dressing stations along the route to the embarkation piers. But the stretcher bearers of the Auckland Mounteds, led by Trooper Foley, ignored instructions, carried him all the way to the beach and saw his stretcher onto the hospital ship. He died instead on the operating table in New Zealand.

During the battle for Hill 60 the New Zealand hospital ship *Maheno*, which had been commissioned by the New Zealand government, arrived off Anzac. John Duder was the *Maheno*'s First Officer: 'We have a lighter alongside with the first wounded, poor chaps they all look very bad … We have 50 wounded on board now … two poor fellows aged 21 and 26 passed away half an hour after they came on board, one was shot by shrapnel in the neck and the piece I travelled down his body and lodged in his groin. The other poor fellow had his leg blown off at the knee … he fought hard but we all knew he must die. Our priest tried to comfort him and his last words were for his girl. He asked the priest to write to her … but the horrible part about the poor men is that they are all run down and as soon as they receive a bad wound, mortification sets in. Dr Simpson says that before tomorrow night 20 or more of the severe[ly] wounded will die.'[19]

What shocked the New Zealand nurses and crew most was the state of the men. 'Reading the newspapers only gives a very small idea of what our men are putting up with … All the men that we have on board now are, apart from wounds, just wasted away and broken down for the want of food and rest … '[20]

The surviving Mounteds had little faith. Kitchener's New Army was looked on with distrust. Only the veteran brigades were good enough — Monash's 4th Australians, the Light Horse and themselves. At the end of August there were few enough of these veterans left. Trooper J .W. Watson recorded the last stages of the battle for Hill 60.

'Sun 29 August — Making the captured trenches secure. Our men very bitter against the English troops. Had they come at once we would not have lost so many men. Very solid bomb fight.

'Monday 30 August — Relieved out of trenches by Australian Infantry. Done completely — 21 left out of about 70 men. Was promoted to Corporal. Australian Light Horse charged the trenches on our right at 1230. Last light, our line is straight. We gained about 400 acres in four days fighting, 1000 men killed and wounded. Land is very dear here!'[21]

The 400 acres was an optimistic measurement. Birdwood reported to Hamilton that the crest had been taken and it was seen as a tactical coup. However, the promised land was illusory. Hill 60 remained in Turkish hands and above its low mound and overshadowing the plains were the heights of the Sari Bair Range. Newly promoted Corporal Watson would find himself in command of a squadron of 21 men instead of 150. It was the same throughout the brigade. Bean wrote: 'The burden of the work had been sustained by war weary troops. The magnificent brigade of New Zealand Mounted Rifles, which was responsible for the main advances, had been worked until it was almost entirely consumed.'[22]

Two thousand seven hundred Mounted Rifles had landed on the Peninsula. They now numbered 365, and sick men were reducing this number every day. The Canterburys had 2 officers and 35 men, Wellington 6 officers and 122, Otago 4 officers and 56, and Auckland 4 officers and 136.

In the Roll Book of the Canterbury Mounted Rifles opened on 1 April 1915 are the statistics of the campaign, neatly written in red copperplate handwriting. It tells the story of the New Zealand Expeditionary Force at the end of August 1915.

Strength of Regiment as at 1 April 1915 date of commencement of regimental register prior to embarkation for Peninsula including 3rd Reinforcements, medical personnel, chaplain, dental surgeon, veterinary officer and Armourer	33 officers	673 ORs
Landed on the Peninsula	26 officers	459 ORs
Reinforcements arrived ANZAC at various dates	6	186
Total on Peninsula	32	645
Killed in action and died of wounds	5	108
Died of sickness	2	10
Missing	1	45
Evacuated to hospital sick and wounded	23	443
Total casualties	31	606
Regiment returned from Peninsula to Lemnos on 14 Sep 1915 for a spell and to be re-established	1 officer	39 ORs[23]

Many of the sick were unfit for further active service. As one leafs through the pages, the most common entry is: 'Missing Khiajik Aghala 28.8.15' and then written in red underneath, 'reasonably supposed dead'. Physical and mental exhaustion after the failure of August saw the disintegration of the original ANZAC Corps. During August the New Zealand Field Ambulance admitted 1435 wounded, but far more revealing were the 1693 admitted sick. Sickness from dysentery and enteric fever reached epidemic proportions. By 12 September the New Zealand Infantry Brigade, nominally 4050 strong, was reduced to 1050 all ranks.

The rolls of the 8th Southland Company graphically paint the destruction of the force. It had five officers and 154 men present at the start of the August battle. On 15 August the strength was two officers and 88 other ranks. By the end of August, despite returnees from hospital and its small share of the 5th Reinforcements, its effective strength was reduced to one officer, a lieutenant, and 40 other ranks. Every day men were admitted to hospital. On 11 September, the companies of 8th Southland and 10th North Otago were combined to give a total strength of 93 out of 450. These 93 represented a trench strength of 38, the remainder being detached to numerous other duties, such as batmen, snipers, miners, machine-gunners, trench mortarmen, signallers, runners, sanitary fatigues, stretcher bearers, ammunition storemen and perhaps most important of all in those days of declining morale, one man as regimental postman.

An RMO wrote: 'There is much enteritis among the men of this battalion, many of them come to me in a collapsed condition from strain and overwork … they are quite unfit for more work just now.' Another noted: 'The men have lost their old keenness for sniping and observing. They lie about the trenches taking little of their old interest in the business of fighting.'[24]

12

THE END

Goin ? Yes. But glad to go?
Glad? Well, 'struth I hardly know.
Wouldn't care if we'd put through
All the job we came to do.
Don't like quittin anywhere
Till I'm done. But wouldn't care
That much, if I didn't mind
'Bout the boys we'll leave behind.[1]

Of the 12,256 New Zealanders who had landed on Gallipoli in the Main Body and Reinforcements, 900 sailed back into Mudros Harbour. This figure includes men who landed more than once and it conflicts with total New Zealanders supposedly landed; however, the figure is based on known reinforcement totals. These are:

New Zealand landed 25 April–1 May	4444
Initial Reinforcements from Convoy	522
Third Reinforcements May	839
Fourth Reinforcements	2000
Mounted Rifles, four Regiments	2000
Maori Contingent	477
Fifth Reinforcements	1974
Total	12,256

Left behind on the Peninsula were the artillery, engineers, signallers, and the machine-gun detachments. Many of these were equally weak and exhausted, but they could not be replaced.

The 900 disembarked in Mudros Harbour at midday on 15 September and marched to Sarpi Camp. It was about five kilometres and 'normally the march would have been a pleasant exercise and even with full packs up we should have done it in about an hour. Men were so weakened though that no one thought of carrying anything and as to forming up and marching as a unit it was not to be dreamed of. Each one just did his best. A few of the relatively strong managed the distance in a couple of hours, but others in anything up to twelve. Some came in the next day. We were in an unbelievably bad state.'[2]

At Sarpi Camp they found more of the incompetent administration and neglect that had plagued the campaign. For a start, the camp did not exist. It was a bare site on stony ground with a scattering of marquees set aside for both brigades, but insufficient for even their sadly depleted numbers. As the men straggled in it began to rain. The first night of the rest period was spent crowded standing in the marquees. As no one had the energy to dig ditches, water flooded through and around them. 'We stood with our miserable handful of possessions hugged to our chests and waited for the downpour to cease.'[3]

Lemnos was an enormous hospital. Five brigades of Australians and New Zealanders had been withdrawn to reorganise and rebuild their strength: the 1st and 2nd Australian Infantry brigades of the 1st Australian Division and all of Godley's NZ & A Division, the two New Zealand brigades and Monash's 4th Australian Infantry Brigade. Together the five brigades did not total more than 4000 out of an original establishment of some 18,000.

Conditions would improve, but 'the watchwords for everything and everybody are "inefficiency and muddle" and red tape run mad'.[4] Even in October, 2000 of Godley's division were still without tents; there were tents available but getting approval was the difficulty. Brigadier General John Monash recorded: 'The Canadian Hospital evacuated some forty large marquees for huts. I sent to General Jackson, "Can we have these?" "Why certainly, if the hospital commandant approved!" "Yes, he would approve, if the ADMS did!" The latter said, "Oh yes, but better see Ordnance!" Ordnance said, "Certainly, but Commandant Mudros must authorise." Latter did so. We sent fatigue parties to strike and pack the tents, and we got transport. We brought them two miles to Sarpi Camp. We were actually in the act of pitching them, when peremptory orders came that the whole of these tents must be at once returned to the hospital.'[5]

Conditions were equally bad in the hospitals and convalescent camps. Ewen Pilling had been evacuated with concussion and dysentery on 13 August. 'August 16 — Our treatment turns out to be pretty rotten. Life does not promise to be very interesting, nor with the food we get will a man recover his strength quickly. Could they pump plenty of porridge, fresh vegetables, meat and good bread and butter into a man, he would soon be fit once more. But the food is only a slight improvement on the hard tack of the Peninsula. We have no money and the luxuries of the canteen are beyond us.' Canteen stores were available only for cash and there were no arrangements for pay.

'At pre[sent] I wear a pair of boots, short pants with two bulls eyes in them, a torn jersey and tunic and felt hat. These and my field glasses are my present worldly possessions ...' Even in the hospitals, beds and stretchers were in short supply: 'There are wounded and sick men here on the mend and all that saves us from a bed on the stones is an oil sheet.'[6]

But the men were used to muddle, and Lemnos offered peace. 'We cannot get used to the quietness and peaceful surroundings which seem weird.' The day before, the same writer recorded; 'It seemed very strange hearing no firing …having to dodge no shell, that it was hard to get to sleep … and in the morning it was something to once more hear the twittering of the birds.'[7]

Then pay was arranged for the first time since April and the men happily provided Greek hawkers with fortunes as they purchased bunches of grapes at a penny a bunch, nuts, chocolates and cigarettes. It was a time to visit other battalions, look for friends and try to establish what had become of them, to gorge on the unheard-of luxuries of fresh meat, eggs, condensed milk, and a ration of one bottle of stout between two men.

With money in the pocket and with room to stand without being shot at, gambling flourished. The ubiquitous Crown & Anchor boards appeared and crowds gathered for 'two up'. Gunner Edgar Hassell was recovering from dysentery: 'The convalescent camp was spread over a huge area and contained many thousands of soldiers. At the foot of the hill was a large salt water lagoon which at its deepest part was no more than three feet deep and yet it covered an area of about 20 acres. The infantry camp was across the other side. But the water being so shallow provided an easy means of getting over to the "two up school" … Even the nurses used to tuck up their skirts and wade across sometimes and on one occasion I saw one of them win over £70 in the "two up ring".'[8]

Although relieved from the tension of the trenches, men were still falling sick. They had hung on desperately to stay with their mates but now they broke down. Exhaustion and the change and richness of diet threatened to complete the total disintegration of the force. George Bollinger, who had returned in August, was now Regimental Sergeant Major of the Wellington Battalion: 'Over 25 percent of the men are parading sick, most suffering from terrific pain in the stomach. They seem to have broken up completely.'[9]

On Monday 20 September, the day retraining started in the battalions, he wrote: 'Our battalion fell in 62 strong. Our strength is decreasing every day, our sick parades being as large now as they were when we were up to full strength.'[10]

Godley was well aware that his New Zealanders were spent: 'We are sadly reduced … those of the men who came out originally and landed here on the 25th April are very tired and badly need a rest.' After the August failure he was conscious that as well as their being physically exhausted, the men's morale had plummeted. 'It is difficult to make the men all realise that we have got to stick it out, and there are some of them, who think and say, that it is time they were now withdrawn, and British Infantry put in their place.'[11]

Feeling was widespread among the men that they, and particularly those who had landed in April, had done their share of fighting. It was now time for others. Like their predecessors in the Boer War, they had seen a year of service, and were now due to go back to New Zealand. But it was not to be.

'The first jolt came on Sunday. We shambled out on to church parade … Fielden Taylor preached a sermon to the effect that no one had done his bit while he still had a leg to stand on. Hard talk to those who reckoned that we should be sent home.'[12]

This was followed four days later by an address from the divisional commander: 'General Godley did a great skite about the fighting we had done. He seems to think us as fit as ever, pictures us in the forefront of more slaughters and finally marches at the head of the remainder into Constantinople. I guess they will have to find a few more New Zealanders before that takes place.'[13]

'A proclamation of this sort was a bitter pill to swallow even from such a popular character as Fielden Taylor — from the General, it was the occasion of appalling sentiments in frightful language.'[14]

'From that point on the men viewed Lemnos as an opportunity to fatten lambs for the slaughter.'[15] Godley reviewed his New Zealanders again in November before they returned to Gallipoli. His remarks were equally difficult to swallow but ominously true. 'Make no mistake about it, men,' he said, 'this war is going to last another three years.'[16]

By November the food, the rest and a gradual training programme was restoring the strength of the men. Convalescents were returning and the arrival of the 6th Reinforcements, totalling 2464, slowly built the brigades back up to half strength.

Their arrival marked the end of a chapter. By the end of August, New Zealand casualties numbered 7067 killed and wounded and dead from disease out of a total of 7571 for the campaign. Although nobody yet knew it, the worst was over, and the character of the campaign would change to the monotony of trench warfare. The new arrivals knew nothing of Gallipoli. They had read accounts in the New Zealand papers and had scanned the casualty lists, but on arrival in Egypt they found Gallipoli to be a taboo subject, shrouded in official silence and rumour. Even friends they visited in hospital never discussed it.

Now the new arrivals, such as Alexander Aitken of the Otagos, met with the creators of the legend. 'I felt then, as everyone else must have, an obscure disquiet. Last Post had not yet sounded, it could not be as late as 21.00; yet the marquees were almost silent, voices were subdued, men could be seen through the flaps already under their blankets. There was not a trace of the animation usual in a camp until Last Post. Only one man had the curiosity to walk out a short distance and see us arrive, yet our arrival had been no surprise because dixies of tea stood waiting for us. No one had asked for news of New Zealand or Egypt. There was a mystery somewhere, perhaps even a disaster.'[17]

In the morning the explanation became obvious. The splendidly fit 6th Reinforcements found that these few marquees and these few men were the ANZACs about whom a story had gone round the world'.[18]

'These men ... were seen by daylight to be listless, weak, emaciated by dysentery, prematurely aged. They had suffered also in nerves. The pastoral silence of the ancient island was felt to be deceptive and sinister; it was unnatural to walk abroad at large without the fear of sudden death ... I noted the startling transformation of old friends. There was Paine, known at school only a few years before, last seen among the 5th Reinforcements, as they marched out of Trentham on 12th June to the music of regimental bands; now hardly recognisable, his hollow face matching in colour his sun faded tunic and forage cap; yet he was among the least debilitated ... It was significant that the prime cause, Gallipoli, was under a taboo and barely mentioned.'[19]

The New Zealand Expeditionary Force by now was mainly made up from the 3rd, 4th and 5th reinforcements that had joined it at Gallipoli. There were very few of the Main Body left. The Wellington Battalion had 15 and it was the same throughout the brigades, as Cecil Malthus recorded. 'I think I am the only Main Body man in the company now. The new reinforcements are very friendly, a fine lot in every way. Being Main Body, I find I am regarded, in spite of my weak and wan condition, with a rather amusing mixture of sympathy and awe.'[20]

The arrival of the 6th Reinforcements also marked a change in the character of the force. Though they arrived in regimental lots still with the identifying number of the provincial battalion, they had been drawn from throughout the country. Godley's quota system had broken down; Otago and the rural areas could not keep up with the insatiable demand for reinforcements. They no longer sailed as Otago, Canterbury, Wellington and Auckland 'boys'; they were just 'New Zealanders'.

Godley was loath to see the provincial link die. He wrote to Allen: 'It used to make me very indignant in New Zealand to see that the South African Contingents had no connection with our Citizen Army and altogether looked upon themselves and were looked upon as a thing apart ...

'It is a great pity, and both Johnston and Russell and several of the Commanding Officers have approached me about it, and have asked me to urge upon you the desirability of sticking to a system on which the whole force was planned, namely that each existing Regiment of the New Zealand Citizen Army should furnish its quota to the Expeditionary Force ...'[21]

The regiments would retain their provincial names and a strong regimental spirit, but from the 6th Reinforcements on, reinforcements were really a manpower pool to be allotted to units as required. From the 10th Reinforcements on, the identifying unit number was dropped from the regimental number (see Appendix III). The arrival of the 6ths also marked the end of war service for most of the Main Body of the New Zealand Expeditionary Force, who had sailed away from New Zealand in the heady days 12 months before. Already 2500 New Zealanders were dead, 2233 had returned to New Zealand by the end of October permanently unfit for further active service, and thousands were in hospital or convalescing.

The new arrivals who replaced the veterans of ANZAC had very little awareness of what had gone before. Little was said. The history of the campaign was visible in the eyes of the survivors and in their obvious physical exhaustion. There was a distance between the survivor engrossed in the miracle of living, and the still enthusiastic reinforcement. For newcomers, the other measure of the campaign was the disintegrating mounds of mummified bodies on the seaward slopes of Chunuk Bair.

Sir Heaton Rhodes, a member of Massey's cabinet, visited Gallipoli in this period to satisfy the public clamour at home. He went to Mudros and saw the men. Much of what was lacking at Anzac, rest and food, was now being provided. Rhodes assured the New Zealand government of this, and so allowed Godley to tell Allen how well the men were now being provided for:

'As regards to your cable re our men having been continuously on the Peninsula without rest it is of course quite untrue. Two battalions were at Imbros in July, and the whole of both the Mounted Rifles and Infantry Brigades have been at Mudros now for more than two months. The Artillery Engineers, Army Service Corps and medical services have all also had in relays a good spell of rest off the Peninsula. Altogether, both as regards food and rest, I don't suppose any army in the history of the world before has ever had so much of these two commodities.'[22]

The stay at Lemnos had achieved its purpose. Rest, food and a gradual build-up in training improved the health of the men. By October it was 'Parades as usual. The afternoons are always free. Complaints are being frequently received about the behaviour of our troops on the island and the Authorities are making all sorts of threats. The whole division was (to be) inspected today by General Godley but at the last minute was cancelled.' The inspection was held the following day: 'He simply walked through the lines and had nothing to say. We are back on biscuit rations today but the Old Body swear that as long as they have a sixpence in their pockets they will not eat an Army biscuit.'[23]

By the beginning of November, the men were bored. 'We are getting impatient about moving off. The novelty of life here is completely worn off. The men have picked up a lot in health, evidence of which is shown by the vigorous way they pursue football, etc.'[24]

On 8–9 November the New Zealand brigades returned to the Peninsula. They were still well below full strength. Russell's Mounted Rifle Brigade, including the Otago Mounted Rifles, was 1400 strong. Johnston's New Zealand Infantry Brigade, including the Maoris, was 2200 strong.*

The engineers had also been rested and had returned to Gallipoli on 17 October: 'Up at 4.00 a.m. breakfast 5.30 a.m. which I had to prepare for the officers. Left camp at 7.00 a.m. marching to and reaching West Mudros about 9 a.m., leaving the paddleboat for HMS *Partridge* which moved away at 4.00 p.m. After our spell it was hard to realise we were once more to face the music and we were only too soon to face the guns once again. As we neared Gallipoli the reports grew louder and louder and we could plainly see the flashes of guns and shells, while miles away. Arrived at Anzac at 10.00 p.m. disembarked, lining up on the beach and marching in open order to No. 2 Outpost, this time taking the beach nearly all the way. At 11.00 p.m. we bivvied for the night. Heavy rain falling and having to sleep in the mud and slush — wet through and miserable. We soon got our rechristening for one or two of our number were knocked out.'[25]

The landings were mainly uneventful — the 'pit pot' of rifle fire overhead, and one or two casualties from spent bullets. Only Lieutenant Colonel Herbert Hart, now

---

* Godley divided the Maori Contingent between the four battalions of the Infantry Brigade, a half company to each battalion. Four Maori officers were sent home for unsatisfactory conduct during the August offensive. It appears the fault was both with the initial methods of selection and the personality and command style of the Contingent Commanding Officer, Lieutenant Colonel A.H. Herbert NZSC. This caused an outcry among Maori tribes in New Zealand. See Christopher Pugsley, *Te Hokowhitu A Tu*, Reed, Auckland, 1995.

Commanding Officer of the Wellington Battalion, recorded a major disaster: 'During unloading a sling broke and a Vickers machine gun and a box of mess stores (which included a couple of bottles of Johnny Walker) were dropped into the sea and lost, whereupon we nearly wept tears of blood.'[26]

The brigades found themselves on the new ground to the north of Anzc, which had been won in the August offensive. The Infantry reoccupied Rhododendron Ridge, Cheshire Ridge and the Apex, while the Mounted Rifles occupied the upper ridges of the Damakjelik Bair. The 2nd Australian Division, the previous occupants, had worked hard. For the old hands, it was a different Gallipoli. 'Huge improvements have been made here. The quarters are comfortable, being dug into the sides of the saps and they are also rainproof. Good rations were issued today, plenty of water is supplied.'

For the new arrival it was still the first experience of war: 'We landed in the dark, just in the midst of what the old soldiers call a "demonstration" … well I must admit that fear dominated most feelings for at least half an hour after.'[27]

It was also their first experience of shelling and it was obvious that Bulgaria's entry into the war on Germany's side had increased the flow of howitzers and supply of ammunition to the Turkish positions, as the newly arrived Private J. Johnson of the Otagos experienced. 'Soon as a shell whizzed past … we new men started fearingly, though its destination was a mile off … I found myself very unwilling to move … at all, but in the afternoon took my turn to go for water in which journey I got my baptism of fire. My course lay down the gully, then along the beach "sap" to No. 2 Post — an open space and then down a long sap at right angles out onto the beach to tanks, almost to the very sea itself. Well, when near No. 2 Post, the Turks started a fierce shelling with both high explosive shells and shrapnel, and it went strong for an hour or so … Meanwhile I had gradually by short runs and creeps (not altogether necessary, but I was afeared and the snipers were busy on the sap down to the tanks) got down and filled the bottles. I was tempted to turn back without doing so but felt that was rank cowardice! and gradually worked back up the sap in an awful funk, sweating profusely in the head for I could see some shells landing and tossing up bivvies, and I could hear all the shells coming — the HE ones always come slowly with an awful hiss, and I didn't know where the next one was going to land: a shell or bullet always sounds nearer than it really is. Yes I was just done and exhausted when I got back about 1600 and wanted nothing but to rest.'[28]

Both old hands and new quickly adapted to life in the trenches. Saps and trenches were now 2.5–3 metres deep and climbed tortuously up the ridges along the paths won in August. Except for the Apex, where the trenches to the Turkish blockhouse on the Pinnacle were 30 metres apart, and at Hill 60, where opposing trenches were ten metres apart, the deep gullies on the Kaiajik Dere, Aghyl Dere and Sazli Beit Dere separated the opposing front lines. Above them the heights of Sari Bair were lined with the brown earth of recent digging, and the forward slopes of Chunuk Bair were festooned with barbed wire barricades. For both sides it was dig, tunnel, watch and wait.

The high expectations of the Gallipoli enterprise had foundered. Britain's experiment in traditional maritime strategy had failed and the Western Front had again become paramount. Gallipoli was now an embarrassing backwater, expensive in men, material and effort and difficult to shrug off.

French efforts in Salonika had forced Hamilton to surrender three divisions to the Salonika Expeditionary Force, and on the Peninsula there were no thoughts of further offensives. Both sides were well aware that the Allied Forces at Helles, Anzac and Suvla were bottled up. Godley wrote to Allen: 'I am afraid there is little doubt that we shall winter here. The failure of the 9th Corps to take advantage of our desperate fight from the 6th to the 10th, and so push on our left has produced another stalemate, and it does not seem likely that we shall now get sufficient reinforcements before the winter to do anything more. The prospect of wintering here is not a pleasant one, but I have no doubt we shall manage it somehow.'[29]

In the Balkans, Serbia had fallen and there was a direct route for German howitzers and munitions to Turkey. Digging to defeat this threat was the priority: 'Wright and I in our spare time worked hard at a new bivvy — everybody was doing the same. We first made terraces and then went in as far as possible, getting at least 15' of rock overhead to be safe against the heavy shells which were expected before long. We called these "funk holes", a name however very unpopular with our Colonel, who decried its use.'

The Apex was considered the most vulnerable and dangerous post in the division's area. The crowded scenes on the Apex in August had given way to tunnel and sandbag with no movement above ground. Defences included an array of five machine guns, four mortars, and a local improvisation of four catapults that would throw grenades either singly or in volleys. The Wellingtons manned the Apex with the Otagos. Lieutenant Colonel Hart wrote: 'I am surrounded by a perfect maze of trenches, the front lines on three sides of my bivouac being only 25 yards distant, and the Turk trenches a further 49 yards away. Three or four times a day I run along the firing line to ensure that all is correct and everyone alert.

'Rifle fire, shelling and bombing go on incessantly day and night, but one hardly notices it except during occasional heavy bursts.

'Most of the men are accommodated in dugouts or recesses, undercut at the bottom of gaps or communication trenches 8 or 9 feet below the surface. Each dugout is 10 feet long with two side recesses on each side thus. This holds eight men, two in each side recess. Each recess is 3'6" high, 3'6" wide, 6' long, so the men have to lie down always. The food and water supply is most difficult. It is all packed on mules along the beach at night, and up the dere to a point about 250 yards below the summit of the Apex, the last part being too steep for mules. The cookhouses are located there and at each meal men are detailed to carry the dixies of stew, tea, etc up the steep saps to the trenches, and it is very heavy and tiring work.'[30]

Life in the trenches was the routine of eight hours on and sixteen hours off. Those in the support and reserve trenches were on fatigues, carrying parties for food and water, digging parties for dugouts and saps, or assisting engineers remove the spoil from the tunnels which, as at the old Anzac lines, worked their way forward under the Turkish trenches opposite the Apex.

'It is rather weird to listen to the pick pick of the Turkish miner not many feet away, to see some of our men at the end of a sap, listening, which goes on for 24 hours a day and to see others preparing a charge to blow up the Turk while at the same time one wonders if he is doing likewise.'[31]

Casualties were few. In the six weeks the Wellington Battalion manned the Apex, five men were killed and 17 men were wounded. In the months of November and December, New Zealand casualties totalled 27 killed, 25 dead from wounds, 53 dead from disease and 125 wounded. Many who died of wounds and disease had been among those evacuated in August and September. By contrast, the Australians, with two divisions as well as brigades in the NZ & A Division, suffered a total of 390 killed, 308 dead from disease and 1129 wounded. On 29 November alone, Turkish shelling of Australian positions at Lone Pine killed 58 and wounded 204. It was an ominous indication of the growing power of the Turkish artillery.

Sickness had declined with the onset of the colder weather. 'The flies were mostly dead though the lice, much stouter hearted, went on with undiminished vigour.'[32] Diary entries record this period as one long anticlimax. 'Nov 2 — Hardly know a war is on today — very little firing', and, 'Nov 8 — Getting quite stale doing nothing.'[33] They were 'Quiet Days', and the Turkish lines, now manned by second-rate troops, were happy to live and let live.

On 16 October, Hamilton was replaced by General Sir Charles Monro. C.E.W. Bean saw Hamilton the day he left: 'The poor old chap looked to me very haggard — almost broken up; so were some of the staff. They told us privately that the telegram had only come the day before in a cypher telegram.

'It is rather fault of character than of intellect that has caused him to fail. He has not the strength to command his staff— they command him; especially Braithwaite, his chief of staff, with whom he is on the worst of terms, I believe, has commanded the expedition. Braithwaite is a snob — only a snob could support this lazy GHQ, and so far as I know he has only been to Anzac once … Hamilton has not the strength to give those with whom he is surrounded a straight out blow from the shoulder — however much the situation demands it.'[34]

Birdwood took temporary command of the force until Monro arrived, Godley commanding the ANZAC and Russell the NZ & A Division. In early November, Kitchener came to see for himself. Ormond Burton was one of the spectators: 'Down near the beach one day I ran into a scene of the greatest excitement. The area, though crowded, was not usually bursting with energy. Everyone seemed suddenly to have come to life. A platoon of Indian troops was drawn up in an immaculately dressed line, turbans at the right angle, tunics on and buttoned. No one had ever seen a sight like this at Anzac before. Some Tommies were almost as bad. All New Zealanders and Australians within sight and sound were converging rapidly on a point where a big crowd was assembling, the centre of which was moving slowly. Everywhere men were diving into their bivvies for cameras. In the centre of the crowd was General Birdwood and with him unmistakably Field-Marshal the Earl Kitchener. To any decently brought up English officer the scene must have been incredible. A Field-Marshal, one rank only below God Almighty, ringed by a crowd of privates, none of them in the correct military posture, hands in their pockets, commenting freely to their mates, moving only just sufficiently to allow the exalted one to make slow progress, and taking snaps of him under his very nose. Yet in a strange way there was no disrespect. The same men back at home at an agricultural show would have gathered round a super bull and discussed his points admiringly in much the same fashion.'[35]

Although the soldiers did not realise it, it was the beginning of the end. Kitchener recommended evacuation, but for the men on the Peninsula the main worry was the approach of winter: 'This morning was very bitter and reminded me of New Plymouth. The Turks put in a lot of heavy shells today, we are busy getting winter quarters ready.'[36]

There had been a storm in early October and the November weather got progressively worse: 'Thurs 18 Nov — The wind has been strong all day and the dust frightful. The men in the trenches had a bad time; we all prayed for rain and got it at 8 o'clock tonight. For fifteen minutes it came down in torrents.' The next day: 'The air this morning was thin, very thin. The last 18 months our blood has got very thin and we feel the cold.' By the end of November: 'Today has been cold and miserable and tonight snow is falling, a sleet having set in. Hardships have begun ... Mud everywhere and everywhere so steep. Taranaki cow yards are nothing to it.' And on Sunday 28 November: 'Several inches of snow fell last night and this morning; all day long a driving snow fell. There was no inclination amongst the men to go snowballing. We were miserable. No one had contemplated this. Trees, shrubs and everything are white down to the shores of the Aegean ... Perhaps it is well this has set in so early as it gives fair warning as to what we have to provide against.'[37]

Gone was the naked army of ANZACs, the cut-down shorts and bare chests. Greatcoats and balaclavas were the dress of the day. Men 'devoured bully beef and bacon in a way that would have seemed incredible a few weeks before'.[38]

The November storms had emphasised the weakness of the sea links with the Anzac bridgehead. Godley wrote to Allen: 'The gale which I wrote you about on November 19 veered suddenly round to the north without warning and caught everybody by surprise, with the result that a great many of the craft sheltering in Imbros were wrecked and when I was there a few days afterwards you never saw such a scene of devastation as the beach presented. A torpedo boat, a big water ship, trawlers, lighters, barges, picket boats etc. all liberally heaped on the beaches ...

'Our men did not suffer so badly as many, as we are so much on the high ground, but the valleys and water courses leading up to the hills became practically impassable, and they had to go very short of water for a couple of days. On our left, where we have the Indian Brigade, the ground low lying and the conditions there very much worse, and we had a good deal of frostbite. And further still to the left, and further North at Suvla, where the 9th Corps are, they had no fewer than 210 men actually either drowned or killed by frostbite or exposure, and had to evacuate 6500 in three days with frostbite.

'What our fate is to be for the winter is not yet quite settled. We are now anxiously awaiting developments and a final decision ... I am afraid we are too late to help Serbia,

Surviving members of the 1000-strong Wellington Battalion Main Body still serving at Gallipoli on 16 September, although many had returned to the Peninsula after being sick or wounded. *(L.M. Playford Collection – PAColl-0251, Alexander Turnbull Library)*

Lieutenant Colonel Herbert Hart commanding the Wellington Battalion in the snow outside his Headquarters at the Apex, November 1915. *(WF-002271-03, Wairarapa Archive)*

and our impotence here fills one with shame, especially in view of the magnificent gallantry displayed by these troops, and the frightful casualties we have incurred.'[39]

Planning for the evacuation had started in early November. Sir Charles Monro had assumed command of the Mediterranean Expeditionary Force and recommended evacuation to the British government. The British Cabinet, split on the course of action to take, delayed its decision until early December. However, on 4 November, Birdwood, as acting Commander of the Mediterranean Expeditionary Force, was instructed by Kitchener to prepare 'in concert with the naval authorities and your staff … in the utmost secrecy a complete plan for evacuation if and when it should be decided upon'.[40]

On 25 November, this position was confirmed. Birdwood was given command of the Dardanelles Army, Godley the command of the ANZAC Corps. Russell assumed command of the NZ & A Division, and Meldrum that of the New Zealand Mounted Rifles.

Colonel C.B.B. White, the Australian Chief of Staff to the ANZAC Corps, had completed the preliminary planning for the evacuation from Anzac. 'The principle on which it was done was to gradually trickle away the men, leaving the front trenches gradually thinner and thinner, and supports and reserves gradually disappearing, but to the very end, always holding the front trenches exactly as they were held with full garrisons.'[41]

Before any major evacuation of troops and equipment took place, White devised a scheme to condition the Turkish command to less activity on the Anzac front. 'At 8 o'clock last night we ceased fire for 48 hours, just as a ruse.' The troops in the trenches thought that the 'Silent stunt' was 'to try and make the Turks think we were evacuating from Anzac and thus induce them to attack'.[42] Turkish patrols investigating the silence were permitted to move up to the ANZAC front trenches and in one case into the front line, only to find the line fully manned. This convinced the Turkish authorities that the silence was due to ANZAC preparations for winter.

The troops involved, as well as the Turks, were kept unaware of the impending evacuation. The planning was confined to the corps commanders and their immediate staffs. From November, guns and equipment were thinned out on the pretext of reinforcing the Salonika front. White had planned, and Birdwood and Godley agreed, that over a period of ten days the 42,000 men at Anzac would be reduced to 20,000. During this period, most of the guns would be sent away, one gun from each battery remaining. The final evacuation would be completed over two nights: 10,000 would be sent off each night in three parties of about 3000, all the time maintaining an appearance of normality, and everything proceeding as usual with no unnecessary movement. The trenches would be held with a reduced number of men, but the same amount of firing carried out with rifles, bombs and guns, as when the full garrison had occupied the trenches.

From late November and early December, the men began to note the change in routine. On 12 December Private Johnson of the Otagos was at Anzac Cove: 'One funny thing I had noticed was a storeship loading heavy guns and also stores from a barge, not into it, which seemed unusual. At "home" people also knew something was doing. And that night as I was in the signal office at Divisional HQrs on a "run" I found them all conjecturing and comparing notes: someone else had seen guns going away and we remembered that for some days those who were near the Apex had been drawing our stores from the Brigade Reserve up near there and not from the beach as usual.'[43]

In early December, Turkish shelling increased all along the Anzac front. At the Apex on 4 December, 'the enemy gave us nerve racking entertainment today. At 9 o'clock they sent in 22 x 8" howitzer high explosive shells. The biggest we have had yet, they send huge bits of iron everywhere as the shell casing 1 ¼ inches thick breaks in thousands of pieces.' The Apex was shelled again at midday but, with the underground network of dugouts, there were only two casualties. However, Hart concluded, 'but a few days of this would send everyone nervy'.[44]

Despite the weather, the Turkish shelling and the increasing signs that something was up, many refused to believe in an evacuation. 'Rumours are becoming current that we are to evacuate Anzac, as many troops and some guns have already left Suvla. No one here yet believes it [as it] means throwing up the sponge.'[45]

Hart's view was shared by his soldiers. George Bollinger had been sent with a party to Imbros to buy canteen stores. His entries become a record of growing certainty and despondency: 'Sunday 12 December — Anzac Garrison Apex. This morning we returned to Anzac via Suvla Bay being told we would be unable to buy any canteen stores. It is ours but to do and die and not to reason why, but our minds think strangely and think one thing "evacuation" but I sincerely hope our thoughts are wrong.

'Monday 13 December — Garrison Apex. Intelligence department reports Turks have 13 in[ch] Howitzer in position also several more in Constantinople. Austrian Regt in Capital and Turks likely to make a big attack in the next few days. Otago Battalion and remainder of Maori Contingents moved out today. It is said they go to Imbros Island for a rest but take into consideration above notes and what does it suggest? Should evacuation take place you can imagine the feelings of the men left of those who effected the landing on April 25 last. Artillery was fairly active today.

'Tuesday 14 December — Garrison Apex. Everyone has fully got it into his head that we are about to evacuate Gallipoli. These times it does not pay to think. One would get despondent. The old hands are the heart and soul of the place. We are in best of spirits and make light of all rumours etc. Today we got out handicaps for the "Gallipoli Runaway Stakes" etc.

"Turks — 30 yds behind scratch."

"Wellington Battalion — scratch. Canterbury Battalion — 10 yds. Auckland Battalion — 1/2 acre. Otago Battalion — 2 days."

'This caused a terrible lot of merriment.

'Wednesday 15 December — Garrison Apex. We are quietly moving off. The weather is rough and windy. Tonight our battalion advance party moves off. Hawke's Bay Coy will be the last to leave. It is a sad business and should, I think, have a big morale effect on neutral nations. Everything is being done calmly and quietly and the enemy no doubt have not the slightest suspicion of any movement. We have not yet thought of our future destination. Will it be Egypt, Salonika, or England? Most probably Egypt to again meet our old enemy in the same place as we met him last February. We will not be terribly proud of our Gallipoli "Bar". Ours is not to reason why, but just to do and die; but who has blundered?'[46]

Even the men of the Main Body were now forced to accept the reality of evacuation. 'Fatigue parties and others who return from the beach tell the most weird stories about picks, shovels, engines, piping, iron, etc. being towed out to sea and jettisoned, about ordnance stores being opened to anyone and kerosene being tipped over huge stacks of supplies. Some of these are true and some not, maybe? However it can only mean one thing, evacuation. So all we have suffered and sacrificed here has been in vain, a most glorious chance in the history of this war, absolutely foiled and lost by the most absurd and ridiculous manner the scheme was commenced.'[47]

On 14 December, commanding officers were briefed in secret on the evacuation plan. On 15 December details were confirmed for the evacuation, and Godley issued a corps order informing all ranks of the evacuation. In the New Zealand brigades, advance parties of the remaining units were embarked on the evening of the 15th, and units briefed their men on the evacuation plan. The NZ & A Division on the left of Anzac would file down the principal deres to piers on Ocean Beach. The Australian divisions in the centre and right would embark from the piers at Anzac Cove. Everything was to a strict timetable and each party numbered 400 men, the capacity of the motor lighters or 'beetles' that were taking the men to the transports offshore.

Battalion orders were drafted to meet this timetable. The Apex was garrisoned by the Auckland and Wellington battalions. Hart's Wellingtons were 465 strong; 38 were sent away in the advance party. On the first night troops were to embark in two parties. The first, 141 strong, would move from the Apex at 8.30 p.m. The second, 45 strong, would leave the Apex at 10.45 p.m. and embark at midnight. On the second night there were three parties: A Party, 95 strong, would leave at 5.40 p.m. and embark at 6.30 p.m. B Party, 79 strong, would leave at 9.15 p.m. and embark at 10.30 p.m. The last to leave would be C Party, 67 strong; it would leave the Apex at 2.00 a.m.[48]

If necessary, C Party would stay and cover the evacuation of the remaining troops. Orders emphasised: 'All movements will be made expeditiously and in silence … All movement will be performed with no talking, calling out, smoking, striking of matches, or showing any lights whatever …

'Troops will embark with 150 rounds per rifle and two iron rations. Troops moving off the first night will each carry three blankets, that is 2 of their own and one belonging to men going the final night.

'The second blanket of the men going the final night should be rolled up, clearly labelled and sent on mule transport with the … parties of the first night. All troops leaving on the 2nd night will carry two Mills Bombs.

'On no account whatever, will destruction of ammunition, grenades, bombs, etc by explosion be permitted. No action of any sort is to be taken which is not normal. Preparations are to be made at once to bury or otherwise dispose of trench mortars, ammunition, bombs and other trench stores that cannot be carried away. No attempt will be made to remove large numbers of wounded on the second day. The following hospitals will be available: No. 1 Australian Casualty Clearing Station, No. 13 Casualty Clearing Station. At the camps of vacated hospitals and dressing stations, bandages and certain appliances have been deposited in the tents.'[49]

Heavy casualties were anticipated in the rear guard. In the Anzac area, 30 stretcher bearers from the two New Zealand field ambulances were to stay behind with the regimental medical officers and attend to casualties who could not be evacuated on the last night. Two medical units, the 13th Casualty Clearing Station and the 1st Australian Casualty Clearing Station, would remain behind at Walker's Ridge, near the pier. They had room for 2000 casualties, blankets, dressings, drugs, and food and water for 14 days. If casualties were exceptionally light the medical personnel would be thinned out. 'The post of honour will be given to the 1st Aust CCS: the first to land, the last to embark.'[50]

No one wanted to go. 'Well sir, I hope our poor pals who lie all around us sleep soundly, and do not stir in discontent as we go filing away from them forever.'[51]

Men in all the battalions, and particularly those who had been at the landing, demanded the right to be in the last party. Companies volunteered to a man. Those who missed out lodged complaints with their officers. All through the force, men were dejected at the thought of leaving. Hart wrote: 'It jars very, very heavily upon one. Hundreds have volunteered to stay and fight it out or to stay as a covering party to sacrifice their lives if required to get even with the enemy and save their pals. We do not like admitting it is a failure.'[52]

In every battalion it was the same. George Tuck of the Auckland Battalion wrote in his diary: 'I am no hero but I would sooner go over the Ridge in frontal assault with all its chances of death with honour than do this thing.'[53]

Joe Gasparich was also a member of C Party and wrote: 'We could not understand two things; one was withdrawing in front of an enemy and the other was leaving our cobbers behind. You don't know how that hurt the blokes. Only those who were there would know. We had been together so long and had been through so many things together. We belonged to one another.'[54]

For all it was the agony of pals left behind. Graves were visited for the last time, new headstones and markers erected and the surrounds lined with stones. The grief was not only for men: 'Today the artillery horses were shot. One despatch rider who gallops daily along the beach from Chailak Dere to Walker's Ridge went into hysterics when he was informed that his horse, which had been wounded under him three times, had to be destroyed.'[55]

The bitterness showed in many ways. Among those troops not manning the forward trenches or involved in destroying stores there were outbreaks of drunkenness: 'Hospitals on Flat already evacuated and we had orders to stroll across about one mile to hospital on beach and move about a bit to throw dust in eyes of Turks. Boys went over bringing back cases of beer, spirits and wine — about two or three kegs of rum — and we had a royal time. It was the same all over the position — boys the worse for liquor everywhere. God knows how we would have fared had the Turks attacked us while in this state.'[56]

Finally: 'Salmon found most of the boys drunk today and found also the hoard, so he and Sgt Jones smashed every bottle and poured the rum down the sap, thus making boys wild. Orders reached us that we were to move off at 8.30 p.m. After a makeshift meal at 6.30 p.m. we got ready for a move, falling in, all that was left of us, 17 in all. At 8.30 p.m. and after presenting arms to our dead comrades, moved off with rifle magazines loaded … We reached the embarkation point OK only once standing to arms as the Turks started some rapid fire and we thought we were in for it.'[57]

The 19th was the last night of evacuation. The thought of leaving hurt Godley as much as his men. Defiantly optimistic on how it would have gone, he wrote to Allen: 'This is probably the last letter I shall write to you from this place, as we begin to evacuate it tonight. We are all very sad at this, as unpleasant though it would be, we know perfectly well we could stick the Winter out better than the Turks, and that it is only a matter of endurance in which, even if we were not reinforced, we could defeat them in the end if we remained.'[58]

The evacuation went off successfully. On both nights the men stole away and gathered where it had all begun, in Mudros Harbour.

At Mudros, the fate of the rear party was on everyone's thoughts, as Ormond Burton recalled. 'Some did more than think — they prayed and prayed hard. I shall never forget Chaplain Taylor's prayer that night: we were holding a voluntary service in the open air in the dark. He spoke of his belief in prayer and asked our agreement and then he just wrestled with God for the lives of those men, our comrades, who were to leave Anzac that night; then as we sang "Jesus, Lover of my Soul" we felt it could not be in vain, that He would save them, and it was with great peace that we concluded that service with "Abide with Me".'[59]

The prayers and the careful planning were answered. On the final night at Anzac the parties faded away from the firing lines. 'At 9 o'clock we said goodbye to the covering party and filed down Chailak Dere. The night was very still. Scarcely a shot was fired and near us no bullets fell. In the brilliant moonlight every familiar feature showed clearly, the bends, the bracken, the forsaken bivouacs, the graves of men marked by gathered stones and the pitiful crosses of box wood, pencil marked.'[60]

Finally in the early hours of the 20th the rear guard crept away. Joe Gasparich was one: 'I came down — I got off my perch [the firing step] … I walked through the trench and the floor of the trench was frozen hard … and when I brought my feet down they echoed right through the trench, down the gully, right down, and you could hear this echo running ahead … Talk about empty, I didn't see a soul … It was a lonely feeling. Here I was on my own at last.'[61]

C Party, with its machine guns, marched down through the communication trenches, out of the gate in the wire at the mouth of Chailak Dere, where they were checked off, along to the pier onto the lighters, and out onto the warships and transports offshore. It was over. Godley left a letter for GOC (General Officer Commanding a division), Turkish Troops, Ari Burnu Front.

Soldiers at Anzac helping themselves to the supply dumps, which were thrown open to all in the last days. *(WF-002269-21, Norman Prior Collection, Wairarapa Archive)*

Self-firing rifles were set up to deceive the Turks on the night of the evacuation. Duncan Stout with his time-delayed rifle. *(Thomas Stout Collection – PAColl-4173-09, Alexander Turnbull Library)*

December, 1915

Excellency,

In withdrawing my troops from this portion of Ottoman Territory, I am glad to recall that the struggle in which for eight months past our two armies have been engaged, has been characterised on either hand by a scrupulous regard for the usages of civilised war. I am, therefore, fully confident that the Graveyards of British soldiers buried in Turkish soil will be respected by your troops, but I should be grateful if your Excellency will take measures for their special preservation in the territory under your command. They have fallen far from home, fighting gallantly in their country's cause, and deserve that a gallant foe, such as we have found the Turkish soldiers to be, should take special care of their last resting place.

Thanking you in advance, and assuring you of my highest consideration,

Lieut-General, Commanding British Troops in the Ari Burnu and Sari Bair Area.[62]

13

GALLIPOLI — THE NEW ZEALAND STORY

Men of our islands and our blood returning
Broken or whole, can still be reticent;
They do not wear that face we are discerning
As in a mirror momentarily lent,
A glitter that might be pride, an ashy glow,
That could be pity, if the shapes would show.
Allen Curnow, 'Attitudes for a New Zealand Poet II'

It would be 1918 before New Zealanders once more saw the Narrows. They were men of the Canterbury Mounted Rifles, sent with the 7th Australian Light Horse Regiment as part of the garrison for the Peninsula. Most of the time was spent searching for graves and trying to identify the skeletons that still littered the seaward slopes of Chunuk Bair. It was the first pilgrimage. Overton's grave was found and marked by an edging of stones. So too were the graves at the outposts.

There was little sense of elation, only a sadness and a longing to return home to New Zealand. Sadly, having seen and crossed the Narrows, more New Zealanders stayed behind. Today in the Consular Cemetery at Canakkale lie 11 of the Canterbury Mounteds, who died of Spanish influenza. Gallipoli was exacting its final toll.

Much had passed since the evacuation from Gallipoli. The years had cost New Zealand a generation of young men back to that Christmas of 1915, still remembered by survivors as one of the most bitter of the war. It had been particularly gruelling for the Auckland Battalion at Lemnos.

'On Christmas Day in the morning Major Alderman fell the Battalion in and told us that while he regretted that there was nothing for breakfast we were to strike tents, embark before midday on the *Morsova* where we would find Christmas dinner waiting for us. This was fair enough so we got to work with a will and duly embarked with some other New Zealand units. We settled down to wait with reasonable patience. All appeared to be going well because we could see and smell the preparations for what afterwards turned out to be the officers' mess. Minor murmuring began about three o'clock. About 4.00 p.m. some boxes of bully beef and some of army biscuits were dumped on the deck. Christmas dinner was served. When some optimist clamoured for hot tea the ship's quartermaster coldly indicated a water tap.

'The mood of the troops was bitter — blackly, sourly bitter. To make things worse flunkeys were running backward and forward to the officers' mess with dishes that fairly stank of Christmas cheer. Only on one other occasion have I known such bitterness among New Zealanders. The decks were crowded with men glowering and smouldering in cold rage. Fielden Taylor stepped out into the middle of it all and proposed a concert. A mutter of unquotable language went round. He called for a volunteer to give an item. More language and not much muttering about it. So in his high, cracked, and utterly untuneful voice he himself started to sing. If there had been stones to throw he would have been stoned on the spot. No response! So he croaked — again and again. After his seventh effort someone either thawed or could not bear to listen to the eighth. Another followed with a song. The crowd laughed at a joke, the gloom lifted, and the evening finished in a very happy fashion.'[1]

Other New Zealand battalions made sure that the gall of defeat was sweetened with Christmas cheer but all were conscious of a battle lost.

> *Dear Harvey,*
>
> *... The present state of things at the front have no interest for me at all, and for this reason. Gallipoli Peninsula was ours anytime after the attack in August last (if we had enough men). It's the same old tale, 4 men and a sergeant to do the work of a regiment, anyway it fed me up with war, and now I'm war sick and only want to get home. Don't mistake me I've not lost heart and I know that the scrap is ours, but at the present way of going about it, it has lost thousands of valuable lives and will cost thousands more yet ...*
>
> *Kia Ora*
> *Your affectionate brother*
> *Fred*[2]

Churchill's lightning stroke to shorten the war had failed. Optimistic from the start, the British government was dragged into a conflict the effort and cost of which were never appreciated. British expectations had focused solely on the fruits of victory, never on what that victory might cost. Gallipoli consumed men and material that were piecemeal, always too little and always too late, and that, if available to Hamilton in April 1915, should have given him the Narrows. In January 1916 Gallipoli was Turkish once more. Helles was evacuated in an operation as successful as the Anzac one. The campaign was finally over, the cost enormous.

The Turks and Allies suffered savagely, approximately 252,000 casualties each.[3] British casualties, including the ANZACs', numbered 115,000 killed, wounded and missing out of 410,000 soldiers engaged. Another 90,000 were evacuated sick. French casualties numbered 47,000, including 10,000 dead, out of 79,000 soldiers engaged. Within the British total the Australians suffered 26,094 casualties, including 7594 killed. Of 8556 New Zealanders who served in the campaign, 2515 were killed in action, while 206 died of disease and of other causes, a total of 2721; 4752 were wounded.[4]

The figures of New Zealand casualties include those who were wounded more than once; for example, Lieutenant Colonel Bauchop appears three times, as he was twice wounded before being killed in August. The brunt of the Gallipoli campaign was borne by a small number of New Zealanders. The 8556 New Zealanders who served on the Peninsula made 14,720 landings (see Appendix III). Men would be wounded or evacuated sick, then return again, and again. To the men on the Peninsula before August it must have seemed as if there was no escape, as if they were condemned to return to Gallipoli until they were killed or permanently maimed.

Indeed, the true cost of Gallipoli is not with the known casualties. For every New Zealander killed or wounded, another went sick, and by September 1915, attrition was so bad that there were more New Zealanders convalescing in England (2927) than serving at Gallipoli (2840).

For most of the New Zealanders who served at Gallipoli before August 1915, this was their only war. The majority of those who survived were back in New Zealand, permanently unfit for further active service, by the end of 1916. Private Newell was one of these. He lasted until the evacuation but, on reaching Egypt, 'saw Doctor who said there was nothing for me but hospital. All my joints stiff and sore and hands almost useless. Can only walk with great difficulty.' Five days later on 3 January, he 'saw Doctor … who told me I would never be fit for active service so guess that I'm about played out now'.[5]

Only a very small percentage saw service in France and Palestine, and these were mainly men of the later reinforcements. By January 1916, the original ANZAC was a figure of legend:

> Not many are left, and not many are sound,
> And thousands lie buried in Turkish ground,
> These are the ANZACs; the others may claim,
> Their zeal and their spirit, but never their name.[6]

But it was the Gallipoli veterans who provided the framework of experience within which to absorb the stream of reinforcements and the New Zealand Rifle Brigade that had arrived in Egypt by late 1915. In January 1916, the New Zealand Division was formed. It was made up from the original Infantry Brigade, which became the 1st New Zealand Infantry Brigade, and provided cadres of officers and NCOs who, together with reinforcements, formed the 2nd New Zealand Infantry Brigade (the New Zealand Rifle Brigade becoming the 3rd Brigade).

This was the 'national army' that Sir Ian Hamilton had identified in his inspection tour of May 1914. It marked the culmination of New Zealand's experience at Gallipoli, and appropriately represented our identity as New Zealanders. The division was commanded by Major General Sir Andrew Russell, one of the few commanders to emerge from the Gallipoli campaign with an enhanced reputation. Godley remained a Corps Commander of the II ANZAC, with Birdwood Commander of the I ANZAC. Godley would remain Commander of the New Zealand Expeditionary Force, as well as Corps Commander, for the remainder of the war, while Russell led the division in France and Flanders, and Brigadier General Chaytor stayed with the New Zealand Mounted Rifles in Egypt.*

Despite the 'ANZAC' label, Gallipoli cemented our identity as New Zealanders — a national army in miniature. The Australian Imperial Force grew to five divisions, and within the British Army there was the tendency to lump us together as 'Australasians' or 'ANZACs'. In 1916 the British Commander in Egypt considered merging the administration of both countries' forces. Godley's answer demonstrated how far we had come: 'It would not be satisfactory to the New Zealand Government that any office should be established for the combined Australasian Forces. This was tried when we went to the Dardanelles last year and did not prove satisfactory, with the result that last December the Australian and New Zealand [Administrative] headquarters were definitely separated, each under a Commandant, entirely independent of the other.'[7]

Independence and integrity would become principles to be jealously guarded by every New Zealand commander from that time forth. This is the debt that we owe Alexander Godley.

At Gallipoli, Godley lost the trust of his New Zealanders. The high standards he demanded in the raising and training of the force were not matched by his own abilities in battle. He failed the test that he had set: 'What is needed is that officers ... should understand clearly that they are, for the time being fathers and mothers to the lads entrusted to them for a brief period by the state. They must know each man — not the name only, but the nature of the man.'[8]

It was the man's nature that crippled Godley's development of understanding of his New Zealanders. They did not want the praise and platitudes that he gave in plenty towards the end of the campaign, and which had been so lacking at the start. No — they would accept him as a 'hard bastard' as long as he was a capable leader. But discipline without understanding bred resentment and distrust. Godley was measured by the New Zealand corpses lying forward of Quinn's and Pope's and on Chunuk Bair. Gallipoli exposed Godley's limitations as a commander in the field. He faithfully carried out, without question, Birdwood's directions but never added a personal dimension.

His diaries show a perception of the difficulties in hindsight, but never in action. Rhodes James refers to him as the 'Hunter-Weston of Anzac'. In tactical ability this is a fair comparison, but as Rhodes James also noted, there was a difference, because Hunter-Weston retained the affection of his men to the end. Godley's strength lay in the administration and preparation of the New Zealand Defence Forces for war, and

---

* Chaytor would later command the ANZAC Mounted Division.

in the mobilisation and administration of the New Zealand Expeditionary Force. 'I was appointed to command the New Zealand Expeditionary Force on 1st September, 1914, and have commanded it since and am still commanding it. I am still paid by the New Zealand Government, and, as regards the NZ Expeditionary Force am a servant of that Government.'[9]

The New Zealand Division paid a heavy price for the failure of the Gallipoli campaign. In France and Belgium, with the Canadian and Australian divisions, it became a spearhead force. Here, for three more bloody years, our small national army learnt well the full meaning of 'attrition'.

By 1918, New Zealand, with a population of 1,099,449, had raised 128,525 for service in the Expeditionary Force. Of these, 100,444 served overseas, 16,645 were killed or died of wounds, 41,317 were wounded, and 530 were reported prisoners — a total of 58,500 casualties. Only Britain mobilised a higher number of troops as a percentage of population: 11.2 percent compared to New Zealand's 8.9 percent and Australia's 6.8 percent. Casualties numbered 58.6 percent of the New Zealand Force, second only to Australia with 64.8 percent, and compared with Britain's 47.1 percent.[10] It was a terrible price exacted from a small country isolated from the events of an essentially European conflagration. The failure of Gallipoli condemned us to three more years in the mud and obscenity of France and Flanders. But never again did New Zealand troops stand centre stage or hold for a moment the power to directly influence the course of world events as they did on Chunuk Bair in those August days of 1915.

Initially, New Zealanders were more bitter than Australians about Gallipoli's cost. The British government established a Dardanelles Commission to examine the conduct and administration of the Gallipoli campaign. The high commissioners of Australia and New Zealand were members of the commission. In Australia there were strong feelings that it was disloyal to rake over the ashes while the war was being fought, and the Australian High Commissioner found pressing reasons for not attending the commission's sessions and did not sign the final report that was concluded on 4 December 1917.

New Zealand took a far more critical stance. The New Zealand High Commissioner, Sir Thomas McKenzie, included a supplementary report as 'I hold stronger views upon certain of the findings which I feel it is my duty to put forward.'[11] McKenzie criticised the lack of War Office planning in the campaign, the expenditure of lives instead of shells 'almost with futility' at Helles, and the maladministration of the wounded, recording the opinion of the Australian Surgeon General Howse, VC, 'That he personally would recommend his Government, when this war is over, under no conceivable conditions to trust to the medical arrangements that may be made by the Imperial Authorities'.[12]

It was an important stand. It marked one of the last flickers of independent assessment of Britain's conduct of war until New Zealand's Labour government in the Second World War.

Such considerations were beyond the realm of the New Zealand veterans still serving. The years of war would further reduce their number; Ewen Pilling, Jimmy Swan and Colvin Algie were among the many to die. George Bollinger, in his last letter before his death, wrote of how he hated the thought of returning to the trenches. This war took the best we had and sapped the spirit of those who were left. 'I could stand up to anything in the way of shell fire for the first couple of years but the last year or so was my undoing. Every burst used to set me all quivering and if Armistice had been delayed much longer I would probably have been a "shell shock" case.'[13]

The effects of war became a private battle that the survivors faced alone. Outwardly nothing might have been evident, but the cumulative pressures had taken their toll. 'I was in a hospital in England before coming back and then moved up to Kamo Sanatorium and I was there for seven months recovering from shell shock they called it? The effect of slaughter and death, and the smell of death and blood and people killed in the most fearful way all around ... so that one became over familiar with death. They were lying out in No Man's Land to begin with, then swell up, as you can imagine, the body would, and then after a time they would collapse slowly into the ground and Mother Earth would fold them into her arms once more and they would disappear into the mud. So you couldn't talk to people back home about death? Could they understand that? I don't think so.'[14]

The spirit and nationalism that bound New Zealanders together, first at Gallipoli and then in France and Palestine, were born of comradeship and of a 'tribe' assailed from without and knowing that survival meant living and striving together. 'Anyone on 15 September 1916, on the battlefield of the Somme, who at zero hour looked back and saw the whole torn earth filled with the files of the New Zealand Division moving onto the Switch Line and Flers was lifted into a certain ecstasy. He was caught up into a movement of people — for behind the men and about them were the hopes and fears of all New Zealand. But such happenings are costly and when in four years they have surged through the life of the community not once but twenty times there is at the end a mood of exhaustion.'[15]

Men lived for home, and thoughts of New Zealand kept them sane. They had endured much, and had established a sense of belonging and identity, but they had also seen this consumed in the years of war. Those who returned to New Zealand were shadows of the men who had sailed away.

The first Gallipoli wounded returned in July 1915. They came home as heroes to civic receptions and paraded through every town to cheering crowds. New Zealand was proud of her sons and anxious to show it. 'We must not let our welcome end here. I would not have these brave men think that when they leave this hall they will be forgotten. Voices: "No! No!"'[16]

But as the boatloads of sick and maimed kept arriving, to reach 24,015 by November 1918, the cheers and greetings were replaced by silent agony on the faces of crowds waiting for ships to dock or hospital trains to pull in.

Those who arrived were unlikely heroes, diffident and laconic, only wanting to pick up civilian life where they had left off. Too great a fuss was embarrassing, but after the first boatloads there was little fear of that. Brereton arrived in January 1916 with 120

The first Anzac Day celebration, 1916. Birdwood inspects New Zealand convalescents at Codford Camp.
(NAM Waiouru)

The unveiling of the New Zealand Chunuk Bair Memorial, 2 May 1925, by General Sir Alexander Godley, formerly commanding officer of the NZEF. Major-General Sir Andrew Russell is standing on the right. Sir James Allen, former Minister of Defence, is nearest to the memorial. *(IA 1,32/3/136, Archives New Zealand)*

Fred Rogers, who fought on Gallipoli with the Otago Battalion, addresses the crowd at the New Zealand Anzac Day Ceremony on Chunuk Bair, 25 April 1990, which was the 75th anniversary of the Gallipoli Campaign. *(New Zealand Defence Forces)*

wounded on the *Rotorua*: 'We were very displeased with our reception in Auckland, possibly contrasting it with our welcome in London. A stout sergeant major began by bullying the unfortunate men on the wharf, repeating as fast as he could shout, "Shun", "Stand at ease", not understanding that a man with only one leg can do neither and all of them were more or less crippled. Immediately afterwards a rascally expressman took me down for 7s 6d. We began to wonder if we were in an enemy country.'[17]

The cost of war tore the fabric of New Zealand society apart. Town questioned the effort of country, and country that of town. The cost was so high that no one could dare question the worth of the war. Minorities were persecuted and conscientious objectors hounded. Even the men at the front were not immune. Those with German names or relatives, such as George Bollinger, were subject to a series of police checks instigated by 'well meaning' citizens at home who wanted to be sure that they had not enlisted to shoot good New Zealanders in the back.

Gallipoli veterans found themselves strangers in the prosperous land they now called 'Home'. There was plenty of work for those prepared to get stuck in, but they could not. They were hospitalised or required continuing outpatient care. The years of prosperity into the 1920s became for them years of recovery from wounds or the after-effects of dysentery and disease. They were years of frustration and bitterness as well: 'Well you would go for an interview, everything was satisfactory until they saw your discharge certificate and that you were no longer fit for active service, and they would say, "Oh well, we will let you know" and they didn't let us know.'[18]

New Zealand has never lived comfortably with its heroes. Before 1914, such heroes won fame overseas, perhaps returned briefly to be idolised, then maintained their heroic status by going again. The heroes of Gallipoli were all too obviously human. When they came back they were far from heroic, and after all they were just the 'boys' who had been sent away. Those at home were quick to applaud their sacrifice, but also wanted it recognised that there were 'heroes and heroines' who had stayed behind.

The men wanted most of all to put the war and the memory of war behind them: 'For sixty years, of course, I hardly mentioned Gallipoli, even to my own family.'[19] But for veteran and bereaved, Gallipoli and its cost kept intruding for years after:

4th October, 1923.
re 11192 — McCandlish, R. — dec'd.

Dear Madam,
It is with deep regret that I have to inform you of the receipt of advice from the Imperial War Graves Commission that although representatives of the Commission have searched and re-searched the area in which the above named soldier fell the grave has not been identified. Exhumation operations in this sector have been completed as far as possible, and a great many New Zealanders who were originally buried on the field of battle have been brought into the central cemeteries, each reinterment being reverently carried out in the presence of an Army Chaplain. Many now rest in 'unknown' graves, which are being tended by the overseas authorities with the same care as those of our men whose names are known. Over each 'unknown' grave a headstone will be erected bearing the words, by Rudyard Kipling.

In Memory of
A New Zealand Soldier
Known unto God.

By arrangement with the Imperial War Graves Commission the New Zealand Government will erect memorials to the missing in selected cemeteries in the various theatres of war, each memorial bearing the names of the missing in the area represented by the memorial. The above soldier's name will be inscribed on the Missing Memorial to be erected in Chunuk Bair Cemetery, 1½ miles from the Landing Anzac, and I hope in due course to forward you a photograph.

Although exhumation operations have now been completed the
Commission is willing to make further search where additional evidence
of the location of a grave is available. Should you be in possession of such
information I shall be pleased to forward the particulars overseas in the hope
that the grave may be traced.

Yours faithfully,
Mrs M.A. McCandlish,
184 Guyton Street,
Wanganui.
Secretary[20]

Douglas Robb, an undergraduate of Auckland University in 1917, later surgeon and Chancellor of the University of Auckland, wrote: 'Almost a generation of the best young men were wiped out, and throughout my life I have been conscious of this deprivation. In all walks of life many of those who would have been the leaders were missing. The ineptitudes of the decades between the two wars, both in Europe and in New Zealand may in large measure be due to this. Not only these men, but those who would have been their children are missing, and we have had to do our best without them. It is hard to estimate what human loss and depreciation was the result of these experiences ...'[21]

In the grey years of the 1920s and 1930s, Anzac Day for the veterans took on increasing significance. In looking back on 'those years of insane destruction, it remained unhappily true, that for the first and only time, they had identified with a cause bigger than themselves and had known what it meant to be a man'.[22]

This was an identity that the veterans had experienced overseas as New Zealanders; it was something they could not find in New Zealand after 1919. It could not be shared, except in the fellowship of the Returned Services Association and in gathering each Anzac Day.

Anzac Day — the anniversary of the landing at Anzac Cove — was first celebrated in 1916 with a memorial service, and games and sports among the men of the Expeditionary Force. It became a day of increasing sombreness as the years went by, 'a day of wreaths, a day without work or play — even the hotel bars and racecourses were closed'.[23]

So it was that Anzac Day had two meanings for New Zealanders. For the New Zealand public at home it signified the legend created by Ashmead Bartlett's despatches, and a proclamation to the world that a junior partner in the British Empire had come of age. Anzac Day became the symbol of our willingness to share the burdens of Empire, and those that died were our payment towards this.

To the soldiers of the New Zealand Expeditionary Force, Anzac Day, or Landing Day, was a myth, as 25 April was Australia's Day. They deserved the credit for gaining that foothold, while the New Zealand role came later. It was a legend created by a naval staff officer when he included 'New Zealand' and 'New Zealanders' wherever appropriate in Ashmead Bartlett's despatches. However, as the war went on and the toll mounted, each Anzac Day became the day the nation remembered its war dead.

It became a symbol of something found in war, something akin to that expressed by a passage Malone at Chunuk Bair had marked in Ruskin's *Crown of Wild Olive*: 'I found, in brief, that all great nations learned their truth of word, and strength of thought, in war: that they were nourished in war, and wasted by peace, taught by war, and deceived by peace; trained by war and betrayed by peace — in a word, that they were born in war and expired in peace.'[24]

To the New Zealand soldiers, Anzac Day became the touchstone of an identity, a sense of purpose, a growing recognition of themselves as New Zealanders. It is true that it was a day of sadness, of men gone, but there was also joy and comradeship. Comradeship was vital because it made the obscenities endurable. It overlaid the bitterness and suffering.

Anzac Day was a day of shared experiences remembered. A day of competitions and sports, of a beer with mates, and a toast to those they had served with and loved. This was never recognised by the public at home. As time passed one only saw old men growing older and boozing after each Dawn Service. One could only ask, 'How could they dishonour the memory of the dead like that?' One never realised that, far from dishonouring, it was keeping alive, however fitfully, a memory that had been 'born in war and expired in peace'.

Anzac Day means much more to Australians. It was planned and largely fought as Australia's day. Today in Australia, 'Anzac' is another word for 'Australian'. Unlike the New Zealanders, the Australians went to war to live out a myth they already believed. 'Because of this, the war years magnified the Australian legendary image which became personified in the Australian soldier. Australians verified beliefs about themselves on a world stage.'[25]

Anzac Day is an Australian national day, a paean to Australian manhood. It is an image that continues to fascinate Australians. It was 'the proving of a nation's soul' and they celebrate it with a continuing stream of novels, plays, paintings, and films exploring their nationalism.

New Zealanders have never been so confident or prepared to subject themselves to such open self-examination. 'Anzac' as a symbol of nationalism was an image too large for most New Zealanders to absorb. Self-proclaimed nationalism was out of character and in the post-war years the country was still led by the men who had taken it to war in 1914. Both Massey and Ward remained fervent Imperialists, and an enormous gulf grew between the ideals they had fought for and the youth who rightly asked what it had all been for. Only the generation in between, those who had fought and wasted their strengths in war, knew what it meant to be a New Zealander and found it again in the company of their mates each Anzac Day.

> *A glitter that might be pride, an ashy glow*
> *That could be pity, if the shapes would show.*

Post-war years were years of conservatism, and the puritanical streak that is part of New Zealand's make-up showed in the manner of its remembrance of the dead.

There was no war literature as in Australia; New Zealand fashioned its memorials in stone. There was little encouragement to remember. Because of this, the Gallipoli watercolour landscapes of New Zealander Horace Moore-Jones are now one of the principal exhibits of the Australian War Memorial in Canberra.

Gallipoli stayed undisturbed: it inspired only a popular history, a place in the regimental histories, one novel and a handful of personal memoirs. It was only in the 1960s that all the books that had been written in the 1920s, or should have been written, started to appear: Alexander Aitken's *Gallipoli to the Somme*, Cecil Malthus' *Anzac, A Retrospect* and then Maurice Shadbolt's play, *Once On Chunuk Bair*.

We are now old enough in national terms to re-examine our history, to understand the carnage and admire the spirit which enabled men, through a bond with each other, to endure such conditions. What possessed and drove them still exists today. We are still conscious of our isolation and we are still prepared to set out at any excuse to see the world.

The first occasion after the First World War was the Chanak Crisis in 1922. Winston Churchill again raised the spectre of the Dardanelles and our government offered a force: 14,333 volunteered, 70 percent of them too young to have served in the 1914–18 War. It has been the same in every war since; it seems to be a New Zealand tradition to fight in foreign wars not of our making.

Anzac Day has grown to mean much more than the memory of a landing in the dawn by an Australian division. It is part of the story of our country at war, of the history of New Zealand for much of this century, and a symbol of a growing consciousness of our own identity. But Anzac Day, in terms of Gallipoli alone, better stands for another day and another dawn uniquely ours — 8 August 1915, the day we 'beheld the Narrows from the hill'.

Consciously or not, Gallipoli has etched its mark. Although the veterans remained in many ways a race apart, living for something they saw in their past, part of their experience eventually flowed through and was shared by New Zealand at large. 'You were comrades in arms, that was something you can't explain, it's between them and when you get back to your own country; become married and settle down with your families, that feeling simply grows in your family and it has that effect upon the whole community.'[26]

Our society today has been moulded by the Gallipoli experience. This was when we began to think for ourselves and for the first time to put New Zealand's interests first. We are the sum of what our soldiers did, what they found, and what they lost. It was the loss of innocence.

'It would make us grow up as it were — if you can understand the idea behind the thought of growing up.'[27]

APPENDICES

I. Prisoners of the Turks

Twenty five New Zealanders were taken prisoner by the Turks during the Gallipoli campaign: one on the first day, 21 during the battle for Chunuk Bair, and three during the attacks on Hill 60. All were wounded when captured; six would die in captivity, and one after repatriation. New Zealand's story of Gallipoli is incomplete without an understanding of their experiences in Turkey from 1915 to 1918.

Private William Robert Surgenor was captured in the crest-line trench on Chunuk Bair on 8 August 1918: 'Every man in the trench I was in was killed or wounded, including myself. I was hit in the mouth and leg. The Turks got into the trench and bayonetted or clubbed every man wounded except myself and Trooper Davis, Wellington. They eventually bayonetted Davis in the arm but did not kill him. They took my surrender. One or two of the wounded men made attempts to get up and they were immediately clubbed to death or bayonetted.

'They took me to a dressing station. We met some Germans, who seemed to make our passage pretty safe — a German corporal in particular. The Turks were not the good sorts I have heard them said to be. This corporal said he had been sent to the Eastern front for his pro-ally feelings. We went to a hospital ship and were sent to Constantinople. We were placed in the Maltese Hospital with Lt Stone, of the Worcesters. The treatment there was better than we expected. We remained a fortnight and were sent on to another hospital — called a punishment hospital. There Enver Pasha visited us and addressed us — he said we were under punishment because Turkish troops in Egypt were badly treated. The treatment he said would not improve, but would get worse. All the British prisoners were concentrated there. We had no beds and three men went to a mattress, with one cloth to cover them. My wound, which was very bad, was dressed once in three or four days. They only put iodine on it. One piece of shell was taken out of my nose. Their hospital arrangements were very crude indeed. One orderly

had to dress over 100 men — but he could not possibly get through, so a Norfolk officer used to help him. We have made a sworn statement about this hospital and sent it to the authorities. From this place we were taken to a prison in Constantinople and placed [with] about 100 men — in a small room without space enough to lie down. I was still under treatment by our own fellows, who used to dress my wound. The room was infested with vermin and very dirty, but nothing was done by the authorities to try and clean it. We ate our food there also. The food consisted of a dish of boiled wheat for every 12 men, morning and night. There was plenty of water. After a while I was sent to the interior, to Angora, and was a fortnight there and then went to Changri, marching for 100 kilometres. This march was a terrible business for most of the men were just out of hospital and weak, and were in consequence lagging behind. For that they were knocked about and badly treated. En route we were lodged in cow sheds, and Armenian churches, packed in like sardines. At Changri we were lodged in a big barracks which were infested with vermin. We had no soap and no changes of clothing. We did not work there. The only clothing I had issued during captivity was a shirt and a pair of socks. From this place I went to Belemidik, where I worked on a tunnelling job for a German firm, receiving 2/- [two shillings] per day. Our food was better. There I contracted fever and was sent to hospital at Afion.

'At Afion Camp the Turks took young fellows by force away to the officers' quarters. The chaps had no option. They would come back looking horribly ashamed and would talk to no one. At last one of them made a clean breast of it. It was reported to the Swiss Commission. I don't know what the result was. On one occasion two Turks tried to get me away but I knocked them out. The Commandant was the worst of all at it. Sometimes fellows tried to escape but they got "hell", and were sent to prison with the lowest types of criminals and diseased persons.

After three days I was set to work. The men on this job were mostly sick, and were constantly whipped because they could not do enough. The work was carrying stone. I had a couple of whippings myself. I could not retaliate — one received a great deal more. Some of the fellows struck the Turks, and they only got three months gaol, and it was terrible being interned in these places. The usual punishment was to put you into a dirty closet with a ration of half a pound of bread a day, and keep you there a fortnight.

This was their usual form of light punishment and it generally ended up with hospital. The insanitary condition of the place was too awful. I have seen a lot of Russian prisoners bastinadoed, but we British escaped that. Their screams were awful. From this place we went to Adapazari, working on the roads. We were lodged 114 men in one house whose dimensions were 30 ft x 30 ft. It was the dead of winter and we had no fires, and often the snow leaked through into the rooms. After a spell there we went to Sans Stefano and worked on loading waggons under German masters. I was afterwards put on to carpentering. One day because I was standing waiting for another chap to finish and enable me to get on, I was pounced upon and put into prison for two days with two Turks doing long sentences. One of the Turks had VD, and was treating himself for disease on the face. They used to have to urinate out of the windows and could not get out except when the sentry was present. The Turks also used to urinate against the door, and the condition of the place can be imagined. The German responsible for this was named Benemann. It was no use appealing to him. I had three days of this. I was at Stefano when the armistice was signed and got away to Constantinople.'

II. A Gallipoli Chronology

This is based on the Gallipoli Diary included in Major Fred Wake's book, *The New Zealanders at Gallipoli* (Whitcombe and Tombs Ltd 1919).

1914

June

28   Assassination of Archduke Ferdinand at Sarajevo.

July

28   Austria declared war on Serbia.

30   Preliminary arrangements made in New Zealand for the Expeditionary Force.

August

2   Germany declared war on Russia. Germans entered France. Russians entered Germany.

3   Germany declared war on France.

4   Britain declared war on Germany.

7   The NZ government cabled to the Imperial government offering the services of an Expeditionary Force.

8   British Expeditionary Force landed in France.

10   Goeben and Breslau reported at Constantinople.

12   Services of NZ Expeditionary Force (NZEF) accepted by Imperial authorities.

15   Samoan Force of 1350 New Zealanders and four guns sailed.

28   German Samoa surrendered.

September

24   Main Body embarked on transports.

25   Force ordered to await a more powerful escort.

October

14   *Minotaur* and *Ibuki* arrived in Wellington Harbour.

15   Main Body again embarked on transports.

16   Convoy sailed from Wellington.

21   Arrived at Hobart.

22   Left Hobart for Albany.

28   Arrived at Albany.

November

1   Australian and NZ convoy left Albany.

2   First shelling of the Dardanelles forts by French and British squadrons.

5   Britain and France officially declared war on Turkey.

9   HMAS *Sydney* destroyed the *Emden* at the Cocos Islands.

15   NZ transports arrived at Colombo.

17   NZ transports left Colombo for Aden.

25   NZ transports arrived at Aden.

26   Combined Australian and NZ convoy left Aden for Suez.

28   Received wireless to prepare for disembarkation in Egypt.

30   Arrived at Suez.

December

1   NZ ships passed through the Suez Canal.

3   Commenced disembarkation at Alexandria.

4   First troop train arrived at Helmieh station for Zeitoun Camp.

8   German naval defeat at the Falkland Islands. Australian Light Horse Brigade and Ceylon Planters Rifle Corps attached to NZEF.

12   British Section of NZEF trained on Salisbury Plain left Southampton for Egypt.

14   2nd Reinforcements left NZ.

18   Proclamation of a British Protectorate in Egypt; the Khedive Abbas deposed.

19   His Highness Prince Hussein proclaimed Sultan of Egypt.

23   March of NZ troops through the streets of Cairo.

24   British section arrived at Zeitoun Camp: 6 officers and 229 other ranks.

25   Christmas Day spent in the desert.

1915

January

18   Division named the 'New Zealand and Australian Division'.

25   NZ Infantry Brigade ordered to Suez Canal.

26   Infantry Brigade left Zeitoun for Ismailia and Kubri.

February

1   Advance parties 4th Australain Infantry Brigarde arrived at Zeitoun.

3   Turks attacked Suez Canal. New Zealanders engaged; one man died of wounds and one wounded.

14   3rd Reinforcements left NZ.

19   Naval attack on the forts at the entrance of the Dardanelles.

26   NZ Infantry returned from Suez Canal to Zeitoun.

March

18 Dardanelles naval attack. *Queen, Irresistible* and *Bouvet* sunk.

26 3rd Reinforcements, consisting of 63 officers and 2417 other ranks, arrived at Zeitoun.

29 Inspection of Division by Sir Ian Hamilton.

April

9 NZ & A Division, less mounted units, entrained for Alexandria.

10 First transports left for Mudros.

15 Transport *Lutzow* with Divisional Headquarters on board arrived in Mudros Harbour.

17 4th Reinforcements left NZ.

24 French, British, Australian and NZ transports left Mudros Harbour.

25 French landed at Kum Kale. British landed at Cape Helles. NZ & A Army Corps landed at Anzac Cove; 3rd Australian Infantry Brigade forced a landing at dawn. NZ Divisional Headquarters and details ashore at 10.00 a.m.; Auckland Battalion all ashore by 12 noon with two companies of the Canterbury Battalion; No. 1 Field Company NZ Engineers and Canterbury and Otago Infantry came ashore during the afternoon.

26 6.00 a.m.: two guns of NZ Howitzer Battery landed and came into action. Turkish counter-attacks beaten off at Anzac.

27 2nd Battery NZ Field Artillery (NZFA) landed at 3.00 a.m. Battle for Walker's Ridge involving Wellington and Canterbury battalions.

28 Portsmouth and Chatham battalions (Royal Marine Brigade) arrived 6.00 p.m. No.2 Company Divisional Train arrived at night.

29 Heavy Turkish attacks all along the Anzac line. Naval Brigade (Nelson and Deal Battalion) arrived at night.

May

2 Turkish observation post destroyed at Lala Baba by Canterbury Battalion.

2/3 Otago attack on Baby 700 fails.

3 Turkish warship in straits fired on transports; *Annaberg* hit.

4 Australian raid on Gaba Tepe beaten off.

5/6 NZ Infantry Brigade and 2nd Australian brigade left for Cape Helles.

6 3rd Reinforcements arrived at Anzac (839) — sent down to Helles. Combined French, British and Imperial forces commenced Second Battle of Krithia.

7 New Zealanders in support of 29th Division. Sinking of *Lusitania* in the Atlantic.

8 NZ Infantry and 2nd Australian Brigade attacks on Krithia defeated.

10 Australians at head of Monash Gully attacked Turks, but withdrew.

12 NZ Mounted Rifles (1500 men) arrived at Anzac to fight as infantry. General Chauvel with 1400 men of the Australian Light Horse arrived.

14 HMS *Goliath* sunk at mouth of straits. Queens-landers made a sortie from Quinn's Post.

15 General Birdwood slightly wounded in the head at Quinn's Post. General Bridges mortally wounded.

16 6-inch howitzer with Royal Marine Light Infantry crew arrived in support of the Division. Machine gun detachment of Otago Mounted Rifles arrived.

17 2nd Australian Infantry Brigade returned. Three guns of 2nd Battery NZFA manhandled up to Plugge's Plateau.

18 German Taube flew over Anzac.

19 Turkish attack at Anzac defeated. NZ Infantry Brigade returned from Helles.

20 Otago Mounted Rifles (dismounted) arrived (500). Turks first ask for an armistice.

24 Armistice day to bury dead.

25 HMS *Triumph* torpedoed off Gaba Tepe.

27 HMS *Majestic* torpedoed off Cape Helles.

28 Late at night Turks fire mine in front of Quinn's Post. Canterbury Mounted Rifles take Old No. 3 Post.

29 Attack on Quinn's Post. Major Quinn killed. NZ Infantry Brigade relieves 4th Australian Brigade No. 3 Section.

31 Turkish blockhouse blown up in front of Quinn's by two sappers. NZ Mounted Rifles (NZMR) forced to abandon Old No. 3 Post.

June

3 2nd Field Company NZ Engineers arrived (239).

4 Slight advance made at Cape Helles. Canterbury Infantry raided from Quinn's Post late at night.

5 Another sortie against German officers' trench opposite Courtney's Post.

7 4th Reinforcements arrived Anzac Cove (1761). Sortie from Quinn's Post night of 7/8th.

8 First Monitor appeared off Anzac.

10 Scouting parties of NZMR driven back to No. 2 Post.

12 4.5 inch howitzer taken from Howitzer Gully up to Plugge's Plateau.

21 French captured the Haricot Redoubt at Cape Helles.

28 Successful British attack at Helles.

29/30 The last Turkish attack on Anzac fails.

July

2 Determined Turkish attack at Helles unsuccessful.

4/5 Another heavy attack beaten off by British at Cape Helles.

10 Turks at Cape Helles asked for armistice to bury their dead. Armistice refused.

11 NZ Hospital ship *Maheno* left Wellington.

12 General Masnou, commanding the 1st French Division at Helles, mortally wounded.

31 200 men of the 11th West Australian Battalion took Turkish trenches opposite Tasmania Post.

August

3 13th (New Army) commenced landing at Anzac.

6/7 British attack at Cape Helles. Australians attack at Lone Pine, Quinn's Post and Russell's Top at The Nek. Old No. 3 Post retaken and Table Top and Bauchop's Hill taken by NZMR. Damakjelik Bair captured by Left Covering Force (Traver's 40th).

7 9th Corps land at Suvla Bay before dawn. Rhododendron Ridge in the hands of New Zealanders. Auckland attack fails.

8 Wellington Battalion captures Chunuk Bair. Reinforced by Auckland Mounted Rifles during day. Relieved by Otago Battalion and Wellington Mounted Rifles that night. New Army remains inactive at Suvla. 5th Reinforcements reach Anzac and go into the firing line.

9 Gurkhas reach the Saddle between Hill Q and Chunuk Bair. New Zealanders hold Chunuk Bair, relieved at night by New Army troops.

10 New Army troops driven from Chunuk Bair by Turkish counter-attack.

11 Stalemate at Suvla.

14 6th Reinforcements left NZ.

21 First attack on Hill 60. Italy declared war on Turkey.

26 *Maheno* arrived off Anzac.

27 Battle renewed for the possession of Hill 60.

28 New Zealanders hold and consolidate their position on Hill 60.

September

Troops withdrawn to rest camp at Sarpi on Lemnos.

20 Bulgaria Treaty with Turkey announced, thus opening the Balkan corridor.

29 British and Indian troops enter Kut-el-Amara.

30 10th (Irish) Division left Suvla for Salonika.

October

3 2nd French Division left Helles for Salonika.

7 Britain offered Cyprus to Greece.

9 Belgrade captured by Austro-Germans.

11 Lord Kitchener asked Sir Ian Hamilton the estimated cost of evacuation.

12 Sir Ian Hamilton replied that evacuation was unthinkable.

14 In the House of Lords, Lord Milner and Lord Ribblesdale urged evacuation of Gallipoli.

15 Britain declared war on Bulgaria.

16 Kitchener telegraphed recalling Sir Ian Hamilton.

17 Sir Ian Hamilton departs.

20 General Monro, in London, received instructions to proceed to the Near East and take over command of the Mediterranean Expeditionary Force.

23 Wreck of *Marquette* carrying 1st NZ Stationary Hospital to Salonika. Ten NZ nurses drown.

30 General Sir Charles Monro first visits the Peninsula.

November

2 4th Australian Infantry Brigade arrived from Sarpi rest camp.

10 NZMR returned to Anzac.

13 Lord Kitchener visited Anzac. Mr Winston Churchill resigned from British Cabinet.

24 Period of silence ordered, lasted 72 hours. Major General Russell assumes command of NZ & A Division.

26 Major General Godley assumed command of Army Corps.

27/28 Commencement of the Great Blizzard.

December

3 General Townshend besieged at Kut-el-Amara.

8 General Monro ordered General Birdwood to proceed with evacuation of Anzac and Suvla.

10/11 All sick, wounded, surplus troops, vehicles and valuable stores removed.

12 Announced at Anzac that a winter rest camp would be formed at Imbros. Surplus guns removed.

15 Detailed orders issued for evacuation.

16 All ranks warned of impending operations.

19 The last night of evacuation of Anzac and Suvla.

20 Evacuation of Anzac and Suvla completed by daylight. Troops disembarked at Lemnos.

25 Christmas Day mostly spent at sea on transports returning to Egypt. Troops transferred to Egypt between December 21 and 31.

1916

January

9 Evacuation from Cape Helles completed.

1918

October

31 Turkey surrenders.

December

CMR return to Gallipoli.

III. Gallipoli: New Zealand Statistics

New Zealanders landing at Gallipoli

(These are approximate as small numbers of New Zealanders were constantly being returned to the Peninsula after convalescence from Lemnos or Egypt.)

New Zealanders landed 25 April 1915	3100
New Zealanders ashore by 1 May 1915	4444
Initial Reinforcements from transports offshore	522
3rd Reinforcements for Infantry Brigade in early May	839
4th Reinforcements	2000
NZMR Brigade (four regiments) 2000 Maori Contingent	477
5th Reinforcements	1974
6th Reinforcements	2464
Total landings on the Peninsula by New Zealanders	14,720

Despite this figure of 14,720 only 8556 New Zealanders served on the Peninsula, so this means many of the 4th, 5th and 6th Reinforcements were convalescents who had already fought there and been evacuated with sickness or wounds to Egypt or England and were returning.

Where they lie

There are few known New Zealand graves at Gallipoli. Of the 2721 dead:

265	are buried in known graves or known to be buried in a cemetery on the Peninsula
76	are buried in cemeteries on Lemnos
3	are buried in Haidar Pasha Cemetery, Istanbul (Prisoners of War)
344	known graves

1669	lie in unknown graves and are commemorated by the New Zealand Memorials of Twelve Tree Copse (179), Lone Pine (708: also commemorates 252 buried at sea), Hill 60 (182) and Chunuk Bair (852)
252	buried at sea
2265	

The remainder of the 2721 lie in Britain, Malta, Egypt, Gibraltar and New Zealand.

New Zealand Casualties by Months for the Dardanelles Campaign 1915*

Month	Killed		Died of wounds		Died of disease		Total deaths		Wounded		Missing & Prisoners		Total Casualties	
	Offrs	ORs	Offrs	ORs	Offrs	ORs	Offrs	ORs	Offrs	ORs	Offrs	ORs	Offrs	ORs
25–30 April	8	267	3	75	..	19	11	361	26	672	..	5	37	1038
May	18	578	7	91	..	7	25	676	31	815	..	13	56	1504 ⎫1
June	6	57	2	73	..	7	8	137	29	516	..	..	37	653 ⎭
July	1	49	3	31	2	50	6	130	9	223	..	..	15	353
August	39	842	9	169	3	62	51	1073	100	2150	..	..	151	3224 ⎫2
September	..	6	6	27	2	38	8	71	5	123	..	..	13	194 ⎭
October	..	6	1	5	1	26	2	37	3	25	..	..	5	62 ⎫3
November	..	10	1	10	1	32	2	52	2	54	..	..	4	106 ⎭
December	1	16	..	14	2	18	3	48	3	66	..	..	6	114
TOTAL	73	1831	32	495	11	259	116	2585	208	4644	..	18	324	7247

* Major T.J. Mitchell and Miss G.M. Smith, *The Official History of the Great War: Casualties and Medical Statistics*, (HMSO 1932).

APPENDICES

Notes:
1. Decrease in casualties offset by increase in sickness.
2. Majority of New Zealanders on Lemnos.
3. Sickness also decreased. It was a different war.

Official New Zealand Casualties*

Figures in the previous table vary from final New Zealand official figures. These are listed as:

Killed		Died of wounds		Died of disease		Other causes		Totals		Grand totals
Offrs	ORs	Offrs	ORs	Offrs	ORs	Offrs	ORs	Offrs	ORs	All ranks
80	1829	29	57	5	195	..	6	114	2607	2721

Official New Zealand wounded number: 4752 (includes those wounded more than once).

Summary of Statistical Information, New Zealand Expeditionary Force (15/11/1914)**

I.	Strength of Force (all ranks)		8417
II.	Those with previous military training		
	(a)	Serving at time of enlistment	
		(1) In Permanent Forces of Dominion	214
		(2) In Territorial Force, including Unattached List	3602
		(3) General Training Section and Rifle Clubs	174
		(4) Regular Army	53
		(5) Home Territorials	33
		Total	4076
	(b) Not serving at time of enlistment but previously serving in		
		(1) Regular Army	271
		(2) Home Territorials	289
		(3) Permanent Forces of Dominion	14
		(4) Territorial Force and Rifle Clubs	515
		(5) Volunteers	1543
		(6) Foreign or other Dominion Forces	217
		Total	2849
		Total with previous military training	6925
III.	Those without previous service		1492
IV.	Those with war service		432
V.	Musketry qualifications of Mounted Rifles and Infantry		
	(a)	Marksmen	721
	(b)	Qualified	2415
	(c)	Not qualified	765
	(d)	Not completed	2042
	(e)	Not classified	1043
VI.	Ages		
	(a)	Under 21	1614
	(b)	21 and under 25	3686
	(c)	25 and under 40	3528
	(d)	40 and over	89
VII.	Family Status		
	(a)	Single men and widowers without children	7922

---

* *The Great War 1914–1918: New Zealand Expeditionary Force Roll of Honour* (Govt Printer 1924).

** Taken from NZEF (1914) Europe War Diary.

	(b)	Widowers with children	25
	(c)	Married men with children	325
	(d)	Married men without children	145
VIII.	Religion		
	(a)	Protestants	7287
	(b)	Roman Catholics	977
	(c)	Hebrews	19
	(d)	Unspecified	134
IX.	Parentage		
	(a)	Born in New Zealand	6241
	(b)	Born in British Isles or other parts of Empire	2157
	(c)	Naturalised British subjects	19

First World War New Zealand Expeditionary Force: key figures prefixed to regimental numbers

1. Samoan Advance
2. Artillery
3. New Zealand Medical Corps
4. Engineers
5. Army Service Corps
6. Canterbury Infantry
7. Canterbury Mounted Rifles
8. Otago Infantry
9. Otago Mounted Rifles
10. Wellington Infantry
11. Wellington Mounted Rifles
12. Auckland Infantry
13. Auckland Mounted Rifles
14. Army Service Corps Divisional Train
15. Headquarters
16. Maori Infantry
17. Veterinary Corps
18. Chaplains Department
19. Samoan Relief Infantry
20. Samoan Relief Mounted
21. Pay Department
22. Nursing Service
23. 1st Battalion, New Zealand Rifle Brigade
24. 2nd Battalion, New Zealand Rifle Brigade
25. 3rd Battalion, New Zealand Rifle Brigade
26. 4th Battalion, New Zealand Rifle Brigade

The above key numbers were in use only until the formation of the 10th Reinforcements. After that, a strict numerical sequence was used with no distinguishing numerical prefix. This change was instituted as it was found that the regimental number was not an accurate guide to a soldier's unit because personnel were not returning to their original units on posting from hospital, training camps, and so on.

NOTES

1.   That Awful Dardanelles Muddle

1.   pp.1744–1747, H.H.S. Westmacott diary.
2.   p.121, O.E. Burton, *The Silent Division. New Zealanders at the Front 1914–1918* (Angus and Robertson, 1935).
3.   p.39, Gallipoli Correspondent. *The Front Line Diary of C.E.W. Bean* (George Allen & Unwin, 1983).
4.   Tpr C. Pocock, CMR, diary, 25 March 1915.
5.   p.61, Suzanne Welborn, *Lords of Death. A People, A Place, A Legend (*Fremantle Arts Centre Press, 1982).
6.   Tpr R. McCandlish, WMR, letter dated 1 Oct. 1914.
7.   p.120, Sir Ian Hamilton, *Gallipoli Diary*, Vol. I (Edward Arnold, 1920).
8.   Major General Sir Alexander Godley to Sir James Allen, NZ Minister of Defence, letter dated 24 April 1915.
9.   p.1746, Westmacott diary, *op. cit.*
10. Sgt F.N. Hardey, CIB, letter dated 29 Aug. 1915.
11. p.83, C.E.W. Bean diary, *op. cit.*
12. Pte P.M. Thompson, OIB, diary, 9 May 1915.
13. Lt Col. W.G. Malone, WIB, letter to Maj. H. Hart, WIB, dated 20 June 1915.
14. Sgt G.W. Bollinger, WIB, diary, 9 June 1915.
15. p.112, O.E. Burton, unpublished manuscript, *A Rich Old Man.*
16. Bollinger, *op. cit.*, 15 Dec. 1915.
17. p.9, O.E. Burton, *Spring Fires* (The Book Centre Ltd, The Pilgrim Press).
18. p.18, Hon. A. Herbert, *Mons, Anzac, Kut* (Edward Arnold, 1919).
19. p.230, K. Sinclair, *A History of New Zealand* (Penguin, 1980).
20. M.H. Holcroft, *Reluctant Editor* (A.H. & A.W. Reed, 1969).
21. p.15, John Mulgan, *Report on Experience* (Blackwood & Paul, 1967).
22. 'The Real Anzacs', *Punch*, 1 Nov. 1916.
23. p.27, John Mulgan, *op. cit.*
24. 'Attitudes for a New Zealand Poet II', Allen Curnow, *Collected Poems 1933–1973* (A.H. & A.W. Reed, 1974).
25. Pte W.A. Hampton, WIB, Introduction to Gallipoli Slide Collection, n.d.

2.   The Loud Beating of the Drum

1.   'Once the Days', Denis Glover, *An Anthology of New Zealand Verse* (OUP, 1956).
2.   p.206, Alice F. Webb, 'The Patriot', *New Zealand Short Stories* (OUP, 1957).
3.   L. Cpl C. Clark, WIB, IV Author/ TVNZ 1982.
4.   p.16, E.P. Malone, 'The New Zealand School Journal and the Imperial Ideology', *The New Zealand Journal of History*, 7(1), April 1973.
5.   p.208, K. Sinclair *op. cit.*, also M. Pugh, unpublished manuscript, *New Zealanders at War — A Fresh Look*'(Massey, 1978).
6.   p.9, Lt E.G. Pilling, 'An Anzac Memory'. *Extracts from a Rough Diary* (Stanton Bros, 1933).
7.   Sgt D.W Curham, WIB, IV Author/TVNZ 1982/83.
8.   A.A. Grace, 'Our Little Army', *NZ Herald*, 1 Aug. 1914.
9.   p.121, O.E. Burton, *The Silent Division*, *op. cit.*
10. Pte C.L. Lovegrove, WIB, papers.
11. Clark, IV, *op. cit.*
12. p.83, K.M. Stevens, 'Maungatapere: A History and Reminiscence' (*Advocate*, n.d.).
13. Pte H.B.G. Lewis, OIB, IV Author/ TVNZ 1982.
14. Pte G. Skertet, OIB, IV Author/TVNZ 1982.
15. Curham, IV, *op. cit.*
16. Cpl J.B. Austin, FdAmb, IV 1982.
17. Tpr J.E. Parrant, WMR, IV 1982.
18. Sgt J.S. Skinner, OIB, IV Author/TVNZ 1982.
19. p.201–202, Spencer Westmacott, *The After-Breakfast Cigar. Selected Memoirs of a King Country Settler* (A.H. & A.W. Reed, 1977).

20. Telegram, Liverpool to Harcourt, London 5.45 a.m., 4 Aug. 1914. p.176, *The Times Documentary History of the War, Vol. X, Overseas, Part 2* (London 1919).
21. Telegram, Harcourt to Liverpool, 12.20 a.m., 6 Aug. 1914, *ibid.*
22. *New Zealand Herald*, 6 Aug. 1914.
23. p.1594–1595, Westmacott diary, *op. cit.*
24. The Defence Act 1909 (NZ Govt Printer).
25. Lord Plunket to Crewe, 2 Feb. 1910, CO 209/271. p.147, John Gooch, *The Plans of War. The General Staff and British Military Strategy c.1900–1916* (Routledge, Kegan Paul, 1974).
26. p.137 General Sir Alexander Godley GCB, KCMG, *Life of an Irish Soldier* (John Murray, 1939).
27. p.472, 'Report by the Inspector General of Overseas Forces on the Military Forces of New Zealand', by General Sir Ian Hamilton. *The Times Documentary History of the War, op. cit.*
28. p.71, Godley to Wilson, 6 Sep. 1911. WO 106/59. Gooch *op. cit.*
29. Godley to Allen, Secret Memo for Minister of Defence, 9 Oct. 1912.
30. ibid.
31. p.146, Godley, *op. cit.*
32. *Rolls of the Special Squadrons* (QEII Army Museum, Waiouru).
33. p.150, Godley, *op. cit.*
34. p.559, *The Encyclopaedia of New Zealand*, Vol. III (R.E. Owen, 1966).
35. p.471, Hamilton's report, *The Times Documentary History of the War, op. cit.*
36. p.487, ibid.
37. p.147, R.L. Weitzel, 'Pacifists and Anti-Militarists 1909–1914', *New Zealand Journal of History*, Vol. III.2 (1973).
38. *New Zealand Herald*, 14 May 1914.
39. Col. Robin, QMG, Memo Minister of Defence, 22 Aug. 1914 (National Archives).
40. Appendix III, *NZEF (Europe) 1914 War Diary* (Army General Staff, 1915).
41. Sgt Fred Rogers, OIB, IV Author/TVNZ 1982.
42. Clark, IV, *op. cit.*
43. McCandlish, letter dated 14 Aug. 1914.
44. *Southland Daily Times*, 13 Aug. 1914.
45. p.l, Gnt N. Hassell, NZFA, unpublished manuscript, *Memories of 1914.*
46. Godley to Allen, letter dated 16 Dec. 1914.
47. Major J.B. McClymont papers (QEII Army Museum, Waiouru).
48. p.177, *The Times Documentary History of the War, op. cit.*
49. p.154, Godley, *op. cit.*
50. Lt Col. H. Hart, WIB, diary, 12 Aug. 1914.
51. Sgt E.R. Norman, CIB, letter dated 18 Aug. 1914.
52. Thompson diary, *op. cit.*, 11 Aug. 1914.
53. Roll Book CMR compiled from 1 April 1915 (QEII Army Museum, Waiouru).
54. McCandlish, letter dated 6 Oct. 1914.
55. Lt Col. W.G. Malone, WIB, diary, 20 Aug. 1914.
56. p.12–13 Clutha McKenzie, *Tales of a Trooper* (John Lane, 1921).
57. Malone Diary, *op. cit.*, 24 Sep. 1914.
58. p.5, 2Lt C.W Saunders, DCM, NZE, diary.
59. p.8, ibid.
60. Bollinger diary, *op. cit.*, 14 Oct. 1914.
61. ibid.

3. A Ragtime Army

1. p.30, Thompson *op. cit.*
2. p.20, C. McKenzie *op. cit.*
3. Bollinger, *op. cit.*, 17 Oct. 1914.
4. Hart, *op. cit.*, 20 Oct. 1914.
5. Malone, *op. cit.*, 25 Oct. 1914.
6. Godley to General Davies (AAG), letter dated 5 Sept. 1914 (NZ/WA252).
7. Appendix VIII, *NZEF (Europe) 1914 War Diary, op. cit.*
8. p.6, O.E. Burton, *The Silent Division, op. cit.*
9. C. Pocock, *op. cit.*, 3 Nov. 1914.
10. p.78, 'Tahitian Tatler', quoted in Peter Liddle, *Men of Gallipoli* (Allen Lane, 1976).
11. C. Pocock, *op. cit.*, 19 Nov. 1914.
12. p.21, C. Malthus, *ANZAC A Retrospect* (Whitcombe & Tombs, 1965).
13. Bdr AA. Currey, NZFA, letter to Major E.V Bevan dated 3 June 1915 (Auckland Institute & Museum).
14. C. Pocock, *op. cit.*, 25 Nov. 1914.
15. p.5, O.E. Burton, *The Silent Division, op. cit.*
16. C. Pocock, *op. cit.*, 29 Nov. 1914.
17. ibid, 6 Nov. 1914.
18. Bollinger, *op. cit.*, 26 Oct. 1914.
19. Malone, *op. cit.*, 20 Nov. 1914.
20. Godley to Allen, letter dated 24 Nov. 1914.
21. Hart, *op. cit.*, 19 Nov. 1914.
22. Pte W.N. Anderson, OIB, letter dated 24 March 1980 (London Papers).
23. C. Pocock, *op. cit.*, 28 Nov. 1914.
24. ibid, 26 Nov. 1914.
25. p.4, O.E. Burton, *The Silent Division, op. cit.*

26. Godley to Allen, letter dated 21 Oct. 1914.
27. R. McCandlish, *op. cit.*, letter dated 1 Oct. 1914.
28. E.R. Norman, *op. cit.*, letter dated 27 Oct. 1914.
29. p.1665, Westmacott diary, *op. cit.*
30. Bollinger, *op. cit.*, 1 Nov. 1914.
31. ibid, 9 Nov. 1914.
32. Malone, *op. cit.*, 10 Nov. 1914.
33. Thompson, *op. cit.*, 12 Nov. 1914.
34. Sgt A.C. Barker, NZFA, diary, 16 Nov. 1914.
35. C.E.W. Bean, diary, *op. cit.*, 16 Nov. 1914.
36. p.61, Welborn, *op. cit.*
37. Godley to Allen, letter dated 24 Nov. 1914.
38. C. Pocock, *op. cit.*, 17 Nov. 1914.
39. Godley to Col. Robin, letter dated 29 Nov. 1914.
40. ibid.
41. p.189, Howard Robinson, *A History of the Post Office in New Zealand* (R.E. Owen, 1966).
42. *NZEF (Europe) 1914 War Diary, op. cit.*, 1 Dec. 1914.
43. Godley to Allen, letter dated 1 Dec. 1914.
44. Hart, *op. cit.*, 7 Dec. 1914.
45. Thompson, *op. cit.*, 7 Dec. 1914.
46. p.12, C.L. Lovegrove, *The History of the Wellington Regiment 1914–1916*, Volume 2, unpublished manuscript (Wanganui Public Library).
47. Bollinger, *op. cit.*, 9 Dec. 1914.
48. p.2, introduction, author unknown, Lt Col. W.G. Malone's diary (QEII Army Museum, Waiouru).
49. Malone, ibid, 4 Jan. 1915.
50. Thompson, *op. cit.*, 3 Jan. 1915.
51. p.678, Westmacott, *op. cit.*
52. Thompson, *op. cit.*, 11 Dec. 1914.
53. p.13, C.L. Lovegrove, *op. cit.*
54. p.1718, Westmacott ,*op. cit.*
55. Barker, *op. cit.*, 16 Dec. 1914.
56. *NZEF (Europe)1914, War Diary, op. cit.*, 30 Nov. 1914.
57. Godley to Allen, letter dated 10 Dec. 1914.
58. Malone op. cit, 29 Dec. 1914.
59. Barker, *op. cit.*, 11 Dec. 1914.
60. p.3, Sgt T.N. Holmden, AIB, unpublished manuscript, Chapter III 'Egypt'.
61. p.4, ibid.
62. Maj. WH. Cunningham to Col. Hughes, letter dated 8 Jan. 1915 (Lovegrove Papers, Wanganui Public Library).
63. p.4, Holmden, *op. cit.*
64. Mrs Bessie Lee Courie's *Song of the Mothers to the Brewers*, quoted on p.95, *The New Zealanders at War*, by Michael King (Heinemann, 1981).
65. p.13, C.L. Lovegrove, *op. cit.*
66. Godley to Allen, letter dated 26 Dec. 1914.
67. p.39, C.E.W. Bean diary, *op. cit.*
68. Letter Lt Gen. Sir William Birdwood to Maj. Gen. WT. Bridges, dated 27 Dec. 1914 (K.M. Little Papers, QEII Army Museum, Waiouru).
69. Godley to Allen, letter dated 10 Jan. 1915.
70. Malone, *op. cit.*, 11 Nov. 1914.
71. Capt. C.S. Algie, AIB, diary, 27 Dec. 1914.
72. C. Pocock, *op. cit.*, 25 March 1915.
73. R. McCandlish, *op. cit.*, letter dated 5 Jan. 1915.
74. C. Pocock, *op. cit.*, 25 March 1915.
75. Godley to Allen, letter dated 10 Jan. 1915.
76. Godley to Allen, letter dated 17 Jan. 1915.
77. Hart, *op. cit.*, 20 Dec. 1914.
78. R. McCandlish, *op. cit.*, letter dated 5 Jan. 1915.
79. ibid, 28 Jan. 1915.
80. E. Norman, *op. cit.*, letter dated 6 Jan. 1915.
81. R. McCandlish, *op. cit.*, letter dated 21 March 1915.
82. Godley to Allen, letter dated 25 March 1915.
83. Allen to Godley, letter dated 23 March 1915.
84. Godley to Allen, letter dated 15 Feb. 1915.
85. C.S. Algie, *op. cit.*, New Year's Day, 1915.

4. Rumours of the Dardanelles

1. E. Norman, *op. cit.*, letter dated 28 March 1915.
2. C.S. Algie, *op. cit.*, 26 Jan. 1915.
3. Hart, *op. cit.*, 30 Jan. 1915.
4. p.26, C. Malthus, *op. cit.*
5. Bollinger, *op. cit.*, 3 Feb. 1915.
6. ibid., 5 Feb. 1915.
7. ibid, 9 Feb. 1915.
8. ibid, 26 Feb. 1915.
9. Thompson, *op. cit.*, March entry.
10. Capt. A.B. Morton, N.Z.S.C., N.Z. Inf. Bde. HQ diary, 26 March 1915.
11. C. Pocock, *op. cit.*, 25 March 1915.
12. C.S. Algie, *op. cit.*, 13 March 1915.
13. Bollinger, *op. cit.*, 27 March 1915.
14. Malone, *op. cit.*, 25 Dec. 1914.
15. p.21, Saunders, *op. cit.*
16. p.49, P.S. O'Connor, 'The Recruitment of Maori Soldiers 1914–1918', *Political Science*, XIX.2 (1967) pp.48–83.
17. Malone, *op. cit.*, 5 April 1915.

18. Hart, *op. cit.*, 3 April 1915.
19. Kitchener to Gen. Maxwell, quoted on p.42, Robert Rhodes James, *Gallipoli* (Batsford, 1965).
20. p.42, ibid.
21. p.52, ibid.
22. p.257, H.H. Asquith, *Letters to Venetia Stanley.* Selected and edited by Michael and Eleanor Brook (OUP, 1982).
23. p.303 Martin Gilbert, *W.S. Churchill 1914–1916*, Vol. III (Heinemann, 1971).
24. Hamilton to Kitchener, quoted p.65, Rhodes James, *op. cit.*
25. Hart, *op. cit.*, 28 March 1915.
26. Saunder,s *op. cit.*, 10 April 1915.
27. Godley to Allen, letter dated 25 March 1915.
28. Godley to Allen, letter dated 2 April 1915.
29. E.G. Pilling, *op. cit.*, 4 April 1915.
30. Bollinger, *op. cit.*, 2 April 1915.
31. C. Pocock, *op. cit.*, 5 April 1915.
32. Sgt L.J. Poff, N.Z.E., Div. Sig. diary and letters, letter dated 8 April 1915.
33. Bollinger, *op. cit.*, 10–11 April 1915.
34. Saunders, *op. cit.*, 18 April 1915.
35. Spr P.R.M. Hanna, Div. Sig. Bde. HQ, diary, April (AT ms 1647).

36. Malone, *op. cit.*, 14 April 1915.
37. p.1736–1740, Westmacott, *op. cit.*
38. Godley to Lady Godley, letter dated 22 April 1915.
39. p.87, Rhodes James, *op. cit.*
40. Lt Col. W.E. Braithwaite, Royal Welsh Fusiliers, GSOI NZ & A Div., private diary and notes, 21 April 1915.
41. ibid.
42. Contained in S. Sgt K.M. Little, Div. HQ, on staff ANZAC, diary and papers (QEII Army Museum, Waiouru).
43. p.1743, Westmacott, *op. cit.*
44. Malone, *op. cit.*, 23 April 1915.
45. p.l, Spr F.V Senn, NZE, Div. Sig., *Gallipoli Recollections.*
46. ibid.
47. 12/335, Sgt G. Dittmer, AIB, quoted in 'Anzac 50 Years Ago', *NZ Weekly News Commemorative Issue*, 21 April 1965.
48. Godley to Lady Godley, letter dated 22 April 1915.
49. ibid, 24 April 1915.
50. A.B. Morton, *op. cit.*, 24 April 1915.

5. The Greatest Day in Our Lives

1. Sgt Richard Ward, Auckland Infantry Battalion, diary, 25 April 1915.
2. 6/752 Pte E.J. Baigent, quoted in *Anzac 50 Years Ago*, *op. cit.*
3. C.S. Algie, *op. cit.*, 25 April 1915.
4. Godley to Allen, letter dated 24 April 1915.
5. p.52, C. Malthus, *op. cit.*
6. p.68, quoted in Patsy Adam-Smith, *The Anzacs* (Hamish Hamilton, 1978).
7. p.69, ibid.
8. A.B. Morton, *op. cit.*, 23 April 1915.
9. Godley to Allen, letter dated 24 April 1915.
10. p.1746, Westmacott, *op. cit.*
11. p.86, Rhodes James, *op. cit.*
12. p.102, C.E.W. Bean, *Gallipoli Mission* (Australian War Memorial 1948).
13. Lt Col. P.C. Fenwick, NZMC, DADMS, NZ & A Div., diary, 25 April 1915.
14. p.112, quoted in Rhodes James, *op. cit.*
15. p.113, ibid.
16. p.171, Godley, *op. cit.*
17. p.61, Saunders, *op. cit.*
18. Braithwaite, *op. cit.*, 25 April 1915.
19. p.1747–1748, Westmacott, *op. cit.*
20. p.2, F.V. Senn, *op. cit.*

21. R.F. Ward, *op. cit.*, 25 April 1915.
22. Hardey, *op. cit.*, 29 August 1915.
23. p.70, Major C.B. Brereton, CIB, *Tales of Three Campaigns* (Selwyn & Blount, 1926).
24. p.1748–1749, Westmacott ,*op. cit.*
25. p.1749–1750, ibid.
26. p.42, Malthus, *op. cit.*
27. p.26, Capt David Ferguson MC, *The History of the Canterbury Regiment NZEF 1914–1919* (Whitcombe & Tombs, 1921).
28. C.S. Algie, *op. cit.*, 25 April 1915.
29. p.1750–1751, Westmacott, *op. cit.*
30. p.1751, ibid.
31. Pte H.S. Sing, AIB, 25 April 1915 (WA10/2/2 NA).
32. p.27, 2Lt O.E. Burton, *The Auckland Regiment, being an account of the active service of the First, Second and Third Battalions of the Auckland Regiment* (Whitcombe & Tombs, 1922).
33. Pte R.B. Steele, AIB, 25 April 1915.
34. p.302, C.E.W. Bean, *Official History of Australia in the War 1914–18. The Story of Anzac*, Vol. I (Angus & Robertson, 1936).
35. ibid.
36. p.1753–1758, Westmacott, *op. cit.*

37. Ward, *op. cit.*, 25 April 1915.
38. p.302, C.E.W. Bean, *The Story of Anzac*, Vol. I, *op. cit.*
39. p.1758, Westmacott, *op. cit.*
40. Pte A.E. Smith, CIB, letter dated 20 June 1978 (AT ms 1542 Folder 1).
41. p.1759–1761, Westmacott, *op. cit.*
42. Ward, *op. cit.*, 25 April 1915.
43. H.S. Sing, *op. cit.*
44. p.307, C.E.W. Bean, *The Story of Anzac*, Vol. I, *op. cit.*
45. p.310, ibid.
46. p.312, ibid.
47. ibid.
48. Pte F.W Watson, AIB, to Mr Lambert, letter dated 7 Sep. 1915.
49. ibid.
50. p.4, Senn, *op. cit.*
51. p.313, C.E.W. Bean, *The Story of Anzac*, Vol. I, *op. cit.*
52. Cpl R.J. Petre, CIB, diary, 25 April 1915 (AT ms 1833 Folder 1).
53. p.433, C.E.W. Bean, *The Story of Anzac*, Vol. I, *op. cit.*
54. p.435, ibid.
55. ibid.
56. Braithwaite, *op. cit.*, 25 April 1915.
57. p.314, C.E.W. Bean, *The Story of Anzac*, Vol. I, *op. cit.*
58. Thompson, *op. cit.*, 25 April 1915.
59. Hart, *op. cit.*, 25 April 1915.
60. Malone, *op. cit.*, 25 April 1915.
61. p.7, Roy F. Ellis MM, *By Wires to Victory* (INZEF Divisional Signal Company War History Committee).
62. p.69, Brereton, *op. cit.*
63. Thompson, *op. cit.*, 25 April 1915.
64. p.4, Senn, *op. cit.*
65. p.2, Pte F.E. McKenzie, AIB, diary.
66. p.3, ibid.
67. p.15, L. Cpl H.V. Howe, 11th Aust. Bn, 'ANZAC: Sparks from an Old Controversy', *Australian Army Journal.*
68. p.16, ibid.

69. ibid.
70. p.210, Cpl G.A. Tuck, AIB, diary.
71. ibid.
72. p.48, Malthus, *op. cit.*
73. p.48, E. Ashmead Bartlett, *The Uncensored Dardanelles* (Hutchinson, 1928).
74. Godley to Lady Godley, letter dated 29 April 1915.
75. ibid.
76. Braithwaite, *op. cit.*, 25 April 1915.
77. p.114, Eric Bush, *Gallipoli* (George Allen &C Unwin, 1975).
78. p.164, Brigadier General C.F. Aspinall-Oglander, 'The Official History of the Great War. *Military Operations Gallipoli, Vol. I* (Heinemann, 1929).
79. p.144, *Hamilton, Gallipoli Diary*, Vol. I, *op. cit.*
80. Fenwick, *op. cit.*, 25 April 1915.
81. p.47, Malthus, *op. cit.*
82. p.1763–1767, Westmacott, *op. cit.*
83. p.100, O.E. Burton, *A Rich Old Man, op. cit.*
84. Pte Tony Fagan, AIB, IV Author/TVNZ 1982.
85. Godley to Allen, letter dated 6 May 1915.
86. Capt T. Rhodes, Grenadier Guards, ADC to Maj. Gen. Godley, GOC's diary, 25 April 1915.
87. Ward, *op. cit.*, 25 April 1915
88. *NZ Herald*, 29 April 1915.
89. Pte W.J. Surgenor, WIB, POW, report dated 13 Dec. 1918.
90. p.2, Capt N. Fitzherbert, NZAPC, OC NZ Records Section, letter to High Commissioner for N.Z. dated 15 May 1915 (Wanganui Museum).
91. The *Press*, 4 May 1915.
92. ibid, 4 May 1915.
93. *NZ Herald, op. cit.*, 6 July 1915.
94. The *Press*, 6May 1915.
95. ibid., 6 May 1915.
96. *The Lyttelton Times*, 8 May 1915.
97. The *Press*, 10 May 1915.
98. ibid., 20 May 1915.
99. Godley to Allen, letter dated 14 June 1915.

6. Hanging On

1. Poff, diary, *op. cit.*, 26 April 1915.
2. Gnr J.D. Hutchison, NZFA, diary, 26 April 1915.
3. p.27, Lt J.R. Byrne, NZFA, *New Zealand Artillery in the Field 1914–18* (Whitcombe & Tombs, 1922).
4. Godley to Lady Godley, letter dated 29 April 1915.
5. Bollinger, *op. cit.*, 26 April 1915.
6. Hart, *op. cit.*, 26 April 1915.
7. ibid.
8. p.168, Rhodes James, *op. cit.*
9. Saunders, *op. cit.*, 27 April 1915.
10. p.74–76, Brereton, *op. cit.*

11. p.506, C.E.W. Bean, *The Story of Anzac*, Vol. I, *op. cit.*
12. Sgt Maj. A.W. Porteous, MC OIB, diary, 26 April 1915.
13. Algie, *op. cit.*, 26 April 1915.
14. Sgt AT. Morris, CIB, diary, 27 April 1915.
15. Fenwick, *op. cit.*, 5 May 1915.
16. p.82, Brereton, *op. cit.*
17. Algie, *op. cit.*, 27 April 1915.
18. Barker, *op. cit.*, 10 May 1915.
19. Fenwick, *op. cit.*, 3 May 1915.
20. ibid.
21. Hardey, *op. cit.*, 29 Aug. 1915.
22. Bollinger, *op. cit.*, 27 April 1915.
23. Malone, *op. cit.*, 25 April 1915.
24. Saunders, *op. cit.*, 27 April 1915.
25. Hart, *op. cit.*, 27 April 1915.
26. Bollinger, *op. cit.*, 27 April 1915.
27. Malone, *op. cit.*, 25 April 1915.
28. Curham, IV, *op. cit.*
29. Saunders, *op. cit.*, 27 April 1915.
30. Bollinger, *op. cit.*, 27 April 1915.
31. Malone, *op. cit.*, 25 April 1915.
32. Hart, *op. cit.*, 27 April 1915.
33. Malone, *op. cit.*, 25 April 1915.
34. ibid, 28 April 1915.
35. ibid, 28 April 1915.
36. p.110, Capt R.W. Campbell, *The Kangaroo Marines* (Cassell, ND).
37. p.184, Rhodes James, *op. cit.*
38. p.82–83, C.E.W. Bean, diary *op. cit.*, 29 April 1915.
39. Malone, *op. cit.*, 28 April 1915.
40. Saunders, *op. cit.*, 28 April 1915.
41. Malone, *op. cit.*, 29 April 1915.
42. ibid, 30 April 1915.
43. Braithwaite, *op. cit.*, 29 April 1915.
44. Report on the Action of Night 2/3 May 1915. Maj. Gen. Godley dated 24 May 1915. (MS 0017 QEII Army Museum, Waiouru).
45. p.35, Pilling *op. cit.*
46. Pte W.N. Anderson, OIB, diary, 2 May 1915.
47. Thompson, *op. cit.*, 3 May 1915.
48. ibid.
49. Saunders *op. cit.*, 2 May 1915.
50. p.36, Pilling, *op. cit.*
51. Rogers, IV, *op. cit.*
52. W.N. Anderson, *op. cit.*, 2 May 1915.
53. Skinner, IV, *op. cit.*
54. p.36, Pilling, *op. cit.*
55. p.593, C.E.W. Bean, *The Story of Anzac*, Vol. I, *op. cit.*
56. p.2 Spr E.C. Clifton, NZE, Memoirs.
57. p.597 C.E.W. Bean, *The Story of Anzac*, Vol. I, *op. cit.*
58. Rogers, IV, *op. cit.*
59. p.59, Lt A.E. Byrne, MC, *Official History of the Otago Regiment in the Great War 1914–1918* (J. Wilkie & Co., ND).
60. Rhodes, *op. cit.*, 25 April 1915.
61. Thompson, *op. cit.*, 3 May 1915.
62. p.36, Pilling, *op. cit.*
63. Hardey, *op. cit.*, 29 Aug. 1915.
64. p.201, Brereton, *op. cit.*
65. Malone, *op. cit.*, 2 May 1915.
66. Saunders, *op. cit.*, 2 May 1915.
67. p.598, C.E.W. Bean, *The Story of Anzac*, Vol. I, *op. cit.*
68. p.5, Report on the Action of Night 2/3 May 1915, *op. cit.*
69. Godley to Allen, letter dated 6 May 1915.
70. Malone, *op. cit.*, 4 May 1915.
71. p.95, A. Herbert, *op. cit.*
72. Capt. A.B. Motton, NZSC papers (AT MS1310).
73. Fenwick, *op. cit.*, 11 May 1915.
74. A.B. Morton papers, *op. cit.*
75. p.601, C.E.W. Bean, *The Story of Anzac*, Vol. I ,*op. cit.*
76. p.194, Hamilton, *Gallipoli* Diary Vol. I, *op. cit.*
77. Hutchison, *op. cit.*, 5 May 1915.
78. McKenzie, *op. cit.*, 5 May 1915.
79. Capt. H.T. Palmer, SMR, letter/diary, 5 May 1915.
80. ibid, 8 May 1915.
81. Fenwick, *op. cit.*, 4 May 1915.

7. Helles

1. p.213, Hamilton, *Gallipoli Diary*, Vol. I, *op. cit.*
2. p.343, Aspinall-Oglander ,*op. cit.*
3. p.207, Hamilton, *Gallipoli Diary*, Vol. I, *op. cit.*
4. Malone, *op. cit.*, 7 May 1915.
5. McKenzie, *op. cit.*, 7 May 1915.
6. p.342, Aspinall-Oglander, *op. cit.*
7. p.117, Brereton, *op. cit.*
8. p.106, L. Cpl E.P. Williams, CIB, *A New Zealanders Diary, Gallipoli & France 1915–1917* (Melbourne Publishing Co. ND).
9. Bollinger, *op. cit.*, 8 May 1915.
10. McKenzie ,*op. cit.*, 10 May 1915.
11. Sgt J.G. Gasparich, AIB, IV author/TVNZ, 1982.
12. p.119, Brereton, *op. cit.*
13. Pte H.V Palmer, CIB, IV author/TVNZ, 1982.
14. p.120, Brereton, *op. cit.*

15. p.71, Malthus, *op. cit.*
16. p.211, Hamilton, *Gallipoli Diary*, Vol. I, *op. cit.*
17. Malone to Hart, letter dated 20 June 1915, Malone papers *op. cit.*
18. p.211, Hamilton, *Gallipoli Diary*, Vol. I, *op. cit.*
19. p.94, C.E.W. Bean diary, *op. cit.* McCay, Comd. 2 Aust. Bde, to Bean.
20. Gasparich, IV, *op. cit.*
21. W.N. Anderson, *op. cit.*, 8 May 1915.
22. Thompson, *op. cit.*, 9 May 1915.
23. p.107, Brereton, *op. cit.*
24. Malone to Hart, letter dated 20 June 1915, *op. cit.*
25. Pte R.J. Weir, DWHQ/WIB, diary,
26. Algie, *op cit.*, 9 May 1915.
27. McKenzie, *op. cit.*, 10 May 1915.
28. ibid, 19 May 1915.
29. Fenwick, *op. cit.*, 11 May 1915.
30. Gnr R.J. Wait, NZFA, diary, 6 June 1915.
31. Bollinger, *op. cit.*, 11 May 1915.
32. Skinner, IV, *op. cit.*
33. Bollinger, *op. cit.*, 12 May 1915.
34. p.207, Hamilton, *Gallipoli Diary*, Vol. I, *op. cit.*
35. Hardey, *op. cit.*, 29 Aug. 1915.

10 May 1915.

8. The Siege of Anzac

1. Fenwick, *op. cit.*, 12 May 1915.
2. ibid, 11 May 1915.
3. p.193, Hamilton, *Gallipoli Diary*, Vol. I, *op. cit.*
4. p.50, C.E.W. Bean, *The Story of Anzac*, Vol. II, *op. cit.*
5. Saunders, *op. cit.*, 10 May 1915.
6. p.112, C.E.W. Bean, diary, *op. cit.*
7. Saunders, *op. cit.*, 13 May 1915.
8. Tpr C. McKenzie, WMR, diary, 12 May 1915.
9. p.87, K.M. Stevens, *op. cit.*
10. p.88, ibid.
11. H.T. Palmer, *op. cit.*, 15 May 1915.
12. Maj. P.J. Overton, CMR, letter dated 16 May 1915.
13. Lt L.C. Chaytor, CMR, diary, 14 May 1915.
14. Overton, *op. cit.*, letter dated 30 May 1915.
15. Malone, *op. cit.*, 14 May 1915.
16. Braithwaite, *op. cit.*, 15 May 1915.
17. p.189, C.E.W. Bean, *The Story of ANZAC*, Vol. II, *op. cit.*
18. p.283, Hamilton, *Gallipoli Diary*, Vol. I, *op. cit.*
19. Saunders, *op. cit.*, 3 May 1915.
20. Fenwick, *op. cit.*, 14 May 1915.
21. Braithwaite, *op. cit.*, 15 May 1915.
22. Saunders, *op. cit.*, 18 May 1915.
23. Tpr WC. East, WMR, IV, author/ TVNZ, 1982.
24. Pte F.H. Palmer, WIB, IV, author, 1983.
25. ibid.
26. Sgt J.W. Wilder, WMR, diary, 19 May 1915.
27. p.48, Sgt C.G. Nicol, *The Story of Two Campaigns, Official War History of the Auckland Mounted Rifles Regiment 1914–1919* (Wilson & Horton, 1921).
28. p.153, C.E.W. Bean, *Gallipoli Diary*, Vol. I, *op. cit.*
29. C. McKenzie, diary, *op. cit.*, 19 May 1915.
30. R. McCandlish, *op. cit.*, 19 May 1915.
31. p.89, K.M. Stevens, *op. cit.*,
32. Hardey, *op. cit.*, 7 Oct. 1915.
33. Pte Ben Smart, WIB, diary, 21 May 1915.
34. Hardey, *op. cit.*, 7 Oct. 1915.
35. Saunders, *op. cit.*, 4 May 1915.
36. Bollinger, *op. cit.*, 24 May 1915.
37. Fenwick, *op. cit.*, 24 May 1915.
38. p.119, C.E.W. Bean, diary, *op. cit.*
39. Godley to Allen, letter dated 29 May 1915.
40. Fenwick, *op. cit.*, 25 May 1915.
41. R. McCandlish, *op. cit.*, 28 May 1915.
42. Wilder, *op. cit.*, additional note at back of diary, 'No. 3 Post'.
43. ibid.
44. L.C. Chaytor, *op. cit.*, 30 May 1915.
45. ibid.
46. Braithwaite, *op. cit.*, 1 June 1915.
47. p.197, C.E.W. Bean, *Gallipoli Diary*, Vol. II, *op. cit.*
48. Saunders, *op. cit.*, 29 May 1915.
49. Hardey, *op. cit.*, 7 Oct. 1915.

9. Summer

1. R.J. Weir, *op. cit.*, 27 May 1915.
2. Malone, *op. cit.*, 31 May 1915.
3. Saunders, *op. cit.*, 9 June 1915.
4. p.128, E.P. Williams, *op. cit.*
5. p.18, Hassell, *op. cit.*
6. Lt J.L. Anderson, Div. HQ, APM, diary, 30–31 May 1915.
7. p.84, Malthus, *op. cit.*
8. p.86, ibid.
9. Bollinger, *op. cit.*, 2 June 1915.
10. p.63, Capt. Home RMO, WIB, quoted in Lt Col. A.D. Carbery, *The New Zealand Medical Services in the Great War* (Whitcombe & Tombs, 1924).
11. Malone, *op. cit.*, 1 June 1915.
12. ibid, 2 June 1915.

13. ibid.
14. ibid.
15. Pte J.W. Swan, WIB, diary/letter, 14 June 1915.
16. p.249, C.E.W. Bean, *The Story of ANZAC*, Vol. II, *op. cit.*
17. Sgt H. Johns, WIB, IV, author/TVNZ, 1982.
18. Smart ,*op. cit.*, 8 July 1915.
19. p.232, C.E.W. Bean, *The Story of ANZAC*, Vol. II, *op. cit.*
20. F.E. McKenzie, *op cit.*, 3 June 1915.
21. Hardey, *op. cit.*, 7 Oct. 1915.
22. Saunders, *op. cit.*, 4 June 1915.
23. Memo, ANZAC Corps Headquarters, dated 6 June 1915 (K.M. Little Papers, QEII Army Museum, Waiouru).
24. Braithwaite, *op. cit.*, 7 June 1915.
25. ibid, 8 June 1915.
26. Godley to Lady Godley, letter dated 4 June 1915.
27. p.142, E.P. Williams, *op. cit.*
28. Pte W.J. Newell, AIB, diary, 19 June 1915.
29. Smart, *op. cit.*, 14 June 1915.
30. J.S. Skinner, IV, *op. cit.*
31. Sgt F.S. Cooper, NZFA, Div. HQ, diary, 16 May 1915.
32. ibid, 3 Jury 1915.
33. ibid, 13 July 1915.
34. Hardey, *op. cit.*, 29 Aug. 1915.
35. J.L. Anderson, *op. cit.*, 30 May 1915.
36. Quoted by Fenwick, *op. cit.*, 2 June 1915.
37. ibid, 17 May 1915.
38. Malone to Mrs Malone, letter dated 3 July 1915.
39. Malone, *op. cit.*, 9 June 1915–24 July 1915.
40. ibid.
41. Bollinger, *op. cit.*, 9 June 1915.
42. p.11, Maj. A.C. Temperley, Norfolk Regt, BM NZ Ini. Bde, *A Personal Narrative of the Battle of Chunuk Bair August 6th–10th, 1915I,* ms 0017 (QEII Army Museum, Waiouru).
43. p.139, C.E.W. Bean, diary *op. cit.*
44. Malone to Mrs Malone *op. cit.*, 3 July 1915.
45. p.62, Capt Home, RMO, WIB, quoted in Carbery, *op. cit.*
46. Pte V.J. Nicholson, WIB, IV, author/ TVNZ 1983.
47. Curham, IV.
48. H.V. Howe, letter to D.G.W. Malone, dated 12 May 1964.
49. Saunders, *op. cit.*, 30 May 1915.
50. H.V. Howe, *op. cit.*
51. Curham, IV, *op. cit.*
52. Saunders, *op. cit.*, 22 June 1915.
53. ibid, 30 May 1915.
54. Malone, *op. cit.*, 9 June–24 July 1915.
55. Smart, *op. cit.*, 31 May–1 June 1915.
56. p.18, Hassell, *op. cit.*
57. Bollinger, *op. cit.*, 12 June 1915.
58. p.41, Pilling, *op. cit.*
59. p.18, Hassell, *op. cit.*
60. Smart, *op. cit.*, 1 July 1915.
61. Pte RA. Childs, CIB, diary, 30 June 1915.
62. p.380, C.E.W. Bean, *The Story of ANZAC*, Vol. II, *op. cit.*
63. Saunders, *op. cit.*, 21 June 1915.
64. Smart, *op. cit.*, 14 July 1915.
65. H.V. Palmer, IV, *op. cit.*
66. J.W. Swan, *op. cit.*, 28 May 1915.
67. F. Rogers, IV, *op. cit.*
68. R.A. Childs, *op. cit.*, 20 June 1915.
69. Smart, *op. cit.*, 11 July 1915.
70. p.22, Barbara Harper (ed.), 'Letters from Gunner 7/516 and Gunner 7/517', letter from Lt Gordon Harper, CMR, dated 25 July 1915 (Anchor Communications, 1978).
71. Tpr R. Rawcliffe, WMR, letter dated May 1915, ms 2758 (QEII Army Museum, Waiouru).
72. p.43, Pilling, *op. cit.*
73. Bollinger, *op. cit.*, 26 June 1915.
74. ibid, 27–29 June 1915.
75. Godley to Allen, letter dated 6 June 1915.
76. McKenzie ,*op. cit.*, 5 Aug. 1915.
77. J. Swan, *op. cit.*, 25 June 1915.
78. Barker ,*op. cit.*, 29 May 1915.
79. Saunders ,*op. cit.*, 8 June 1915.
80. Hutchison, *op. cit.*, 1 June 1915.
81. Saunders, *op. cit.*, 27 June 1915.
82. Smart, *op. cit.*, 30 June 1915.
83. Godley to Allen, letter dated 14 June 1915.
84. p.65, Carbery, *op. cit.*
85. S. Sgt K.M. Little, Submission to Dardanelles Commission dated 19 Jan. 1917 (K.M. Little Papers, QEII Army Museum, Waiouru).
86. Fenwick, *op. cit.*, 7 June 1915.
87. Saunders, *op. cit.*, 17 July 1915.
88. p.43, Pilling, *op. cit.*
89. Smart, *op. cit.*, 18 June 1915.
90. ibid, 28 June 1915.
91. ibid, 5 July 1915.
92. Johns, IV, *op. cit.*
93. Malone to Lt Col. Richardson, NZSC, dated 19 June 1915.
94. Hardey, *op. cit.*, 29 Oct. 1915.

10. The Battle for Chunuk Bair

1. John Masefield, *On the Dead in Gallipoli, Poems* (Heinemann, 1948).
2. Nicholson, IV, *op. cit.*
3. Malone, *op. cit.*, 4 Aug. 1915.
4. Godley to Lady Godley, letter dated 5 Aug. 1915.
5. Barker, *op. cit.*, 6 Aug. 1915.
6. Wilder, *op. cit.*, 4 Aug. 1915.
7. F.E. McKenzie, *op. cit.*, 1 Aug. 1915.
8. p.108, O.E. Burton, *A Rich Old Man*, *op. cit.*
9. W.N. Anderson, *op. cit.*, 4 Aug. 1915.
10. Malone to Mrs Malone, letter dated 5 Aug. 1915.
11. Hardey, *op. cit.*, 30 Oct. 1915.
12. Hutchison, *op. cit.*, 4–6 Aug. 1915.
13. A.A. Currey, *op. cit.*, 9 Nov. 1915.
14. ibid.
15. p.566, C.E.W. Bean, *The Story of ANZAC*, Vol. II, *op. cit.*
16. Wilder, *op. cit.*, 6 Aug. 1915.
17. p.100, K.M. Stevens, *op. cit.*
18. ibid.
19. Draft of letter to editor, *Reveille*, official publication of the NSW Branch of Returned Sailors and Soldiers Imperial League of Australia, in reply to 19 May 1932 request for an article on fighting of New Zealand Mounted Rifles at Sari Bair in Aug. 1915 (W. Meldrum).
20. ibid.
21. p.65, Maj. G.A. King, NZSC, HQ NZMR Bde, diary (Gp Capt E.G. King).
22. Pte P. Tahitahi, Maori Contingent, IV, author/ TVNZ 1983.
23. p.576, C.E.W. Bean, *The Story of ANZAC*, Vol. II, *op. cit.*
24. Malone, *op. cit.*, 4 Aug. 1915.
25. p.12, Temperley, *op. cit.*
26. W.N. Anderson, *op. cit.*, 6 Aug. 1915.
27. Pte O.W. Howe, AIB, letter dated 7 Sep. 1915.
28. Hardey, *op. cit.*, 30 Oct. 1915.
29. ibid.
30. ibid.
31. Malone papers, *op. cit.*, 7 Aug. 1915.
32. p.637, C.E.W. Bean, *The Story of ANZAC*, Vol. II, *op. cit.*
33. Malone, *op. cit.*, 4 Aug. 1915.
34. p.7, Temperley, *op. cit.*
35. p.18, ibid.
36. p.6, ibid.
37. p.638, C.E.W. Bean, *The Story of ANZAC*, Vol. II, *op. cit.*
38. p.148, C.E.W. Bean, diary, *op. cit.*
39. p.606, C.E.W. Bean, *The Story of ANZAC*, Vol. II, *op. cit.*
40. Barker, *op. cit.*, 7 Aug. 1915.
41. Wilder, *op. cit.*, 8 Aug. 1915.
42. Hart, *op. cit.*, 15 Sep. 1915.
43. p.220, quoted in C.E.W. Bean, 'Gallipoli Mission', *op. cit.*
44. *Battle of Chunuk Bair*, C.L. Lovegrove, *op. cit.*
45. p.65, Burton, *The Auckland Regiment*, *op. cit.*
46. Pte W. Howe, *op. cit.*
47. ibid.
48. Algie, *op. cit.*, 7 August 1915.
49. Sir Ernest Harston, 'Gallipoli. What Did Happen?' *Voice of the Veteran April 1957* (Malone Papers).
50. C. Clark, IV, *op. cit.*
51. Hardey, *op. cit.*, 29 Oct. 1915.
52. W.N. Anderson, *op. cit.*, 7 Aug. 1915.
53. New Zealand Infantry Brigade, *War Diary*, 8/9 Aug. 1915 (NZ WA 70/1).
54. J. Swan, *op. cit.*, 9 Aug. 1915.
55. Smart, *op. cit.*, 8 Aug. 1915.
56. C. Clark, IV, *op. cit.*
57. J. Swan, *op. cit.*, 9 Aug. 1915.
58. C Clark, IV, *op. cit.*
59. Curham, IV, *op. cit.*
60. p.13, Temperley, *op. cit.*
61. ibid.
62. p.15, ibid.
63. ibid.
64. Capt E.S. Harston, WIB, letter dated 9 March 1965 (Malone papers).
65. C. Clark, IV, *op. cit.*
66. H. Johns, IV, *op. cit.*
67. Harston, *op. cit.*, letter dated 5 March 1942 (Malone papers).
68. Swan, *op. cit.*, 9 Aug. 1915.
69. p.2, Temperley, *op. cit.*
70. H. Johns, IV, *op. cit.*
71. C. Clark, IV, *op. cit.*
72. ibid.
73. H. Johns, IV, *op. cit.*
74. ibid
75. Pte R.J. Davis, WIB, *Statement of Capture by the Turks at* Anafarta, *Gallipoli Peninsula*, dated 29 Aug. 1919.
76. W.R. Surgenor, *op. cit.*
77. Harston, *op. cit.*, letter dated 5 March 1942.
78. ibid.
79. H. Johns, IV, *op. cit.*
80. Curham, IV, *op. cit.*
81. Spr B.L. Dignan, NZE, Div. Sig., letter dated 23 Aug. 1915 (Bassett Papers).
82. p.104, K.M. Stevens, *op. cit.*
83. ibid.

84. ibid.
85. C. Clark, IV, *op. cit.*
86. Nicholson, IV, *op. cit.*
87. Maj. W.H. Hastings, Indian Army, MG OC, 3ALH Bde, letter dated 5 Nov. 1929 (Malone papers).
88. p.184, Godley, *Life of an Irish Soldier, op. cit.*
89. p.185, ibid.
90. p.17, Temperley, *op. cit.*
91. p.19, ibid.
92. Harston, *op. cit.*, 5 March 1942.
93. W.H. Hastings, *op. cit.*
94. Harston, *op. cit.*, 5 March 1942.
95. p.679, C.E.W. Bean, *The Story of ANZAC*, Vol. II, *op. cit.*
96. p.20, Temperley, *op. cit.*
97. p.185, Godley, *op. cit.*
98. p.146, C.E.W. Bean, diary, *op. cit.*
99. p.7, Temperley, *op. cit.*
100. p.51, Pilling, *op. cit.*
101. p.123, Lt Col. W. Meldrum, WRM, quoted in Ted Andrews, *Kiwi Trooper* (*Wanganui Chronicle* 1967).
102. Appendix B to NZ & A Div. *Instructions Issued to Commanders in accordance with Divisional Order No. 11*, dated 5 Aug. 1915 (NA WALL).
103. Tpr H.E. Browne, WMR, letter (AT Misc ms 1196).
104. Nicholson, IV, *op. cit.*
105. H. Johns, IV, *op. cit.*
106. C. Clark, IV, *op. cit.*
107. p.108, O.E. Burton, *A Rich Old Man, op. cit.*
108. ibid.
109. p.93, Carbery, *op. cit.*
110. p.156, A. Herbert, *op. cit.*
111. L. Cpl L.M. Hart, OIB, letter dated 1 Jan. 1916.
112. Lt E.L. Hunt, OIB, letter to author 24 Oct. 1981.
113. L.M. Hart, *op. cit.*
114. p.24, Ronald Lewin, *Slim: The Standardbearer* (Leo Cooper, 1976).
115. p.692, C.E.W. Bean, *The Story of ANZAC*, Vol. II, *op. cit.*
116. H.E. Browne, *op. cit.*
117. p.123, Andrews, *op. cit.*
118. H.E. Browne, *op. cit.*
119. p.123, Andrews, *op. cit.*
120. H.E. Browne, *op. cit.*
121. p.24, Temperley, *op. cit.*
122. Curham, IV, *op. cit.*
123. p.21, Temperley, *op. cit.*
124. F.E. McKenzie, *op. cit.*, 6 Aug. 1915.
125. Childs, *op. cit.*, 12–17 Aug. 1915.
126. Godley to Lady Godley, letter dated 12 Aug. 1915.
127. Godley to Allen, letter dated 14 Aug. 1915.
128. p.86, Hamilton, *Gallipoli Diary*, Vol. II, *op. cit.*
129. 'Despatch of Sir Ian Hamilton 11th December 1915', included as an Appendix to *The Final Report of the Dardanelles Commission* (Part II — Conduct of Operations) (HMSO Cmd 371).
130. H.V. Howe to Harston (Malone papers).
131. p.112, O.E. Burton, *A Rich Old Man, op. cit.*
132. p.99–120, O.E. Burton, *The Silent Division, op. cit.*
133. Keegan, *Six Armies in Normandy*, quoted in a review by Beddow, *The Guardian*, 1 Aug. 1982.
134. p.120, O.E. Burton, *The Silent Division op. cit.*

11. Hill 60

1. p.128, Hamilton, *Gallipoli Diary*, Vol. II, *op. cit.*
2. p.38, Lt G.C. Harper, *Letters from Gunner 7/516 and Gunner 7/517, op. cit.*
3. Tpr E.D. Templar, CMR, letter to author 12 Oct. 1981.
4. ibid.
5. p.735, C.E.W. Bean, *The Story of ANZAC*, Vol. II, *op. cit.*
6. p.736, ibid.
7. p.130, Hamilton, *Gallipoli Diary*, Vol. II, *op. cit.*
8. Sgt J. Wilson, NZE, diary, 26 Aug. 1915.
9. Kingo, *op. cit.*, 19 Sep. 1915.
10. Tpr J.W. Watson, AMR, diary, 23 Aug. 1915.
11. King, *op. cit.*, 19 Sep. 1915.
12. Wilder, *op. cit.*, 21 Aug. 1915.
13. ibid, 26 Aug. 1915.
14. ibid, 27 Aug. 1915.
15. Tpr J.F. Rudd, CMR, IV, Author/ TVNZ, 1982.
16. W. East, IV, *op. cit.*
17. p.749, C.E.W. Bean, *The Story of ANZAC*, Vol. II, *op. cit.*
18. p.69, *In Memoriam, Chaplain-Major William Grant*, his letters from the Front (Gisborne, 1915).
19. First Officer J. Duder, *Maheno*, diary, 26 Aug. 1915.
20. ibid, 28 Aug. 1915.
21. J.W. Watson, *op. cit.*, 29–30 Aug. 1915.
22. p.761, C.E.W. Bean, *The Story of ANZAC*, Vol. II, *op. cit.*
23. Roll Book of Canterbury Mounted Rifles, *op. cit.*
24. p.101, Carbery, *op. cit.*

12. The End

1. L. Cpl Cobber, *The ANZAC Pilgrim's Progress*, (Simkin, Marshall, Hamilton, Kent & Co.).
2. p.114, O.E. Burton, *A Rich Old Man, op. cit.*
3. ibid.
4. p.70, E.M. Cutlack (ed.), *War Letters of General Monash'* (Angus & Robertson, 1934), letter dated 26 Sep. 1915.
5. p.74, ibid, letter dated 3 Oct. 1915.
6. p.55–56, Pilling, *op. cit.*
7. Newell, *op. cit.*, 18–19 Sep. 1915.
8. p.22, Hassell, *op. cit.*
9. Bollinger, *op. cit.*, 18 Sep. 1915.
10. ibid, 20 Sep. 1915.
11. Godley to Allen, letter dated 3 Sep. 1915.
12. p.114, O.E. Burton, *A Rich Old Man, op. cit.*
13. p.61, Pilling, *op. cit.*
14. p.115, O.E. Burton, *A Rich Old Man, op. cit.*
15. Hart, *op. cit.*, 21 Sep. 1915.
16. p.19, Alexander Aitken, *Gallipoli to the Somme* (OUP 1963).
17. p.7, ibid.
18. p.114, O.E. Burton, *A Rich Old Man, op. cit.*
19. p.9, Aitken, *op. cit.*
20. p.133, Malthus, *op. cit.*
21. Godley to Allen, letter dated 10 Oct. 1915.
22. Godley to Allen, letter dated 10 Nov. 1915.
23. Bollinger, *op. cit.*, 5–6 Oct. 1915.
24. ibid, 29 Oct.–7 Nov. 1915.
25. Newell, *op. cit.*, 17 Oct. 1915.
26. Hart, *op. cit.*, 8 Nov. 1915.
27. Sgt Major J.M.T. Downey, NZFA, diary, 9 Sep. 1915.
28. Pte J. Johnson, OIB, letter dated 22 Dec. 1915.
29. Godley to Allen, letter dated 24 Aug. 1915.
30. Hart, *op. cit.*, 12 Nov. 1915.
31. ibid, 14 Nov. 1915.
32. p.117, O.E. Burton, *A Rich Old Man, op. cit.*
33. Newell, *op. cit.*, 2 Nov.; 8 Nov. 1915.
34. p.170, C.E.W. Bean, diary, *op. cit.*
35. p.l 19, O.E. Burton, *A Rich Old Man, op. cit.*
36. Bollinger, *op. cit.*, 13 Nov. 1915.
37. ibid, 28 Nov. 1915.
38. p.117, O.E. Burton, *A Rich Old Man, op. cit.*
39. Godley to Allen, letter dated 9 Dec. 1915.
40. p.853, C.E.W. Bean, *The Story of ANZAC*, Vol. II, *op. cit.*
41. Godley to Allen, letter dated 20 Dec. 1915.
42. Bollinger, *op. cit.*, 25 Nov. 1915.
43. J. Johnson, *op. cit.*
44. Hart, *op. cit.*, 4 Dec. 1915.
45. ibid, 11 Dec. 1915.
46. Bollinger, ibid, 13–15 Dec. 1915.
47. Hart, ibid, 13 Dec. 1915.
48. Wellington Infantry Battalion Special Operation Order, by Lt Co. Hart, DSO, 17 Dec. 1915 (Hart Papers).
49. ibid.
50. Carbery, *op. cit.*
51. Quoted in Hart ,*op. cit.*, 15 Dec. 1915.
52. ibid.
53. Tuck, *op. cit.*, see also, p.121 Burton, *A Rich Old Man, op. cit.*
54. Gasparich, IV, *op. cit.*
55. Hart, *op. cit.*, 15 Dec. 1915.
56. Newell, *op. cit.*, 18 Dec. 1915.
57. ibid.
58. Godley to Allen, letter dated 18 Dec. 1915.
59. J. Johnson, *op. cit.*
60. p.121, O.E. Burton, *A Rich Old Man, op. cit.*
61. Gasparich, IV, *op. cit.*
62. Godley, letter dated Dec. 1915 (Godley Papers).

13. Gallipoli — The New Zealand Story

1. p.123, O.E. Burton, *A Rich Old Man, op. cit.*
2. Tpr A.D. Blanks, AMR, letter dated 20 Oct. 1915 (3rd Auckland & Northland Battalion).
3. p.955, R. Ernest Dupuy and Trevor H. Dupuy, *The Encyclopedia of Military History* (Janes Publishing Co. 1977).
4. Lt Col. John Studholme, *New Zealand Expeditionary Force record of personal services during the war of officers, nurses, and first class warrant officers, and other facts relating to the NZEF* (Govt. Printer, 1928).
5. Newell, *op. cit.*, 29 Dec. 1915–3 Jan. 1916.
6. *The Real Anzacs*, Punch, *op. cit.*
7. Godley memo to Birdwood, 17 March 1916.
8. p.476, Hamilton's Report, *The Times Documentary History of the War, op. cit.*
9. Godley, *op. cit.*, 17 March 1916.
10. p.532, C.E.W. Bean, *Anzac to Amiens* (Australian War Memorial 1946).
11. p.93, *The Final Report of the Dardanelles Commission*, Part II, *op. cit.*
12. p.95, ibid.
13. p.15, Hassell, *op. cit.*
14. Tony Fagan, IV, *op. cit.*
15. p.6–7, Ormond Burton, *Spring Fires* (The Book Centre, 1956).
16. Record of Civic Reception, Auckland Town Hall, *NZ Herald*, 17 July 1916.

17. p.132, Brereton, *op. cit.*
18. Lewis, IV, *op. cit.*
19. Pte R.J. Weir, Div. HQ/WIB, IV, author/ TVNZ, 1982.
20. R. McCandlish, papers (Mulvey family).
21. p.74, quoted in Keith Sinclair, *A History of the University of Auckland 1883–1983* (AUP, 1983).
22. L.C.F. Turner, '1914–1919' in *A New History of Australia* (Heinemann, 1974).
23. p.314, E.J. Gibbons, 'The Climate of Opinion', *The Oxford History of New Zealand* (OUP, 1981).
24. General Sir Alexander Godley to D.G.W Malone, letter dated 7 June 1932 (Malone Papers).
25. p.4, Welborn, *Lords of Death op. cit.*
26. H. Johns, IV, *op. cit.*
27. Gasparich, IV, *op. cit.*

BIBLIOGRAPHY

Adam-Smith, Patsy, *The ANZACs*, Hamish Hamilton 1978

Adcock, A. St John, *Australasia Triumphant*, Simkin, Marshall and Hamilton 1916

Aitkin, Alexander, *From Gallipoli to the Somme*, Oxford University Press 1963

Andrews, Ted, *Kiwi Trooper: The Story of Queen Alexander's Own*, Wanganui Chronicle 1967

Annabell, Norman, *Official History of the New Zealand Engineers during the Great War 1914–1919*, Evans, Cobbe & Sharpe 1927

'ANZAC', *On the Anzac Trail: Being Extracts from the Diary of a New Zealand Sapper*, Heinemann 1916

The ANZAC Book, written and illustrated in Gallipoli by the men of ANZAC, Cassell 1916

Aspinall-Oglander, Brig.-Gen. C.F., *The Official History of the Great War: Military Operations Gallipoli, Vols 1 & 2*, Heinemann 1929, 1932

Asquith, H.H., *H.H. Asquith Letters to Venetia Stanley*, selected and edited by Michael and Eleanor Brock, Oxford University Press 1982

Baker, Paul, *King and Country Call*, Auckland University Press 1988

Barber, L.H., *Kia Kaha: A History of the Haurakis 1898–1978*, (6th Hauraki) Battalion RNZIR 1978

Bartlett, E. Ashmead, *The Uncensored Dardanelles*, Hutchinson 1928

Bean, C.E.W., *Official History of Australia in the War: The Story of ANZAC Vols I & II*, Angus and Robertson 1935/1936

—— *ANZAC to Amiens*, Australian War Memorial 1946

—— Gallipoli Correspondent, *The Frontline Diary of C.E.W. Bean*. Selected and annotated by Kevin Fewster, Allen & Unwin, 1983.

—— *Gallipoli Mission*, Australian War Memorial 1948

—— *Two Men I Knew: William Bridges and Brudenell White, Founders of the AIF*, Angus and Robertson 1957

Benson, Sir Irving, *The Man with the Donkey, John Simpson Kirkpatrick, The Good Samaritan of Gallipoli*, Hodder & Stoughton 1965

Buley, E.C., *Glorious Deeds of Australasians in the Great War*, Melrose 1915

Burdon, R.M., *The New Dominion, a social and political history of New Zealand 1918–39*, A.H. & A.W. Reed 1965

Burton, O.E., *The Silent Division: New Zealanders at the Front 1914–1919*, Angus & Robertson, 1935.

—— *Spring Fires*, The Book Centre Ltd, The Pilgrim Progress 1956

—— *The Auckland Regiment, being an account of the going on active service of the First, Second and Third Battalions of the Auckland Regiment*, Whitcombe & Tombs 1922

Bush, Eric, *Gallipoli*, Allen & Unwin 1975

Brereton, Major C.B., *Tales of Three Campaigns*, Selwyn & Blount 1926

Brugger, Suzanne, *Australians and Egypt 1914–1919*, Melbourne University Press 1980

Byrne, Lt Arthur Emmett, *Official History of the Otago Regiment NZEF in the Great War 1914–1918*, J. Wilkie & Co. 1921

Byrne, Lt John Richard, *New Zealand Artillery in the Field 1914–18*, Whitcombe & Tombs 1922

Callwell KCB, Major General Sir C.E., *The Dardanelles*, Constable 1924

Campbell, Capt. R.W., *The Kangaroo Marines*, Cassell ND

Carbery, Lt Col. A.D., *The New Zealand Medical Services in the Great War 1914–1918*, Whitcombe & Tombs 1924

Cobber, L. Cpl, *The Anzacs' Pilgrims Progress*, Simkin, Marshall, Hamilton, Kent & Co. ND

Condliffe, J.B., *Te Rangi Hiroa: The Life of Sir Peter Buck*, Whitcombe & Tombs 1971

Cowan, James, *The Maoris in the Great War*, Whitcombe & Tombs 1925

Cunningham, W.H., Treadwell, C.A.L., and Hanna, J.S., *The Wellington Regiment NZEF 1914–1919*, Ferguson and Osborn 1928

Cutlack, F.M., *War Letters of General Monash*, Angus & Robertson 1934

Crowley, F.K. (ed.), *A New History of Australia*, Heinemann 1974

Davin, D.M. (ed.), *New Zealand Short Stories*, Oxford University Press 1951

Dardanelles Commission, *First Report*, HMSO Cd 8490 1917

——— *The Final Report of the Dardanelles Commission (Part II — Conduct of Operations Etc) With Appendix of Documents and Maps*, Cmd 37 HMSO

Delarge, Edmond, *The Tragedy of the Dardanelles*, John Lane 1932

Denham, H.M., *Dardanelles: A Midshipman's Diary 1915–16*, John Murray 1981

Drew, Lt H.T.B., *The War Effort of New Zealand*, Whitcombe & Tombs 1923

Dupuy, R. Ernest, and Dupuy, Trevor N., *The Encyclopedia of Military History*, Janes Publishing Co. 1977

Ellis, M.M., and Finlayson, Roy, *By Wires to Victory, 1st Divisional Signal Company War History Committee Encyclopedia of New Zealand, Vols. I–III*, Government Printer 1966

Ferguson, Captain David, *The History of the Canterbury Regiment, NZEF 1914–1919*, Whitcombe & Tombs 1921

Fortesque, Captain Granville, *What of the Dardanelles?* Hodder & Stoughton 1915

Gammage, Bill, *The Broken Years: Australian Soldiers in the Great War*, Australian National University Press 1974

Gasson, James, *Travis VC: Man in No Man's Land*, A.H. & A.W. Reed 1966

Gellert, Leon, *Songs of a Campaign*, Angus & Robertson 1917

Gilbert, Martin, *Winston S. Churchill 1914–1916, Vol. 3*, Heinemann 1971

Godley, GCB, KCMG, General Sir Alexander, *Life of an Irish Soldier*, John Murray 1939

Gooch, John, *The Plans of War, The General Staff, and British Military Strategy 1900–1916*, Routledge & C. Kegan Paul 1974

Grant, William, *In Memoriam: Chaplain-Major William Grant, His Letters from the Front, Gisborne Herald* 1914

Haigh, J. Bryant, *Men of Faith and Courage*, The Word Publishers 1983

Hamilton, Sir Ian, *Gallipoli Diary, Vols I & II*, Edward Arnold, 1920

——— *Gallipoli Despatches*, HMS0 1915–1916

Hand-Newton, DSO, C.T., *A Physician in Peace and War*, N.M. Peryer 1967

Hankey, Lord, *The Supreme Command 1914–1918*, Allen & Unwin 1961

Harper, Barbara (ed.), *Letters From Gunner 71516 and Gunner 71517*, Anchor Communications 1978

Head, DSO, Lt Col. C.O., *A Glance at Gallipoli*, Eyre and Spottiswoode 1931

Herbert, The Hon. Aubrey, *Mons, ANZAC and Kut*, Edward Arnold 1919

Hill, A.J., *Chauvel of the Light Horse*, Melbourne University Press

Idriess, Ion, L., *The Desert Column*, Angus and Robertson 1951

Imperial War Graves Commission Memorial Registers, Imperial War Graves Commission 1925

James, Robert Rhodes, *Gallipoli*, Batsford 1965

Johnston, George, *My Brother Jack*, Collins 1964

Keyes, Admiral of the Fleet, The Lord, *Amphibious Warfare and Combined Operations*, Cambridge University Press 1943

——— *The Fight for Gallipoli*, Eyre & Spottiswoode 1941

King, Michael, *The New Zealanders at War*, Heinemann 1981

Laffin, John, *Damn the Dardanelles*, Doubleday 1980

Latter, E.G., *Together Onward: A Short History of the Canterbury Regiment, The Nelson Marlborough West Coast Regiment and the Second Battalion (Canterbury Nelson Marlborough West Coast) Royal New Zealand Infantry Regiment*, 2 RNZIR 1970

Liddle, Peter H., *Men of Gallipoli: The Dardanelles and Gallipoli Experience August 1914 to January 1916*, Allen Lane 1976

McGibbon, Ian, *Blue Water Rationale: The Naval Defence of New Zealand 1914–1942*, Government Printer 1981

——— *The Path to Gallipoli*, GP Books 1991

McKenzie, Clutha N., *The Tales of a Trooper*, John Lane 1921

McKenzie, Compton, *Gallipoli Memoirs*, Cassell 1929

McKernan, Michael, *Australian Churches at War*, Sydney Catholic Theological Faculty and Australian War Memorial 1980

——— *The Australian People and the Great War*, Nelson 1980

Malthus, Cecil, *ANZAC, A Retrospect*, Whitcombe & Tombs 1965

Manson, Cecil & Celia, *Doctor Agnes Bennett*, Joseph/Whitcombe & Tombs 1960

Masefield, John, *Gallipoli*, Heinemann 1916

May, Philip Ross (ed.), 'Len Richardson's Politics and War: Coal Miners and Conscription 1914–18', *Miners and Militant Politics in Westland*, Whitcoulls 1975

Mitchell, Major T.J. and Smith, G.M., *The Official History of the Great War: Casualties and Medical Statistics*, HMSO 1932

Mulgan, John, *Report on Experience*, Blackwood & Janet Paul 1967

Nevinson, Henry W., *The Dardanelles Campaign*, Nisbet & Co. 1920

New Zealand Expeditionary Force, *Alphabetical List of Casualties in order of units*, Vol. I 15 Aug. 1914 to 14 Aug. 1915, Vol. II 15 Aug. to 14 Nov. 1915, Vol. III 15 Nov. 1915 to 14 Feb. 1916,

Coulls, Culling & Co. Vol. I, 1915, John Mackay/ Government Printer Vols II & III 1916

New Zealand Expeditionary Force, Its Provision and Maintenance, prepared in the branch of the Chief of General Staff HQ NZ Military Forces, Marcus F. Marks, Government Printer 1919

New Zealand Expeditionary Force (Europe) 1914 War Diary, Government Printer 1915

Nominal rolls of New Zealand Expeditionary Force, Vol. 1 Alphabetical Roll from 15 Aug. 1914 to 31 Dec. 1915, Government Printer 1917–1919

The Great War, 1914–1918 New Zealand Expeditionary Force Roll of Honour, Government Printer 1924

Nicol, Sgt C.G., *The Story of Two Campaigns: Official War History of the Auckland Mounted Rifles Regiment 1914–1919*, Wilson & Horton 1921

North, John, *Gallipoli: The Fading Vision*, Faber & Faber 1966

Oliver, W.H. (ed.), with Williams, B.R., *The Oxford History of New Zealand*, OUP 1981

Palmer, Hartley Valentine, *The Trail I Followed*, Butler Printing Ltd, 1970

Pemberton, T.J., *Gallipoli Today*, Ernest Benn 1926

Phillips, Jock, Boyack, Nicholas and Malone, E.P., *The Great Adventure*, Allen & Unwin 1988

Pilling, Lt Ewen George, *An Anzac Memory: Extracts from a Rough Diary*, Stanton Bros. 1933

Powles, Lt Col. C. Guy, *The New Zealanders in Sinai and Palestine*, Whitcombe & Tombs 1922

—— (ed.), *The History of the Canterbury Mounted Rifles, 1914–1919*, Whitcombe & Tombs 1928

Robertson, John, *Anzac and Empire*, Hamlyn, 1990

Robinson, Howard, *A History of the Post Office in New Zealand*, R.E. Owen 1966

Roskill, Stephen, *Hankey, Man of Secrets, Vol. I 1877–1918*, Collins 1970

Ross, Captain Malcolm and Ross, Noel, *Light and Shade in War*, Edward Arnold 1916

Ross, Noel, *Noel Ross and His Work*, Edward Arnold 1919

Sanders, Liman von, *Five Years in Turkey*, US Naval Institute 1927

Shadbolt, Maurice, *Once On Chunuk Bair*, Hodder & Stoughton 1982

Sinclair, Keith, *A History of New Zealand*, Penguin 1980

—— *A History of the University of Auckland, 1883–1983*, Auckland University Press 1983

Stephen, John Smith, *The Samoan (NZ) Expeditionary Force*, Ferguson & Osborn 1924

Stevens, K.M., *Maungatapere: A History and Reminiscence*, *Whangarei Advocate* ND

Studholme, CBE, DSO, Lt. Col. John, *Some Records of the New Zealand Expeditionary Force* (unofficial but compiled from official records), W.A.G. Stunner, Government Printer 1928

—— *The Times Documentary History of the War Vol. X Overseas Part 2*, 1919

Thomson, Alistair, *Anzac Memories*, Oxford University Press 1994

Tomlinson, J.E., *Remembered Trails*, *Timaru Herald*, June 1968

Treadwell, OBE, C.A.L., *Recollections of an Amateur Soldier*, Thos Avery & Sons 1936

Varnham, MC, ED, Lt Col. F.S., *Primus in Armis: 1st Battalion, Taranaki Regiment* (includes The Taranaki Regiment, Great War 1914/19)

Waite, DSO, NZE, Major Fred, *The New Zealanders at Gallipoli*, Whitcombe & Tombs 1919

Welborn, Suzanne, *Lords of Death: A People, A Place, A Legend*, Fremantle Art Centre Press, 1982.

Westmacott, Spencer, *The After-Breakfast Cigar: Selected Memoirs of a King Country Settler* (ed. by H.E. Westmacott), A.H. & A.W. Reed

Weston, Lt Col. C.H., *Three Years with the New Zealanders*, Skeffington & Son 1918

White, T.W., *Guests of the Unspeakable: The Odyssey of an Australian Airman — Being a Record of Captivity and Escape in Turkey*, Angus & Robertson 1935

Wilkie, Major A.H., *ANZAC* (23–page poem published recounting Mounteds' deeds at Anzac — copy with Meldrum Family)

—— *Official History of the Wellington Mounted Rifles Regiment in the Great War 1914–1919*, Whitcombe & Tombs 1924

Wilkinson, R.I., Norman, *The Dardanelles: Colour Sketches from Gallipoli*, Longman Green 1916

Williams, L. Cpl E.P., *A New Zealander's Diary. Gallipoli and France 1915–1917*, Melbourne Publishing Co. ND

Winter, Denis, *25 April 1915*, University of Queensland Press, 1994

Periodicals and Articles

'Anzac 50 years Ago', *NZ Weekly News* commemorative issue, 21 April 1965

'Gallipoli Recalled The Spirit of Anzac', Wellington Gallipoli Veterans Association, 1955, ed. Leo Fanning

'New Zealand at the Dardanelles', *Special War Issue of The Weekly Press*, Christchurch, September 1915

'New Zealand's Roll of Honour', *Auckland Weekly News* 1915

Graham, John McK., 'The Voluntary System,

Recruiting 1914–16', MA thesis, Auckland 1971

Harson, Sir Ernest, 'Gallipoli: What Did Happen?', *Voice of the Veteran* April 1957

Howe, H.V., 'ANZAC: Sparks from an Old Controversy', *Australian Army Journal*

McGeorge, 'Military Training in New Zealand Primary Schools 1900–1912', *ANZHES Journal* III.2 1974

McLeod, John, 'De-Mythologising the Australian ANZAC' (Draft in author's possession)

Malone, E.P., 'The New Zealand School Journal and the Imperial Ideology', *NZ Journal of History* V7 (1) 1973, pp.12–27

Mayhew, W.R., 'The Returned Services Association 1916–1943', MA thesis, Otago 1943

O'Connor, P.S., 'The Recruitment of Maori Soldiers 1914–1918', *Political Science* XIX 2, 1967, pp.48–83

——— 'The Awkward Ones — dealing with conscience 1916–18', *NZ Journal of History* VIII.2, 1974, pp.118–36

Weitzel, R.L., 'Pacifists and Anti-Militarists 1909–1914', *NZ Journal of History* VIII.2, 1973

Unpublished Sources

During the research for the television documentary on New Zealanders at Gallipoli (*Gallipoli, the New Zealand Story*, TVNZ 1984), the Bluestockings research team interviewed all the surviving New Zealand Gallipoli veterans they could locate. The tapes and transcripts of these interviews were an essential source for this book. Those quoted are listed in the notes but the many not quoted enabled incidents to be corroborated and mood ascertained. These interviews are too numerous to be listed here but the transcripts and tapes are now part of the Queen Elizabeth II New Zealand Army Museum Archives in Waiouru and form a unique primary reference source for this campaign.

Unpublished sources are listed by location. The first group were located during the research interviews, and unless otherwise shown, copies have been deposited with the QEII Army Museum, Waiouru.

Anderson, W.M., Diary

Arnold, Rory, Letters of Rory Arnold. *Nelson Evening Mail* 18 April 1980

Baker, V.H., Diary and description of activities on NZ Hospital Ship *Maheno* 1 July 1915–Jan. 1916

Chaytor, Lt C., Diary, extract 9 May 1915–19 Aug. 1915 (original in possession of Chaytor Family)

Childs, Reginald Alfred, Diary

Fenwick, NZMC, Lt Col. P.C., Anzac Diary 24 April to 27 June 1915 (Mrs G.V. Goodwin/C. Fenwick)

Fitzherbert, Capt. N., Letter to High Commissioner for New Zealand, Report on casualties dated 15 May 1915 (original in Wanganui Museum)

Harris, Sgt Robert Hugh, A Short Account of Operations on Gallipoli as seen by 12/561 Sgt R.H. Harris, AIB, NZEF (24 April 1972)

Hunt, F.L., Letters to author 1981

King, NZSC, Lt Col. George Augustus, Diaries (GP Capt E.G. King)

Little, Keith Melvyn, Papers including Diary 2 vols: 15 Oct. 1914–5 June 1915, 20 May 1915–19 Oct.1915. Ships' newspapers, articles. Routine orders, etc. Submission to the Dardanelles Commission and copies of the Dardanelles Commission's Reports.

London, H.D., Papers and Letters relating to the Gallipoli campaign

McCandlish, Roderick, Letters, Diary and Condolences on death in action. Nov. 1914–Aug. 1915 (Mulvey Family)

McKenzie, F.E., War Diary of Pte F.E. McKenzie, 3 Auck. Inf. Main Body NZEF

Meldrum, CB, CMG, DSO, Brig. Gen. W., Miscellaneous Papers (Meldrum Family)

Morris, Sgt Alfred Thomas, Extract from Diary (Elaine Jenkins)

Malone, Lt Col. William George, Diaries, Letters and Papers including son's correspondence with Aspinall-Oglander, Rhodes James and John North (D.G.W. Malone)

Newell, Pte William Jabez, Copy of Diary from time of being warned for active service during leave and Gallipoli campaign to the evacuation and admission to hospital — 1915 and 1916

Poff NZE, Sgt Leo John, Diary and Letters

Richardson, Maj.-Gen. George Spafford, Letters and Diary (Massey University Library/Richardson Family)

Rogers, Fred, Diary/Roll Book 8th Southland Company 2 May–Dec. 1915

Templar, E.D., Personal Recollections of Gallipoli, Letter to Author 12 Oct. 1981

Vincent, Sgt Henry McDonald ('Mac'), National Film Unit Script on Gallipoli (H.M. Vincent)

Wakelin, Bdr Bertram R., Letters detailing torpedoing of the *Southland* and Gallipoli experiences, dated July 1978

Watson, F.W., Letter on death of Sgt R. Lambert, dated 7 Sept. 1915

Watson, M.M., James, W., Diary

Weir, Russell J., Diary 23 Mar. 1915–8 Sep. 1915

Alexander Turnbull (AT)

Algie, Capt. C.S., Diary (MS 1374)

Baker, Pte R.D., Four Months at Anzac, April–August 1915 (MS 1560)

Browne, Tpr H.E., Account of the fighting for Chunuk Bair 6–10 Aug. 1915 (MS 1196)

Burton, O.E., *A Rich Old Man* (unpublished manuscript)

Clifton, Spr E.C., Diary

Cooper, Sgt Frank Simpson, Diary (MS 1676)

Hanna, Spr P.R.M., Diary (MS 1647)

Holmden, Sgt T.N., Unpublished Manuscript (MS 2223)

Morton, Capt. A.B., Diary and Letters (MS 1310)

Petre, Cpl R.J., Diary (MS1833)

Rhodes, Capt. Tahu, GOC's Diary April–June 1915 (PMS)

Senn, Spr F.V., Gallipoli Recollections (MS 1697)

Smith, Pte A.E., Letter dated 20 June 1978 (MS Papers 1542)

Tuck, Sgt G.A., *Narrative of Experiences at Gallipoli* (MS Bound)

Westmacott, Lt H.H.S., Diaries Vols 12 and 13 (Micro MS 847) (originals with Westmacott family)

Wilson, Sgt John, Gallipoli Diary 1915

Auckland Institute & Museum

Currey, Bdr Arthur A., Letters and Diary extracts 15 June 1915–9 Nov. 1915 (MS 858)

Duder, John, Diary of Hospital Ship *Maheno* 11 Jul. 1915–31 Oct. 1915

McKenzie, Clutha N., Diary of Trooper Clutha McKenzie 6th Manawatu Mounted Rifles, 11 Dec. 1914–7 Jan. 1916 (MS 1078)

Newton, Ernest W, Papers of E.W. Newton and A.J. Newton Otago Regiment, 1 NZEF (MS 921)

Defence Headquarters Library

Details of Service and details of individuals in British Section NZEF 1914 (NZEF —Vertical File)

Canterbury Public Library

Anderson, J.L., Diary Tues 4 May-Fri 6 Aug. 1915

Stevens, Pte Herbert H., Diary

Canterbury University Library

Johnson, John, Letter detailing Anzac experience in Nov-Dec. 1915 at Gallipoli dated 22 Dec. 1915. (Dorothy Johnson Papers)

Kennedy, Alexander S., Diary, in particular 6–18 Aug. 1915 describing Chunuk Bair offensive

National Museum Wellington

Cox, WIB, Major E.P., Diary and Letter dated 16

Aug. 1915 describing action on Chunuk Bair and death of Lt Col. W.G. Malone

Palmerston North Library

Hassell, Gnr Norman Edgar, Memories of 1914

National Archives (NA)

War Diaries of the NZ & A Division and the NZ Mounted Rifles Brigade, Infantry Brigade, Mounted Regiments and Infantry Battalions

Alexander, DSO, Maj. H.M., Letters

Black, Lt A.J., Letters 30 May–26 Aug. 1915

Braithwaite MC, 2 Lt J.L., Letters 18 May–25 May 1915

Braithwaite, Col. W.G., Private Diary including copies of reports and operation orders of the NZ & A Division

Coleman, Sgt W.S., Letters

Davis, Pte R.J., Statement of Capture by the Turks at Anafarta, Gallipoli Peninsula, dated 29 Aug. 1919

Godley, GCB, KCMG, General Sir Alexander J., Godley-Allen Official Correspondence, Lady Godley Correspondence

Harper, Lt Gordon, Letters dated 15 and 30 May 1915

Maxwell, Sig. Alan C., Diary of events after leaving Egypt for the Dardanelles 8 May–July 1915

Overton, Maj. P.J., Letters

Palmer, Capt. H.T., Letter covering events 22 April–28 May 1915

Surgenor, W.J. Pte, POW Report dated 13 Dec. 1918

Queen Elizabeth II NZ Army Museum Waiouru

Barker, A.C.M., Diary New Zealand to Egypt and That Awful Dardanelles Muddle

Bollinger, G.W., Diary 28 Sep. 1914–11 Feb. 1916

Canterbury Mounted Rifles, The Roll Book of the Canterbury Mounted Rifles compiled from 1 April 1915

Cooksey, L/Sgt John R.H., Gallipoli Diary (RV2669)

Darby, Pte John H., Miscellaneous papers/newspaper clippings re Gallipoli service

Des Forges, Herbert Leslie, Letters from 6 Aug. 1914 (RV 2411)

Downey, Sgt Major J.M.T., Gallipoli Diary

Hampton, Pte W.A., Introductions to 'Gallipoli Slides'

Hardey, Sgt Frances Norman, Letters describing Gallipoli service (RV 1328)

Hart, CB, CMG, DSO, Brig. Hubert, Diaries 12 Aug. 1914–19 Feb. 1916 including Evacuation Orders of the Wellington Battalion dated 17 Dec. 1915

Hart, Leonard Mitchell, Letter dated 1 Jan. 1916 describing story of 5th Reinforcements during the Battle for Chunuk Bair

Howe, Pte O.W., Letter dated 7 Sep. 1915, describing night advance on Chunuk Bair and attack by Auckland Battalion on morning of 7 Aug. 1915

Hutchinson, Gnr J.D., Extract from Diary 28 Mar. 1915–28 Nov. 1915

Lynch, Sgt Charles David, Letters and Certificate of Discharge 29 May–7 Jul. 1915 (MS 0228)

Morgan, Spr Garland Oswald, Diary 18 Sep.–9 May 1915 (also dysentery remedy) (RV3281)

Norman, Sgt Edward Robert, Letters (RV 1573)

Peers, Sgt George, Diary 10 April–4 Aug. 1915 (RV 0595)

Pocock, Tpr Claude, diary 1 Nov. 1914–5 June 1915 (RV 1298).

Porteous, MC Sgt Maj. A.W., Diary (RV 0510)

Robieson, L. Cpl Norman Athelston, Letters and letter to brother by A.L. Berry on Robieson's condition in hospital

Rowe, Pte Norman Clarence, Diary 14 Aug. 1915–30 April 1916

Saunders, DCM, 2 Lt C.W., Diary

Smart, Pte Ben, Diaries

Sutherland, Pte Peter J., Letters 9 Mar. 1915–15 July 1915 (RV 3114)

Swan, DCM, Pte James Whiteford, Letter/Diary detailing Gallipoli experiences (RV 3498)

Temperley, Col. A.C., A Personal Narrative of the Battle of Chunuk Bair 6–10 Aug. 1915 (MS 0017)

Thompson, Pte P.M., Diary 13 Aug. 1914–15 Sep. 1915.

Tilsey, MC, DCM, Sgt Robert, Diary

Ward, Sgt Richard Frederick, Diary 23 Sep. 1914–31 Oct. 1914, also 25–26 April 1915

Wilder, Sgt J.W., Diary 3 April–27 Aug. 1915

2nd Wellington West Coast Squadron Wellington Mounted Rifles, Roll Book of 2nd Q.A. W.W.C. Sqn

Wanganui Public Library — C.L. Lovegrove Papers

Company Diary 7th Wellington West Coast Coy of Wellington Battalion NZEF sent as letters by Maj. W.H. Cunningham to Lt Col. R. Hughes.

Various letters to Col. Hughes from officers in Egypt and Gallipoli, commentary to W.A. Hampton's glass slides (now in QEII Army Museum, Waiouru)

Diary of the Wellington Regiment 31 Mar. 1915–31 Dec. 1915

A Brief History of the 2nd Sqn W.M.R.

The History of the Wellington Regiment 1914–1916 (unpublished manuscript)

GLOSSARY

Units

AIB	Auckland Infantry Battalion.
AIF	Australian Imperial Force, The Australian Expeditionary Force.
ALH	Australian Light Horse.
AMF	Australian Military Forces.
AMR	Auckland Mounted Rifles.
ANZAC	Australian and New Zealand Army Corps. Also name of the area held by the ANZACs.
ASC	Army Service Corps.
Bde	Brigade. A formation commanded by a brigadier general, which in 1915 comprised four battalions of infantry or three regiments of mounted rifles. A brigade of artillery consisted of a number of gun batteries.
Bn	Battalion. A unit of infantry commanded by a Lieutenant Colonel and made up of four companies of infantry, a total strength of 1010 men.
Bty	Battery. A sub-unit of four field guns.
CIB	Canterbury Infantry Battalion.
Corps	A group of divisions commanded by a Lieutenant General.
Coy	Company. A sub-unit commanded by a Major. An infantry company numbered some 227 men.
CMR	Canterbury Mounted Rifles.
Div.	Division. A formation commanded by a Major-General and consisting of a number of brigades of infantry or mounted rifles, plus artillery and engineers, signals and administrative units.
Div. Sig.	Divisional signals.
Engr	Engineer.
Fd Amb.	Field Ambulance. The medical unit in the division responsible for the treatment and evacuation of casualties. There was a Field Ambulance on the establishment of each brigade.
HQ	Headquarters.
Inf.	Infantry.
MG	Machine gun.

MEF	Mediterranean Expeditionary Force.
NZ & A Div.	New Zealand & Australian Division. A mixed division, made up of the two brigades of the NZEF plus the 4th Australian Infantry Brigade and the 1st Australian Light Horse Brigade, under the command of Major-General Sir Alexander Godley. Initially only the two infantry brigades went to Gallipoli.
NZE	New Zealand Engineers. In 1915 the signallers were also part of the NZE.
NZEF	New Zealand Expeditionary Force.
NZFA	New Zealand Field Artillery.
NZMC	New Zealand Medical Corps.
NZMR	New Zealand Mounted Rifles.
NZPS	New Zealand Permanent Staff. Regular Non-commissioned Officers and Warrant Officers of the New Zealand Military Forces.
NZSC	New Zealand Staff Corps. Regular Officers of the New Zealand Military Forces.
OIB	Otago Infantry Battalion.
OMR	Otago Mounted Rifles.
pl.	Platoon. A sub-unit of some 50 men led by a junior officer. There were four platoons in a company.
regt	Regiment. A unit of Mounted Rifles or Light Horse commanded by a Lieutenant Colonel and comprising three squadrons, a total strength of 549. In the Turkish Army a regiment was the approximate equivalent of a brigade.
sqn	Squadron. A sub-unit of Mounted Rifles or Light Horse made up of four troops, totalling 158. Fighting strength 80 excluding horse holders.
tp	Troop. The equivalent of a platoon in the Mounted Rifles. Mounted strength 27, fighting strength 20, excluding horse holders.
WIB	Wellington Infantry Brigade.
WMR	Wellington Mounted Rifles.

Ranks and Appointments

AA & QMG	Assistant Adjutant and Quarter Master General. The principal administrative officer of a division.	DAPM	Deputy Assistant Provost Marshall.
		Gnr	Gunner.
		GOC	General Officer Commanding a division.
AAG	Assistant Adjutant-General. Principal staff officer responsible for the administration of personnel and their welfare in a division.	GSO	General Staff Officer on the headquarters of a division.
		Lt/2 Lt	Lieutenant/Second Lieutenant. A junior officer commanding a platoon or troop.
ADMS	Assistant Director of Medical Services. The principal medical officer in a division.	Lt Col.	Lieutenant Colonel.
		Maj.	Major.
Adjt	Adjutant. The staff officer in the headquarters of a regiment or battalion responsible to the Commanding Officer for operational and personal matters.	NCO	Non-commissioned officer.
		OC	Officer Commanding a squadron or company.
		Pte	Private.
AQMG	Assistant Quarter-Master General. Principal staff officer responsible for administration of services and logistics in the division.	RSM	Regimental Sergeant-Major. Senior NCO in a unit
		Sgt	Sergeant.
		Spr	Sapper of the Engineers, including signallers in 1915.
BM	Brigade Major. The principal staff officer for the co-ordination of operations in a brigade.	Tpr	Trooper
		Fate	
Capt.	Captain.	DOW	Died of Wounds.
CO	Commanding Officer. Lieutenant Colonel in command of a regiment or a battalion.	DOD	Died of Disease.
		KIA	Killed in Action.
Cpl	Corporal.	MIA	Missing in Action.
CSM	Company Sergeant-Major. The senior non-commissioned officers in a company.	POW	Prisoner of War.
		RTNZ	Returned to New Zealand.

Awards

DCM	Distinguished Conduct Medal
DSO	Distinguished Service Order
ED	Efficiency Decoration (Territorial Force)
MC	Military Cross
MM	Military Medal
MID	Mentioned in Despatches
VC	Victoria Cross
VD	Volunteer Decoration

INDEX

Index of Persons

Born England 1876. Commercial traveller. WIA
April 1915, RTNZ 11.9.15. Died 1955. 167

Lovegrove 10/410 Pte Cecil Laurence, WIB. Born
Blenheim 1892 Compositor. WIA. Died 1972.
369, 371

Luxford CMG 8/307 Chap. John Aldred. Born
Wellington 1854. Clergyman. WIA 9.10.15, leg
amputated. Died 1921. 229, 328

Mackesy CMG, CBE, DSO 13/610 Lt Col Charles
Earnest Randolph, AMR Born Ireland 1861. Real
estate agent, CO AMR. Died 1925. 214, 223

Mackesy 13/254 2 Lt Henry Frederick Ernest,
AMR. Born Kansas, 1882. Commercial traveller of
Kamo. KIA 7.8.15. 272, 274

MacLagan Brig Sinclair E.G. Born Edinburgh 1868.
Comd 3 Aust. Inf Bde. British Regular Officer.
Died 1948. 16, 94, 106, 108, 110, 114, 117,
127–32, 146

Malone MID (3) Lt Col William George. Born
London 1859. Lawyer/farmer of Stratford. CO
WIB. KIA 8.8.15. 24, 60 passim, 172, 204, 218,
239 passim, 369 passim

Malthus 6/291 Cecil, CIB. Born Timaru 1890.
Teacher. Evac. sick. Author *ANZAC A Retrospect*.
Died 1976. 144–45, 360, 370

Manders Col N. Born Marlborough, Eng. ADMS,
NZ & A Div. KIA 9.8.15. 116, 147, 307

Manning 12/402 Pte Langley, 6th Haurakis, AIB.
KIA 25.4.15. 155

Margetts Capt IS., 12th Aust. Bn. Born Launceston
1891. KIA 23.7.16. 115

Massey William F. Born Limavady, Nth Ireland
1856. Farmer/politician. Leader of Opposition
1903–12. Prime Minister, leader of Reform Party
1912–25. Formed National Government Aug
1915. Died 1925. 33, 44, 50, 64, 89, 158, 335, 359

Maxwell Gen Rt Hon Sir John G. (1859–1929).
GOC Brit Army in Egypt Sep 1914–March 1916.
84, 96, 194, 372

McCandlish 11/92 Tpr Roderick, WMR. Born
Kaiapoi 1892. Farmer. KIA 8.8.15. 54, 60, 225,
231, 357–58, 369 passim

McCay Maj Gen J. W (1864–1930). Comd 2nd
Aust. Inf Bde. Lawyer of Melbourne. Member
Legislative Assembly (Castlemaine) 1895–99,
1900 State Minister for Public Instruction, 1899
Commission for Trade and Customs. Member
House of Representatives (Corinella) 1901–06,
Minister for Defence 1904–05, Lt Governor Vic
1920. 375

McClymont 8/1072 Maj John Bell. Born Milton
1877. Outfitter. OC 10th North Otago Coy.
RTNZ from Egypt 31.12.14. Died 1963. 56, 370

McDonald Lt Col Thomas W, OIB. Born Tasmania
1869. Regular Officer NZSC, CO OIB. Gastric
ulcer Egypt 5.1.15 RTNZ 21.5.15. 56

McInnes 7/367 Tpr Malcolm, CMR. Born 1887.
Labourer. Scargill Cant. KIA 7.8.15. 216

McKay 13/205 Tpr Alexander Duncan, AMR. Of
Waipu. KIA 8.8.15. 302

McKay 13/250 Sgt Alexander Peter, AMR. Of
Waipu. KIA 8.8.15. 302

McKenzie 11/511 Tpr Clutha Nantes, WMR. Born
Balclutha 1895. Farmhand. WIA (blinded) 8.8.15.
Director NZ Institute for the Blind 1923–38.
60n, 224–25, 310, 370, 374

McKenzie 12/190 Frank Ezekiel, AIB. Born
Kimbolton 1891. Lawyer. WIA 20.6.15, 10.8.15.
Died 1967. 193–94, 373

McKenzie Sir Thomas GC, MG (1854–1930).
Born Edinburgh. MP (Clutha) 1887–1896, MP
1900–1912, PM 28 Mar–10 Jul 1912. 1912–20
NZ High Commissioner in London. 60n

McLean 12/192 Sgt Mathew John, AIB. Born 1886.
Traveller. Evac. sick Aug 1915. 143

McRae 2/680 Gnr Reginald, NZFA. Born Sth
Australia. Bushman/farrier of Gisborne. KIA
26.9.15. 35, 37, 38, 70

Mead 6/296 Lt Owen Herbert, CIB. Born 1892.
Produce salesman of Blenheim. Evac. sick. Died
1942. 135

Meekan 12/1055 Pte Samuel, 16th Waikatos, AIB.
KIA 25.4.15. 155

Meldrum CB, CMG, DSO 11/675 Lt Col William.
Born 1865. Farmer/solicitor of Hunterville. CO
WMR 1914–17, Comd NZMR 1917–19. Died
1964. 55, 225, 233, 274, 277, 304, 306, 310, 312,
315, 377

Mercer Maj Gen Sir D., KCB. Born London 1864.
Later Adjutant General RM. Died 1920. 213

Mitchell 8/1173 Maj/Lt Col George. Born Balclutha
1877. Company manager. OC 10th North Otago
Coy. WIA 12.5.15. Died 1939. 168, 366n

Moir 8/1061 John Harper, 2IC OIB. Born 1869.
School master. WIA Aug, Gallipoli. Died 1944.
56, 184, 188

Monash Brig J. (1865–1931). Comd 4th Aust. Inf
Bde, GOC 3 Aust. Div 1916–18, Lt Gen May
1918, GOC Aust. Army Corps. 86, 111, 144,
181 passim, 212, 230, 236, 267, 286, 302, 305, 314,
319, 326

Monro General Sir Charles (1860—1929). C in C
Dardanelles, Oct 1915 and MEF 1915, Comd
1st Army in France 1916. C in C India 1916–20,
Governor and C in C Gibraltar 1923–28. 339, 365

Mooney 12/917 RSM/2 Lt Robert. Born England
1889. NZPS, RSMAIB. KIA 8.8.15. 118

Index of Military Units

Index of Places